Issues in Pricing

Issues in Pricing

Theory and Research

Edited by

Timothy M. Devinney
Vanderbilt University

Lexington Books
D.C. Heath and Company/Lexington, Massachusetts/Toronto

Library of Congress Cataloging-in-Publication Data

Issues in pricing.

  Bibliography: p.
  1. Pricing. I. Devinney, Timothy Michael, 1956–
HF5416.5.I77   1988   658.8'16   86–45337
ISBN 0–669–13215–2 (alk. paper)

Published simultaneously in Canada
Printed in the United States of America
International Standard Book Number: 0–669–13215–2
Library of Congress Catalog Card Number 86–45337

The paper used in this publication meets the minimum requirements of
American National Standard for Information Sciences—Permanence of
Paper for Printed Library Materials, ANSI Z39.48–1984. ∞

88 89 90 91 92 8 7 6 5 4 3 2 1

To my grandparents

Contents

Acknowledgments

Numerous individuals aided in the development of this book. Glenda A. Hudson and David Livert provided expert editorial assistance. Rebecca J. Sanderson handled much of the graphics work. M. Cordy Cades, Kelly J. Newell, and Erica Meeter were responsible for typing several of the chapters. In addition, Guy N. Lever and Janet M. Kim proved miscellaneous research assistance. The individual authors deserve highest appreciation for their willingness to contribute their work to this book and their immense patience during the period of its completion. Finally, the Owen Graduate School of Management, Vanderbilt University, must be thanked for providing financial support through the Dean's Fund for Faculty Research. Additional funding was received from the University Research Council at Vanderbilt University.

Part I
Introduction and Overview

Timothy M. Devinney

O ur understanding of the microfoundations of pricing behavior—the pricing behavior of firms and its impact on consumers, competitors, and society—has undergone dramatic developments in the past several decades. Although applied pricing research has existed as long as people have observed the changing nature of prices in marketplaces and unsuccessfully attempted to control them, there existed little systematic understanding of the determinants of price until the publication of Adam Smith's monumental *Wealth of Nations* in 1776. Since that time, concomitant with the development of other areas of economic science, the study and understanding of the determinants of price have expanded dramatically. However, the traditional economic perspective was to view price as an equilibrium entity simultaneously determined along with quantity in an open marketplace. Little room was left for the role of individual strategic decision making. This somewhat restrictive viewpoint has led to a noticeable lack of theoretically based normative pricing models and an underestimation of the role that price could play as a strategic management variable.

The developments in economics in the past half century (most notably developments in game theory, information economics, industrial organization, and more sophisticated mathematical techniques) have set the stage for a second view of price—that of price as a strategic decision variable. This new role for pricing has led to a more applied field now known as *pricing strategy*. The present book represents an introduction into, and integration of, recent developments in the area of pricing strategy. Specifically, eight areas of interest to both academics and technically oriented practitioners are addressed:

1. the role of economic theory in pricing strategy
2. the role of behavioral theory in pricing strategy
3. the role of informational uncertainty in pricing strategy
4. long-term dynamic pricing strategy
5. pricing strategy under competitive conditions

6. empirical studies of pricing strategy
7. the relevance of pricing-strategy research
8. the development of a general-pricing-strategy paradigm

The book is divided into six parts with each part focusing on one or more of the eight issues. Each part contains an introduction to the topics discussed by the chapters in that section. Each chapter is intended to make an original contribution to our understanding of pricing strategy.

Part I addresses the first two issues by providing an introduction into the area of pricing strategy from more general theoretical perspectives. Chapter 1 gives an introduction into how the basic precepts of neoclassical economics can be expanded upon to address the more complex issues associated with the pricing of multiattribute products under different market-structure conditions. Chapter 2 provides an introduction into the role that price expectations play in determining consumer purchasing decisions. A background review on behaviorally based pricing models is given, followed by the detailed creation of a theory of consumer expectations using recent developments in rational expectations theory.

Part II discusses the role that information plays in the marketplace. Chapter 3 focuses on the role of signaling in markets—how price, advertising, and production can reveal information about quality to consumers. An introduction into the economic theory of information is followed by an integrated discussion of the conditions under which information can be disseminated to consumers through the manner in which a product is priced or marketed. Chapter 4 discusses how insurance mechanisms, such as product warranties, can affect market outcomes. This research is particularly important for understanding the pricing of products where performance is affected by consumer usage. Chapter 5 examines the strategic–durable-good pricing problem of a monopolist under different cost and consumer-expectation assumptions. It is shown that under some conditions, a monopolist may choose to raise costs in order to affect consumer expectations and be able to increase its price-cost margin further.

Part III addresses the issues associated with pricing in a multiperiod framework. Chapter 6 serves as a general introduction into the subject of dynamic pricing. Chapter 7 discusses the roles of price and advertising in the case of nondurable new products. Chapter 8 investigates the role of price discounts in shifting consumer purchases through time.

Part IV is concerned with the role of competitive behavior. Chapter 9 examines the pricing of durables in a game theoretic scenario. Chapter 10 examines the pricing implications of different channels-of-distribution assumptions. Chapter 11 looks at the pricing strategies when firms use goals other than pure profit maximization.

Part V focuses on empirically based pricing research. Chapter 12 provides an examination of price sensitivity over the product life cycle. Chapter 13 looks at the interesting problem of pricing when different stores sell similar but not identical products. Chapter 14 is an analysis of why price markups vary so radically both within and across stores.

Part VI, the conclusion to the book, contains two general chapters. Chapter 15 addresses the extremely important issue of what of managerial relevance can be gotten from pricing research. Chapter 16 provides a survey and synthesis of pricing strategy research that includes the research in the present book.

Pricing strategy is an expanding area of both practical and theoretical importance. From a theoretical perspective, it provides an avenue through which previously unrelated economic and behavioral theories can be integrated, hopefully leading to a better understanding of strategic behavior in the marketplace. From a practical perspective, it implies that many economic theories, once thought to be relegated only to the ivory towers, can now be used to develop a better practical understanding of pricing behavior, leading ultimately to directly applicable normative decision models. My modest hope is that the present book will increase the appreciation and understanding that practitioners have of pricing strategy while encouraging academics to expand on this area of research.

1

Economic Theory and Pricing Behavior: A General Framework

Timothy M. Devinney

Then primary basis of virtually all normative pricing models is economic theory. Although many applied pricing models attempt to build upon a purely psychological base (e.g., Adam 1970; Monroe 1973; Thaler 1985; Stoetzel 1970), no such models have achieved a generalizability that rivals that of neoclassical microeconomics. Despite the apparent strength and scope of the neoclassical framework, it has failed, in many respects, to gain any consensus within the marketing discipline—although it is recognized as important in addressing specific problems (e.g., pricing, vertical integration, and other miscellaneous marketing issues). The purpose of this chapter is to provide a general framework for pricing decisions using an expanded neoclassical microeconomic basis. It is hoped that such a framework will provide the blueprint on which further research can be developed while providing guidance and structure for more practical management decisions.

The chapter is organized as follows. The first section provides a brief discussion in simple language of the basic framework that is the basis of this treatise. Its components are described and its basic logic is elucidated. The remainder of the chapter examines in detail the components of this economics-based structure. The role of demand and production, industry structure, and information are the primary topics of discussion. This will lead to an exposition of the importance of the structure to specific pricing behavior. The chapter concludes with a wrap-up of the discussion of the framework and a brief look at its managerial implications. An explanation of all mathematical symbols is provided in the chapter's appendix.

An Economic Framework for Pricing Behavior

Many disparate factors influence a firm's day-to-day pricing and strategic behavior. A list of these factors, although interesting, would provide little practical guidance for firms attempting to optimally determine their pricing strategy. Rather than attempting to provide a litany of factors that affect pricing behavior, I will provide a framework within which optimal pricing behavior can be discussed.

Assumptions Underlying the Framework

Any framework requires specific assumptions about how the actors in the marketplace operate; i.e., what are the consumer's and producer's goals? Two assumptions are crucial to the framework and must be accepted before there can be further development. Both assumptions are optimality-based and will engender criticism. The reader is asked only to accept them; discussion of the possibility of their alteration will be given later.

> *Assumption 1:* It is assumed that producers maximize expected economic profits conditional upon their knowledge of available production technologies, product alternatives, demand, competitors' strategic reactions, and the information available to them, their rivals, and consumers.

> *Assumption 2:* It is assumed that consumers maximize the utility from the consumption of specific products conditional upon their income and their knowledge of the supply, composition, and price of the products in the marketplace. Products and utility functions may be single- or multiattribute in nature.

The first assumption states that the producers will attempt to maximize their firm's economic profits conditional upon their knowledge of the firm's environment. The second assumption (the consumer's analog to the prior assumption) states that consumers maximize satisfaction conditional upon their knowledge of their purchasing environment.

Logic of the Framework

The framework is diagrammatically represented in figure 1-1. Before we discuss the exact components, let us briefly outline how the structure should be approached.

A firm is constrained by two primary factors—its own production technology and the level of demand. Although neither is totally exogenous, let us proceed as if they were or as if we were talking about only those aspects of demand and production that were exogenous. A firm is constrained internally by its production technology, which defines the level of production (given a specific technology) and cost (given factor input prices). It is externally constrained by demand (the amount consumers are willing to purchase at a specific price). Therefore, we can define the base constraints facing any firm as *technology* and *demand*.

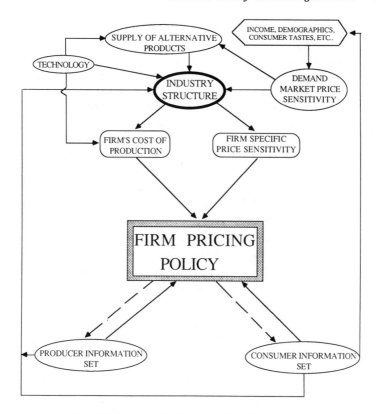

Figure 1-1. The Economic Process in the Determination of Price

Consider a single producer of a product with perfect knowledge of every consumer's demand. Such a monopolist has the power to force consumers to pay the absolute maximum amount they would be willing to spend on the product. From the firm's standpoint, this ability to perfectly price-discriminate would represent the best of all possible worlds.

But in reality, a firm has three sources of major constraints. First, there are *internal constraints*, including the base technology constraint (which may be viewed as given in the industry and also as the most important aspect) plus factors such as managerial knowledge and ingenuity, learning and technical progress, and miscellaneous organizational factors of a more firm-specific nature. Second, there are *external constraints*, primarily the influence that industry structure and its components—technology, demand, competitive reactions, alternative products, and so forth—have upon the firm. Finally, a *firm's decision making* will have an impact upon its rivals as well as consumers in the marketplace. While not a true constraint, firm decision-making impact operate mainly on the information side of the marketplace, although it may have secondary industry-structure effects.

The logic of the framework is simple. Firms attempt to achieve the best of all possible worlds—the ability to charge the maximum number of consumers they desire the maximum price these consumers are willing to pay. However, factors in the environment force the firm to opt for a second-best solution. The role of our economic framework is to define the first-best pricing model and to categorize how the constraints discussed influence this ideal. The key to a successful pricing strategy is understanding which constraints are binding and what are the appropriate responses.

A Brief Description of the Framework

The framework outlined in figure 1–1 represents the causal flows in the economic process determining price. Two factors are exogenous in this framework: technology and demand determinants. Consumer income, demographics, tastes, and so on, determine the level of demand, which influences industry structure. *Industry structure* is defined in the traditional manner as competitive, oligopolistic, or monopolistic based upon the firm's individual market power. Technology, the other exogenous factor in the framework, influences the *firm's cost of production* and also interacts with demand to determine the potential profitability of *alternative products* and producers and, therefore, industry structure. The supply of alternative products will also have some impact upon industry structure. The greater the potential of product alternatives, the more likely the existence of a competitive market structure. It is very easy to imagine additional links between the variables in the process; however, our framework will only concentrate upon primary effects and will ignore the secondary feedback loops common in markets.

The structure of the industry will influence the firm's cost of production and define the firm's demand curve. Technology will determine the nature of the firm's production process and its cost function, while the structure of the industry will affect firm output and, hence, the actual cost and use of productive resources. For example, technology will determine what a plant looks like and the level of the average cost curve, while industry structure will determine the number of plants a firm can profitably operate and the exact average cost of production. Industry structure will also determine what the firm's demand curve looks like. For example, if the firm were a monopolist, firm and market demand would be the same. If the firm were a perfect competitor, its demand would be a horizontal line at the reigning market price. If the firm were an oligopolist, its demand curve would be steeper than the market demand curve as well as bound from above by it.

Up to this point, we have ignored how information affects this market. Consumers do not possess perfect knowledge; what knowledge they have is affected by the *firm's pricing behavior* in the marketplace. For example, advertising can affect tastes and preferences by fostering certain image-types while also providing very specific product information. Markets with more informed consumers have a tendency to be more competitive. Therefore, firms can affect and will be affected by the *consumer information set.*

The *producer information set* refers to the knowledge producers possess about each other's behavior, and it has a direct impact upon industry structure and the firm's pricing behavior. Markets with a very knowledgeable, small group of firms will have a greater likelihood of collusive behavior. The firm may affect the producer information set through what it chooses to reveal to its rivals.

The framework proposed is a simple one that views technology and basic demand determinants as providing the environment within which the firm operates. The interaction of these factors along with the endogenously determined information structure of the market affect the firm's pricing decision. In the sections that follow, the components of the framework are elaborated upon and specific implications are discussed.

The Framework

Basic Determinants of Demand

The demand for a particular product category, as distinct from individual product demand, can be viewed as primarily exogenous with some endogenous components. In traditional economic theory structures, demand is driven by three completely exogenous factors: income, Y; tastes and preferences given by a utility function, $U(\cdot)$; and the price of alternative products, P_{AOG}. Market price, P, and quantity, Q, are then determined endogenously. Information about all product alternatives in the market is assumed to be complete—consumers and producers possess perfect knowledge.

Although taxing, in reality this formulation of demand allows for easy categorization of products based upon their sensitivity to the underlying parameters of the model. Products can be easily categorized into useful groups by defining an elasticity as the percent change in one factor with respect to another, holding everything else constant ($\epsilon_{AB} = [\partial A/\partial B][B/A]$). Table 1-1 provides a summary listing of these categorizations; their importance is discussed next.

Products are categorized as luxury, normal, or inferior based upon the value of the income elasticity, $\epsilon_{QY} = (\partial Q/\partial Y)(Y/Q)$, which measures the sensitivity of quantity demanded to income changes. (The definition has nothing to do with quality, despite the words used to describe the products.) The income elasticity concept is useful in two respects. First, the consumption of normal and luxury products will be positively correlated with income over time, with luxuries being more strongly correlated. The consumption of inferior goods

Table 1-1
Elasticity Definitions in a Neoclassical Demand Curve

Elasticity Definition	Values	Description
Income elasticity: $\epsilon_{QY} = \dfrac{\partial Q}{\partial Y}\left(\dfrac{Y}{Q}\right)$	$\epsilon_{QY} < 0$	Inferior
	$0 < \epsilon_{QY} \leqq 1$	Normal
	$\epsilon_{QY} > 1$	Luxury
Cross-price elasticity: $\epsilon_{QP_{AOG}} = \dfrac{\partial Q}{\partial P_{AOG}}\left(\dfrac{P_{AOG}}{Q}\right)$	$\epsilon_{QP_{AOG}} > 0$	Substitutes
	$\epsilon_{QP_{AOG}} > 0$	Complements
	$\epsilon_{QP_{AOG}} = 0$	Neuters
Price elasticity: $\epsilon_{QP} = \dfrac{\partial Q}{\partial P}\left(\dfrac{P}{Q}\right)$	$\epsilon_{QP} < -1$	Elastic
	$-1 < \epsilon_{QP} < 0$	Inelastic
	$\epsilon_{QP} = -1$	Unitary Elastic

is negatively correlated. Normal and luxury goods would be expected to move with the business cycle, inferior goods against the business cycle. Second, consumers with rising incomes, as is typical in a family life cycle, would purchase more normal and luxury products and fewer inferior products as they progressed through the cycle.

The cross-price elasticity, $\epsilon_{QP_{AOG}} = (\partial Q/\partial P_{AOG})(P_{AOG}/Q)$—the magnitude and direction in which the quantity demanded changes with respect to the price of an alternative product—has been traditionally used to gauge the substitutability of products. Using the cross-price elasticity, products are categorized as substitutes (demand falls when the price of an alternative is lowered, $\epsilon_{QP_{AOG}} > 0$), as complements (demand rises when the price of an alternative is lowered, $\epsilon_{QP_{AOG}} < 0$), or as neuters (demand is independent of other product prices, $\epsilon_{QP_{AOG}} = 0$). For example, automobiles and public transportation are substitutes—they possess a positive cross-price elasticity; computers and software are complementary products—they possess a negative cross-price elasticity.

The final factor that traditionally has a specifically defined elasticity is product price. The price or own-price elasticity, $\epsilon_{QP} = (\partial Q/\partial P)(P/Q)$, measures the sensitivity of product demand with respect to its own price; it is always negative. Demand is called price-elastic or price-sensitive when $\epsilon_{QP} < -1$, and price-inelastic or price-insensitive when $-1 < \epsilon_{QP} < 0$. The concept of price elasticity has traditionally been perceived as much more important than the other elasticities because of its obvious direct relevance to product pricing.

Table 1-2
The Relation between Product Revenue and Price Elasticity

Price Elasticity	Product Revenue Effect
$\epsilon_{QP} < -1$	If price is increased, total revenue will fall. If price is decreased, total revenue will rise.
$-1 < \epsilon_{QP} < 0$	If price is increased, total revenue will rise. If price is decreased, total revenue will fall.
$\epsilon_{QP} = -1$	If price is changed, total revenue will remain unchanged.

In conclusion, two aspects of the price elasticity concept deserve mentioning. First, there is a direct relation between product revenue and price elasticity. (See table 1-2.) This implies that firms will ultimately attempt to drive consumers into the price-elastic range of demand. Second, there are two primary factors that affect price elasticity. These are:

- *Product substitutability.* The greater the number of substitutes available, the greater the price sensitivity. However, the opposite does not hold true. The lack of substitutes does not imply lower price sensitivity.

- *Price elasticity of luxuries versus nonluxuries.* Luxuries will have a more price-sensitive demand than normal or inferior goods. This follows only when a luxury or nonluxury is defined based on the income elasticity.

The traditional neoclassical demand framework has proved remarkably valuable in addressing many issues. However, its application to marketing has always been limited owing to the unidimensional manner in which it modeled product demand. While many theories (e.g., Robinson 1933; Chamberlin 1936) attempted to model product diversity in terms of imperfect competition, these attempts were criticized because they proved difficult to apply and were very sensitive to their assumptions about barriers to entry (e.g., Stigler 1968). It was not until the work of Rosen [1974] and Lancaster [1971, 1979], which built upon that of Becker [1965], Griliches [1961], and other developments of the sixties, that economists began viewing demand in terms similar to marketers. The next section builds upon the work of Rosen and Lancaster in providing a more marketing-oriented pricing framework.

Expanded Demand Formulation

With the basic model of demand explained, the simple neoclassical formulation can be expanded in a simple and interesting way. Suppose that products are multiattribute in nature, that they differ across suppliers, and that consumers possess incomplete information. Products are represented by x, an $n \times m$ matrix representing each of the n products' level of the m attributes.

The consumers' information set is represented by a ξ, an m-element vector indicating consumers' perception of each of the m attributes. We have simplified the exposition by assuming that all consumers possess or distort information in the same manner regardless of consumer or product. All consumers view all products in the same manner; that is, what distortions exist are identical across consumers or products. For example, if one consumer overestimates the gas mileage of automobiles, all consumers overestimate the mileage by the same amount. Different automobiles will, of course, have different gas mileages. Therefore, $x\xi$ represents the viewed attributes of the products. If attribute 1 is unobservable, then $\xi_1 = 0$; if it is correctly surmised, then $\xi_1 = 1$; and if it is overestimated, then $\xi_1 > 1$. I will discuss the effect of different consumers possessing different information at a later point in the chapter.

In this market, consumers are facing a set of n product prices, P, with attributes given by x, and an information set, ξ. The information set will clearly be affected by many factors that will be discussed when the role of information is analyzed separately. We will assume that ξ is a given for all consumers. It can not be altered by either consumers or producers.

The consumer's maximization problem is to choose the quantities of each product, $q^t = (q_1, q_2, \ldots, q_n)$, to maximize expected utility subject to the faced constraints:[1]

$$\underset{q_1, \ldots, q_n, q_{AOG}}{\text{MAX}} \quad \{EU(q^t x, q_{AOG}) = U(q^t x\xi, q_{AOG})\} \tag{1}$$

subject to: x, ξ, $Y = \sum_{\forall j} P_j q_j + P_{AOG} q_{AOG}$.

The solution to this maximization is straightforward, differing little from the traditional model. Consumers would choose those $q^{*t} = (q_1^*, q_2^*, \ldots, q_n^*)$ and q_{AOG}^* so that:

$$\frac{MU_h(q^*, q_{AOG}^*)}{P_h} = \frac{MU_j(q^*, q_{AOG}^*)}{P_j} = \frac{MU_{AOG}(q^*, q_{AOG}^*)}{P_{AOG}} \quad \forall h, j \tag{2}$$

In this case, $MU_j(q^*, q_{AOG}) = \partial U(q^{*t}x\xi, q_{AOG}^*)/\partial q_j$ is the marginal utility associated with the consumption of product j. Note that consumers expect to receive attribute levels corresponding to $q^{*t}x\xi$, but actually receive the levels given by $q^{*t}x$. In addition, there is no implication that there will be a price-weighted equalization of the marginal utilities of the attributes since only the total product can be purchased in the market.[2]

The base demand for any single product, q_j^D, can be derived using Roy's identity and the indirect utility function. If $\mu^*(P, P_{AOG}, Y, x\xi)$ represents the maximum utility attainable at the given prices, income, and the perceived attribute levels, the demand for product j will be

$$q_j^{\mathrm{D}} = \frac{\partial \mu^\star(P, P_{\mathrm{AOG}}, Y, \underset{\sim}{x}\underset{\sim}{\xi})/\partial P_j}{\partial \mu^\star(P, P_{\mathrm{AOG}}, Y, \underset{\sim}{x}\underset{\sim}{\xi})/\partial Y}. \tag{3}$$

The optimization given in equation (1) can be easily converted into an attribute-mix solution, since the choice of $(q^\star, q^\star_{\mathrm{AOG}})$ will imply an optimal attribute mix for the consumer. Difficulties do arise when consumers are viewed as choosing attributes because more than one product mix can arise when the same attribute mix is chosen. Under these circumstances, the solution in attribute space would be unique while that in product space would not.

We may further elaborate upon this foundation by recognizing that the price of the product in the market will be equal to a weighted sum of the hedonic or attribute prices (Rosen 1974; Griliches 1961), $P_j = \sum_{k=1}^{m} \omega_k \rho_{jk}$. Several things should be noted about the hedonic prices. First, the hedonic price of attribute k is not necessarily going to be the same across all products. The rationale for this will be shown shortly. Second, the weights will be the perceived values rather than the actual values of the attributes, $\omega_k = \xi_k x_{jk}$. This follows simply because no consumers would pay for more than they perceived they were receiving.

This implies that the following system of equations holds in the marketplace:

$$P_1 = \rho_{11}\xi_1 x_{11} + \rho_{12}\xi_2 x_{12} + \ldots + \rho_{1m}\xi_m x_{1m}$$

$$P_2 = \rho_{21}\xi_1 x_{21} + \rho_{22}\xi_2 x_{22} + \ldots + \rho_{2m}\xi_m x_{2m}$$

$$\vdots \tag{4}$$

$$P_n = \rho_{n1}\xi_1 x_{n1} + \rho_{n2}\xi_2 x_{n2} + \ldots + \rho_{nm}\xi_m x_{nm}$$

or, $\underset{\sim}{P} = \underset{\sim}{\rho}^{\mathrm{t}}[\underset{\sim}{x}\underset{\sim}{\xi}]$. This set of equations is interesting, in that, while the P_js and x_{jk}s may be observable by an investigator, the ρ_{jk}s and ξ_ks must be solved for statistically. However, this requires $m(n + 1)$ parameters to be solved for from n equations. On the surface, this is impossible since $n < m(n + 1)$. However, if further structure can be imposed upon the system by finding more equations, it is conceivable that a solution may be found. We shall return to this point later with an approximate solution to the dilemma.

The demand for specific attributes can also be obtained by the use of Roy's identity and the indirect utility function. The demand for attribute k would be

$$x_k^{\mathrm{D}} = \frac{\partial \mu^\star(\rho, P_{\mathrm{AOG}}, Y, \underset{\sim}{x}\underset{\sim}{\xi})/\partial \rho_k}{\partial \mu^\star(\rho, P_{\mathrm{AOG}}, Y, \underset{\sim}{x}\underset{\sim}{\xi})/\partial Y}. \tag{5}$$

Several interesting implications follow from this expanded framework. The most important of these is the role played by perceptions in the determination of attribute and product demand. Note that although not all aspects of a consumer's information set are modeled, the role of perception has not been operationalized in a vague manner. The bias associated with each attribute has been focused upon. This allows the demand formulation to be expanded using psychological theories of how product attributes are perceived (e.g., Bettman 1979). A simple example should suffice to highlight how this can be done. Work by Payne [1976] and Johnson [1984, 1986] has focused upon how individuals fill in the gaps when specific pieces of attribute information are missing or when alternatives are imperfectly comparable. What they are effectively saying is that the ξ matrix possesses no zero elements when a decision is ultimately made, even though no information is available about a specific product-attribute level. The ease with which this work can be integrated into the framework is clear.

The second implication of the model is that all of our normal elasticity definitions will still hold. Attributes can be viewed as substitutes or complements and also as luxuries, normal commodities, or inferior commodities. The demand curve of an attribute can be elastic or inelastic, with the consequent implications as to how the price affects attribute revenues. However, it must be remembered that what is relevant in this case will not be the total product price but the hedonic prices.

One typically assumes that a product being marketed is an economic good and that utility rises with consumption of the product (rather than that it is an economic bad with utility falling with increasing consumption). Attributes can, however, be economic bads. For example, automobiles give off pollution, which is inhaled by the driver. The larger the engine, the larger the amount of pollution. Since engine and pollution are technologically linked, they will be supplied together. (The consumer would clearly take none of the bad if it could be separated at no cost.) Since a consumer would pay to remove a bad, its hedonic price would be negative. The only condition necessary for the whole product bundle to be a good is $\partial U(\cdot)/\partial q_j > 0$ or $P_j > 0$.

A final implication of the expanded demand formulation is the link it provides between product demand and attribute demand. Attribute demand will always be unique; product demand may not be. Attributes are *the* commodity being demanded. More than one product or combination of products can satisfy demand, while only one attribute mix will be optimal for the consumer. (This assumes that the continuity assumption traditionally used with utility functions holds.)

Basic Determinants of Production

The internal constraints facing a firm are defined by the underlying nature of the production technology and the factor prices. Traditional economics-based marketing models have failed to account adequately for the important role these factors play in determining firm policy.

In the traditional neoclassical model, the production process is determined by a production function that translates factor inputs into a product output. Such a function would be $q = g(f_1, f_2, \ldots, f_z)$ where f_h, $h = 1, \ldots, z$ are the quantities of the input factors. The production process itself would be categorized by how output changes when the specific factors are changed. For example, if all factors were increased by some proportion $\alpha > 1$ and output increased a proportion $\beta > 1$, $\beta q = g(\alpha f_1, \alpha f_2, \alpha f_3, \ldots, \alpha f_z)$, then if $\alpha > \beta$, the production process is subject to decreasing returns to scale (DRS); if $\alpha < \beta$, the production process is subject to increasing returns to scale; and if $\alpha = \beta$, it is subject to constant returns to scale (CRS). Firms will want to exhaust all economies of scale; i.e., they will operate in the ranges of production subject to DRS or CRS. Production processes are also broken down into short-run and long-run production. This distinction simply differentiates between the ability to switch between different production techniques over time.

Just as there is a direct relation between the demand curve and the utility function, there is also a direct relation between the production function of a firm and the firm supply curve. We can define a firm's cost curve as $C^*(q) = \text{MIN}[\theta_1 f_1 + \theta_2 f_2 + \ldots + \theta_z f_z] = \text{MIN}[\theta^t f]$ subject to $q = g(f_1, f_2, \ldots, f_z)$ where $\theta^t = (\theta_1, \ldots, \theta_z)$ represents the factor prices of the z input factors. $C^*(q)$ will imply an f^* representing the optimal amounts of the input factors to produce q units of output at minimum cost. (Each producer would be doing this optimization. For simplicity of exposition, the subscripts j have been left off.)

The firm's productions problem is then solved as:

$$\text{MAX}_q \{\Pi = P_q - C^*(q)\} \tag{6}$$

subject to: $q = q^D$; $\quad \Pi \geqq 0$.

The solution to this problem is well recognized. Production will occur up to the point where marginal revenue (MR) = marginal cost (MC), or $P + q(dP/dq) = C_q^* = P(1 + 1/\epsilon_{qP})$. This is the well-known elasticity-pricing formula. Rearranged, it is $P = C_q^*/[1 + 1/\epsilon_{qP}] = \Gamma C_q^*$ where $\Gamma \geqq 1$ can be viewed as the markup over marginal cost. If the industry is perfectly competitive, $\Gamma = 1$ and $P^* = C_q^*$. Alternatively, if the firm possesses some market power, then $\Gamma > 1$ and $P^* > C_q^*$.

This formulation is built upon in many ways. For example, the production process can be viewed as evolving with time either through endogenous learning or exogenous technical processes (e.g., Arrow 1961; Gold 1981; Nelson 1981; Oi 1967). There is also a growing amount of literature on the role that multiproduct production processes play in markets (e.g., Baumol, Panzar, and Willig 1982; Bulow, Geanakoplis, and Klemperer 1985; Devinney and Stewart 1988; Rosen 1972). The latter work will be integrated in our discussion in the next section.

Expanded Production Formulation

The simple neoclassical production formulation, like its demand counterpart, sacrifices realism for the sake of simplicity. In this section, the neoclassical model is expanded upon to account for attribute production, and a discussion of multiproduct production is given.

Unlike with the demand-formulation expansion, we cannot approach the production problem as either a product-quantity or attribute-quantity choice problem. The reason for this is that consumers can mix products to achieve an attribute mix but also must choose from the products in the market. The producers must choose not only attributes, but also how they are packaged. Both have profitability implications.

As before, we can define the firm's cost function as

$$C^{*}(\theta, x^{\dagger}, q) = \operatorname*{MIN}_{f}\{C = q\theta^{t}\underset{\sim}{T}(x^{\dagger})\}. \tag{7}$$

$C^{*}(\theta, x^{\dagger}, q)$ represents the minimum cost to produce q units of a product with attribute mix $x^{\dagger}$ when factor input prices are θ. $\underset{\sim}{T}(x^{\dagger})^{t} = (f_{1}^{\dagger}, f_{2}^{\dagger}, \dots, f_{z}^{\dagger})$ represents the attribute-product technology of the quantities of the z input factors needed to produce one unit of a product of configuration $x^{\dagger}$. If the packaging and attribute-choice costs are separable, then the firm's attribute and quantity choice becomes, first, an attribute-choice problem and, then, a packaging problem. The attribute-choice problem is:

$$\operatorname*{MAX}_{x^{\dagger}}\left\{\Pi = \sum_{\forall k}\xi_{k}\rho_{k}x_{k}^{\dagger} - C^{*}(\theta, x^{\dagger}, q)\right\} \tag{8}$$

subject to: $\Pi \geq 0$; x^{D} (firm attribute demand); q^{D} (firm demand),

with a solution $x^{\dagger*}$ that implies a ρ^{*}. As will be discussed, ρ^{*} will be given to the firm if the attribute market is separable and perfectly competitive; otherwise, it will be determined by the quantity of that attribute in the market and the product configuration chosen by the firm. The level of each attribute will be determined by setting

$$MC_{x_{k}^{\dagger}} = MR_{x_{k}^{\dagger}} = dC^{*}/dx_{k}^{\dagger} = \xi_{k}\rho_{k} + x_{k}^{\dagger}\xi_{k}(d\rho_{k}/\partial x_{k}) = \xi_{k}\rho_{k}(1 + 1/\epsilon_{x_{k}\rho_{k}}). \tag{9}$$

The hedonic price would be $\rho_{k} = [dC^{*}/dx_{k}^{\dagger}]/\xi_{k}(1 + 1/\epsilon_{x_{k}\rho_{k}}) = \Gamma_{k}MC_{x_{k}^{\dagger}}$. The hedonic price has all the attributes of a product price with the addition of the perception factor ξ_{k}. The lower the perceived value of the attribute, the lower the quality of information, the greater the markup.

Now that the firm has chosen the optimal quantity of attributes to purchase, the packaging decision needs to be made. This is done by choosing q given $x^{\dagger*}$:

$$\underset{q}{\text{MAX}} \{\Pi(\underset{\sim}{\rho}, \underset{\sim}{x}^{\dagger*}, \theta, \underset{\sim}{T}, \underset{\sim}{\xi}, \underset{\sim}{\phi}, q) = q \sum_{\forall k} \xi_k \rho_k x_k^{\dagger*} - C^*(\theta, \underset{\sim}{x}^{\dagger*}, q)\} \tag{10}$$

subject to: $\Pi \geqq 0$; $\underset{\sim}{x}^D; q^D$.

The solution q^* will satisfy the condition that $MR_q = MC_q = 0 = C_q^*$. This will determine the quantities of each of the attributes that will be in a product bundle. The product price will be $P = \sum_{\forall k} \xi_k \rho_k x_k^* = \sum_{\forall k} \xi_k \rho_k (x_k^{\dagger*}/q^*)$. Remember that $x_k^{\dagger*}$ is the total quantity of the attribute produced by the firm, and x_k^* is the quantity of the attribute in one unit of the product—$x_k^* = x_k^*/q^*$.

The $MR_q = MC_q = 0$ relation is interesting and requires some explanation. Since consumers demand products for their attributes, packaging has no real economic impact. All profits will be generated from attribute production, and packaging will be expanded until it no longer covers its additional cost. This aspect of the problem could be changed if the attributes and packaging were not separable in demand or if bundling served as an information-revelation or consumer-surplus–extracting mechanism (Adams and Yellen 1976). In this case, the $MR_q > 0$ and a packaging markup would be profitable.

Up to this point, we have ignored two major issues—the role of multiproduct firms and the role of producer information.

The key to understanding multiproduct firms is understanding the production and demand synergies being faced. Although this issue is too broad to be discussed in the present chapter, I can outline it briefly. Baumol, Panzar, and Willig [1982] discuss the notion of an economy of scope that is the multiproduct analog to economy of scale. Economies of scope would exist when a joint-production process is more efficient than a group of single-production processes. Only when economies of scope exist would multiproduct production by a single firm prove sustainable. This framework would then be altered in several respects. Production would still be in attributes, but the cost function would need to be generalized to $C^*(\theta, \underset{\sim}{x}^{1\dagger}, \underset{\sim}{x}^{2\dagger}, \dots, \underset{\sim}{x}^{\ell\dagger}, q^1, q^2, \dots, q^\ell)$, which would represent the minimum cost to produce q^1 units of product 1 with attribute configuration $\underset{\sim}{x}^{1\dagger}$ and so on for all ℓ products. The profit function would also be altered owing to the fact that demand interrelations now need to be accounted for. That is, the firm's products may be substitutes, complements, or neuters in demand. The demand for one product will not necessarily be independent of the demand for the other.

The second issue is the role of the producer information set, ϕ. Unlike the consumer information set, this concept is less quantified and encompasses information of a very different type. I have purposely ignored this point until now. Two simple aspects of this information set will be discussed, but details will be left until later. In equation (8), the firm's maximization was subject to both the attribute and quantity demand facing the firm. These are clearly functions of the basic market demand for attributes and quantities conditional upon the supplies put into the market by other producers. It is here that the producer information set influences the model in the estimation of q^D and x^D.

The Determination of Industry Structure and Industry Equilibrium

We have structured the two sides of the market and are now ready to structure the equilibrium. According to the theory of contestable markets, the nature of the structure of an industry is related to the ease of entry into and exit from a market. We shall keep this definition but assume that such entry and exit costs are already included in the firms' cost functions.

Marketing pricing models have traditionally ignored the role that entry- and equilibrium-stability conditions imply for firm behavior. This oversight is alarming since the nature of the equilibrium structure of the market will often fully determine the pricing structure of the market. We will begin by using a very generalized equilibrium structure under perfect contestability and afterwards ease the latter assumption.

The market will be said to be in equilibrium when no one consumer can become better off by switching either producers of the same product (in terms of attributes) or producers of products with different attribute mixes. Producers cannot earn additional profits either by switching the attribute mix of their existing product(s) or, in the case of multiproduct firms, by adding new products.

Mathematically, this equilibrium would be stated as follows for all consumers, i, and producers, j:

$$\nexists \text{ any } \underset{\sim}{x}', q', q'_{AOG}, \text{ such that}$$

$$EU_i(q^{*t}\underset{\sim}{x}^*, q^*_{AOG}) < EU_i(q^{'t}, \underset{\sim}{x}', q_{AOG}) \qquad \forall i \qquad (11)$$

and

$$\Pi_j(\underset{\sim}{\varrho}^*, \underset{\sim}{x}_j^{t^*}, \theta, T, \xi, \phi, q_j^*) < \Pi_j(\underset{\sim}{\varrho}', \underset{\sim}{x}_j', \theta, T, \xi, \phi, q_j') \qquad \forall j \qquad (12)$$

$$\Pi_j^* = 0 \qquad (13)$$

The second equilibrium condition (equations [12] and [13]) implies that zero economic profits are earned in equilibrium. The equilibrium is competitive in the sense that it is perfectly contestable. The first equilibrium condition (equation [11]) implies that no other combination of market parameters dominates the equilibrium. This does not mean that the equilibrium is unique, but that it is not dominated. Two or more equally preferable solutions could exist.

What does this equilibrium look like? The equilibrium is nothing more than an extension of the hedonic pricing equilibrium of Rosen [1974]. Given all other attributes, the price of some more of one attribute must be equal to the additional utility gained by the consumer. Therefore,

$$C_{x_k}^\star = \frac{\partial \Pi_j^\star}{\partial x_k} = \frac{\partial U_i^\star}{\partial x_k} = \xi_k \rho_{jk}^\star \qquad \forall \quad i, j, k. \tag{14}$$

That is, for an additional unit of x_k, the additional profitability to be expected by the firm is $\xi_k \rho_{jk}^\star$; however, since $\Pi_j^\star = 0$, this must equal the marginal cost $C_{x_k}^\star$ of producing that unit, as well as the average cost. Since the change cannot be preferred by consumers (otherwise it would not be an equilibrium), the additional utility must have exactly the value of the expected price, $\xi_k \rho_{jk}^\star$.

If the firm were a monopolist or imperfect competitor, only the condition given by equation (13) would change. For entry to be stopped, the only condition that is necessary for stability is $\Pi_{n+1}(\cdot) < 0$. If there are n firms in the industry, the profits of the $(n + 1)$st, for whatever reason, will be negative. If this is the case, equation (14) will become

$$\frac{\partial \Pi_j^\star}{\partial x_k} = \frac{\partial U_j^\star}{\partial x_k} = \xi_k \rho_{jk}^\star \neq C_{x_k}^\star \qquad \forall \quad i, j, k. \tag{15}$$

The equilibrium levels given by equation (15) will not be the same as those given by equation (14).

Figure 1-2 provides a graphic representation of the equilibrium. $\pi_j^0(x_{jk} \mid \bar{x}_j^\star, \theta, T, \xi, f_j, q_j^\star, \Pi = 0)$ in frame I of the figure represents those combinations of price, P_j, and attribute k supplied by firm j given that optimal choices are made with respect to all other attributes $\bar{x}^\star$, and so on, such that economic profits are zero. (The line above x implies the x matrix excludes attribute k.) This isoprofit curve represents two things: the feasible offerings of P_j and x_{jk} available in a purely competitive market where all producers use the same technology, or the minimum offerings of x_{jk} available (the opportunity cost to the firm of providing x_{jk} conditional on all other attributes and factors). If the market were perfectly competitive, consumers would view $\pi_j^0(\cdot)$ as their product offerings from this firm and would go to point A. At point A, equation (14) is satisfied with the firm and consumer trading off x_{jk} versus all other attributes at a marginal rate of $\xi_k \rho_{jk}^\star$, where $\rho_{jk}^\star$ is the equilibrium market-determined hedonic price of attribute k for firm j. $\phi^0(x_{jk} \mid \bar{x}^\star, Y, q_{AOG}^\star, x\xi, U = U^0)$ is the consumer's isoutility curve. It represents those combinations of P_j and x_{jk}, conditional upon all other factors being chosen optimally, such that the consumer achieves utility U^0. Note the difference between the consumer's isoutility curve and the producer's isoprofit curve. Since the con-

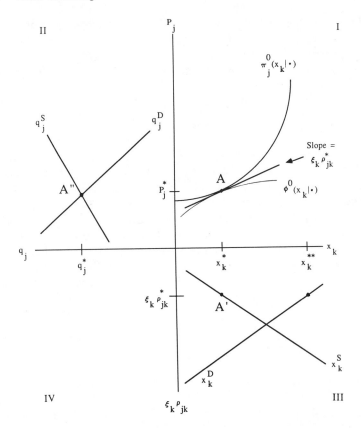

Figure 1-2. Competitive Equilibrium with Multiattribute Products

sumer can receive quantities of x_k from other producers, the $\tilde{\bar{x}}^*$ matrix represents the optimal choices of all other attributes and products except the amount of attribute k to purchase from producer j. Even the choice of how much of attribute k to purchase from all other producers has been made. This condition would be repeated for all m attributes.

Frame III represents attribute k's market demand and supply. The hedonic price of x_k for firm j is $\xi_k \rho_{jk}^*$. If this was the reigning market price, and the attribute was sold separately rather than bundled with the remaining $m - 1$ attributes, total market demand would be x_k^{**}. However, firm j's product only provides the consumer with x_k^*; therefore, $x_k^{**} - x_k^*$ represents the quantity of x_k that would be received from other products if the attribute were separable and its price were $\xi_k \rho_{jk}^*$. This brings up an interesting point. Since x_k is bundled with all other attributes, we cannot expect the supply for and demand of x_k to be equalized. However, what frame III implies is that if the attributes could be unbundled, the consumer would demand much more of that attribute than was forthcoming from producer j. We would therefore expect other products in the market to satisfy this excess demand even if imperfectly. One implication is that the hedonic prices of x_k for other products could be higher—the result of the excess demand. Alternatively, if $x_k^{**} = x_k^*$, there would be no excess demand, and consumers would only accept more x_k if it were absolutely necessary to get another attribute(s). In these cases, the hedonic prices of the other products would be less than $\xi_k \rho_{jk}^*$. If an infinite number of products existed, each containing infinitesimal amounts of each attribute, so that all possible combinations of attribute levels were achievable, or if all attributes were separable, only then would we expect attribute demand to equal supply with one reigning market price, $x_k^S = x_k^D$ at $\xi_k \rho_k^*$

Frame II translates the firm's demand and supply into quantity terms. If, as we have assumed, packaging has no real economic impact, then product quantity equals supply, given the configuration of the product, $q_j^S(P_j \mid x_j^*) = q_j^D(P_j \mid x_j^*)$. The firm will satisfy all demand for its product at the reigning price. This will of course be a function of other factors (e.g., the producer information set), which have been left out of the function for simplicity.

Figure 1–3 repeats figure 1–2 with the firm now acting as a monopolist in attribute k. $\pi_j^M(\cdot)$ is now the isoprofit curve representing the maximum profit offers of P_j and x_k. It differs from $\pi_j^o(\cdot)$ only with respect to the level of profits. Equilibrium condition 3, equation (13), would simply be $\Pi_2(\cdot) < 0$. All other factors (e.g., technology) are the same. The consumer would go to point B with the firm earning $P^* - C^{**}$ on each unit of x_k sold. It is interesting to note the difference between the results in figure 1–2 and 1–3. First, when acting as a monopolist, firm j's product contains more of attribute k than in the competitive case—although in the latter case, consumers purchased more of that attribute over all other products. A monopolist may supply more of that attribute over which it has a monopoly than it would as a competitor. This is one of the reasons why a monopolist would desire to increase the per unit quality of a product. However, the total market amount of that attribute must be less under monopoly. Second, the relation in frames I and III is now more direct. Note that in frame III of figure 1–3, the monopolist equates $MR(x_k)$ and $MC(x_k)$ to get exactly the same monopolistic hedonic price found in frame I.

The Role of Information

One of the key aspects of the structure described is the role information plays in determining the important market parameters—price, quantity, product composition, and so on. The reason for its importance is straightforward. For consumers, what is important is not the true level of the attributes, but how they are perceived by the market participants. For producers, what is important is not market demand, but what part of the market is expected to be available

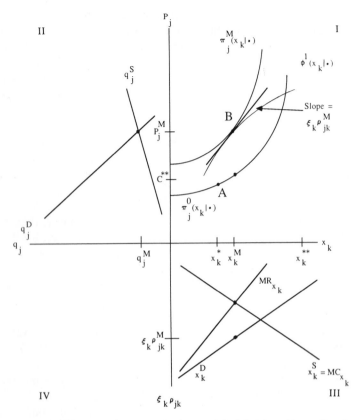

Figure 1–3. Monopolist Equilibrium with Multiattribute Products

to the firm. The framework can be expanded upon quite simply by altering the informational factors in the market.

We have also proceeded as if the information structure of the market were exogenously determined. This is clearly incorrect, and some of the more interesting aspects of this formulation can be found by elaborating on the endogenous aspect of the information structure in the market.

The Consumer Information Set

The consumer information set was modeled in a very simplistic manner with all products being perceived similarly by all consumers. There are four ways in which this can be elaborated upon. First, different consumers, or consumer groups, could possess their own biases in perceiving product-attribute information that differs across products. This implies that ξ would be an $n \times m$

matrix, with each element being a random variable representing the distribution of the perceptions of consumers in the marketplace. The underlying distribution would be affected by many of those factors that affect consumer search—income, advertising, experience, and so on (Burdett and Malueg 1981; Lippman and McCall 1976; Stuart 1979). These will be discussed shortly.

Second, the consumer information set construct could be expanded by segmenting the consumer information set into unique groups. For example, in a traditional separating equilibrium, the consumers differ significantly enough in terms of preferences to warrant unique products. The producers would wish to separate them on their information structure. This would imply a separate ξ^i for each group.

Third, when we allow firm behavior to affect the consumer information set, more interesting implications arise. The most obvious role is that played by advertising or promotional mechanisms. As the consumer gathers more information, the true levels of the attributes do not change; they are simply perceived differently, though not always more correctly. Therefore, ξ can be viewed as a function of advertising and promotional expenditure. Such expenditures can either bias or unbias perceptions of the whole product, or they can lead to the possibility of perceptual product separation. If advertising can be specifically targeted, groups can be separated on their perceptions rather than actual preferences, with, for example, two groups desiring different products merely purchasing identical products that they perceive as different. Mathematically, if A represented an $n \times m$ matrix of targeted advertising effectiveness, $A^t \xi$ would represent the net of advertising perceptions.

The fourth and final aspect of the consumer information set that requires elaboration is its evolution with time or experience. It is reasonable to view the accuracy of a consumer's perceptions as becoming better with time, providing that other factors do not intervene to upset this evolution. Therefore, $\lim_{t \to \infty} \xi_{jk}^i = \bar{\xi}_{jk}^i$ where $\bar{\xi}_{jk}^i$ represents consumer i's limiting perception of attribute k of product j. The most obvious limit for all i, j, k would be $\bar{\xi}_{jk}^i = 1$; however, many factors, such as search costs or the variance in the value of the underlying attributes, could lead to $\bar{\xi}_{jk}^i \leq 1$. The speed of this evolution will be a function of the behavior of firms through advertising and promotions as well as the consumer's cumulative experience with the product (Nelson 1974).

The consumer information set has been modeled in a robust but still rather limited fashion. In a more general definition, this set would represent all aspects of the consumers' product knowledge, including how preferences are formed (see chapter 2 by Winer) and nonquantifiable attributes.

The Producer Information Set

The behavior of producers in a marketplace is critically linked to the ability of each producer to predict its rival's actions. The developments in game theory and its applications to marketing (Moorthy 1985) have made this point abundantly clear. There are several ways in which rivals can react or attack a firm, through price and quantity decisions, product/attribute-mix decisions, and promotional-expenditure decisions. Each of these will clearly have an impact on the firm under investigation.

Two questions with respect to the producer information set are: (1) what are the appropriate assumptions to be made with respect to how expectations are formed and (2) how does one quantify the relevant components of the producer information set?

Unlike consumer expectations, producer expectations would be expected to be formed in a much more rational manner. While one may quibble as to exactly how such expectations are formed or how they evolve with time, there is little doubt as to the underlying force behind their formation—profits (Sheffrin 1983). Moorthy [1985], as well as others (e.g., Myerson 1984; Bresnahan 1981), gives a complete analysis of the factors affecting information in markets under varying rationality assumptions. Therefore, it seems logical to assume in our formulation that producers' expectations are formed rationally under common knowledge—a parent firm can only expect another firm to do the same as it would if it were faced by the same circumstances, knew what the parent firm knew, and knew that the parent firm knew this. For example, if firm 1 were introducing a new product of a specific configuration at a specific price and promotional expenditure, it would expect rival(s) to act as it would if the circumstances were reversed, fully knowing what it already knows (about price, configuration, and so on) and knowing that the rival knows.

In answer to (2), the producer information set must possess, at a minimum, the expectations of rivals' quantities, q^e, and product configurations, x^e, as well as promotional expenditures, A^e. Each of these matrixes is of dimensionality one element smaller than the analogous nonexpectational matrixes, q, x, and A. $\phi_j = \{q^e, A^e, x^e\}$ would now represent producer j's complete information set. Note, as we have emphasized, it contains more than one unique piece of information.

Integration of the producer information set into the supply side of the framework is possible at several points. Let us ignore advertising and see how a firm's expectations of the quantity and attribute mix of rivals affects its behavior. The demand facing a firm will only be an expected demand that can be simply operationalized as E{*firm demand* | x, x^e, ξ} = {*market demand* | $x\xi$} − E{*alternative product equilibrium supply* | x^e}. Market demand may also be uncertain, but we will ignore this possibility. This demand may also be a quantity or attribute demand. Thus, firm demand will be a function of the firm's choices of its key decision variables conditional upon its expectations of what its rivals' effective impact will be. Note that what is important is not the rivals' choices, but how they will ultimately effect the market.

Elaboration of the Framework

The framework can be elaborated on and expanded in two primary ways. First, the paramaters structured in the previous sections can be altered at the margin. This can provide useful insights without major changes to the basic core underlying the framework. Second, new parameters can be added to the framework. Caution needs to be exercised in this latter case since such alterations may require other basic changes in the framework (for example, in the conditions necessary for equilibrium). This section will briefly discuss some interesting implications of marginal changes to the framework.

Demand-Side Alterations

A number of demand-side elaborations (e.g., the role of advertising and the evolution of the information set), have already been discussed in our general consideration of demand. A particularly interesting elaboration of the framework, and one that is easily added, is consumer heterogeneity.

Suppose that two types of consumers exist; type 1 and type 2. These consumers can differ according to their perceptions of products or their basic demand. For the sake of simplicity, we will assume their difference is in their basic demand. Several interesting conclusions follow from the change in the framework. The groups can consume different products of completely different configurations; both groups can consume the same product; or the groups can consume two different products that vary only in one attribute. This last possibility is a special case of the first possibility.

Figure 1–4 presents the situation where consumers separate only on attribute k. Producer j supplies both consumer group 1 and group 2 with the same levels of the non-k attributes. $\bar{x}_j^*$ represents these levels of the attributes (excluding k). Group 2 receives an enhanced attribute-k product represented by point B with x_k^{**} of attribute k. Group 1 receives a product with only x_k^* units of attribute k. This case would be similar to two individuals purchasing the same type of automobile with the exception that one chooses a powerful stereo and the other a simple AM/FM radio. Note several things about this "separating" equilibrium. First, neither group wishes to switch products. Both would reduce their utility by a switch to the other group's product. Group 1 would be on a lower isoutility curve (given by $\phi_1^1[\cdot]$) at point B, while group 2 would be on a lower isoutility curve (given by $\phi_2^1[\cdot]$) at point A. Second, while they consume the same non-k attribute set from producer j, there is no reason to believe that they are consuming the same products from other producers. All the isoprofit curve $\pi_1^0(\cdot)$ represents is that all the non-k attributes offered by firm j are the same. Nothing is said about the consumer's other product choices. Finally, this equilibrium analyzed is a competitive

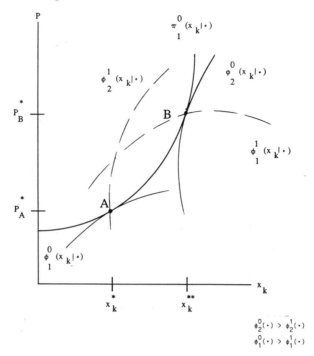

Figure 1-4. A Competitive Separating Equilibrium

equilibrium. Both products are offered competitively. Product differentiation exists in this competitive equilibrium.

Figure 1-5 presents the case where the two groups consume completely different products. $\pi_1^0(\cdot)$ represents a technology under which the product consumed by group 1 is produced. $\pi_2^0(\cdot)$ represents the technology under which the product consumed by group 2 is produced. The products consumed by each group may differ on any number of attributes. This would be akin to a case where not only are these individuals purchasing different sound systems in their automobiles but also different engines and roominess. We will return to this example in the next section since it has technological implications, but two points will be highlighted here. First, consumer group 2 chooses to consume the alternative technology product—point F dominates point B. Second, if only consumer group 1 existed, or if consumer group 2 were fairly similar to group 1, whether or not the technology were there would be unimportant. Consumers would only select from the possible product configurations given by $\pi_1^0(\cdot)$.

Figure 1-6 presents a case where the consumers choose the same product

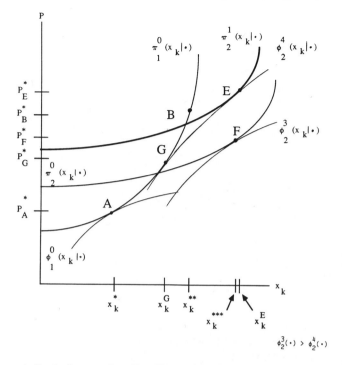

Figure 1-5. A Separating Equilibrium with Differing Technologies

even though their preferences differ. Note that in this case, what is important is the structure of the technology as shown by the kinks in the isoprofit curve $\pi_3^0(\cdot)$. In the previous examples, where the isoprofit curves were smooth, different preferences implied different products being consumed. This will generally be the case. It is the technology that will determine whether or not different preferences lead to different products. (This assumes that preferences are represented by smooth utility surfaces. If choice is determined through some type of disjunctive or lexicographic process, product differentiation may arise more readily.)

Many other elaborations of the demand side of this framework are possible. Search costs can be directly modeled through an alteration in the budget constraint. Multiproduct or various monopoly models can also be integrated within the methodology. There is, however, one aspect of the framework that must remain sacrosanct. Although different elaborations of consumer information and expectations can be built into the framework, optimizing behavior must remain as the mechanism through which choices are made. Without this assumption, equilibrium solutions would be impossible.

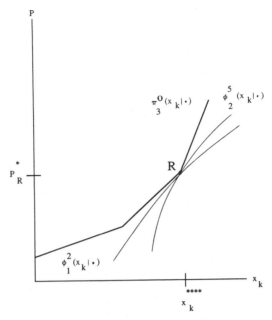

**Figure 1-6. Equilibrium with Heterogeneous Consumers Choosing the
Same Product**

Supply-Side Alterations

The primary firm-based alterations that can be introduced into the model surround the evolution or change in technology. This can occur at several levels. One may want to think of learning as altering product cost over time. Multiproduct-production technologies are a second possibility. Finally, alternative technologies for the same product can exist.

The previous section elaborated on a case (given in figure 1-5) where two technologies existed, and consumers separated according to their preferences for the products made under these technologies. This works in equilibrium since neither technology is dominating; that is, $\pi_1^0(\cdot)$ is not strictly above or below $\pi_2^0(\cdot)$. This leads to several interesting conclusions. Suppose that two firms were identical except that one had a monopoly on the technology given by $\pi_2^0(\cdot)$ in figure 1-5. This firm's monopoly would be constrained because of the possibility that consumer group 2 could switch to the products being produced under the technology given by $\pi_1^0(\cdot)$. The limitations of a monopoly over a technology will therefore be constrained by the heterogeneity of the consumers and the range over which a technology dominates. The monopolist would be constrained to earn the level of profits given by $\pi_2^1(\cdot)$ since at $\pi_2^1(\cdot)$, the consumer's isoutility curve, $\pi_2^4(\cdot)$, is tangent to both $\pi_2^1(\cdot)$ (at point E) and $\pi_1^0(\cdot)$ (at point G). Any attempt to raise price above P_E^* would cause consumers to switch away from the monopolist's product. Second, this highlights the role that the interaction of technology and consumer preferences play in determining market structure. Traditional market structure models have had a tendency to strongly fixate on demand's role in market-structure determination, missing this critical point (e.g., Grover and Dillon 1985; Day, Shocker, and Srivastava 1979).

A second interesting supply-side elaboration, also mentioned earlier, is multiproduct production. This is a highly complicated issue that will only be touched on briefly. If the two technologies given by $\pi_1^0(\cdot)$ and $\pi_2^0(\cdot)$ were not independent, the graphic solution is complicated considerably. The reason being that the level of one curve will be determined by the amount produced using the other technology. $\pi_1^0(\cdot)$ becomes a function of what is produced using the $\pi_2^0(\cdot)$ technology and vice versa. While not logically complicated, the firm will be faced with the difficult problem of knowing what the value of the production synergies will be.

In the examples discussed here, the changes to the framework are marginal. The firm's decision variables may be expanded to include technology choice or the production processes may possess more complicated functional forms. However, its basic logic and methodology is left consistent.

Estimation of Perceived Hedonic Prices

It was noted earlier that market prices and attribute values alone would be insufficient to generate statistical estimates of the hedonic prices of the attributes. There are several solutions to this dilemma.

The easiest solution is when the market is close to or completely competitive. Equilibrium would imply that $C_{jx_k}^* = \xi_k \rho_{jk}^*$ for all j, k. Therefore, an estimate of marginal cost would be an estimate of the perceived hedonic price and the marginal utility received from the consumption of attribute k within product j. This is the clearest case, but is interesting since firm production actually reveals information about consumer utility.

If the market is imperfectly competitive, the marginal-cost–hedonic-price relation becomes $\xi_k \rho_k = \Gamma_{jk} C_{jk}^*$ with equation (4) becoming $P = \Gamma^t[\underset{\sim}{x}\underset{\sim}{\xi}]$. Γ_{jk} is firm j's markup on attribute k. Since C_{jk}^* is observable (it can be estimated independently), the number of unknowns is reduced to nm. The problem is still insolvable, but conditions can now be imposed upon the markups, which can simplify the problem to the point of solvability. For example, if we impose a condition $\Gamma_{jk} = \Gamma_k$, we now have n equations and m unknowns, which is potentially solvable.

Conclusion

The major strengths of the framework discussed in this chapter are its ease of expansion and the synergies that it allows between economics and marketing. One of the major weaknesses of the traditional neoclassical model has been its representation of products as commodities. The current framework brings into line many aspects of economics and marketing by extending the neoclassical model to account for the manner in which most marketers think product-purchasing decisions are made.

The general discussion throughout the chapter has amply highlighted areas where the framework can be expanded and elaborated upon. In this conclusion, I will refrain from repeating these points and instead focus upon some managerial implications. These will represent the basic general conclusions that follow from our framework.

First, perhaps the most valuable managerial implications follow from the role that both demand and technology play in determining industry structure. The most straightforward manner in which to phrase this conclusion is to note that technology defines what is feasible, while demand determines which of the feasible possibilities will actually survive in reality. Therefore, market-structure determination must necessarily encompass an analysis of demand and technology. Traditional marketing market-structure techniques ignore this latter aspect of the problem.

The actual nature of product differentiation is a demand-based phenomenon. As was shown, heterogeneous consumers will imply pressure toward heterogeneous products. The degree of the magnitude of the difference will also have technology implications. The more heterogeneous the consumer groups, the more likely it is that firms will produce products in the same categories (e.g., stereos, automobiles) under widely divergent production technologies.

Second, the existence of heterogeneous consumers and production processes will imply that a monopoly in any one area (e.g., a technology or attribute) will be constrained. The fact that consumers can switch to alternative technology products will serve to limit the monopolist's market power. We would therefore expect that the actual influence of a monopolist's market power will be more limited in the case of multiattribute product markets.

Third, looking at the more consumer-oriented implications, we immediately focus upon the consumer information set. Consumers are heterogeneous because of differences in tastes or perceptions. The firm, therefore, has the potential to separate consumers on one or both dimensions. While it may potentially be more reasonable to separate on the basis of tastes, short-term differentiation based upon perceptual differences may be more profitable.

Fourth, the final implication involves product versus attribute demand. While attributes are the things in primary demand, products are the things supplied and with which consumers maximize their satisfaction. It has been shown that this will imply a tendency toward equal per-dollar marginal utility of products but not necessarily attributes. Put more clearly, firms should not attempt to equate their supply and demand for attributes unless the attributes are separable from the product. If the attributes are nonseparable, then attributes can be oversupplied and undersupplied without any detrimental effects to the firm.

This chapter has not attempted to provide a complete answer to how economic models can be integrated into marketing theory and practice. Rather it has, using the words of Lakatos [1978], set up the framework upon and within which a "scientific research program" can be built. Its contribution should be seen not so much as answering questions, but as providing a manner of answering questions.

Notes

1. Each consumer would be doing the optimization. For simplicity of exposition, the subscripts i have been left off. A superscript t implies the matrix or vector is transposed.

2. This can be seen by realizing that equation (2) can be expressed in attributes as

$$\frac{\sum_{vk} MU^{\star}_{hx_k} \cdot \frac{\partial x_{hk}}{\partial q_h}}{\sum_{vk} \rho^{\star}_{hk} \xi_k x_{nk}} = \frac{\sum_{vk} MU^{\star}_{jx_k} \cdot \frac{\partial x_{jk}}{\partial q_k}}{\sum_{vk} \rho^{\star}_{jk} \xi_k x_{jk}} = \frac{MU^{\star}_{AOG}(\cdot)}{P_{AOG}} \quad \forall \quad h, j, k$$

In this equation, $MU^{\star}_{hk} = \partial U(\cdot)/\partial x_{hk}$ where x_{hk} is firm h's level of attribute k, and the * implies that the quantities of products are chosen optimally. This does not imply that

$$\frac{MU_{hx_k}}{\xi_k \rho^{\star}_{hk}} = \frac{MU_{jx_k}}{\xi_k \rho^{\star}_{jk}} \quad \forall \quad j, k, h.$$

Appendix A-1:
Explanation of Mathematical Symbols

Expression	Definition
ϵ_{AB}	Elasticity of A with respect to B
Y	Consumer income
P_B	Price of product B
Q_B	Market quantity of product B
$U(\cdot)$	Consumer utility function
ξ	Consumer information set
$\underset{\sim}{x}$	Matrix of product-attribute combinations
$E\{\cdot\}$	Expectations operator
q_B	Firm B's quantity of its own product
MU_B	Marginal utility with respect to B
$\mu^\star(\cdot)$	Indirect utility function
ρ_{BD}	Hedonic price of firm B and attribute D
$g(\cdot)$	Firm production function
f_B	Quantity of input factor B
θ_B	Price of input factor B
$C(\cdot)$	Cost of production
Π	Profits
Γ	Markup factor
$\underset{\sim}{\phi}$	Producer information set
$T(\cdot)$	Attribute technology function
$\pi(\cdot)$	Isoprofit function
$\phi(\cdot)$	Isoutility function

Expression	*Definition*
A	Advertising and promotion
B	Implies that B is a vector, matrix, or set
$\tilde{\bar{B}}$	Implies that B excludes some information
$\tilde{B}^{\dagger}$	Implies that only a subset of all possible Bs is being considered.
$B^{\star}$	Implies that B is an optimum or equilibrium
$\tilde{I}$	An identity matrix
$\tilde{B}^{D}$; B^{S}	Demand (D) and supply (S) of B
i	Index used for consumers
j	Index used for producers or products
k	Index used for attributes

2
Behavioral Perspective on Pricing: Buyers' Subjective Perceptions of Price Revisited

Russell S. Winer

T he amount of research on pricing from the manager's perspective is voluminous. In addition to most of the chapters in this book, other reviews (Monroe and Della Bitta 1978; Nagle 1984; Rao 1984) have dealt with optimal pricing policies over time, with experience curve effects, with unbundling, and so on. This research stream provides a highly useful base from which normative pricing rules can be developed to handle most situations.

However, relatively little research has been conducted on developing demand models incorporating the behavioral or psychological aspects of price. Indeed, as Rao [1984, p. 550] points out, relatively little is yet known about how price enters the choice process. This is a rather interesting state of affairs since, as price is the only marketing variable that generates revenue, it would seem to be of paramount importance to understand how the pricing rules used in practice affect the consumers to whom the prices are targeted and how the impact on consumers affects ultimate demand.

Much of the behavioral pricing literature is oriented toward the price-quality relationship, a stream that started with the seminal article by Scitovsky [1944-45]. However, another stream of research involves understanding what are called reference prices. A reference price is an internal price to which consumers compare observed prices. The idea of the existence of reference prices may go back as far as Ricardo [1948], who mentions something called a "just" price conceived by consumers or the price a good "ought" to cost. (More will be said about this later.) Defining p^o to be the observed retail price and p^r to be the individual's internal reference price, the underlying assumption of this literature is that positive values of $(p^o - p^r)$ are perceived negatively in that they are unwelcome surprises, while negative values of $(p^o - p^r)$ are viewed positively.

It is easy to show that the optimal pricing decision will be affected by reference prices. Assume the following profit function of a firm:

$$\Pi = pq - cq - FC, \tag{1}$$

where p = price

q = quantity demanded

c = variable cost rate

FC = fixed costs

Define the demand function to be

$$q = a + bp \tag{2}$$

where a and b are parameters, b being negative. It is easy to show that the price that maximizes profits is $(bc - a)/2b$. If the demand function is

$$q = a + b(p^o - p^r) \tag{3}$$

where p^o and p^r are the observed and reference prices, respectively, then the profit-maximizing price becomes $(bp^r + bc - a)/2b$. Since b is negative, the optimal price is lower when there are reference prices. This is an expected result since companies are penalized by maintaining prices much higher than consumer reference prices and are thus given an inducement to keep p^o in line with p^r. While this simple model does not produce a general result, an implication is that pricing decisions may indeed change if consumers form reference prices and use them to make purchasing decisions.

Three areas of potential discussion have arisen from the literature on reference prices. First, there are several psychological theories that could explain a consumer information processing scheme based on an internal comparison procedure. While some of these have been previously reviewed (Monroe 1973), other theories have recently emerged that have quite different implications for models of consumer demand.

A second area is the definition of reference price. Many definitions of the price to which retail price is compared have been offered. It is shown in this chapter that the reference-price concept is in fact multidimensional; that is, no one concept can or should capture it as the alternative operationalizations that have been offered are quite different.

Finally, a point that is often made in the literature on reference prices is that little research has been conducted empirically to study either how they are formed or how they impact demand. The acid test of the reference-price concept should not be based solely on whether acceptable price ranges can be elicited from people but also on whether maximum and/or minimum prices affect the demand for goods. Excellent reviews of the behavioral aspects of pricing have appeared before (Jacoby and Olson 1977; Monroe 1973; Monroe and

Petroshius 1981); more recent work (Gurumurthy and Little 1986; Raman 1986; Winer, 1985, 1986) has attempted to incorporate the concept of reference price into empirically estimable demand functions. Therefore, our focus will be to take the behavioral pricing literature and demonstrate its implications for estimating consumer demand.

The purpose of this chapter is to address three issues. First, psychological theories relevant to reference price formation are reviewed both for their content and for their implications for demand models. Next, various operationalizations for reference prices are surveyed. Third, the available empirical research in the relationship of reference prices to demand is examined. Finally, implications and directions for future research on reference prices are given.

Foundations of Reference Prices

Basic Economic Model

The classical Hicks-type economic model of household demand posits a downward-sloping demand curve whose location depends on the level of income, the prices of other goods, and the tastes of the household. This model has been often used to estimate household demand functions (Guadagni and Little 1983; Narasimhan 1984; Raj 1982; Winer 1980). The general form of these models is:

$$Q_t = a + bp_t^o + cX_t + \epsilon_t, \tag{4}$$

where Q_t = a demand-related variable such as household purchase quantity at time period t

p_t^o = observed retail price

X_t = other exogenous variables such as advertising and demographics

ϵ_t = stochastic disturbance

The expected sign of b is, of course, negative in keeping with economic theory.

The model represented by equation (4) represents our null model (the model against which the reference-price models will be compared). Although no empirical testing will be performed in this chapter, it will be clear how such testing can be done to (1) test the reference-price models against the basic demand framework and (2) test the theoretical reference-price models against each other.

At least four different psychological theories can be drawn upon to justify the concept of a reference price: the Weber-Fechner law of psychophysics, adaptation-level theory, assimilation-contrast theory, and prospect theory.

These are briefly reviewed along with several other theories. Finally, I allude to theories related directly to the formation of the reference prices themselves.

The Weber-Fechner Law

Weber's law of psychophysics relates proportional changes in a stimulus to a response, or

$$\Delta S/S = K$$

where S is the stimulus and K is the response. In a pricing context, the expression implies that the impact of a price change is perceived in percentage terms; i.e., a \$20 change matters more on a \$100 item than on one costing \$1,000. Fechner adapted Weber's law to account for subjective sensations not directly measurable. (See Monroe 1971.) His derivation was

$$R = k \log S \tag{5}$$

where R is the sensation derived from changes in the stimulus S. The implication of (5) is that, assuming S is price and R is demand. Fechner's formulation posits a logarithmic relationship between price and quantity purchased.

The original applications of the Weber-Fechner law were in the area of price thresholds (Adam 1970; Fouilhe 1970; Gabor and Granger 1966; Monroe 1973; Stoetzel 1970)—i.e., the range of prices for goods considered acceptable by consumers. In this context, S in equation (5) is the price change implemented by a firm and R is the response in terms of change in the maximum and minimum prices people are willing to pay for a good. In addition, the relationship between price changes and the response is logarithmic. Many authors have used this result to develop logarithmic price scales based on thresholds elicited from households.

From a managerial perspective, the Weber-Fechner law indicates possible responses to promotional campaigns (see Sawyer and Dickson [1984]) and other price changes. First, the price change or promotion must be large enough to provoke a reaction and the size of the change is related to the current price (or current reference price; see equation [9]). However, the price change cannot be too large or it will exceed either the upper or lower threshold, causing no sale to occur. As Gabor [1977, chapter 12] and others have shown, these price thresholds can vary widely between products.

One implication of the Weber-Fechner law in the context of demand models is the implied relationship between price and reference price. Assuming a household demand function containing both p^o and p^r, given that p^r is often unobserved (and is unobservable), a reduced form could be constructed eliminating p^r by substituting $\ln(p^o)$ for p^r. For example, given the following household demand function (Gurumurthy and Little 1986; Raman 1986; Winer 1986):

$$Q_t = a + b(p_t^o - p_t^r) + cX_t + \epsilon_t, \qquad (6)$$

where X represents other marketing stimuli and ϵ a random disturbance, and the following relationship between p^o and p^r:

$$p_t^r = d + f \ln(p_t^o) \qquad (7)$$

equation (6) becomes

$$Q_t = (a - bd) + \left[p_t^o - f \ln(p_t^o)\right] + cX_t + \epsilon_t \qquad (8)$$

If one of the X's is perceived quality, Cooper [1970] found empirical support for equation (7) where the dependent variable is quality. Clearly, both (7) and a quality function could not be simultaneously tested.

An interesting implication of equation (6) is that if $p^o = p^r$, then price drops out of the equation. (See Winer 1985.) This is an interesting and intuitive inference as it means that when observed prices meet the reference price, the other marketing-mix variables become more important.

A second way to operationalize equation (5) is to consider $\Delta S/S$ to be $(p^o - p^r)/p^r$. Then, (5) would imply that R (in this case, demand) is a logarithmic function of the percentage higher or lower than retail price is over the reference price. Equation (6) would then become

$$Q = a + b \ln\left[(p_t^o - p_t^r)/p_t^r\right] + cX_t + \epsilon_t. \qquad (9)$$

The obvious problem with this formulation, however, is that negative values of $(p_t^o - p_t^r)$ are inadmissible. Thus, this formulation may primarily be useful only in an inflationary period when reference prices may not be able to keep pace with retail price changes.

The Adaptation-Level Theory

Another theory to which researchers on behavioral pricing frequently allude is Helson's [1964] adaptation-level theory. (See also Emery [1970] and Monroe [1973].) Helson's belief was that the response to a stimulus is determined by the relationship of that stimulus to preceding stimuli. The preceding stimuli create what are called adaptation levels. The current response, therefore, is a function of the relationship between the current stimulus level and the adaptation level.

To put this in our present context, the consumer's response to price is determined by the relationship between the price and the adaptation level or reference price. Emery [1970] refers to this reference price or adaptation level as the normal or standard price. As noted by Emery and summarized by Monroe [1973], the standard or reference price

serves as an anchor for judgments of other prices,

is an average of prices of similar products,

is compared to other products' prices, and

need not be equivalent to any actual price.

The managerial implications of Helson's theory are not as well defined as those for the Weber-Fechner law. While we can infer more about how reference prices are formed using adaptational-level theory, its predictions about consumer reaction to variation about that level are imprecise. What can be said, however, is that prices above the adaptation level for brand A are likely to be negatively received by the consumer, particularly if the gap is higher for brand A than it is for brand B. Some authors have justified the publication of suggested list prices by adaptation-level theory (Sawyer and Dickson 1984) as this then creates a favorable discrepancy between the current value of the reference price—the list price—and the actual retail price. In addition, adapatation-level theory supports implementing price increases through gradual changes that permit similar gradual shifts in the reference price. Finally, constant promotions can hurt a brand as consumers will adapt to a lower transaction price and resist the higher, off-deal price.

Like the Weber-Fechner theory, Helson's theory has implications for consumer-demand modeling at both the structured model and reduced-form levels. The implied structural-model implications are, first, that at least two equations are necessary to model demand: the demand model itself with the observed-price–reference-price (i.e., adaptation-level) contrast and the model describing the formation of the adaptation level. For example, Helson's theory implies a structure like equation (6) with the following reference-price-formation–model possibilities (see also Gurumurthy and Little [1986], Raman [1986]):

$$\ln(p_t^r) = d + f \ln(p_{t-1}^o) \tag{10a}$$

$$p_t^r = d + f p_{t-1}^o. \tag{10b}$$

Equation (10a) embodies a simplified version of Helson's idea of a weighted log-mean functional relationship between historical observed stimuli and the updated adaptation level. The alternative form follows Gurumurthy and

Little's [1986] argument that since only small changes in prices are likely, a simple linear formulation might suffice. The reduced-forms produced are

$$Q_t = a + b(p_t^0 - e^{d+f \ln p_{t-1}^0}) + cX_t + \epsilon_t \tag{11a}$$

$$Q_t = (a - bd) + b(p_t^0 - fp_{t-1}^0) + cX_t + \epsilon_t. \tag{11b}$$

The Assimilation-Contrast Theory

This is a theory closely identified with Sherif and Hovland [1961]. They hypothesize a price range internal to consumers called a latitude of acceptance that is a range of acceptable prices. This is similar to Gabor and Granger's [1964] acceptable price ranges and the region within the price thresholds discussed earlier. According to the theory, if a consumer sees a brand's price that is within the latitude of acceptance, the price is assimilated into the range and becomes acceptable. It also becomes less noticeable relative to prices outside the range. A price that is outside the range is contrasted to the acceptable range and become noticeable.

Figure 2–1 is a pictorial representation of this theory (Sherif and Hovland 1961, p. 49; Sawyer and Dickson 1984, p. 10). It indicates the two main characteristics of the theory: (1) within the latitude of acceptance, there is no effect of price differences on the reference price (or what Sherif and Havland

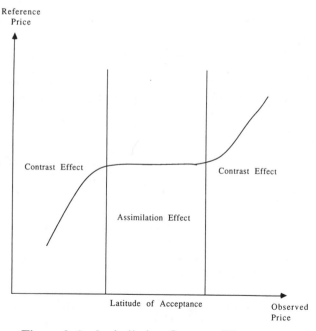

Figure 2–1. Assimilation-Contrast Theory

term the median judgment of the stimulus). (2) for prices outside of the range, the reference price is affected in approximately a linear fashion. In other words, assimilation-contrast theory predicts roughly a cubic relationship between observed and reference price with the flat spot occurring in the latitude of acceptance.

The managerial implications of this theory are clear. As with adaptation-level theory, increasing price is best achieved using small increments as these may stay within the price-acceptance range and thus not provoke brand switching. Unfortunately, sales promotions worth small amounts of money may have the same impact and thus not be effective. In both cases, the width of the range is critical; if a product category has undergone heavy dealing or the price level has remained constant for a period of time, any termination of a promotion or price increase may fall outside of the range, which could have become quite narrow.

A two-equation model similar to those proposed earlier can be specified based upon this theory. Again, as with the other theories, assimilation-contrast theory specifies a relationship between the observed stimuli, market prices, and the internal reference prices. The relationship between stimulus and behavior is not studied. Therefore, again assume that equation (6) is the basic demand model. However, the second equation is now

$$p_t^r = d + f p_t^o + g p_t^{o2} + h p_t^{o3}, \qquad (12)$$

leading to a reduced-form of

$$Q_t = (a - bd) + b\left(p_t^o - f p_t^o - g p_t^{o2} - h p_t^{o3}\right) + c X_t + \epsilon_t. \qquad (13)$$

Equation (13) thus has three price terms and, ignoring possible multicollinearity problems, can be compared to prior models emanating from the other theories.

The Prospect Theory

Kahneman and Tversky [1979] developed an alternative to classical economic utility theory by describing economic agents as making choices relative to a neutral outcome or a "frame." In other words, the particular context in which a decision is being made is hypothesized to affect the choice made. In standard economic theory, the frame or context does not have any impact on the choice that maximizes expected utility.

The most convenient way to describe prospect theory is through figure 2–2, panel a. This figure captures the three important characteristics of prospect theory. First, the value function $v(x)$ is defined over gains and losses, not absolute amounts. Therefore, $v(x)$ is a function of the difference between two stimuli; i.e., there is some reference point being utilized. Second, $v(x)$ is concave for gains and convex for losses. This captures part of the Weber effect

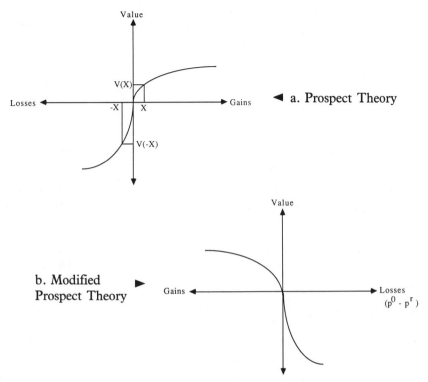

a. Prospect Theory

b. Modified
Prospect Theory

Figure 2–2. Prospect Theory

in that the perceived difference between gains of $2,000 and $1,990 is less than
that between $30 and $20. Finally, consumers are assumed to be more averse
to losses than to gains in that the loss curve is steeper.

Prospect theory can be slightly reconfigured to adapt to reference-price
theory. (See also Gurumurthy and Little [1986].) In panel b of figure 2–2, the
horizontal axis has been redefined to represent the difference between the
observed price of a good and a reference price; i.e., the current reference price
is the frame. In this case, negative values of $(p^o - p^r)$ are "gains" in that
lower observed prices relative to the reference price are desirable, and positive
values are "losses." The key behavioral implication is that positive values of
$(p^o - p^r)$ are treated more harshly than negative values; that is, there is an
asymmetry that is not captured by other psychological theories. (See Nwokoye
[1975] for an alternative explanation of this phenomenon.)

As with assimilation-contrast theory, where knowing the width of the
acceptance range is key to understanding the managerial implications, it is
critical with prospect theory to know, in particular, the steepness of the loss
section of the curve. Otherwise, it is obvious that prospect theory is consistent

with the observed–reference–price–discrepancy hypothesis mentioned throughout this chapter. In addition, prospect theory is not concerned with the formation of the framing or reference price.

Prospect theory offers some interesting prescriptions for how to handle some combinations of price changes and promotions. For example, consider the following two scenarios. (Any differential demand effects and any differential costs of implementation will be ignored.)

Scenario 1: A marketing manager wishes to raise the price of a product by a net of 20¢. Should he raise the retail price by 20¢ or raise it by 23¢ and use a 3¢ coupon simultaneously?

Scenario 2: A marketing manager wishes to lower the price of his product by a net of 10¢. Should he lower the retail price by 10¢ or raise it by 5¢ and offer a 15¢ coupon simultaneously?

To answer these questions (see Thaler [1985] for the theoretical discussion), define a joint outcome (x,y). If the outcomes are valued as $v(x,y)$, they are said to be integrated. If they are valued as $v(x) + v(y)$, they are said to be segregated. In the first scenario, x is a loss of 23¢ and y is a gain of 3¢. According to prospect theory, these should probably be segregated rather than integrated; i.e., use the coupon rather than cut the price, due to the large discrepancy between the loss and the gain (Thaler 1985, p. 202). On the other hand, for scenario 2, with a loss of 5¢ and a gain of 15¢, $v(+15¢) + v(-5¢) < v(15¢ - 5¢)$ due to the steepness of the loss function. Therefore, integration is preferred; i.e., the price should be cut by 10¢. Thus, there are some rather interesting normative implications from prospect theory for combination price strategies.

The modeling implications of this theory affect equation (6) through the asymmetric loss function of figure 2–2. As it is currently specified, the coefficient b should be negative. However, prospect theory indicates that positive values of $(p^o - p^r)$ should be more harshly received than negative values. Respecifying (6), we obtain

$$Q_t = a + b_1(p_t^o - p_t^r)d_1 + b_2(p_t^o - p_t^r)d_2 + cX_t + \epsilon_t, \qquad (14)$$

where $d_1 = 1$ if $(p_t^o - p_t^r) > 0,$

$\qquad = 0$ otherwise

$\quad d_2 = 1$ if $(p_t^o - p_t^r) < 0,$

$\qquad = 0$ otherwise.

Both b_1 and b_2 should be negative; and, under prospect theory, $|b_1| > |b_2|$.

Thaler [1985] takes the value function of prospect theory as a starting point for developing a theory of transactions. He defines total utility from a purchase as the sum of acquisition utility—the value of the good relative to how much is being spent—and transaction utility—how good a "bargain" it is. The latter is defined using value function notation as $v(p_t^o : p_t^r)$, that is, the value of paying p_t^o when the reference price is p_t^r. Clearly, the smaller the gap between p_t^o and p_t^r if the former is greater, the less the loss in utility. Thaler provides implications of his theory for pricing policy, but they apply only to the monopolist.

Other Relevant Theories

Several other theories that substantiate the existence of reference points in human judgment are worth briefly mentioning, although they do not result in quantifiable models of demand different from those already posited.

The research of Wertheimer [1938] and Rosch [1975] elaborates on the Gestalt psychology notion of cognitive reference points. They suggest that there are certain stimuli that act as ideal types or anchoring points for perception. Wertheimer [1938, p. 271] gives the example of how the number 101 is perceived relative to the anchoring point of 100 rather than as an absolute quantity. Rosch [1975] shows that colors shaded just slightly differently from primary colors are perceived relative to the primary color. In our context, the stimulus of an observed or advertised price would be hypothesized to be perceived relative to an anchor that we have termed the reference price.

Jacoby [1976] discusses the application of equity theory to the behavioral pricing literature. Equity theory (Pritchard 1969) describes the individual as seeking to compare his situation relative to those of others. If the individual perceives an imbalance, he will be motivated to take some action that restores equity. An important implication is that the individual develops internal standards based on experience against which the "other" is compared. Jacoby extends this theory to a consumer who is seeking equity in an exchange and therefore compares an observed price to some internal standard or "fair" price.

Sawyer and Dickson [1984] discuss a theory they term an uncertainty theory, which is really a slight reinterpretation of assimilation-contrast theory. They call the latitude of acceptance region in figure 2–1 an area of uncertainty in that the width of the flat region of the curve may be due to high price dispersion of close-substitute products, price variation of a product across stores, or the price of the product varying greatly over time.

Loomes and Sugden [1982] introduced what they called regret theory as a theory of choice under uncertainty. In their model, the amount of utility one derives from choosing a product is a function not only of the product selected but from the regret experienced from the forgone alternatives as well. Thus, the utility that would have been derived from the alternatives not chosen acts as a reference point against which the utility derived from the chosen product is compared.

Finally, Jacoby and Olson [1977] introduce two price-related terms: an "o" (objective) price, and a "p" price (the psychological price). The former is equivalent to p_t^o, while the latter is a qualitative assessment of p_t^o, such as "cheap." It is clear, therefore, that the "p" price is formed by comparing the "o" price to some internal reference point. They refer to this comparison process as "encoding" the "o" price and indicate that the "o" price is judged relative to some general adaptation level (p. 78).

Reference-Price Models

Note that in several of the equations, the reference price remains in the model to be estimated. In these two cases (the alternative Weber-Fechner and prospect-theory models), the appropriate theory of comparison does not specify the formation process for the reference price. As a result, models specifically applicable to the formation of reference prices must be used.

The set of variables that might be used to form a reference price is quite diverse (Oliver and Winer 1987). Any such model could be specified and used to substitute for the usually unobserved p_t^r. However, one that is commonly used is the adaptive-expectations process (Raman 1986; Winer 1986). The adaptive-expectations or error-learning process is

$$p_t^r - p_{t-1}^r = (1 - k)(p_{t-1}^o - p_{t-1}^r) \tag{15}$$

where k is a constant and $0 \leq k < 1$. It can be shown that by repeated substitution for p_t^r, equation (15) produces a distributed lag model of the form

$$p_t^r = (1 - k)p_t^o + (1 - k)kp_{t-2}^o + (1 - k)k^2 p_{t-3}^o + \ldots \tag{16}$$

Since k is between zero and one, higher-order terms of (16) become small quickly. Therefore, using two terms of (16), the prospect-theory model would become

$$Q_t = a + b\left[p_t^o - (1 - k)p_{t-1}^o - (1 - k)kp_{t-2}^o\right]d_1$$

$$+ b_2\left[p_t^o - (1 - k)p_{t-1}^o - (1 - k)kp_{t-2}^o\right]d_2 + cX_t + \epsilon_t. \tag{17}$$

This model may become difficult to distinguish from the linear form of the adaptation-level–theory model, equations (6) and (10b).

Table 2-1
Demand Models Developed from Psychological Theories

Theory	Model
Standard demand model	$Q_t = a + b p_t^o + c X_t + \epsilon_t$
Weber-Fechner models	$Q_t = (a - bd) + b(p_t^o - f \ln p_t^o) + c X_t + \epsilon_t$
	$Q_t = a + b \ln[(p_t^o - p_t^r)/p_t^r] + c X_t + \epsilon_t$
	$\forall (p_t^o - p_t^r) > 0$
Adaptation-level theory	$Q_t = a + b(p_t^o - e^{d + f \ln p_{t-1}^o}) + c X_t + \epsilon_t$
	$Q_t = (a - bd) + b(p_t^o - f p_{t-1}^o) + c X_t + \epsilon_t$
Assimilation-contrast theory	$Q_t = (a - bd) + b(p_t^o - f p_t^o - g p_t^{o2} - h p_t^{o3}) + c x_t + \epsilon_t$
Prospect theory	$Q_t = a + b_1(p_t^o - p_t^r)d_1 + b_2(p_t^o - p_t^r)d_2 + c X_t + \epsilon_t,$
	where $d_1 = 1$ if $(p_t^o - p_t^r) > 0,$
	$= 0$ otherwise
	$d_2 = 1$ if $(p_t^o - p_t^r) < 0,$
	$= 0$ otherwise

p_t^o = current observed price.
p_t^r = current reference price.
X_t = other marketing variables.
Q_t = demand.
$a, b, c, d, f, g, h,$ = parameters.

Summary

The weight of the theoretical evidence is heavily on the side of justification for the concept of reference prices. As can be seen, there are a large number of theories that can be drawn upon to assert that consumers do have some internal standard against which they compare communicated prices.

Some of the preceding theoretical arguments have been presented before. However, additional insights into empirically testing the competing theories have been gained, as can be seen by examining the summarizing table 2-1. Model comparison is quite easy in this situation as choosing the model with the largest $\bar{R}^2$ is equivalent to a likelihood ratio test of the non-nested alternatives (Theil 1971). The logical standard of comparison is a basic demand model incorporating price as p_t^o alone. Other tests besides that based on explained variance in Q_t would be based on the signs of significant parameters. For example, b should be negative based on all the structural models; the prospect-theory form implies a more specific relationship in terms of size between the split b coefficient. The parameters f, g, and h, where appropriate, are recoverable, but significance testing is difficult.

Operationalizations of the Concept

Eight Concepts of Reference Price

Up to this point, we have been proceeding as if there is universal agreement about the definition of a reference price. In concept, it is a standard against which observed prices are compared. In practice, however, as several authors have noted (Jacoby and Olson 1977; Zeithaml and Graham 1983), a wide variety of operationalizations have been proposed for the internal standard. Some of them are, in fact, so different from each other that it makes little sense to even consider the possibility that the set of reference prices consists of only one element. The behavioral prices proposed to act as contrasts with observed price include the following.

"Fair" or "Just" Price. This has been proposed by several authors including Ricardo [1948], Kamen and Toman [1970], and Gabor [1977]. Gabor [1977, p. 179] notes that it is a term that defies precise definition although he attempts to define it as a concept of what a good ought to cost. Clearly, based on the definition, people are assumed to pay only the "just" price or below it. Rao and Gautschi [1982] use the term *evoked price* instead of *just price* to refer to the consumer's conception of the fair price of a new product concept.

Price Frequently Charged. Olander [1970] describes the results of a small study indicating that consumers form perceptions of whether a given price being charged is high or low by comparing it to the price the consumer thinks is that most frequently charged for the good. Thus, the consumer is hypothesized to form a mental frequency distribution of historical prices and choose the mode as the reference price.

Last Price Paid. Uhl [1970] suggests that the last price paid for a good is its reference price. Gabor [1977] calls this the price image of the good and makes it clear that he thinks this reference point indicates how a consumer will react to a price change.

Reservation Price/Upper Threshold Limit. Economists (e.g., Scherer [1980, p. 17]) define a consumer's reservation price as the price just low enough to overcome resistance to buying a good or alternatively, the price at which a good leaves the budget. Rao and Gautschi [1982] define it simply as the highest price a consumer is willing to pay for a product. The consumer's reservation price has been used by Winer [1985] as a reference price in a durable-goods purchasing model.

The reservation-price concept is identical to the upper threshold limit discussed earlier (Adam 1970; Fouilhe 1970; Gabor and Granger 1964; Stoetzel 1970). This can be seen by looking at an example of the question put to consumers in evaluating the upper threshold (Stoetzel 1970): "Above what price would you judge a _____ to be too dear?"

Lower Threshold. The lower threshold in the acceptable-price-range theories acts as an internal reference point. Stoetzel's [1970] operationalization of this lower bound demonstrates this quite clearly: "Being what price would you suspect that a _____ was of poor quality?" In other words, contrary to economic theory, price can become too low for a good if there is a perception of concomitant low quality.

Price of the Brand Usually Bought. Tull, Boring, and Gonsior [1964] conducted a series of experiments examining the price–quality relationship. They asked consumers to judge the quality of products at different prices relative to a reference price they defined as the price of the brand usually bought. Thus, they feel that the reference price for product category is based on the price information from a single brand.

Average of Price Charged for Similar Goods. Emery [1970] and Monroe and Petroshius [1981] argue that consumers have an internal standard or reference price that is the average of the prices of similar goods. It is unclear whether this concept applies to a brand within a category or even between categories, but it is somewhat similar to Olander's [1970] notion of using the price most frequently charged for a product as the reference price.

Expected Future Price. Emery [1970] hypothesizes that consumers not only create current values of prices to be used as reference prices, but they also forecast future levels to make current consumption decisions. This concept has its foundations in Katona's work [cf. 1960] on how consumer expectations of future economic conditions affect purchasing plans. Winer [1985] uses this expectation of future prices as a comparison to current prices as the foundation for a model describing durable-goods purchasing behavior.

Implications for Demand Models

Based on the preceding discussion, it appears that there are really five different, independent operationalizations of the concept of reference price:

"just" price

reservation price

lowest acceptable price

expected price

perceived price

This latter construct, the consumer-perceived price, is an amalgamation of the price most frequently charged, last price paid, price of the brand usually bought, and the average price of similar goods. These quantities are actually different ways of computing what the consumer thinks is the current price, or, as Zeithaml and Graham [1983] express it, the price one is expected to pay for a good.

The concept of reference is clearly multidimensional in nature as it consists of what the consumer thinks is the fair price of a good, the maximum and minimum he would pay for it, the expected price of it in the future, and the current perceived or estimated price. A revised version of the basic reference-price model represented by equation (6) that incorporates the five operationalizations of reference price would be

$$Q_t = a + \underset{\sim}{b}'(\underset{\sim}{1} \times p_t^o - p_t^r) + cX_t + \epsilon_t \qquad (18)$$

where $\underset{\sim}{b}$ = 5 × 1 vector of coefficients

$\underset{\sim}{1}$ = 5 × vector of ones

p_t^r = 5 × 1 vector of reference prices

In other words, household-demand models must not only use the concept of reference price supported by the psychology literature, but should also specify a reference-price vector to account for the distinct types of reference prices that have been hypothesized in the marketing literature to affect consumer behavior.

This multidimensional notion of reference price has important implications for the models in table 2–1. Clearly, the same variables cannot be used to specify the five different reference prices as the reduced form would be highly multicollinear. In addition, it is not logical that the same process generating a consumer's "just" price would produce a minimum or reservation price. A research issue therefore raised at this point is the appropriate alternative specifications for the five reference-price concepts and how these affect the estimation of demand functions. This issue will be addressed in the section of the chapter devoted to research issues raised.

Empirical Evidence

Considerable evidence has been accumulated that some form of reference price serves as a basis for making price judgments (Monroe 1973; Monroe and Petroshius 1981; Zeithaml 1984). Scant research has been conducted linking reference prices to demand; that is, there have been few attempts to empirically validate the reference-price concept in a consumer-demand context.

There are essentially three types of studies linking demand with consumer comparison of price to some reference point: experiments relating price to demand, the work of Gabor and his colleagues, and econometric models using consumer-diary or scanner-panel data.

Experimental Research

Perhaps the earliest example of this approach is Pessemier's [1960] study attempting to estimate demand curves for frequently purchased branded goods. His approach was as follows. First, he estimated a base point on a brand's demand curve by determining how many subjects would buy the brand at its normal price. To estimate the upper half of the curve, he determined how many respondents would buy the brand if its price were raised in one-cent increments while holding prices of other brands in the category constant. To estimate the lower half of the curve, he used information from respondents' brand choices when each brand's prices in rotation was held fixed and the others dropped in one-cent decrements. This experiment does not explicitly use the concept of a reference price. However, the manner in which the demand curves were elicited implies a comparison to a reference price. For example, if brand *A* is normally priced at 31¢ and it is raised to 32¢ while the other brands remain fixed at 31¢, then a logical interpretation of the decline in demand for *A* at the higher price is that respondents developed 31¢ as some kind of reference point and judged a change to a higher price negatively.

Doob et al. [1969] report the results of five field experiments testing the differential impact in terms of sales of a low introductory price with a subsequent rise versus introducing the product at its ultimate intended price. The experiments consistently supported the strategy of introducing the product at the normal price. The authors used cognitive dissonance theory to predict the outcome in that the dissonance aroused by the higher price is justified by a greater liking for the product and more subsequent brand loyalty.

These results can also be easily explained by the reference-price theories reviewed earlier. For example, the low price becomes an adaptation level comparing unfavorably to the higher price and is a median point for a region of assimilation; the higher price is then contrasted to the acceptable range and produces a change in behavior.

Kamen and Toman [1970] reported the results of an experiment that rejected Weber's Law in favor of their "fair-price" theory. This theory stated that even small increments in price can have a negative impact on demand if the resulting price levels are above what consumers consider to be "fair." Weber's Law would dictate that small changes in high price levels would not produce a noticeable difference to consumers. Using gasoline price as the experimental variable and a mail questionnaire, they found that as price levels increase, a fixed difference in prices becomes more important, consistent with their "fair"-price theory, rather than less important. However, Gabor, Granger, and Sowter [1971], Monroe [1971a], and Stapel [1972] raised concerns about the validity of the fair-price theory developed by Kamen and Toman.

Nevin [1974] described an experiment designed to test the external validity of laboratory approaches to estimating price sensitivity. Of interest to us here are the lab experiments. His design incorporated price changes preceded by "cooling-off" periods that represented a return to the price existing before the experiment. Since all his results were in the expected direction (price cuts following the cooling-off periods had positive effects on market share and vice versa), the hypothesis of the returns to normal prices acting as adaptation levels for the subsequent price changes cannot be rejected.

Research by Gabor and His Colleagues

Much of the research by Gabor and his associates (see Gabor [1977] for a summary) has focused on what they have called the buy-response curve. Based upon their earlier cited work related to price thresholds and logarithmic price scales, they developed what is termed a buy-response curve. This is a plot of the percentage of customers for whom a given price is neither too high nor too low. In a 1971 article, Gabor, Granger, and Sowter map a buy-response curve versus last price paid for sausages and show that the two peak at a similar price. The implication is that higher sausage prices will meet resistance from a large portion of the consumer set.

Gabor [1977, appendix 2] derives a two-brand market-share model based on the reservation price or upper threshold limit. The model is

$$MS_b = \phi \left(\frac{p_a^o - p_b^o - m_{ab}}{\sigma_{ab}} \right), \tag{19}$$

where MS_b = market share of brand b

ϕ = normal distribution function

m_{ab} = mean of the distribution of $r_a - r_b$, the difference between the reservation prices of the two brands

σ_{ab} = standard deviation of m_{ab}

The implication of (19) is that MS_b and p_a/p_b are linearly related after a lognormal transformation. This relationship has been empirically verified by Gabor, Granger, and Sowter [1971].

Econometric Models

Winer [1985] developed a model for durable goods that incorporated both expected future prices and perceived prices contrasted with current actual price. Although he did not have actual measures of either reference price, he developed estimates of the quantities using a method for estimating missing observations. Using household-durables–purchasing data from the University of Michigan's Survey Research Center, he found that the probabilities of purchasing color TVs, washers, and dryers were significantly influenced by discrepancies between the reference prices and actual prices.

Gurumurthy and Little [1986] incorporate adaptation-level (AL) theory, assimilation-contrast theory, and prospect theory into a logit model of brand choice. The impact of AL theory is that the reference price is hypothesized to be a function of both the previous reference price and purchase price. The prospect-theory implications were stated earlier as positive values of $\left(p_t^o - p_t^r\right)$ deflating choice probabilities more than negative values add to them. Assimilation-contrast theory produces a range of acceptance around p_t^r. The results based on coffee scanner panel data support prospect theory but do not produce a latitude of acceptance and are insensitive to the smoothing parameters used in the adaptation function for p_t^r.

Raman [1986] defines reference price to be the expected actual price. He defines the latter to be a Box-Jenkins autoregressive model of historical prices. The current reference price captures, therefore, the information inherent in the past prices. He also tests for a minimum threshold effect and prospect-theory–like implications. Using aggregate market-share and price data, he finds strong support for the model in that for several of the brands, (1) there is a positive value for the threshold, indicating a minimum price deviation from the threshold is necessary to provoke a response, and (2) greater sensitivity exists for price deviations above the reference price than for deviations below it.

Winer [1986] specifies the following probability-of-purchase function for a household:

$$PROB_t = a + bPURCH_{t-1} + cADV_t + d\left(Rp_t^r - Rp_t^o\right) + fRp_t^o + \epsilon_t$$

$$(20)$$

where $PURCH_{t-1}$ = indicator of whether the brand was bought on the previous occasion

ADV_t = relative advertising

Rp_t^o, Rp_t^r = relative versions of the observed and reference prices

He specifies two formation models for the reference prices—adaptive expectations and rational expectations. Using coffee scanner panel data, he finds little to choose between the two formation processes but strong support for the model represented by equation (20). The results for the three brands studied are shown in table 2–2 based on logit estimation of (20).

Table 2–2
Probability-of-Purchase–Model Estimates (from Winer 1986)

Brand	Expectation Assumption	$PURCH_{t-1}$	$Rp^r - Rp^o$	ADV_t	Rp_t
A	Extrapolative	1.51**	2.22**	3.19**	−3.15**
		(.74)	(.85)	(.94)	(.64)
	Rational	1.47**	19.72**	2.53**	−23.47**
		(.10)	(5.45)	(.99)	(5.37)
B	Extrapolative	1.94**	5.71**	2.01**	−3.96**
		(.10)	(1.00)	(.83)	(.69)
	Rational	1.90**	7.59**	.97	−13.67**
		(.10)	(4.69)	(.89)	(4.54)
C	Extrapolative	1.46**	1.30	2.55**	−3.95**
		(.14)	(1.10)	(.56)	(.81)
	Rational	1.47**	5.65	2.69**	.92
		(.14)	(6.48)	(.62)	(6.37)

Note: Numbers in parentheses are asymptotic standard errors.
*Significant at $p < .10$, one-tail test.
**Significant at $p < .05$, one-tail test.

Although the literature supporting the empirical relationship between demand and reference prices is small, evidence is growing that it is a valid concept. Unfortunately, each area of research has drawbacks. The experimental literature does not actually mention reference prices, but produces results consistent with the concept. The econometric literature studies reference prices directly, but does not employ actual measures of the concept from consumers. The work of Gabor and his associates does not cover a very wide range of alternative reference-price theories. Thus, there is much yet to do; this is the subject of the next section.

Directions for Research

Validation of the Reference-Price Concept

Despite the significant amount of theoretical support for the reference-price concept, there is still relatively little empirical support. This has led Olson [1980, p. 15] to note that there is no "compelling published evidence for the psychological reality of a reference of adaptation-level price."

The existence of reference prices could be tested in several ways. Olson [1980] suggests the use of protocols. A second way might be to use an information-board approach (that is, allow respondents to choose from a set of information bits in order to select a preferred brand and offer "normal" price or "price last paid" as a bit). A method for examining the price-comparison process itself was proposed by Rosch [1975], who tested for cognitive reference points using linguistic hedges (terms such as *almost* or *virtually* that represent metaphorical distance).

Multiple Reference Prices

As developed earlier in this chapter, reference-price research has really produced five distinct prices consumers may use to compare against observed price. Like the reference-price concept itself, the multidimensional nature of reference prices has yet to be established. Many questions exist in this area. For example, which reference prices are relevant for different product categories or types (e.g., durables versus services versus grocery products)? Do all enter into a demand model in the same manner? Observed prices higher than a consumer's reservation price do not create the same customer response as prices above the customer's minimum acceptable price. Finally, as noted earlier, each reference price may be formed in a different manner.

Normative Pricing Models

As was shown in the introduction using a simple model, the existence of reference prices may alter the prescriptions obtained from normative pricing models. Only Rao and Shakun [1972] have used reference-price concepts in this context. They adapt the price-limit model developed by Gabor and Granger to the new-product–introduction pricing problem.

Perhaps the best normative application of the reference-price concept is for optimal promotion policy. Kinberg, Rao, and Shakun [1974] used the Rao-Shakun model to develop optimal promotion policies in a two-brand market. They show that the optimal size of a price-off promotion and profits of the premium brand being promoted decrease as the share of the brand doing the promoting increases. Kinberg and Rao [1975] develop a model showing that when consumers do not know the duration of the promotion, the optimal duration and profitability of the promotion are positively related to the initial switching probability. However, what is needed is some control theoretic approach that, as opposed to static models, allows the determination of the optimal time path of both promotion-adjusted and unadjusted prices. This would allow for the fact that a promotion running for a period of time may create a lowered adaptation level that would be unfavorably contrasted to a normal price level. See Winer [1986] for supporting arguments.

The Effects of Different-Sized Deviations

There has been some research examining the impact of different-sized price discrepancies from a reference price. Della Bitta, Monroe, and McGinnis [1981] report the results of an experiment that, among other things, looked at the effect of advertised discounts from a "regular" price on perceived value of the offer, interest, and information search. They found that increasing the size of the discount tended to increase the perceived value of the discount, heighten interest, and diminish intent to search for brand information.

Several research questions arise in this area. First, does the effect of the size of a deviation on demand or there purchase-related factors vary by reference price? For example, a 10 percent deviation from perceived price may affect brand choice differently than the equivalent deviation from reservation price. A second issue relates to optimal size of a promotion. Wright [1975] finds that consumers tend to simplify decision tasks when faced with a moderate information load and some time pressure, a situation somewhat akin to supermarket shopping. The finding of Della Bitta, Monroe, and McGinnis [1981] that large discounts diminish information search (i.e., simplify the decision process) supports large promotions over small ones for them to be noticed. In addition, psychological research (e.g., Moyer and Landauer 1967) has shown the existence of a symbolic distance effect—the greater the psychological difference between two stimuli, the faster people can compare their size. Therefore, the discrepancy size effect needs to be further studied, particularly with respect to the five different reference prices.

Explicit versus Implicit Modeling of p_t^r

There are essentially two ways to estimate the demand models specified earlier in the chapter. First, one could use, say, equation (6), obtain measures of p_t^o, p_t^r, and X_t, and estimate the equation. Alternatively, as was done with several of the models, a separate equation for p_t^r can be developed and substituted into equation (6) to eliminate p_t^r to produce a reduced form that itself can be estimated. The advantage of this latter approach is that p_t^o is usually obtainable from standard data sources, while p_t^r is not.

Each approach has a drawback. For the approach necessitating measures of the vector p_t^r, the problem is whether people can truly state what, say, they feel the current price is of a brand. If it is a concept people only use subconsciously, the act of measurement itself affects the external validity of the study. For the reduced-form approach, no measurement of the p_t^r variables is ever undertaken and, therefore, at the end, one is not completely sure what has been found.

An experiment could perhaps be designed to help resolve this issue. In a simulated shopping environment such as that used by Pessemier [1960] or Nevin [1974], direct measures of the p_t^r could be obtained as well as brand preferences or choices over time. The predictive efficacy of the two estimation approaches would help to determine which method best captures reference-price effects on demand.

Which Theory?

Some research effort must be attempted to discriminate between the alternative reference-price theories. As can be seen from the previous discussion and as is noted by Gurumurthy and Little [1986], some of the theories conflict. For example, prospect theory assumes that the value function rises or falls directly from the reference point, while assimilation-contrast theory has a threshold effect that creates a flat spot around the reference point. The approach developed earlier in this chapter that permits separate estimation of each model implied by the different theories and then an ultimate model comparison would be one way to help answer this question.

Conclusion

In this chapter, two major issues have been raised. First, the concept of a reference price, which has often been alluded to in prior research, is multidimensional in nature. It has been argued that it is, in fact, at least five distinctly different concepts. The second issue raised is the need to empirically relate the reference-price concepts to actual consumer demand. Some suggestions have been made for incorporating the concepts into demand models as well as related research. It is hoped that this research will be stimulated by this chapter and develop into a body of knowledge that will allow us to assess the importance of reference prices in affecting demand.

Part II
Pricing and the Role of
Information in Markets

Anne T. Coughlan

T he three chapters in this part—by Devinney, Cooper and Ross, and Moorthy—all deal with pricing (and, more generally, the informational role of the firm's decision variables in market equilibrium) in different contexts. Devinney shows how advertising, scale of production, or price can all be used as signals of (i.e., information sources about) product quality. He develops similar models for each of the three instruments and shows that production and market-structure alterations can accompany advertising signaling, but not scale or price signaling. He argues that of the three, price signaling is the weakest, because of the strong assumptions that must be imposed to assure a stable equilibrium. Scale is the strongest signal under the assumption that it positively affects quality perceptions. However, this assumption may not be satisfied in product markets where small scale carries a connotation of customization or exclusivity. In general, he shows economic motivations (particularly from the firm side) for using advertising, scale, or price as a quality signal.

Cooper and Ross concentrate on the role of warranties as mechanisms to reduce moral hazard by providing both insurance and incentives for "correct" behavior. Their work generally relegates price to the role of clearing the market rather than to that of disseminating information. In a model with risk-averse buyers, where sellers cannot verify how much care buyers exert in using the purchased product, they show that warranties can serve two purposes: first, they give sellers an incentive to produce a high-quality product, and second, they serve as insurance for the risk-averse buyers. The obvious moral-hazard problem of buyers deliberately misusing the product after purchase in order to benefit from the warranty is controlled by granting a warranty that is less than 100 percent protective.

Finally, Moorthy models a situation where price could be used to deceive, but is instead used to reveal information to consumers who are uncertain about a monopolist's costs. Here, consumers form expectations about future prices according to a rational-expectations rule. Clearly, if their expectations are completely naive (in effect, if they do not have expectations), the monopolist's problem is not a truly dynamic one; instead, the monopolist faces a series of static pricing decisions. But if consumers really do form expectations and might wait until the second period to buy a product, then the pricing issue becomes more complicated: a low-cost monopolist must decide whether to reveal its true nature (here, cost structure) in the first period, or to disguise itself as a high-cost (and, hence, high-price) seller in the first period. Moorthy shows that the low-cost monopolist in fact has an incentive to *reveal* its nature through its first-period pricing decision rather than to fool consumers. In short, the monopolist has a profit incentive to set its first-period price so as to dispel any uncertainty consumers have about its cost structure.

From these chapters, it is first clear that given perfect certainty on both the consumer side and the firm side, price (and, indeed, any other decision variable of the firm) plays no informative role, but, rather, only an allocative role. This is because there is no information left to disseminate—all is already known about all actors in the market. While this has been a handy assumption to economic modelers, it is clearly a strong one. Further, price can play no informational role in perfectly competitive markets, since then price simply equals the marginal cost of the marginally operating firm in the market (as in chapter 4 by Cooper and Ross). In such cases, other mechanisms (such as their warranties) must be brought to bear to manage market uncertainty.

Further, uncertainty can take many forms, as the three chapters in part II illustrate. Manufacturers can be uncertain about consumers' reservation prices or about the time and effort consumers exert to maintain a product after purchase. Consumers can be uncertain about a manufacturer's costs or about product quality. Quality itself can have multiple dimensions (e.g., durability, size, and comfort); uncertainty about these dimensions may or may not be resolved after purchase and use of a product. Cooper and Ross assume quality is perfectly observed ex post, but this assumption is clearly not met in all markets. (Consider the consumption of doctors' services, for instance.) Price is one of the many mechanisms that can be used to reveal information in situations of uncertainty (particularly consumer uncertainty); notice that then, it serves both as a revelation mechanism and as an allocative, or market-clearing, mechanism. This dual use of price (or any other single decision variable) is the source of many of the results in the literature concerning the second-best nature of uncertainty equilibria; it cannot be used to multiple purposes without some sacrifice in social welfare or allocative efficiency.

A natural issue of concern in these contexts is the first-best benchmark against which these equilibria are judged. Frequently (as in, for instance, chapter 4), the first-best equilibrium is the one given *no* uncertainty and given an objective of maximizing social welfare. The distortions from this equilibrium caused by uncertainty are quite real; it is important to keep in mind that in many situations, the first-best is attainable in theory only. That is, the "second-best" is really the best solution to the problem available given the state of the world under uncertainty. Comparisons to the theoretical first-best are useful for diagnostic purposes, but not as much for prescriptive ones. In this sense, all three chapters in part II provide examples of the Le Chatelier principle in economics: a problem with a constraint imposed upon it (such as uncertainty) cannot generate a solution that is superior to that achieved in the problem without the constraint.

What can be done to improve the situation? All three chapters consider the possibility of somehow withdrawing or vitiating the importance of the uncertainty constraint. For instance, Cooper and Ross show that not just uncertainty, but also consumers' risk aversion, is important in generating distortions from first-best behavior. Hence, one way of getting around their second-best problem is by having risk-neutral consumers rather than risk-averse ones—then there is no demand for insurance. Another solution is to provide multiple information mechanisms instead of just one (such as price). This can relieve the difficulties induced by forcing price to play more than one role—informational as well as allocative. Devinney provides some qualitative insights into multidimensional signaling mechanisms, arguing that additional signals improve an equilibrium. Moorthy considers the possibility of the monopolist precommitting to a pricing sequence and shows that this is a superior solution to that without precommitment (although he does not explain how precommitment can be achieved realistically).

Those concerned with social welfare might look at the second-best results and conclude that outside intervention is needed to correct market distortions. Cooper and Ross correctly note that any policies designed to induce a first-best solution must take account of *all* the margins on which decisions are made. In particular, if the government were to enforce greater warranty protection in their model, equal to the socially optimal level, consumers would exert less than the socially optimal level of care with the product. Hence, the warranty problem might be solved, but not the moral-hazard problem. A complete solution in this case would have to take into account incentive effects on both the seller side and buyers side, somehow forcing consumers to take the socially optimal amount of care in using the product.

In general, it is clear from this literature and its antecedents that uncertainty can decrease producer and consumer surplus relative to a world of complete certainty. Further, dealing with that problem may involve completely revealing the hidden information (as in Moorthy's analysis, where it is in the monopolist's interest to resolve consumer uncertainty) or it may mean using imperfect signals that incompletely resolve uncertainty. Because these signals are typically costly, uncertainty generally exacts some deadweight cost on the market.

These three pieces suggest some useful directions for future research in the areas of pricing and information. First, some empirical contributions could be made based on the theories developed here. It would be of interest to discover how much information is revealed through different signals (e.g., price as opposed to advertising or scale of production), how consumers process signals from firms, how firms process consumer signals, and what markets look like after the dissemination of firm and consumer signals.

Of further interest, both from empirical and theoretical points of view, is the issue of how quickly consumers learn from signals in the marketplace. Rational-expectations models that assume consumers can perform complicated game-theoretic problems under either certainty or uncertainty may give biased predictions about pricing and demand in equilibrium (or, indeed, the existence of an equilibrium). Moorthy argues that "nonrational expectations" is not a useful modeling device because of the many ways in which expectations may be wrong. Perhaps this is really an indication that both (1) theoretical investigation of the robustness of modeling results to various types of incomplete processing capabilities and (2) empirical investigation of the nature of processing limitations of firms and consumers will be useful in increasing our understanding of the workings of markets under uncertainty. This may involve explicitly dynamic modeling and empirical work to discover the nature of learning processes for market participants.

In addition, the chapters in part II do not exhaust the applications of pricing and information. For instance, in some market situations (such as employment contracts and auctions), it is the buyer that declares a purchase price, not the seller. There, the price declared can reveal the reservation price of the buyer; or it can serve to identify to the buyer the nature of sellers, since only sellers of a certain "type" might agree to contract with the buyer. In compensation contracts, offering a "menu" of "purchase prices" (compensation plans) can induce employees to reveal their productivity or risk characteristics via their choice of plan. But in any of these cases, it is still true that multiple mechanisms for resolving uncertainty (whether they are multiple prices or price and other nonprice mechanisms) improve upon a system where price is forced to play a combined incentive and allocative role.

3
Price, Advertising, and Scale as Information-Revelation Mechanisms in Product Markets

Timothy M. Devinney

The traditional neoclassical economic theorist's view of a consumer is a rational calculating computer in possession of all pertinent information and armed with the ability to use it. It is hardly surprising that this viewpoint is incorrect. Indeed, no economist would be willing to argue for its literal application. Consumers, operating in an uncertain environment, with only limited abilities and even more limited information, frequently rely on techniques and information that economists have been quick to assume they neither use, possess, nor need to use.

In such an uncertain world, it is frequently found that consumers rely on second-hand pieces of information to gauge the quality of products they are purchasing. Early studies by Gabor and Granger [1966], subsequently confirmed by others (e.g., Gardner [1971], Shapiro [1973]), showed that consumers use price to infer quality. Monroe [1973] further showed that this effect was most dramatic when only price was available. In a single-cue or price-only environment, consumers were found to use price as an indicator of quality. If other nonprice information was made available to consumers in a multiple-cue setting, the inferential relation between price and quality was found to disappear.

Advertising has long been thought to convey quality information. From a psychological perspective, advertising was believed to be a persuasive device that could alter brand image and foster sales. Advertising's informative content was not ignored, but was downplayed relative to its creative and persuasive merits. Economists, unable to formally model such qualitative corporate tools, downplayed the role of advertising as nothing but a parameter in the profit equation similar to investment. Nelson [1970, 1974, 1978] provided the first unique economic approach to the role of advertising. He argued that the information content of advertising is not in the content of the message but in the volume of messages. By providing a high volume of messages, the producer assures that there is a high probability that its product will be selected, if only to evaluate its quality.

A third predictor of product quality is the size of a firm. Although traditional business wisdom has, until recently, held that quality of product is relative to the size of a firm's operation, the role that size of market share has played in revealing information on quality has escaped academic inquiry.

The present chapter provides an introduction to the economics of information and shows how second-hand information can be used as an indicator of quality in product markets. More specifically, the informational content of the three indicators just discussed (price, advertising, and size of firm) will be examined. The next section provides an introduction to the economics of information. The subsequent section discusses each of the mechanisms in detail. The following section provides an extension on multiple signals of quality. The final section contains concluding statements and remarks.

Economics of Information

Recent work in the economics of information has forced economists to realize that the perfect-information assumption made by neoclassical theorists is a simplification of reality. The nature of an economic equilibrium will be determined by whether consumers can costlessly observe valuable information in a marketplace. Although economists have implicitly recognized that the form of an economic equilibrium can be changed by an uncertain environment (see, e.g., Stigler [1961]), it had been traditionally assumed that the basic nature and stability of the equilibrium would remain intact. Akerlof [1970], in an economic analysis of the used-car "lemon" problem, provided the first dominant example of how quality uncertainty on the part of buyers could destabilize an economic equilibrium. In Akerlof's example, retailers knew the quality of the car they were selling, but buyers did not know. Buyers knew what the average quality was and treated all cars as average, bidding a fair price for average quality. However, only sellers of below-average-quality cars would accept the price for an average-quality car. Therefore, only below-average-quality cars were sold. If buyers knew this in advance, they would obviously make their bid lower than the price of the average-quality car. In the market, however, for every price they chose to offer, only those sellers with cars below the quality appropriate for the offered price were willing to sell. As a result, quality collapsed. Only cars of the lowest quality would be sold at the lowest price.

Spence [1973, 1974] and Riley [1975] provided the second critical discovery in the economic theory of information with their development of signaling theory. A signal is a piece of information that can be revealed to the market at some cost to the revealer. Signals are important because they can be related to some underlying valuable economic resource. For example, one implication of Spence's work is that high-ability individuals would be more willing to go to college, particularly an expensive college, since they would receive a higher ultimate payoff in future wages. Educational achievement serves as a signal because low-ability individuals find it either more difficult to succeed in college or receive a lower ultimate payoff in future wages. Educational achievement reveals productivity since it is controllable by the individual and has a differential value for individuals of different productivities.

The findings of Spence and Akerlof define two interrelated but different streams of research in the economics of information. Akerlof's work highlighted the importance of the asymmetry of information in economic markets, and it effectively defined a stream of research that now concentrates on the role played by the differential possession of information by market participants. Spence's work defines an orientation that is more concerned with the role that the actual costs and benefits of information revelation play in those markets. While most research contains elements borrowing from both streams, it is important to keep them separate since they address slightly different issues. The next two sections outline each area of research.

Signaling

In understanding market signaling, it is important to first recognize that not all observable differences are signals. Spence [1974] makes an important distinction between *signals* and *indexes*, both actual and potential:

1. A *potential signal* is an observable alterable characteristic.
2. A *potential index* is an observable unalterable characteristic.
3. An *actual signal* is a potential signal that affects market participants' conditional probability assessments of a relevant market parameter.
4. An *actual index* is a potential index that affects market participants' conditional probability assessments of a relevant market parameter.

A signal is, therefore, a manipulable attribute or activity that conveys information. An index can convey information but cannot serve as a signal. Both signals and indexes can exist in potential form without actually conveying information. For example, the sex of a worker may be a potential index for productivity; however, there is no indication that it possesses relevant information. Alternatively, something as seemingly innocuous as the quality of the attire of a potential employee at an interview can serve as a signal of productivity. It is completely alterable and may possess information of potential presentability. Table 3–1 outlines some potential market indexes and signals.

For a piece of information to serve as a basic signal, the following necessary, though not sufficient, conditions are required:

1. A difference in some underlying economic parameter (e.g., quality or productivity).

Table 3-1
Some Potential Signals and Indexes

Index	Signal	
Individual	Individual	Corporate
Race	Education	Advertising
Sex	Place of residence	Financial data
Nation of origin	Marital status	Warranty coverage
Age	Occupation	Number of employees
Height	Weight	Diversification of product
Handicap status	Length of Employment	offerings
Blood type	Number of children	Centralization
	Asset ownership (e.g.,	Prices
	car, home, boat)	
	Religion	

2. A difference in the cost of provision of some economic output (e.g., quality or production) between individuals of different types.

3. Observability of the economic output or some factor that covaries with that output.

To continue our discussion and highlight the importance of these items, let us use the example of college admissions. Suppose two types of university exist: Ivy League and state schools. Ivy League colleges cost \$I to attend, while state schools cost \$S to attend. A successful graduate from an Ivy League school will receive a discounted lifetime salary of L_I; a state school graduate will earn L_S. Those failing out of an Ivy League school receive a salary of L_F. We will assume that $L_I > L_S > L_F$, and that no one fails out of a state school. Two ability types exist, genius (G) and normal (N). For the sake of simplicity, a genius never fails out of school, while a normal individual has a probability ρ of failing out of an Ivy League school.

Is attendance at an Ivy League school a valid signal that an individual is of the genius ability? The answer will be yes only when normal individuals find attendance at an Ivy League school too expensive *and* geniuses find attendance at Ivy League schools preferable to attendance at state schools. This requires the following. First, $L_I - I > L_S - S$; otherwise, geniuses would go to state schools. In addition $(1 - \rho) L_I + \rho L_F - I < L_S - S$; otherwise, normal people would go to Ivy League schools. Rearranging this last expression, we find that $\rho < [L_S - L_I - (S - I)]/(L_F - L_I)$ for type of school to serve as a valid signal of the intellectual quality of graduate. This implies that the larger ρ is, the smaller need be the difference in tuition since the possibility of failing out of an Ivy League school has the requisite effect. Normal people are unwilling to bear the cost of failing out and will therefore attend only state schools. On the flip side, the lower ρ is, the more tuition cost is important in driving the signal.

This simple example effectively outlines the basics of signaling theory. First, individuals differ in basic ability. Second, the cost of revealing that difference varies. Normal people face an expected cost of $\rho(L_I - L_F)$ by going to an Ivy League school and trying to play on the fact that only the signal and not the true variable is observable. Third, the signal, a diploma, is observable. Note another interesting fact; the benefits of an education are clear up-front. A higher salary goes to the Ivy Leaguers. In basic signaling theory, the cost of the signal is what drives the value of the signal. Logically, one may wish to think of the net benefit of a signal as some return less a cost. Elementary signaling theory, however, only concentrates on the cost difference.

Asymmetric Information

Asymmetric information is said to exist when one party is in possession of information having an impact on the welfare of another participant in the marketplace. Such an asymmetry in information can arise because of a participant's position (e.g., a corporate board member might possess information of value to the financial markets) or because an individual might have some specialization in ability that allows the person to collect information more readily than others can. Although the purpose of this formulation has been limited to a set of specific problems (agency relationships, long-term contracts, and so on), almost any market transaction possesses some aspect of this concept.

In product markets, asymmetry of information with respect to quality is a given. Almost any transaction, from buying an automobile or home to weekly grocery shopping, has the characteristic that the producer possesses more knowledge about the quality of the product than the consumer. Even with years of knowledge, it is unlikely that a consumer would possess information superior to that of the producer. Consumers are concerned with whether or not they can get the producer to correctly reveal the quality of the product. In this sense, the consumer purchasing a product is no different from a stockholder desiring that a manager correctly reveal the financial condition of a firm.

To understand the simple asymmetric information formulation, consider two individuals, A and B, where A takes on actions that affect B. Let E be the set of actions that A can take, and let $e \in E$ denote a specific action. In addition, let θ represent a state of nature drawn from a probability distribution G. The state of nature and A's action jointly determine some outcome, $x = x(e, \theta)$, which has a direct effect on B. Each action costs A some amount, denoted $s(e)$, and the outcome is rewarded in some manner, denoted $r(x)$. Individual B receives some payoff or utility from the outcome, less the amount paid to A. Individual B gains $v(x) - r(x)$, where $v(\cdot)$ is B's utility function. A has a net reward of $u[s(x)] - s(e)$, where $u(\cdot)$ is A's utility function. Both A and B

know the parameters of the problem, G, $x(\cdot, \cdot)$, $u(\cdot)$, $v(\cdot)$, $r(\cdot)$, and $s(\cdot)$, and x is observable. However, only A knows e, hence the informational asymmetry.

The formulation itself is somewhat uninteresting until one looks at its implications. Since e is costly to A, A will not use as high a level of action as B would desire. In addition, any outcome implies an uncertain signal about e since x is affected by θ as well. Ideally, if e were observable, B could condition payment on it and not x, and there would be nothing at issue. Therefore, the major implication that follows is that, if e is unobservable, the better will be the reward system, $r(x)$, the closer is the relationship between x and e.

In product markets, numerous systems of rewards exist where relation between underlying parameter and the reward system are linked. Repurchase, or repeat sales, is nothing more than a de facto long-term contract between consumer and producer. Warranties serve as risk-sharing arrangements between producer and consumer. In addition, the willingness to engage in these actions serves as a signal of quality. The willingness to guarantee has long been seen as an indicator of quality, while word-of-mouth advertising is directly related to repeat sales.

Signaling in Product Markets

This section provides the background for the analyses of the upcoming sections. Terms are defined and basic assumptions outlined.

All industries are competitive with potentially two qualities being produced: high and low. Quality is denoted $Q = H, L$. Demand depends on two factors: quality and a signal, p. Demand is denoted $D(p, Q)$. For our purposes, consumers will be assumed to be of two types: high-quality demanders and low-quality demanders. Low-quality demanders number n_L and will only pay for the lowest-perceived-quality product. High-quality demanders number n_H and will pay a premium up to β above the low-quality price for perceived high-quality products.

Producers will have a signaling strategy denoted $p = g(Q)$, which implies the firm signals p when Q is true. The consumer infers Q from p using $Q = g^{-1}(p)$. The signal is an actual signal only when firms producing different qualities choose different signals. Figure 3–1 shows this graphically. In [1], both high- and low-quality producers signal $p^{\dagger}$ and therefore do not allow consumers to distinguish between high and low quality. In [2], high-quality producers signal $p^{\dagger}$, while low-quality producers signal $p^{\dagger\dagger}$, allowing consumers to distinguish quality based on the signal. Mathematically, frame [2] implies $g(\cdot)$ is invertible.

Firms can produce either low- or high-quality goods, but must commit to producing either one or the other and cannot switch between quality types once a choice is made. The cost of high-quality production is given by

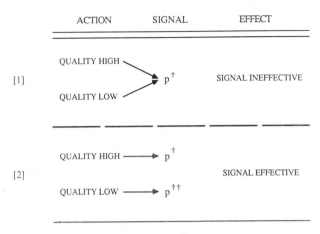

Figure 3–1. Effective and Ineffective Signals

$C(x \mid H)$ and the cost of low-quality production by $C(x \mid L)$. For any given level of output, x^0, $C(x^0 \mid L) < C(x^0 \mid H)$. If high-quality firms were only in competition with other high-quality firms, and quality were freely verifiable ex ante, then the high-quality price would be $P_0^{*H} = C(\hat{x}_0^{*H} \mid H)/\hat{x}_0^{*H}$, firm quantity would be $\hat{x}_0^{*H}$ (point B), and $F_0^{*H} = n_H/\hat{x}_0^{*H}$ high-quality firms would be in operation. If the same was true for low-quality firms, their price would be $P_0^{*L} = C(\hat{x}_0^{*L} \mid L)/\hat{x}_0^{*L}$, firm quantity would be $\hat{x}_0^{*L}$ (point E), and $F_0^{*L} = n_L/\hat{x}_0^{*L}$ low-quality firms would be in operation. These results are shown in figure 3–2 and will serve as our benchmark for later analysis.

When quality is either nonverifiable or only incompletely verifiable, the signal takes on potential value. We will assume that it costs firms $s(p \mid Q)$ to signal p when quality is Q. We have allowed the possibility that $s(p^0 \mid L) \neq s(p^0 \mid H)$ and $s(p^0 \mid L) = s(p^0 \mid H)$. Firms earn discounted profits from operations denoted $\pi(x \mid Q)$ and total discounted profits given by $\pi(x \mid Q) - s(p \mid Q) = Px - C(x \mid Q) - s(p \mid Q)$. Since all markets are competitive, profits must be zero in equilibrium, which further implies that $\pi(x \mid Q) - s(p \mid Q) = 0$.

A signaling equilibrium will exist when it does not pay for low-quality firms to mimic high-quality firms' behavior *and* it pays high-quality firms to behave in a manner different from low-quality firms. Suppose high-quality firms choose the signal $p^H = g(Q = H)$, and low-quality firms choose the signal $p^L = g(Q = L)$. Then, as long as there is no alternative signal, p', such that either high- or low-quality firms choose to switch signals and $p' \neq g(Q = H) \neq g(Q = L)$, then $[p^H, p^L]$ is a viable signaling equilibrium. If profits are zero, it will be both viable and stable. We conclude this section by stating the equilibrium conditions mathematically:

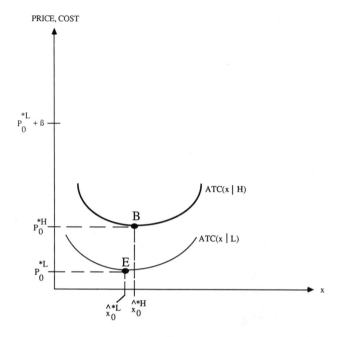

Figure 3-2. Price and Firm Output in Competition with Quality Freely Verifiable ex ante

Signaling condition:

$$\nexists \ a \ \{p', x'\} \text{ such that when } p^{*H} \neq p^{*L}$$

$$\pi(x^{*i} \mid i) - s(p^{*i} \mid i) < \pi(x' \mid i) - s(p' \mid i) \qquad i = H, L \tag{1}$$

and

$$\pi(x^{*i} \mid i) - s(p^{*i} \mid i) < \pi(x^{*j} \mid i) - s(p^{*j} \mid i) \quad i = H, L; \quad j = L, H; \quad i \neq j. \tag{2}$$

Competitive equilibrium condition:

$$\pi(x^{*i} \mid i) - s(p^{*i} \mid i) = 0 \qquad i = H, L. \tag{3}$$

Advertising as a Signal

Advertising has long been regarded as an indicator for the quality of the product advertised. A great deal of psychologically based marketing and policy literature has held that advertising can promote a false image of quality. (For a discussion of this literature, see, e.g., Beales, Craswell, and Salop [1981], Gardner [1975], Peltzman [1981], and Russo, Metcalf, and Stephens [1981].) This literature has served as the primary impetus for much of the government intervention, primarily by the Federal Trade Commission, in the area of false and misleading advertising. Economists have had relatively little to say in the area of false and misleading advertising simply because of the difficulty of considering economically the impact of advertising copy on consumers, the primary focus of misleading advertising studies and cases. Relatively recently, economists have begun to approach this problem as a variant of the work in the formation of expectations. The main thesis in this work is that advertising may have value independent of content. That is, the existence of advertising, or its relative frequency, can serve as a signal for some other characteristic of the product in question (e.g., quality).

The motivating force behind the initial advertising-as-a-signal research was the pioneering work of Phillip Nelson [1970, 1974, 1978]. Nelson [1974] argued that the interaction of familiarity with products and repeat purchase can create the conditions necessary for advertising to reflect a product's quality. High-quality firms should advertise more than low-quality firms. Schmalensee [1978] based his theory on Nelson's main thesis that advertising affects repeat purchases; however, his conclusions were the opposite—high-quality firms advertise less than low-quality firms. Schmalensee's result is driven by one critical assumption. Repeat purchase is negatively related to quality; however, a low-quality firm can attract a higher number of customers dissatisfied by other low-quality firms and will therefore advertise heavily to counteract the attrition it faces from deceived consumers. Such an assumption cannot be viewed as valid in a rational expectations environment since consumers must ultimately learn that they are continually dissatisfied by heavy-advertising firms.

Kihlstrom and Riordan [1984] and Milgrom and Roberts [1986] provide two examples that keep to the spirit of Nelson's argument. The Milgrom and Roberts model investigates the role of joint advertising and price signals, thus falling in the class of multiple-signal models discussed in a subsequent section. Kihlstrom and Riordan provide a model where consumers are initially uninformed and use advertising as a signal. Repeat purchases are driven not by advertising, but by the quality of the product (which is fully revealed with use). Advertising serves as a signal because high-quality firms, achieving more repeat business because of satisfied customers, can recover the advertising cost, while low-quality firms, facing future customer dissatisfaction, cannot. Kihlstrom and Riordan further show that, even if repeat purchasing is not affected by experience with the product, advertising can serve as a signal so long as the marginal cost of high-quality production is lower than for low-quality production. In other words, this implies that advertising may signal quality when most of the cost difference between low- and high-quality products is in the variable production cost and not in the fixed set-up cost.

The model to be illustrated here is a simple variant of Kihlstrom and Riordan. High- and low-quality firms have different production costs and each can advertise at a cost of A per unit of production; using our signaling terminology, $s(p = A) = s(p = A \mid H) = Ax$. Consumers can observe advertising volume costlessly; therefore, the signal cost and value are the same. Consumers only infer quality from advertising. The higher the advertising, the higher the perceived quality.

Figure 3–3 outlines the possible decisions and payoffs for the two types of firms. Each firm can choose to advertise some amount or not advertise. Since it will ultimately be true that advertising is either completely sufficient to signal quality or not sufficient at all, only two possibilities exist as to the level of advertising—firms advertise an amount A or zero. Since two different volumes of advertising always signal two levels of quality, the low-quality producer loses no customers by reducing advertising to zero and saves the advertising cost. Therefore, only cell 2 in figure 3–3 provides a viable signaling equilibrium.

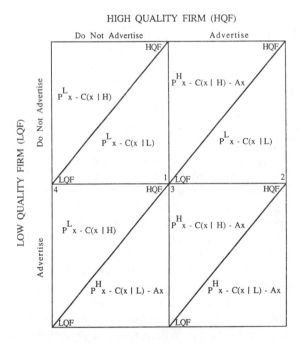

Figure 3–3. Advertising Actions and Payoffs for High- and Low-Quality Firms

The conditions leading to cell 2 being the equilibrium remain to be shown. A high-quality firm will advertise when:

$$P^H x^H - C(x^H \mid H) - A^H x^H \geqq 0. \tag{4}$$

A low-quality firm will not advertise when:

$$P^H x^L - C(x^L \mid L) - A^H x^L < 0. \tag{5}$$

For signaling to be possible, the low-quality firm must be unwilling to advertise at the same level as the high-quality firm, A^H. High-quality firms will always be in competition to force the equilibrium high-quality price to be equal to minimum average total cost, $p^H = [C(\hat{x}^H \mid H) + A^H \hat{x}^H]/\hat{x}^H$, where $\hat{x}^H$ is minimum efficient scale. Combining equations (4) and (5) plus this last relation implies that for advertising choices to be different:

$$\frac{C(\hat{x}^H \mid H) + A^H \hat{x}^H}{\hat{x}^H} < \frac{C(\hat{x}^L \mid L) + A^H x^L}{x^L} \qquad \forall \ x^L$$

or $\qquad\qquad\qquad\qquad\qquad\qquad\qquad\qquad\qquad\qquad\qquad\qquad\qquad\quad$ (6)

$$ATC(\hat{x}^H, A^H \mid H) < ATC(x^L, A^H \mid L) \qquad \forall \ x^L$$

where $ATC(\cdot \mid i)$ is the average total cost of producer of quality i.

What does equation (6) mean? For advertising to be a signal, some level of minimum average total cost for high-quality firms must exist, which is lower than an average cost for low-quality firms advertising at the same level. In addition, it must be remembered that high-quality customers will only pay a premium of β. Therefore, an additional condition is:

$$\frac{C(\hat{x}^H \mid H) + A \hat{x}^H}{\hat{x}^H} - \frac{C(\hat{x}^L \mid L)}{\hat{x}^L} < \beta. \tag{7}$$

Equations (6) and (7) plus the competitive zero-profit condition, equation (3), are necessary and sufficient conditions for a signaling equilibrium.

Figure 3–4 provides a simple example of this case. If both firm types advertise at level A', then some low-quality firms could mimic high-quality behavior since for quantities $x_W < x^L < x_V$, $ATC(x, A' \mid L) < ATC(x, A' \mid H)$. However, at advertising level A^*, $ATC(x, A^* \mid H) > ATC(x, A^* \mid L)$ for all x. Since $P_0^L + \beta < P^{*H}$, high-quality consumers will pay for high quality; hence, an advertising level of A^* would work as a signal. In this equilibrium, $F_0^{*L} = n_L/\hat{x}_0^{*L}$ low-quality firms will be in operation. This will be no different than

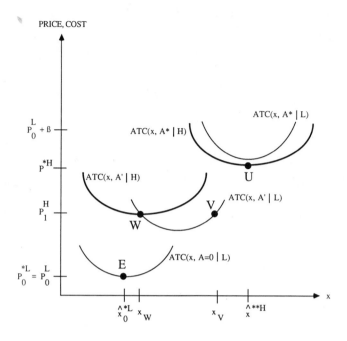

Figure 3–4. Advertising Signaling Equilibrium

when quality is freely verifiable. However, $F^{*H} = n_H/\hat{x}^{*H} \neq F_0^{*H}$ high-quality firms will be in operation (point U). The necessity of advertising to signal quality has changed the cost of high-quality production. It has distorted the nature of the production process and, in this case, increased the size of high-quality firms, leading to fewer high-quality firms in operation. Similar examples could be constructed.

The implications of advertising as a signal are threefold. First, the price paid by high-quality demanders will be higher than when quality is freely verifiable. The necessity of signaling will force the high-quality firms to incur costs that must be recovered. The magnitude of this additional cost is determined not by the high-quality firms but by how efficiently the low-quality firms can advertise. Second, this higher price only reflects the higher cost, not higher profits. Since all firms are in competition, profits will be zero in equilibrium. Third, since we required each unit produced to be advertised, advertising will serve as a signal only when it is related to production. If advertising was independent of production, it may still serve as a signal; however, the level of advertising necessary would be infinitesimal. This is the case because scale would not be affected by advertising, making $ATC(x, \cdot \mid L) > ATC(x, \cdot \mid H)$ for any x sufficient to destroy advertising's signal value.

Scale as a Signal

It is not uncommon for scale of operations to be viewed as a signal of some underlying characteristic of a firm and its products. More often than not, the inference is between size of firm and market power; however, this logic does spill over to the consumer purchasing decision. For example, there has, until recently, been a very strong belief that the size of IBM's operations implied the ability to produce better products. In addition, many nonquantifiable aspects of production, sales, and service are related to the volume of sales. Purchasers of small-manufacturer items may find service (a component of quality) more difficult. Therefore, it is reasonable to believe that scale may have some substantive value as a signal of quality.

The assumptions in the scale-signaling case are identical to the advertising case with the signal now being the level of firm output, x^i where $i = $ H, L. The cost of the signal is the cost of production, or, for simplicity, we will say that the signal has no unique cost. Pricing behavior will be unimportant since consumers will now only be concerned about the level of firm production and how it relates to quality. We will examine one case of scale signaling quality. Devinney [1988] provides a more detailed examination of the issue.

For output level to be a signal, it must be true that a level of output exists for a high-quality firm such that a low-quality firm will choose not to mimic its output. For this to be true, there must be some level of output for which $C(x^0 \mid H)/x^0 = C(x^0 \mid L)/x^0$. In figure 3–5, point Z satisfies this necessary condition. It might appear that for the level of output to distinguish high- and low-quality firms, all that is now required is for the high-quality firms to choose an x such that $C(x \mid H)/x < C(x \mid L)/x$. However, the problem is slightly more complex.

So long as $C(\hat{x}_0^H \mid H) > C(\hat{x}_0^H \mid L)$ it will be impossible for high-quality firms to distinguish themselves and reduce cost. Hence, the solution is to choose an $x^{*H} = x_0 + \epsilon$, $\epsilon \cong 0$. Price will be $P^{*H} = C(x_0 + \epsilon)/(x_0 + \epsilon)$. However, if $C(\hat{x}_0^H \mid L) > C(\hat{x}_0^H \mid H)$, cost can be reduced and separation of qualities achieved. Under these circumstances, $x^{*H} = \hat{x}_0^{*H}$ and price will be $P_0^{*H} = C(\hat{x}_0^{*H} \mid H)/\hat{x}_0^{*H}$. In both circumstances, low-quality price will be $P_0^{*L} = C(\hat{x}_0^{*L} \mid L)/\hat{x}_0^{*L}$. The reader is referred to Devinney [1988] for details of this result.

There are several implications of the scale as a signal result. First, to achieve the crossing of average cost curves, it must be true that the marginal cost of low-quality production must be higher than that of high-quality production over a reasonable range of output. As in the advertising-signaling case, the difference in cost between firms producing different quality must not be solely based on the initial fixed set-up costs. Second, if $C(\hat{x}_0^H \mid L) > C(x_0^H \mid H)$, there will be no difference in the number of firms in operation from the case where quality is freely verifiable. This is different from the advertising-signaling case, where the signal actually changes the nature of production and the

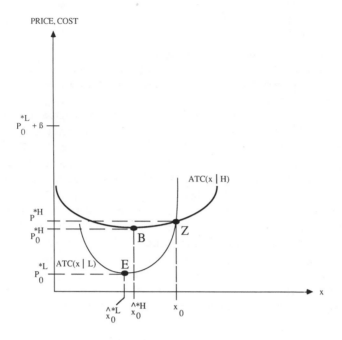

Figure 3–5. Scale Signaling Equilibrium

structure of the industry. These facts imply that scale is potentially an extremely powerful signal in competitive markets. It reveals quality, but does not distort the nature of production.

Price as a Signal

Economic models of price as a signal of product quality arose as analogs to the findings of Grossman and Stiglitz [1980] in financial markets. Grossman and Stiglitz show that the assumption of perfect knowledge in financial markets cannot truly hold if price reveals information. The logic is simple. If price reveals information perfectly, the incentive to invest in information is eliminated. The upshot of this is that information acquisition becomes a public good; once purchased, it becomes available to everyone. All market participants are, therefore, better off waiting for others to acquire information that benefits them. In addition, Grossman and Stiglitz show that there can be an incentive to invest in information under two general conditions. First, the more imperfectly price reveals information, the more value there is in individual information acquisition. This imperfection can take two forms. Information can be private (i.e., specific to a transaction). In addition, randomness in the market may make it less likely that an information based change in price can be detected. The signal cannot be seen because of the noise. Second, if consumers are significantly different, very high demand customers may be willing to accept the fact that others will free-ride on their investment in information. In this last case, it must be recognized that the public-good problem still holds for those individuals in the high-demand groups. One high-demand customer can free-ride on the information gathered by other high-demand customers.

In reality, the fact that not all information acquired by individuals becomes revealed in the market plus the existence of noise, or randomness, in product markets are sufficient to ensure that information investment will occur. In addition, product markets have other unique features that make the analogy with the Grossman-Stiglitz financial market weak. First, in the financial markets, all the players were wealth maximizers; in product markets, consumers are multiattribute utility maximizers. Second, in product markets, information can remain proprietary for a longer period of time because consumers do not always seek the same information. Third, consumers do not act like arbitragers in a financial marketplace. Since most consumers will only purchase a limited quantity of most products, the likelihood of price being affected by one consumer's acquisition of information is low. Price may reflect an underlying distribution of information that is not sufficient for any one individual. Fourth, in the Grossman-Stiglitz world, suppliers are exogenous and their role does not affect price. In product markets, the role of the supplier is very important. Suppliers can and will deceive consumers. Therefore, the difference between the financial markets and product markets lies in that consumers destroy the incentive to invest in financial information, while suppliers destroy the incentive to use price as a signal in product markets.

Chan and Leland [1982] and Cooper and Ross [1984] provide the most comprehensive applications of the Grossman-Stiglitz paradigm to product markets. In both models, it is clear that very specific assumptions become necessary to ensure a stable equilibrium with higher-quality goods being produced. Chan and Leland achieve this by assuming that consumers can observe price and quality at a cost that differs across consumers. They find that when price is costly to observe, but quality is costlessly observable, quality is optimally provided, but price is higher for uninformed consumers. If price is costlessly observable, and quality if costly to observe, the uninformed individual will receive lower quality. If both are costly to observe, then uninformed consumers pay a higher price and receive lower quality.

Cooper and Ross assume that some percentage of the market is always informed. What is important in their model is (1) how large this group is and (2) how the cost of supplying this group affects price. If costs rise quickly as expected sales fall, entry by dishonest firms selling low-quality goods will be limited, and the portion of rip-offs in the market will be low.

In both of these models, it is clear that there must exist some cost from cheating consumers for a relation between price and quality to exist. In the example that follows, we will explicitly model this point to maintain consistency with our previous two cases. It should be kept in mind that the Chan-Leland and Cooper-Ross models fit this logic with special forms of cheating cost.

Suppose that consumers only examine price as an inference of quality. Consumers observing P infer that quality is given as $Q = g^{-1}(P)$. Once again, the issue is whether such a strategy is sustainable. Unlike our previous examples, additional constraints are required for price to signal quality.

Initially, all that is necessary would be for $\pi^L(P^H) < 0$. However, since $P^H > dC(\cdot \mid L)/dq$, this will never be true. Therefore, there must be some cost to low-quality firms mimicking high-quality firms' pricing behavior. Operationally, this is simple to achieve. Let us assume that cheating on quality has some potential penalty. Logically, this penalty can take many forms; however, its most obvious form would be with respect to repeat purchases. That is, some cost exists that is a function of the verifiability of the quality. Each cheating firm has a cost $s(P - g(Q))$, which is the loss from pricing at P. This penalty function is consistent with most consumer theory, both economic and behavioral. It implies that consumers are affected most by larger rip-offs. Therefore, the impact on any firm is larger the more they deceive.

Let us assume that only low-quality firms deceive consumers. In that case, a high-quality firm will raise price so long as profits are positive. If $\pi(P, x \mid Q)$ represents the discounted profits from operations of a firm pricing P, producing x units, and producing quality Q, then as long as:

$$\frac{d\pi(P, x \mid H)}{dP} > 0 \tag{8}$$

a high-quality firm would raise price. A low-quality firm will raise price so long as:

$$\frac{d\pi(P, x \mid L)}{dP} - \frac{ds(P - P^L)}{dP} > 0 \tag{9}$$

or

$$\frac{d\pi(P, x \mid L)}{dP} > \frac{ds(P - P^L)}{dP}.$$

Therefore, for price to signal quality, it must be true that equation (8) is satisfied, but equation (9) is not. As always, the zero-profit competitive condition, equation (3), must also be satisfied. In other words, some P^{*H} must exist such that $\pi(P^{*H} \mid H) = 0$ and $\pi(P^{*H} \mid L) - s(P^{*H} - P^L) < 0$ for all x^L. This can

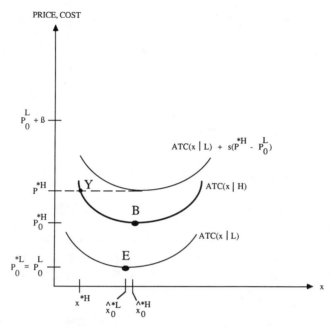

Figure 3–6. Price-Signaling Equilibrium

be seen graphically in figure 3–6. Once the cost of deception is added to the production cost, $C(x \mid L) + s(P^{*H} - P_0^L)$ is strictly larger than point Y, which is the zero-profit level of firm output for firms of high quality.

Two facts stand out about the price-signaling case. First, as in the advertising case, cost must be altered differentially by the same signal. That is, it must be marginally more expensive for a low-quality firm to provide the same signal as a high-quality firm. Second, as in the advertising case, the signal has production distortions; i.e., $\text{ATC}(x \mid L) + s(P^{*H} - P_0^L) \neq \text{ATC}(x \mid L)$. However, if the signal is correct *and* high-quality firms never deceive consumers, then there will be no production distortions. Points B and E in figure 3–6 will be the individual-firm equilibria, which are identical to the full-verifiability case given earlier and represented in figure 3–2. However, if high-quality firms are engaged in deception, which might be the case if the penalty is not significant, it is likely that while low-quality production is not distorted, high-quality production will be. High-quality consumers would end up paying a price higher than P_0^{*H} for high-quality goods.

Summary

Price, advertising, and scale were shown to be viable signals of quality in product markets under reasonable general conditions. Scale was shown to be the most simply achieved mechanism if the production functions, or cost curves, of high- and low-quality products were sufficiently different. In addition, scale signaling has no production distortions because the signal is effectively cost-less. Advertising was the second strongest signal with the return to advertising as a signal being direct related to the efficiency with which low-quality firms could mimic high-quality firms' advertising. Price was also shown to be a feasible signal; however, the conditions necessary for a stable equilibrium with price signaling quality require more stringent assumptions.

Multi-Dimensional Signaling

In realistic terms, the models we have briefly discussed are stylized in both form and substance. Producers and consumers do not act so simply, relying instead on a host of market signals. In addition, consumers are faced by very few products that require only "experience" to judge quality. Price, reputation, firm size, advertising, word-of-mouth, and legitimate rating services (such as the Consumers' Union and specialist publications) all serve to reduce uncertainty about quality.

Wilson [1985] and Milgrom and Roberts [1986] approach this problem in a limited sense by examining joint price and advertising signaling. They come up with similar results. The key finding by Milgrom and Roberts is that an additional signal, advertising, is necessary *only* when the primary signal (in their case, price) is not a sufficient statistic for quality. Wilson considers the case where more than two qualities and signals are available. While he does not conclude this himself, it appears logical to say that his result is similar. The more perfectly the set of signals maps into the set of qualities, and if the signaling strategy is invertible, the more valuable are the signals.

In a multidimensional signaling context, what is important is the number of sources of uncertainty and the number of feasible signals. In Wilson's context, if a continuum of qualities $Q \epsilon [0, 1]$ and a continuum of signals $p \epsilon [0, b]$ exist, such that $g(Q) = p$ and $g^{-1}(p) = Q$, then separation of qualities by signaling is achievable. A somewhat less strict condition would be for the signal set, $p \epsilon [a, b]$, where $b - a > 1$, to be characterized such that a set of orthogonal signals $\bar{p} \epsilon [d, e]$ exist, such that $\bar{g}(Q) = \bar{p}$ and $\bar{g}^{-1}(\bar{p}) = Q$, and $b - a > e - d > 1$.

The implication of a multiple-signaling equilibrium will be subset of the best implications of the single-signal equilibria. A multiple-signal equilibrium will always dominate a single-signal equilibrium. Whether this dominance appears as one signal being used in one set of circumstances and an alternative signal being used in another will depend on the nature of the signals. If the signals are orthogonal (i.e., they have a zero covariance), several signals may be required to provide a sufficient statistic for quality. However, the higher the covariance between the signals, the more likely it will be that one signal is dominant. This will be the case particularly when combining signals is itself costly.

Conclusion

Quality signaling in an uncertain environment has been an issue of discussion in the marketing and policy arena for several decades. Economists' entry into this debate has only been recent; however, they have been successful in changing some of the thinking about how indicators of quality are used in markets. The greatest contribution of economists can be attributed to Nelson, who directed the focus of the discussion away from the content of the signal and aimed it at the existence or nonexistence of the signal.

This chapter shed some light on the role of different signals of quality in product markets. Signals of different types were shown to be modelable under similar and general conditions. Many of the single- and multiple-cue–quality study results can be explained using the results of this chapter. In single-cue studies, production was a given, and consumers were told to make a choice with only price available. As has been shown, what makes price, scale, or advertising into a signal is *not* a consumer's feelings, but firms' production functions and the gains and losses from signaling. These studies have therefore failed to accurately test those factors that cause price to be a viable signal. In multiple-cue studies, it was found that price loses its signal value rapidly. This is consistent with price being highly correlated with the alternative signals in a multiple-signal environment.

The role that signaling plays in uncertain product markets is potentially a large one. However, little research has been conducted on how such signals operate or on what these signals might be. A better understanding of the value of signals in these markets is critical to our understanding of consumer choice and product-market equilibrium.

4
Product Warranties and Moral Hazard

Russell Cooper
Thomas W. Ross

I t may surprise no one to learn that warranties are among the most common written contracts.[1] Most durables, in fact, carry some type of warranty promising compensation from the seller (and/or producer) conditional on poor performance of the product. What purpose or purposes do all these warranties serve?

It may be useful to view warranties as elements of a potentially complicated state-contingent pricing formula. With state-contingent pricing contracts, the price paid by the buyer depends upon the performance of the good. In the form usually observed in practice, the maximum price the buyer would pay is transferred *before* the state is observed. This structure probably minimizes the associated transactions (e.g., collection) costs. Should the state involve observed performance below a specified standard, a warranty payment is made. It may be a cash refund, a replacement unit, or a repair. In any case, buyers effectively pay less, just as they get less, in these states.

There had been, until recently, very little formal analysis of such contracts. Even the obvious (and probably ancient) idea that warranties are insurance instruments did not receive rigorous treatment until Heal offered it in 1977. At about the same time Spence [1977a] suggested that by offering fuller warranties, a seller can signal to the market that its output is of high quality. A signaling equilibrium is possible because it will indeed be less costly for a high-quality firm (with a low probability of breakdown) to offer such contracts.

Some of the most recent work in the area has focused on the incentives aspects of warranties and warranty-like arrangements. (See Kambhu 1982; Mann and Wissink 1983; and Lutz 1985). In an earlier paper [1985], we suggested that warranties can help to solve and, at the same time, create moral-hazard problems. This is because of the two types of incentive problems that

The authors gratefully acknowledge the helpful comments on this chapter received from Debra Aron, David Card, Frank Mathewson, Michael McKee, Louis Wilde, and seminar participants at Carleton University in Ottawa, Columbia University, and the University of Toronto. The authors also wish to thank the Carleton Industrial Organization Research Unit and the Social Sciences and Humanities Research Council of Canada for financial support.

may exist in such markets. First, buyers generally take actions that influence the performance of a product. To the extent that these actions are not observable by the seller, a moral-hazard problem will arise if warranties are present. Second, the actual qualities of many commodities are not directly observable to buyers. In such a situation, the incentives for a seller to maintain high quality are embedded in the warranty. Hence, the degree of warranty protection offered can affect the actions of both buyers and sellers.

The purpose of this chapter is to continue the study of warranties and moral hazard. Our earlier work focused on the double-moral-hazard problem that arises when the buyer does not observe quality and the seller does not observe buyer care when both quality and care affect the probability of satisfactory performance. The buyer and seller were both assumed to be risk-neutral so that there was no demand for insurance in this model. In the next section, we introduce our model and briefly review the most important results of this earlier work.

Though this earlier work shed some light on the effects warranties have on the agents' incentives alone, we still believe that in some cases warranties can provide valued insurance. This would be particularly true, for example, for expensive consumer durables. For this reason, we want to explore a model that has both insurance and incentives features, in a sense, merging Heal's work with our own. This work is begun in the subsequent section. To simplify the problem somewhat, we will focus here on a problem of single-moral hazard. In many cases, the buyer will have good information about the quality of the seller's goods. Perhaps this seller and its product have been around for some time, and the seller has developed a valuable reputation that would be unprofitably damaged were it to lower quality. We will consider quality to be freely observable while the buyer's level of care is still private information. The optimal warranty now must strike just the right balance between providing insurance and providing incentives for care. The final section offers a brief summary and directions for future research.

The Incentive Effects of Warranties— Controlling Double-Moral Hazard

The material in this section draws heavily from our earlier published work. The model involves the market for a good that will break down with some positive probability. The probability that the good works, Π, is a function of the quality built into each unit by the seller (q) and the care or effort exerted by the buyer in its use (e). Both inputs are assumed to be productive but at diminishing rates, thus $\Pi_e \geq 0$, $\Pi_q \geq 0$, $\Pi_{ee} \leq 0$, and $\Pi_{qq} \leq 0$ where subscripts denote partial derivatives. The sign of Π_{eq} is left unspecified and will prove very important in what follows.

To focus on incentive issues, we make both buyer and seller risk-neutral. Each buyer's expected utility is represented by his surplus:

$$V(e, q, p, s) = -p + \Pi z + (1 - \Pi)sz - g(e).$$

Here, p is the price paid for the good and $g(e)$ is the disutility cost of effort or care. We assume that $g'(\cdot) \geq 0$, $g'(0) = 0$, and $g''(\cdot) > 0$. If the unit works (with probability Π), the purchaser enjoys z dollars of benefits. Should the product fail, the contract specifies that a payment of sz dollars be made by the seller to the buyer. s is then a measure of the degree of warranty protection, with $s = 0$ implying no warranty and $s = 1$ a full warranty. Product failure is always assumed to be publicly observable.

The seller's expected profits will be:

$$R(e, q, p, s) = p - C(q) - (1 - \Pi)sz$$

where $C(q)$ is an increasing, convex cost-of-quality function with $C'(\cdot) \geq C'(0) = 0$, and $C''(\cdot) > 0$. The producer's total cost is seen to be a sum of production cost and an expected warranty payment.

In a first-best (FB) contract, all choice variables would be set cooperatively to maximize $R + V$ or total surplus. Notice that in this sum, the terms with p and s drop out since they represent pure transfers. The FB contract (e^*, q^*) will then solve

$$\underset{e,\, q}{\text{MAX}} \quad R + V = \Pi z - g(e) - C(q) \tag{1}$$

yielding first-order conditions

$$\Pi_e(e, q)z = g'(e) \tag{2}$$

$$\Pi_q(e, q)z = C'(q) \tag{3}$$

Warranties have no role in this optimal contract. In fact, both parties will be indifferent between different values of s if the price is adjusted to reflect the changes in the seller's costs. The actual level of price in equilibrium will depend upon market structure. If this was a competitive industry so that the seller was forced to earn zero expected profits, then $p^* = C(q^*)$ (assuming $s = 0$). If the seller was a monopolist capable of raising price until buyers had no expected surplus, then $p^* = \Pi z - g(e^*)$.

We denote the solution to (2), for a given q, as $e^*(q)$ and that for (3) as $q^*(e)$. The FB contract then is simply the (e, q) pair that satisfies (2) and (3) simultanously. In each case, this involves setting the variable (e or q) at a level such that the marginal benefits from further increases—the left-hand sides of (2) and (3)—equal the marginal costs (right-hand sides).

When information about e, q is private, these variables cannot enter the contract. There will then be a role for warranties to provide balanced incentives. Notice that with no warranty ($s = 0$), the seller will have no incentive to provide quality. Similarly, a full warranty ($s = 1$) leaves the buyer with no incentive to take care.

We view the second-best (SB) contract as the outcome of a two-stage game played by the parties to the contract. In the first stage, the players cooperatively select p and s in a binding fashion. The second (noncooperative) stage takes p and s as given and has the players select their inputs e and q. We then look for a Nash equilibrium in these selections.

Given p and s, the buyer will select e to maximize V, yielding the condition

$$\Pi_e(e, q)(1 - s)z = g'(e) \tag{4}$$

while the seller selects q to maximize V, giving

$$\Pi_q(e, q)sz = C'(q). \tag{5}$$

We denote the solution to (4) as $\hat{e}(q; s)$ and that to (5) as $\hat{q}(e; s)$. These are reaction functions and their intersections represent Nash equilibria.

It is obvious from a glance at (4) and (5) that s will have the expected effects on the agents' choices of e and q. An increase in s will raise the private marginal benefit of q and lower the private marginal benefit of e. Thus, we have $\hat{e}_s \leq 0$ and $\hat{q}_s \geq 0$. Further, comparison with (2) and (3) reveals that $\hat{e}(q; s) \leq \hat{e}^*(q)$ and $\hat{q}(e; s) \leq q^*(e)$ for $0 \leq s \leq 1$. Note, however, that a full warranty will induce efficient quality [$\hat{q}(e; 1) = q^*(e)$], while a zero warranty will induce efficient buyer care [$\hat{e}(q; 0) = e^*(q)$].

Whether the SB *equilibrium* levels of e and q are both less than their FB levels will be somewhat sensitive to the slopes of the reaction functions. Note that these slopes will carry the same sign as the cross-derivative Π_{eq}.

Figure 4–1 illustrates the case in which the inputs are complementary, making Π_{eq} positive. It is clear in this case that the SB levels of both e and q (point A) must be below their FB counterparts. Figure 4–2 makes the same point for the case in which $\Pi_{eq} = 0$. Figures 4–3 and 4–4 illustrate that when $\Pi_{eq} \leq 0$, it is possible for both values to be lower in the SB equilibrium (figure 4–3), but it is also possible for one of the two to be higher than at its FB level (figure 4–4). In this case, the inputs are substitutes, so that as one input level, say q, is cut back, the marginal product of the other, e, rises. If it rises enough and its marginal cost does not climb too quickly, the buyer may choose to increase e above its FB level.

The first-stage problem these players face is to cooperatively determine

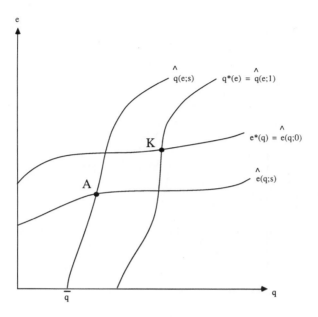

Figure 4–1. $\Pi_{eq} > 0$.

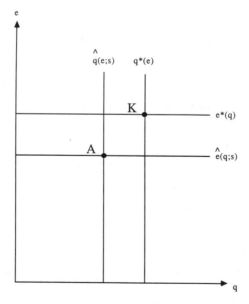

Figure 4–2. $\Pi_{eq} = 0$

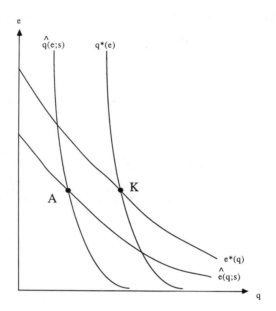

Figure 4–3. SB Has Lower *e* and *q*

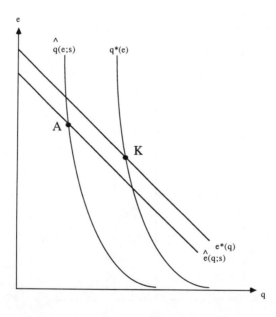

Figure 4–4. SB Has Lower *q* and Higher *e*

p and s, knowing that their choice of s will affect the Nash equilibrium of the second-stage game: higher s will, when $\Pi_{eq} \leqq 0$ for example, lead to an equilibrium with less e and more q. It is in the parties' interest to select the level of s that maximizes $R + V$ subject to the constraints imposed by the game that follows.

That is, we

$$\underset{s}{\text{MAX}} \, \Pi z - g(e) - C(q)$$

subject to $e = \hat{e}(q; s)$, $q = \hat{q}(e; s)$. The first-order condition will give us

$$(\Pi_e z - g')\hat{e}_s + (\Pi_q z - C')\hat{q}_s = 0 \qquad (6)$$

Substituting from (4) and (5), we get

$$\Pi_e s \hat{e}_s + \Pi_q (1 - s)\hat{q}_s = 0$$

Solving this for $s^\star$ we have

$$s^\star = \frac{\Pi_q \hat{q}_s}{\Pi_q \hat{q}_s - \Pi_e \hat{e}_s} \qquad (7)$$

Though this is not a true closed-form solution for $s^\star$ (since s can still enter $\hat{q}_s$ and $\hat{e}_s$), it does highlight some properties of the optimal warranty. $s^\star$ will necessarily lie between 0 and 1 as long as both inputs are productive. Increases in the marginal productivity of some input will lead to a change in s to stimulate the supply of that input: $s^\star$ will rise if Π_q rises or Π_e falls. Similarly, increases in the marginal costs of an input (for example, quality) will reduce $\hat{q}_s$ (from (5)) and move $s^\star$ in the direction that provides a greater incentive for the supply of the other input.

We have just seen here how warranties can affect the incentives of agents on both sides of the market to provide care or quality. With risk-neutral agents, we ruled out any insurance role for the warranty, but in some markets warranties surely do serve an important insurance function. We now turn to an analysis of a model in which insurance *is* desired by buyers, so the optimal warranty will need to balance the desire for insurance on the one hand with the need to provide incentives for buyer care on the other.

Single-Moral Hazard

In this section, we characterize both first-best (FB) contracts and optimal second-best (SB) contracts in the case in which the seller's quality is observable, though the parties still cannot contract over the buyer's level of care.

Consumers, who may now be risk-averse, have preferences represented by a utility function separable in income (y) and effort:

$$V(y, e) = U(y) - g(e)$$

with $U' > 0$, $U'' \leq 0$, $g' \geq 0$, $g'' > 0$. When it works, the good is again assumed to be worth z dollars to the consumer; but when it breaks, it is valueless. Consumers who paid a price p will then have an expected utility of

$$EV = \Pi(e, q)[U(y - p + z) - g(e)] + [1 - \Pi(e, q)][U(y - p + sz) - g(e)]$$

or

$$EV = \Pi U_W + (1 - \Pi) U_B - g(e) = EU - g(e) \tag{8}$$

where U_W is the value of $U(\cdot)$ when the unit works and U_B is the value of $U(\cdot)$ when it breaks.

The competitive firm will face the same two types of costs discussed earlier: the cost of building quality in and the cost of providing the warranty. The expected costs for a typical unit sold will then, for this risk-neutral firm, equal the price it charges:

$$p = C(q) + (1 - \Pi)sz. \tag{9}$$

The nature of equilibrium in a market such as this is highly sensitive to the assumptions made regarding information sets. We maintain throughout that the state (i.e., whether the good works or breaks) is freely observed by all parties, so there is no dispute regarding whether the product performed well enough.[2] Instead, we have chosen to focus on the difficulties of observing and writing contracts on the variables e and q. We begin by characterizing the first-best equilibrium that obtains when e and q are observable to both parties and can be written into the contract. Then we turn to a consideration of the single-moral hazard problem that arises when e is not observable to the firm but q is freely observable to all.

The FB sale-warranty contract will then maximize the buyer's expected utility subject to the break-even constraint (9) for the firm. The problem is then to

$$\underset{q,\, e,\, s,\, p}{\text{MAX}} \quad L^* = \Pi(e, q)\, U(y - p + z) +$$

$$[1 - \Pi(e, q)]U(y - p + sz) - g(e) + \lambda\{p - C(q)$$
$$- [1 - \Pi(e, q)]sz\}$$

and the first-order conditions for an interior solution will be:

$$\Pi_q \Delta U = \lambda[C'(q) - \Pi_q sz] \tag{10}$$

$$U_B' = \lambda \tag{11}$$

$$\Pi_e \Delta U - g'(e) = \lambda \Pi_e sz \tag{12}$$

and

$$EU' = \lambda \tag{13}$$

where we define

$$\Delta U \equiv U_W - U_B$$

$$EU' \equiv \Pi U_W' + (1 - \Pi) U_B'.$$

We denote by q^*, e^*, s^*, and p^* the values that solve this problem.

While we have generated these conditions to serve more as a benchmark than anything else, it is interesting to note the very intuitive and familiar results they contain. Equations (11) and (13) tell us that the warranty will be full; i.e., $s^* = 1$. Then in (10), ΔU becomes zero and the firm chooses q to make marginal cost of quality (C') equal to the social marginal benefit of quality ($\Pi_q z$). With $s^* = 1$, (12) implies that the marginal costs of effort to the buyer just balance the marginal benefits due to lower costs for the firm.

We turn now to study equilibrium in the simple-moral-hazard case in which e is unobservable to the firm so that it cannot be part of the SB contract. In fact, e will be chosen by the buyer after the q and s decisions have been made and after p has been paid. The buyer chooses e to maximize his expected utility knowing that p will now not change. Instead of condition (12) describing effort, we now have

$$\Pi_e \Delta U = g'. \tag{12a}$$

This expression reveals that in order to encourage any strictly positive level of care, the warranty must be less than full so that ΔU is positive. We call this second-best level of effort $\hat{e}$, and we note that the second-order conditions for a maximum will be satisfied; i.e.,

$$K \equiv \Pi_{ee} \Delta U - g'' \leqq 0.$$

It will be important for us to know a little about the $\hat{e} = \hat{e}(p, q, s)$ function. Totally differentiating (12a) with respect to these variables, we find that

$$\hat{e}_p = \Pi_e \Delta U'/K \geq 0$$

$$\hat{e}_q = - \Pi_{eq} \Delta U/K$$

and

$$\hat{e}_s = \Pi_e z U_B'/K \leq 0.$$

With $\Delta U' \equiv U_W' - U_B' \leq 0$ for $s \leq 1$, we find that $\hat{e}_p \geq 0$. The impact of quality on effort depends on the nature of the technological relationship between e and q. If $\Pi_{eq} > 0$, so that effort and quality are complements, we find that $\hat{e}_q$ is positive. For substitutes, Π_{eq} and $\hat{e}_q$ will both be negative. Finally, we find that an increase in warranty protection reduces consumer care; i.e., $\hat{e}_s \leq 0$.

The SB problem is to choose q and s to maximize expected utility, recognizing that price will equal average cost as in (9) and the level of effort, $\hat{e}$, will solve (12a):

$$\text{MAX}_{p, q, s} \quad L = \Pi(e, q)U(y - p + z) + \tag{14}$$

$$[1 - \Pi(e, q)]U(y - p + sz) - g(e)$$
$$+ \lambda[p - C(q) - (1 - \Pi)sz]$$

The reader familiar with the principal-agent literature will see that this is a fairly straightforward adaptation to a sale-warranty context with only two states. An interesting wrinkle is the inclusion of the quality variable q. It turns out that q will be useful to the firm as another instrument (in addition to the more familiar s) with which it can manipulate the buyer's incentive to take care.[3]

The first-order conditions for an interior solution to (14) will be:

$$\partial L/\partial q = \Pi_q \Delta U - \lambda[C'(q) - (\Pi_q + \Pi_e \hat{e}_q)sz] = 0 \tag{15}$$

$$\partial L/\partial s = (1 - \Pi)U_B'z - \lambda z[(1 - \Pi)$$
$$- \Pi_e \hat{e}_s s] = 0$$

or

$$U_B' = \lambda\left[1 - \frac{\Pi_e \hat{e}_s s}{(1 - \Pi)}\right] \tag{16}$$

$$\frac{\partial L}{\partial p} = EU' - \lambda(1 + \Pi_e \hat{e}_p sz) = 0, \tag{17}$$

and, for convenience, we repeat the expression for $\hat{e}$ here,

$$\Pi_e \Delta U = g'. \tag{12a}$$

We label these SB values $\hat{e}$, $\hat{q}$, $\hat{s}$, and $\hat{p}$.

Comparing (15), (16), (17), and (12a) with (10), (11), and (12) readily reveals the nature of the SB distortions. Instead of being able to hold e fixed at a certain level while they solve for optimal q and s, the parties must recognize the effect that changes in these variables will have on the e subsequently chosen.

Conditions (16) and (17) readily reveal the problems we have when trying to set s to provide both incentives and insurance. If incentives were not a problem because, for example, e was somehow verifiable, both $\hat{e}_s$ and $\hat{e}_p$ would equal zero and (16) and (17) would become (11) and (13). That is, the FB would be achievable, with full insurance for the buyer.

On the other hand, if the buyer were risk-neutral so that there was no demand for insurance, $\hat{e}_p$ would equal zero (since $\Delta U' = 0$). This means that $U_B' = EU' = \lambda$ and that the optimal level of s is zero. Again the FB contract is implementable. Only when we try to provide full incentives *and* full insurance at the same time does the informational asymmetry force us into a SB arrangement.

Now that we have the first-order conditions that characterize the SB sale-warranty contracts, there are two interesting things we can do with them. The first involves exploring more carefully the nature of the distortions caused by excluding e from the contract: are q, e, and s too high or too low relative to their FB values? Second, we may want to generate comparative static results telling us how $\hat{e}$, $\hat{q}$, and $\hat{s}$ change with shifts in the values of selected parameters of the model.

It would be very nice indeed to be able to compare the FB and SB values of the variables q, e, and s. For s, this is easy; we have already noted that $s* = 1$ and that $\hat{s}$ must be less than 1 if effort is to be positive. Unfortunately, comparisons for q and e are in general not possible. It is indeed possible to construct examples in which $\hat{e} > e^*$, as unintuitive as that may seem.[4] The inability to compare the FB and SB levels is a weakness common to those sort of models.

What we can do, however, is answer a related question: are e and q "locally" to high or too low? That is, holding all the other variables constant, will a small increase in either of these variables improve or reduce welfare? Looking first at quality, we can rewrite (15) as

$$C'(q) - (\Pi_q + \Pi_e\hat{e}_q)sz = \Pi_q \Delta U/\lambda \qquad (18)$$

The left side of this expression represents the firm's direct marginal cost of q, $C'(q)$, plus the marginal effect of quality on expected warranty payments, $(\Pi_q + \Pi_e\hat{e}_q)sz$. The latter term reflects both the direct effect of q on $\Pi(\cdot)$ as well as the *incentive effect* created by the dependence of $e(\cdot)$ on q. The right side of (18) is the marginal insurance gain to consumers from higher quality. Since $\hat{s} < 1$, $\Delta U > 0$ and the buyer benefits from the increase in $\Pi(\cdot)$ brought about by increasing q. The selection of quality will therefore reflect both insurance and incentive effects.

To evaluate (18), suppose that $\Pi_{eq} = 0$ so that effort was independent of quality; $\hat{e}_q = 0$. With $\Delta U > 0$, (18) implies that $C'(q) > \Pi_q sz$. That is, firms build in quality beyond the point where marginal cost and the marginal benefit of reduced warranty costs are equalized. This "distortion" reflects the insurance role of quality as a *substitute* for warranty protection. If $\Pi_{eq} > 0$ (and therefore $e_q > 0$), the incentive effect of higher q on e reinforces this insurance effect. Finally, when $\Pi_{eq} < 0$ ($\hat{e}_q < 0$), the buyer incentive and insurance effects work in opposite directions and quality can be locally too high or too low.

Buyer care is locally too low in that increases in e can benefit the firm and the consumer jointly. As effort increases, expected warranty payments fall by $\Pi_e sz > 0$. The consumer does not take this into account, however, as can be seen by comparing (12) with (12a).

We digress for a moment to make a fairly obvious point about whether some government intervention into this market can be welfare-improving. It is not unusual these days to hear consumer advocates calling for laws to require sellers to provide fuller warranty protection.[5] It might be thought that the results presented here indicating that s is too low might be construed as theoretical justification for such a public policy. This is clearly not correct. The s the seller offers in the SB equilibrium represents the best that can be done given the constraints due to asymmetric information and moral hazard. The fact that s is below FB level means that if we could hold quality at $\hat{q}$ and effort at $\hat{e}$, we would like to raise s above $\hat{s}$. If s is raised by law, we can expect e and q to adjust. Quality may rise or fall, but the first-order effect on e from (12a) will clearly be negative since $\hat{e}_s < 0$. The probability of breakdown may therefore rise, and we will certainly be shifted to a new third-best equilibrium. A similar story can be told about the effects of laws mandating higher levels of quality.[6]

We turn now to a consideration of comparative statics on the SB equilibrium. We are particularly interested in understanding what happens to the values of the observables, s and q, when various parameters of the model change. The signaling literature suggests that, within markets, s and q should be positively correlated.[7] The story there relies on imperfect buyer information and says simply that firms with high-quality goods will attempt to signal this quality by offering a more complete warranty. Since warranties are less costly to provide when the product breaks less often, high-quality firms will be able to signal more cheaply; therefore, a signaling equilibrium is possible. Signaling theory tells us nothing, however, about how s and q should be related in markets in which quality is well known.

Though positive correlations between s and q are undoubtedly observed in many markets, negative correlations are found as well. An obvious example here is the automobile market in which the Japanese manufacturers sell small cars of higher (by most accounts) quality than the U.S. makers but with inferior warranty protection.

It was our hope that comparative static results on the SB equilibrium would reveal conditions under which positive and negative correlations would be observed. It would seem plausible that certain differences among buyers could generate positive correlations. For example, more risk-averse customers would want more protection from breakdown and it could be that this protection would involve, in general, higher levels of s and q. Similarly, buyers with a greater cost of effort would prefer that the firm provide more risk reduction through s and q.

On the other hand, certain differences among firms in the market may lead them to make different choices regarding how they protect their customers. Some firms (e.g., Japanese auto makers) may have cost advantages in building quality but suffer a cost disadvantage in providing warranty protection.

It turns out that deriving even the most intuitive comparative static results has not been possible. The full comparative static effects of any change seem to be ambiguous. For example, it is not even possible in this simple model to prove that, holding q and s fixed, increasing risk aversion will increase the buyer's chosen level of care.[8]

Nevertheless, there are a few partial results that lend some support to our conjectures about the relationship between observed s and q. To begin, suppose that buyers differed according to their costs of effort. We modify preferences so that

$$V(y, e) = U(y) - \delta g(e)$$

and we ask what happens when δ rises.

While we cannot solve for the total effect of changing δ on the values of s, q, and e, we can look at conditions (15), (16) and (12a) and determine the direction of the first-order effects. From the definitions, it is easy to see that raising δ will lower the values of $(\Pi_{ee} \Delta U - g'')$. This will raise $\hat{e}_s$ and lower $\hat{e}_p$. Effort will become less sensitive to changes in q; that is, a positive $\hat{e}_q$ will fall and a negative $\hat{e}_q$ will rise (i.e., $|\hat{e}_q|$ will fall).

Looking first at (12a), the buyer's choice of effort, it is clear that the first-order effect will be to reduce e below its original level. The marginal cost of effort has risen while the benefits have not. In (16), the rising $\hat{e}_s$ means that $\partial L/\partial s$ will be positive and therefore s should rise. The effect on (15) depends on the sign of $\hat{e}_q$. When quality and effort are substitutes ($\hat{e}_q < 0$), which might seem the more likely case, $\partial L/\partial q$ becomes positive and quality should rise. Thus, these first-order results for the case in which e and q are substitutes suggest that positive correlations between s and q may indeed be due to certain differences among consumers: namely, differences in their cost of care.[9]

To consider differences across firms we add a new term to the cost of the warranty. Now the firm's expected costs are written:

$$C(q) + (1 - \Pi)(sz + x)$$

where x represents some cost of the warranty that does not go to the buyer. It could simply be the costs of verifying that the product is broken and processing the claim.[10]

With this added term, the conditions describing the SB contract become:

$$\Pi_q \Delta U = \lambda[C'(q) - (\Pi_q + \Pi_e \hat{e}_q)(sz + x)] \qquad (19)$$

$$U'_B = \lambda \left[1 - \frac{\Pi_e \hat{e}_s}{(1 - \Pi)} \left(s + \frac{x}{z} \right) \right] \qquad (20)$$

$$EU' = \lambda[1 + \Pi_e \hat{e}_q(sz + x)] \qquad (21)$$

When x increases, we do not observe a first-order change in effort since nothing in (12a) has changed. Looking at (19), we see that the effect on quality is again ambiguous. The added warranty cost raises the direct return to increasing quality. Thus, for a constant level of effort, the optimal SB q will rise. However, the higher level of x also raises the firm's return to stimulating effort by manipulating quality. If $e_q > 0$, this only reinforces the first effect, but when effort and quality are substitutes, it works to depress levels of q.

As x increases, the right side of (20) falls, indicating that $\partial L/\partial s$ becomes positive and that s should therefore be lowered to induce consumers to take more care. A breakdown is now a more costly event and the optimal contract should provide incentives for both parties to supply more of their inputs.

Suppose that firms differ according to their costs of producing units of a certain quality—that is, $C(q)$ becomes $\gamma C(q)$—and we consider the effects of increasing γ. There is no direct effect on e or s in this case since nothing in (12a) or (16) changes. Looking at (15), we find the results very intuitive. As the marginal cost of quality rises, $\partial L/\partial q$ becomes negative and the optimal level of q falls. This lowering of q will in turn affect the buyer's choice of e and the optimal warranty. The change in e depends, of course, on the sign of $\hat{e}_q$ (or Π_{eq}).

The direction of change of s will depend upon how the term $\Pi_e/(1 - \Pi)$ changes with falling q. If Π_{eq} is approximately zero, the value of this term falls as q falls (since $1 - \Pi$ rises). That means that $\partial L/\partial s$ will be positive and that the warranty level should rise. Thus, a higher level of warranty protection is substituted for lower quality as a now marginally more efficient way to ensure buyers against product failure. If $\Pi_{eq} > 0$, the term $\Pi_e /(1 - \Pi)$ must still fall with lower q, and a higher level of s is again the result. Should $\Pi_{eq} < 0$, however, the falling q could make the marginal product of effort (Π_e) so much bigger that a lower warranty, to induce this effort, is called for.

Combining this last pair of comparative static results, we find some reason to believe that negative correlations between s and q within a market may indeed be due to inherent differences between firms in their warranty and quality-producing technologies.

Summary and Directions for Future Research

This study of product warranties has focused on their roles as incentive devices and insurance instruments. To the extent that state probabilities can be affected by the actions of agents, state-contingent pricing can be used to alter behavior and improve outcomes. In the double-moral-hazard model with risk-neutral buyers, we saw that the warranty was being asked to provide incentives for buyer care *and* seller quality. It could not do both perfectly, so we found ourselves in a second-best world, looking for the warranty level that minimized the inefficiencies caused by the asymmetric information.

When warranties were asked to provide insurance for buyers in the single (buyer)-model-hazard case, the same sort of problem arose. Improving insurance protection meant dulling buyers' incentives to take care. Again, some intermediate level of warranty protection proved optimal in this second-best environment.

Our (partial) analysis of the comparative statics properties of this single-moral-hazard and insurance problem were also similar to those derived in our earlier work on the double-moral-hazard problem.[11] Though there is no role for signaling in this model, positive correlations across firms between the level of warranty protection offered and the quality built into the good may be observed if some buyers have higher costs of care than others. These buyers simply prefer more protection of both types: the reduced probability of breakdown due to the higher level of quality, and the higher warranty payment in the event that the unit does fail.

On the other hand, quality and warranty protection may be substitutes for firms with different costs of providing warranties. If providing such protection is very costly for some sellers, they may choose to lower their level of protection and raise their quality to reduce the likelihood that the warranty is needed.

As suggested earlier, this may explain why Japanese automobiles with very low breakdown frequencies carry generally poorer warranties.

There remains much to be done on this topic. We hope to be able, at some point, to do the full comparative static analysis of the single-moral-hazard case. We would particularly like to be able to determine the effects of increasing buyer risk aversion on the optimal quality and warranty levels. Introducing a demand for insurance into the double-moral-hazard model is the next step toward a general model of warranties.

Finally, it would seem desirable to pull together whatever data might be available on product warranties and performance in order to test whether moral hazard and/or insurance are empirically important in shaping warranty contracts.

Notes

1. See Priest [1981].
2. For a discussion of such disputes, see Palfrey and Romer [1983].
3. In this literature, see, for example, Shavell [1979a, b], Holmstrom [1979], and Grossman and Hart [1983]. Similar examples exist in other parts of the agency literature where the parties to the contract cooperatively choose some input other than the agent's effort, which influences the probability of the events. See, for example, Arnott and Stiglitz [1983].
4. See Shavell [1979a].
5. The new so-called lemon laws are the product of some of this agitation.
6. It may be possible to make a case for legislation mandating higher levels of s if it is true that buyers misperceive risks. Rea [1981] makes this point in the context of his model of workmen's compensation.
7. See, for example, Spence [1977a].
8. Comparative static results are next to nonexistent in the principal-agent literature. One exception is the Grossman and Hart demonstration that as risk-aversion increases, the social loss from SB contracting also rises.
9. The astute reader will notice that we have set aside any consideration of the additional problem of adverse selection that might arise in these markets when customers differ.
10. Actually x may be even negative. The firm may not need to spend sz to get the buyer sz dollars of use out of the product. They may be able to repair it perfectly and cheaply, so that the uninsured portion, $(1 - s)z$, represents only the buyer's inconvenience cost.
11. See Cooper and Ross [1985, pp. 110–12].

5
Consumer Expectations and the Pricing of Durables

K. Sridhar Moorthy

T he purpose of this chapter is to study the effect of consumer expectations on the pricing policy of a monopolist. Many authors (e.g., Winer 1985) have noted that consumers form expectations about future prices and technology and use these expectations in deciding when to buy a product. If such expectations exist, then firms ought to take them into account when determining their new product and pricing plans. And, indeed, casual observation suggests they do. In the fast-changing computer industry, where consumer expectations about the future are particularly strong determinants of current buying behaviors, we see both hardware and software manufacturers taking pains to assure the public that future products will be compatible with their current ones. On the pricing front, one effect of consumer expectations—in this case, expectations of future price reductions—is the prevalence of "most-favored customer" clauses allowing the customer to be the beneficiary of any future price reductions (within a specified time period). The objective in either case is to induce the consumer to buy now rather than wait for a new product or a lower price.

Recently a number of people have studied formally the effect of consumer expectations on a monopolist's pricing policy for a durable good. Key references are Coase [1972], Bulow [1982], Stokey [1979, 1981], Kahn [1986], Narasimhan [1987], and Conlisk, Gerstner, and Sobel [1984]. All of these works—as well as the present one—build on Coase's seminal paper so it is useful to review the basic points made there. Coase argued that consumer expectations, if they are rational (i.e., correct), could have a dramatic impact on a monopolist's optimal pricing policy. His argument goes like this. In the absence of any expectations (i.e., each consumer looks at the current price and

---

Part of the research reported here was presented at the Marketing Science Conference at Vanderbilt University in March 1985 and at a marketing workshop at the University of Chicago in May 1985. I thank the participants at these meetings, especially Terry Elrod, for their comments. I am also grateful to Timothy Devinney for his editorial comments and patience.

makes a decision to buy or not to buy based *only* on that price), the monopolist would like to skim the market. He would start with a price equal to the highest reservation price on the market and sell to consumers with that reservation price, then lower the price to the next-highest reservation price, sell to consumers with that (second-highest) reservation price, and proceed similarly down the demand curve until his price reaches his marginal cost. At that point, he stops selling. If consumers have rational expectations, however (i.e., they anticipate the monopolist's incentive to keep lowering the price and selling to lower-reservation-price consumers), then the monopolist's skimming policy unravels quickly. When the first price is announced, consumers simply wait for the price to be lowered; assuming that the monopolist cannot commit to hold a price for any length of time, consumers will wait until the price comes down to marginal cost. And they don't have to wait very long. The monopolist, knowing that people are going to buy only at marginal cost, sees no point in offering a succession of prices. He starts with a price equal to marginal cost and everyone (whose reservation price is at least marginal cost) buys. The effect of consumer expectations has been to change the form of the pricing strategy from a skimming strategy to a constant-price strategy and the monopolist's profits have come down from the maximum level possible—the first-degree price-discrimination outcome—to the lowest level possible (zero).

The other papers just cited have the unifying theme of suggesting real-world features that could "soften" the effect of rational consumer expectations on the monopolist's optimal pricing policy. The papers differ in which real-world feature they focus on. Stokey [1979] shows that precommitment to a pricing policy could help the monopolist. For certain consumer utility functions, the monopolist's optimal precommitment policy is to hold the price constant at the static optimal monopoly price. The monopolist's resulting profits are less than what he would obtain if consumers didn't form expectations (and he could thereby skim the market), but they are obviously greater than his profits in the Coase scenario. Stokey [1981] formalizes Coase's argument and shows that in the absence of capacity constraints, the monopolist must be able to change prices continuously for Coase's result to hold. The reason is, if the monopolist could change prices only at discrete intervals of time (i.e., he could assure consumers in some way that each of his prices will hold for some time), then he achieves a certain amount of precommitment. Even small doses of precommitment are enough to upset the Coase result.

Bulow [1982] shows that by renting a durable for short periods, the monopolist can achieve close to the maximum static level of profits. Renting changes the monopolist's "product" from a durable to a nondurable service—a service that lasts for the duration of the short-term rental. And for a nondurable product, the best pricing policy is to charge a constant price equal to the static monopoly price (see proposition 1). Bulow also argues that if the monopolist is forced to sell rather than rent, then it may benefit him to reduce capacity, produce a less durable product than what is socially optimal, or have high marginal costs. Each of these devices serves to provide some assurance to consumers that future prices will not come down very sharply. Kahn [1986] analyzes the Stokey [1981] model in continuous time and shows that if the monopolist's marginal costs are increasing, then, even though the monopolist is unable to precommit, his prices are still higher than those of a competitive industry (but lower than those of a monopolist who can precommit). Finally, Conlisk et al. [1984] allow new cohorts of consumers to enter in each period in Stokey's [1981] model and show that the optimal policy now is to price cyclically with the prices going down periodically to clear the backlog of consumers waiting for a lower price.

This chapter explores the effect of consumer uncertainty about the monopolist's costs on the monopolist's pricing behavior. Bulow [1982], as just noted, suggests that a monopolist may gain by operating at "high" marginal costs. He assumes that consumers know the monopolist's costs. (In fact, all of the works previously cited assume that. So, in all these analyses, rational consumers can predict exactly the monopolist's strategy.) But typically consumers don't know the firm's costs. Then the following possibility arises. If consumers don't know the monopolist's marginal costs, then even a "low"-cost monopolist may gain by pretending to have higher costs than he actually does. Then he can have the best of both worlds. Low costs are always better than high costs in any static game, which is useful in the "later" periods of a dynamic pricing strategy. At the same time, by pretending to have higher costs than he actually does, the monopolist can affect consumers' waiting behavior. Consumers will not wait as long if they think prices are not going to come down as much. That increases the profits in the "early" periods. The remaining question is: how can a monopolist pretend to have higher costs than he actually does? By charging a higher price initially than what he would otherwise charge! But that is not the end of the story. Any higher price will not do. The higher price chosen must be a price that a higher-cost monopolist would choose. Otherwise, rational consumers will not be fooled by the higher initial price—they will infer correctly that the monopolist does in fact have low costs and expect the price to fall to low levels in subsequent periods. (With these expectations, of course, the low-cost monopolist would see no point in charging the higher price initially.) In other words, if consumers are uncertain initially whether the monopolist is low-cost or high-cost, and if we are talking about a two-period model, then for a low-cost monopolist to successfully masquerade as a high-cost monopolist, it must be the case that the prices offered in the first period by both types of monopolist are the same. That is, we must have a pooling equilibrium and not a separating equilibrium.[1] This chapter shows, however, that in a two-period version of Stokey's [1979] model, a pooling equilibrium in pure strategies does not exist. The only pure strategy equilibria are separating equilibria where the monopolist's first-period price reveals his true cost.

Along the way, the chapter notes the role of product durability in making price discrimination possible. With frequently purchased goods, a skimming strategy of progressively reducing prices is not optimal. The reason is, consumers who buy "early" at a high price return to the market when the price is low. The monopolist's *potential* market is the same on every pricing occasion. This suggests that, for the purposes of the pricing problem analyzed here, the essential difference between a durable and a nondurable is whether the interpurchase time is higher or lower than the time between price announcements. If the interpurchase time is more than twice the time between price announcements, then some price discrimination is possible; otherwise, no price discrimination is possible.

The Model

The monopolist serves a heterogeneous market consisting of a continuum of consumer types with reservation prices distributed uniformly on $[0, X]$, $X >$ 0.[2] Each consumer buys one unit of the durable supplied by the monopolist if the price is not more than the reservation price; otherwise she buys none at all.

There are two time periods, 1 and 2. The monopolist must choose a price for the first period and one for the second. The sequence of moves is that, first, the monopolist announces a price for the first period, p_1, and then consumers decide whether to buy at that price or to wait for the second-period price, p_2, which they do not know yet but about which they have expectations. At the start of the second period, the monopolist announces the second-period price, p_2, and all those who haven't bought yet must buy then or not buy at all. The durable good lasts more than two periods, so once a consumer buys the product, she withdraws from the market. In deciding whether to buy in the first period or the second period, a consumer with reservation price x compares the surplus obtainable if she buys in the first period—$(x - p_1)$—with the surplus she thinks will obtain if she chooses to wait until the second period. If she thinks that the second period price is p_2, then the latter surplus is $(x - p_2)/$ $(1 + r)$ where $r \epsilon [0, 1]$ is the interest rate.

Consumers are uncertain about the marginal cost of the monopolist. With probability $q > 0$, they think it is c_1; with probability $1 - q$, they think it is $c_2 (X > c_2 > c_1 \geq 0)$. The monopolist, of course, knows his marginal cost. If his marginal cost is actually c_1, we will call him a type-1 monopolist; if it is c_2, we will call him a type-2 monopolist. We assume that it is common knowledge (cf. Moorthy 1985) that the marginal cost is constant in quantity and that there are no fixed costs.[3] The monopolist chooses his first- and second-period prices to maximize the discounted sum of first-period and second-period profits. We shall assume that the monopolist also discounts second-period profits at the interest r.

In closing this section, we observe that if a consumer (with reservation price) x chooses to buy in the first period, i.e., $(x - p_1) \geq (x - p_2)/(1 + r)$, then it must also be the case that consumer y, with $y > x$, also prefers to buy in the first period.[4] As a result of this, the set of consumers who buy in the first period is an *interval* of reservation prices $[x^*, X]$ where x^* is the consumer type who is indifferent between buying in the first period and buying in the second period. Reservation prices and impatience are positively correlated.

Some Preliminary Results

In this section, we set up some preliminary results assuming no uncertainty about marginal costs. These results will be useful in developing intuition about the effect of consumer expectations on a monopolist's pricing policy and the role of product durability in mediating this effect. Later, when we study the uncertainty case, these results will be useful in computing the separating equilibria.

Price Discrimination with Naive Consumers. Assume the monopolist's marginal cost is known to be $c (X > c \geq 0)$. It is easy to see what the monopolist's optimal pricing policy would be if consumers were naive and didn't consider second-period possibilities. With the first-period price, p_1, the monopolist will sell to consumers in the interval $[p_1, X]$—every consumer whose reservation price is at least p_1 will buy in the first period. With the second-period price $p_2 \leq p_1$, the monopolist will sell to consumers in the interval $[p_2, p_1]$. What should p_1 and p_2 be? The monopolist's profit function is $(X - p_1)(p_1 - c) + [(p_1 - p_2)(p_2 - c)/(1 + r)]$. Maximizing this with respect to p_1 and p_2, it is easy to see that profits are maximized when $p_1 = [2(1 + r)X + (1 + 2r)c]/(3 + 4r)$ and $p_2 = [(1 + r)X + (2 + 3r)c]/(3 + 4r)$. Note that $p_2 < p_1$, so there is price discrimination. Although we have assumed here that consumers know the monopolist's marginal cost, it should be obvious that introducing uncertainty about costs will have no effect on the solution. Any strategic benefit the monopolist can derive from consumer uncertainty can only happen in a dynamic model. With naive consumers, even a multiperiod model is a static one.

The Role of Durability. It is important to see why we need a durable product to get the preceding result. If the product were a frequently purchased one, then price discrimination would be impossible even with naive consumers who don't look into the future. Suppose, for example, that the people who purchased in the first period—consumers in the interval $[p_1, X]$—returned to the market in the second period. Then the monopolist's first-period profits will be $(X - p_1)(p_1 - c)$ and his second-period profits (discounted to the first period) will be $(X - p_2)(p_2 - c)/(1 + r)$. (Compare the second-period profits here with what we had in the previous paragraph.) It is clear that the monopolist's total profit function is completely separable now between the two periods and, moreover, the pricing problem is identical in the two periods. So the best pricing policy is to hold the prices constant at $(X + c)/2$, the one-period optimal price. There is no price discrimination. What this suggests is that a necessary condition for (at least some) price discrimination is that the interpurchase time be more than twice the time between price announcements.[5] This observation we state as a proposition.

Proposition 1. A necessary condition for a monopolist to price discriminate in a certain time interval is that the interpurchase time of consumers over that time interval (assumed to be homogeneous among consumers) be more than twice the time between price announcements in that interval.

Proposition 1 suggests that, *given* a certain interpurchase time, the monopolist should seek to shorten the time between price changes so that it is less than half the interpurchase time. Said differently, for a given time between price announcements, the monopolist should seek to increase the durability of the product so that the interpurchase time is more than twice the time announcements.

Price Discrimination with Rational Consumers. We go back now to our original assumption of a durable product—the consumers in the first period don't return to the market until the end of the second period when the game is over. But now we assume that the monopolist can precommit to a pricing strategy; i.e., he can precommit to a price pair $(p_1, p_2)(p_1 \geq p_2)$. At the start of the first period, then, the monopolist announces his first- and second-period prices and offers credible assurances to consumers that he will stick to the prices he has announced. All this will make no difference to the monopolist's pricing policy if consumers continue to be naive; we would again get the price-discrimination policy just described. So assume consumers consider future prices when making their current buying decision. In the first period, therefore, they decide whether to buy then or wait until the second period. What is the optimal pricing policy now? Stokey [1979] showed that the optimal pricing policy is to charge the same price in both periods and this price is the one-period optimal price $(X + c)/2$. In other words, if consumers are farsighted, then even with a durable good and precommitment to a pricing policy, the monopolist is unable to price discriminate. It is instructive to see why. If the monopolist precommits to the pricing policy (p_1, p_2), then the marginal consumer x^* who is indifferent between buying in the first period and buying in the second period is given by $(x^* - p_1) = (x^* - p_2)/(1 + r)$. This yields $x^* = [(1 + r)p_1 - p_2]/r$. Therefore, the monopolist's total profit function is $(X - x^*)(p_1 - c) + [(x^* - p_2)(p_2 - c)/(1 + r)]$. Maximizing this with respect to p_1 and p_2, we get $p_1 = p_2 = (X + c)/2$. The monopolist's optimal profits turn out to be $(X - c)^2/4$, less than his profits when consumers were naive. Thus, farsighted consumer can drastically *reduce* the monopolist's ability to price discriminate.[6]

Finally, let us now consider the case where a monopolist *cannot* precommit to a pricing policy. Suppose in the situation considered in the previous paragraph that the monopolist decides in period 2 to renege on his precommitted price $(X + c)/2$. Would he have any incentive to do so? Yes, he would. Facing a residual market $[0, (X + c)/2]$, the monopolist's best price in the second period will be $(X + 3c)/4$, which is less than $(X + c)/2$, the price to which he precommitted himself. *This suggests that rational consumers facing a monopolist who cannot precommit credibly to a pricing policy must realize that in each period, the monopolist will do what is best for him from that period onward. Their expectations about future prices must be conditioned on this realization.* In turn, these expectations will determine when they buy. As for the monopolist, what is best for him in each period depends on who is in the market at that time—and that depends on consumer expectations, as we just argued. The argument seems to be circular, but we can break out of it by working backward from the second period.

In the second period, if the residual market is $[0, x]$, then the best second-period price is $(x + c)/2$. Knowing this, the marginal consumer x will be the one who is indifferent between buying in the first period at p_1 and buying in the second period at $(x + c)/2$. That is $(x - p_1) = [x - (x + c)/2]/(1 + r)$. This yields x as a function of p_1: $x = [2p_1(1 + r) - c]/(1 + 2r)$. Now we come to the monopolist's profit function as it looks at the start of the first period (before he has chosen p_1):

$$\pi(p_1) = [X - x(p_1)](p_1 - c) + \left(\frac{1}{1 + r}\right)\left[x(p_1) - \frac{x(p_1) + c}{2}\right]$$

$$\left[\frac{x(p_1 + c)}{2}' - c\right].$$

Maximizing this function with respect to p_1, we get

$$p_1^* = \frac{X(1 + 2r)^2 + c(1 + 6r + 4r^2)}{2(1 + r)(1 + 4r)}$$

and then

$$p_2^* = \frac{X(1 + 2r) + c(1 + 6r)}{2(1 + 4r)}.$$

The monopolist's optimal profits with no precommitment turn out to be

$$\pi^\star = \frac{(X - c)^2(1 + 2r)^2}{4(1 + 4r)(1 + r)}.$$

It is easy to verify that both first- and second-period prices increase with marginal cost: a higher-cost monopolist's prices are higher than a lower-cost monopolist's. Also, $p_2^\star < p_1^\star$, so there is price discrimination. But the price discrimination here is weaker than when consumers were naive; the price schedule is flatter than before. Correspondingly, the monopolist's profits are also lower when consumers have rational expectations than when they have no expectations. Compared to the precommitment case, the monopolist's profits with no precommitment are lower if the interest rate is positive. *So precommitment is valuable to the monopolist.* Bulow [1982] notes various ways by which a monopolist can signal precommitment. For example, the monopolist can build a plant with capacity $(X - c)/2$ and thereby assure consumers that prices in any period cannot fall below $(X + c)/2$.

The next section reexamines the monopolist's pricing problem with no precommitment when consumers are uncertain about his marginal cost. Again, I will assume that consumers' expectations are rational (i.e., given the information they have in the first period, their expectations about second-period prices are correct). This is quite a strong assumption even in the case of no uncertainty—witness the backward induction calculations required to implement it previously. With uncertainty about costs, rational expectations are even harder to implement. So while it is interesting that Winer [1985] offers empirical evidence for rational expectations, I will not appeal to that evidence for motivating this assumption. Rational expectations, to me, are simply a modeling device—a way to understand how consumer expectations affect a monopolist's pricing policy. The idea is to say something about how expectations—even expectations that are not rational but that are, nevertheless, qualitatively similar to rational expectations—affect a monopolist's pricing policy; modeling these expectations as rational expectations is a tractable way of doing so. "Nonrational expectations" is not a useful modeling device for this purpose because there are many ways to have incorrect expectations.

The Main Results

The first thing to note is that only by *not* precommitting to a pricing policy can the monopolist derive any advantage from the uncertainty in consumers' minds. If the monopolist were to precommit both periods' prices, then the monopolist is left with no options to exploit any signals the announced prices may have conveyed to consumers. The essence of taking advantage of consumer uncertainty, then, is to use the first-period price to convey or not convey information about costs, and use the second-period price to reap the benefits of doing so.

Rational Expectations Equilibrium

As mentioned earlier, I will call the monopolist with marginal cost c_1 a type-1 monopolist and the monopolist with marginal cost c_2 a type-2 monopolist. Of course, there is really only one type of monopolist, and the monopolist knows—before announcing his first-period price—which type he is. The reason for considering both types of monopolist is that the consumers don't know which type of monopolist they are dealing with and therefore their actions will consider both possibilities. In turn, this means that even the monopolist has to consider what he would have done if he were not the type he actually is. In game-theoretic terms, we can express the same idea as follows. Following Harsanyi [1967–68], we convert the game of incomplete information into a game of imperfect information by introducing a third player into the game, "nature," and give nature the first move of choosing a monopolist's type (Moorthy 1985). Nature's choice is then revealed to the monopolist but not to the consumers. The rest of the game unfolds as follows. The next move is the monopolist's first-period pricing decision, followed by the consumers' decision on when to buy. Then comes the monopolist's second-period decision and that ends the game.

It is obvious that the monopolist would play according to his true type in the second period, regardless of what happened before. Therefore, once we specify the monopolist's first-period price and the inference consumers draw from it, the rest of the game unfolds smoothly. If p_1 is the first-period price and q^* the posterior probability of a type-1 monopolist (after consumers see p_1 and draw the appropriate inference from it), then the marginal consumer x^* who is indifferent between period-1 and period-2 consumption is given by $[2(1 + r)p_1 - c^*]/(1 + 2r)$ where $c^* = q^*c_1 + (1 - q^*)c_2$ is the posterior expectation of marginal cost. Furthermore, the optimal second-period price is $(x^* + c_1)/2$ for a type-1 monopolist and $(x^* + c_2)/2$ for a type-2 monopolist. But now we come to the crucial question. How should p_1 be determined for the two types of monopolists and how should we specify the consumers' inference rule? Depending on the inference rule consumers use, the two monopolists will determine their respective p_1s—p_1^1 and p_1^2; and given the choice of p_1^1 and p_1^2, the inference rule may or may not make sense.

To see this, suppose consumers follow the rule of inferring type-1 whenever they see a price below X. (Otherwise they infer type-2.) Given this rule, it is obvious what the type-1 monopolist will do. He will choose his first-period price as $p_1^1 = [X(1 + 2r)^2 + c_1(1 + 6r + 4r^2)]/[2(1 + r)(1 + 4r)]$—the price that maximizes his profits assuming that his type will be revealed. (See the previous section.) As for a type-2 monopolist, the only way to reveal his identity will be to choose a price at least as high as X in the first period—an unattractive possibility because it leads to no sales in the first period. (The discounted total profits will be $(X - c_2)^2/4(1 + r)$.) If he decides to allow himself to be confused as a type-1 monopolist, then the best price for him in the first period is $[X(1 + 2r)^2 + 2rc_1 + c_2(1 + 2r)^2]/[2(1 + r)(1 + 4r)]$.[7] (The profits at this price are $[(X - c_2)^2(1 + 2r)^2 + (c_2 - c_1)^2 - 4r(X - c_2)(c_2 - c_1)]/[4(1 + r)(1 + 4r)]$.) The latter price is clearly below X and it also yields greater profits to the type-2 monopolist than a price of X or higher. So, given the consumers' inference rule, the type-2 monopolist will choose $[X(1 + 2r)^2 + 2rc_1 + c_2(1 + 2r)^2]/[2(1 + r)(1 + 4r)]$ in the first period. If our definition of equilibrium only required that the monopolist's actions be profit-maximizing given the consumers' inference rule, then we would have an equilibrium at this point. But this equilibrium would not make sense. For one thing, the consumers' inferences are wrong. When they see $[X(1 + 2r)^2 + 2cr_1 + c_2(1 + 2r)^2]/[2(1 + r)(1 + 4r)]$ in the first period, the consumers mistakenly infer type-1 when they should be inferring type-2. Second, the inference rule itself is wrong. It doesn't allow the consumers to use the fact that whenever the two types' first-period prices are different, then the monopolist's types are being revealed.

We rectify these problems by defining a rational expectations equilibrium as a sequential equilibrium (Kreps and Wilson 1982b).

Definition

A *rational expectations equilibrium* is a pair of first-period prices (p_1^1, p_1^2), a pair of second-period price functions $(p_2^1(\cdot), p_2^2(\cdot))$, and an inference rule q^*: $[0, \infty) \to [0, 1]$ mapping first-period prices into posterior probabilities of a type-1 monopolist, such that:

1. $p_2^i(x) = (x + c_i)/2$ maximizes $(x - p_2)(p_2 - c_i)$, the second-period profits of a type-i monopolist ($i = 1, 2$), for any marginal consumer $x \in [0, X]$.

2. p_1^i maximizes $[X - x^*(p_1)](p_1 - c_i) + (1/1 + r)[x^*(p_1) - c_i]^2/4$, the total discounted profits of a type-i monopolist ($i = 1, 2$), where $x^*(p_1) = [2(1 + r)p_1 - c^*]/(1 + 2r)$ is the marginal consumer based on $q^*(p_1)$ being the posterior probability of a type-1 monopolist. Here $c^* = q^*(p_1)c_1 + [1 - q^*(p_1)]c_2$.

3. The inference rule, $q^*(p_1)$, follows Bayes rule as long as p_1 has a positive probability of happening under the equilibrium strategies of the two types of monopolist.

We say that a rational expectations equilibrium is *revealing* if $q^*(p_1^1) = 1$ and $q^*(p_1^2) = 0$. A rational expectations equilibrium is *separating* if $p_1^1 \neq p_1^2$. It follows straightforwardly that every separating equilibrium is revealing and every revealing equilibrium is separating. That is, if the two types of monopolist choose different first-period prices in a rational expectations equilibrium, then it must be the case that they reveal their identities. We call a rational expectations equilibrium where $p_1^1 = p_1^2$ a *pooling* equilibrium. In what follows, we are particularly interested in finding out whether there exists a pooling equilibrium that yields greater profits to the low-cost monopolist than what he would get by revealing his type. But first, we specify the form of the inference rule.

Proposition 2. In any rational expectations equilibrium where both types of monopolist use pure strategies, the consumers' inference rule must be of the form

$$q^*(p_1) = \begin{cases} 1, & \text{if } p_1 < \bar{p}, \\ q, & \text{if } p_1 = \bar{p}, \\ 0, & \text{if } p_1 > \bar{p}, \end{cases}$$

for some $\bar{p} \in (0, X)$.

Proof: If the two types of monopolist use the same initial price, then by condition 3 of the definition of a rational expectations equilibrium, the inference rule must not change the consumers' priors upon seeing this price. On the other hand, if the two types choose different initial prices, then the inference rule must infer that the types are being revealed. Then, using the fact that type 1's optimal revealed price is less than type 2's optimal revealed price (see the previous section), it is clear that the inference rule in a rational expectations equilibrium must be of the form shown.[8] ∎

Since we shall be dealing with rational expectations equilibria in pure strategies only, we shall assume that the inference rule is of the form in proposition 2.

Separating Equilibria

We start with some notation. Since neither type of firm is going to price below c_1 or above X in the first or second periods, it is convenient to represent all prices as the fractions $(p - c_1)/(X - c_1)$. We shall denote such fractions by k, a different k for each different p. In addition, let s denote the fraction $(c_2 - c_1)/(X - c_1)$.

Using the $k - s$ notation and noting that the marginal consumer is $[2(1 + r)p_1 - c^*]/(1 + 2r)$ when the posterior probability of type 1 is q^*, we can write the two types' profit functions

$$\pi^1 = (X - c_1)^2 \left\{ \frac{s^2(1 - q^*)^2 + 4k_1(1 + r)[(1 + 2r)^2 + 2rs(1 - q^*)] - 4k_1^2(1 + r)^2(1 + 4r)}{4(1 + r)(1 + 2r)^2} \right\},$$

$$\pi^2 = (X - c_1)^2$$

$$\left\{ \frac{s^2 q^{*2} + 4(k_1 - s)(1 + r)[(1 - s)(1 + 2r)^2 - 2rsq^*] - 4(k_1 - s)^2(1 + r)^2(1 + 4r)}{4(1 + r)(1 + 2r)^2} \right\}$$

Type 1's profit function π^1 is maximized when $k_1 = [(1 + 2r)^2 + 2rs(1 - q^*)]/[2(1 + r)(1 + 4r)]$; i.e., when $p_1 = [X(1 + 2r)^2 + 2rc^* + c_1(1 + 2r)^2]/[2(1 + r)(1 + 4r)]$. Similarly, π^2 is maximized when $k_1 = [(1 + 2r)^2(1 + s) + 2rs(1 - q^*)]/[2(1 + r)(1 + 4r)]$; i.e., when $p_1 = [X(1 + 2r)^2 + 2r\bar{c} + c_2(1 + 2r)^2]/[2(1 + r)(1 + 4r)]$. The two monopolists' profits at these prices are:

$$\pi^{i*} = \frac{(1 + 2r)^2(X - c_i)^2 + (c_i - c^*)^2 - 4r(X - c_i)(c_i - c^*)}{4(1 + r)(1 + 4r)}, \quad \text{for } i = 1, 2$$

When $q^* = q$, the p_1 that maximizes π^1 is nothing but the $\bar{p}$ a type-1 monopolist would like to see in pooling equilibrium; we denote this special value of $\bar{p}$ by p_1^{1nr} (in $k - s$ notation k_1^{1nr}). (The *nr* stands for "not revealed.") When $q^* = 1$, then $c^* = c_1$ and the value of p_1 that maximizes π^1 reduces to $[X(1 + 2r)^2 + 2rc_1 + c_1(1 + 2r)^2]/[2(1 + r)(1 + 4r)]$ (in $k - s$ notation $(1 + 2r)^2/[2(1 + r)(1 + 4r)]$). This price, which we shall denote by $p_1^{1r}(k_1^{1r})$, is the price a type-1 monopolist would like to charge if he thought he was going to be revealed. Finally, when $q^* = 0$, $c^* = c_2$, and we get $p_1 = [(X(1 + 2r)^2 + 2rc_2 + c_1(1 + 2r)^2]/[2(1 + r)(1 + 4r)]$ as the price that maximizes π^1 (in $k - s$ notation $[(1 + 2r)^2 + 2rs/[2(1 + r)(1 + 4r)]$). This price, denoted by $p_1^{1m}(k_1^{1m})$ is the price a type-1 monopolist would like to charge in the first period if he thought he was going to be mistaken for a type-2 monopolist. We can similarly define the corresponding quantities for a type-2 monopolist. When $q^* = q$, we have p_1^{2nr} (and correspondingly k_1^{2nr}); when $q^* = 1$, we have $p_1^{2m}(k_1^{2m})$; and when $q^* = 0$, we have $p_1^{2r}(k_1^{2r})$.

It is easily verified that $p_1^{1r} \le p_1^{1nr} \le p_1^{1m} < p_1^{2m} \le p_1^{2nr} \le p_1^{2r}$. With $r > 0$, all the inequalities are strict.) Also, the type-1 monopolist's profits corresponding to these prices follow the relationships: $\pi^{1m} > \pi^{1nr} > \pi^{1r}$. For the type-2 monopolist, however, things are a bit more complicated. For $(c_2 - c_1) \le 2r(X - c_2)$, π^{2*} is decreasing in q^*. Therefore, when $(c_2 - c_1) \le 2r(X - c_2)$, type-2 prefers to reveal himself. The same is true when $2r(X - c_2) < (c_2 - c_1) < 4r(X - c_2)$. (For $(c_2 - c_1) = 4r(X - c_2)$, type-2 is indifferent between revealing himself and being mistaken for type-1.) Finally, for $(c_2 - c_1) > 4r(X - c_2)$, type-2 would like to be mistaken for type-1. These profits are depicted in figures 5-1 and 5-2.

From figures 5-1 and 5-2 and the price orderings, it is apparent that no $\bar{p} < \hat{L}^1$ can support a rational expectations equilibrium. The reason is that $\hat{L}^1$ is the higher of the two prices at which type 1's "mistaken" profits equal type

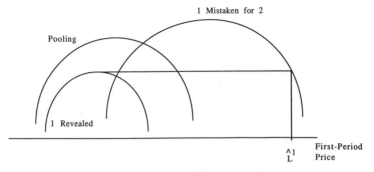

Figure 5–1. Type-1 Monopolist's Profit Functions

A. $c_2 - c_1 > 4r(X - c_2)$

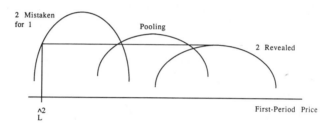

B. $2r(X - c_2) < c_2 - c_1 \leq 4r(X - c_2)$

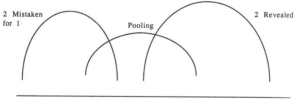

C. $c_2 - c_1 \leq 2r(X - c_2)$

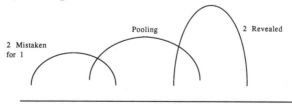

Figure 5–2. Type-2 Monopolist's Profit Functions

1's maximum revealed profits; see figure 5–1.[9] Therefore, for any $\bar{p} < \hat{L}^1$, type 1 will always choose a price where he will be mistaken for type 2, which cannot be allowed in a rational expectations equilibrium. Similarly, in figure 5–2, when $(c_2 - c_1) > 4r(X - c_2)$, $\hat{L}^2$ is the lower intersection of type 2's "mistaken" profit function and type 2's maximum revealed profits.[10] Therefore, when $(c_2 - c_1) > 4r(X - c_2)$, any $\bar{p}$ greater than $\hat{L}^2$ would lead to type 2 choosing to be mistaken as type 1, which cannot be allowed in a rational expectations equilibrium. From these observations and figures 5–1 and 5–2, we can assert the following proposition.

Proposition 3. The rational expectations equilibria in pure strategies are the following:

1. If $r = 0$, then any $\bar{p} \epsilon [p_1^{1r}, p_1^{2r}]$ yields a separating equilibrium. This equilibrium is nothing but the prices in a one-period model: $p_1^{1r} = (X + c_1)/2, p_1^{2r} = (X + c_2)/2$. No sales are made in the second period.

2. If $r > 0$ and $(c_2 - c_1) \le 4r(X - c_2)$, any $\bar{p} \epsilon [\hat{L}^1, p_1^{2r})$ yields a separating equilibrium. In this equilibrium, type 1 chooses p_1^{1r} in the first period and type 2 chooses p_1^{2r}.

3. If $r > 0$ and $(c_2 - c_1) > 4r(X - c_2)$, then there are two cases. If $\hat{L}^1 \le \hat{L}^2$, then any $\bar{p} \epsilon [\hat{L}^1, \hat{L}^2]$ yields the separating equilibrium (p_1^{1r}, p_1^{2r}). If $\hat{L}^1 > \hat{L}^2$, there is no equilibrium.

Conclusion

I have shown in this chapter that in a two-period model with consumers uncertain about the monopolist's costs, the only pure-strategy rational expectations equilibria are of the separating kind. That is, even though consumers are uncertain about the monopolist's costs, the monopolist would prefer to reveal himself in equilibrium. He does this by choosing a price in the first period from which consumers can rationally infer his true cost—a price which the other "type" of monopolist would not choose. Thus, in this two-period model, the monopolist gains no advantage from consumers not knowing his true cost.

We started the chapter with the conjecture that having the opportunity to sell to consumers over time could lead to a low-cost monopolist masquerading as a high-cost monopolist in the early periods—in order to induce consumers to buy early—but in later periods, both types of monopolist would reveal their true cost. This conjecture was not realized in our two-period model, but it is possible that a pooling equilibrium exists with a larger number of periods.

Another possibility is that with only two possible costs, c_1 and c_2, the only pooling equilibria involve mixed strategies, but with a continuum of possible costs $[c_1, c_2]$, a pooling equilibrium in pure strategies exists. These possibilities need to be explored further before we can say categorically whether the asymmetry in cost information has any effect on the monopolist's ability to price discriminate in the face of consumer expectations.

Notes

1. The argument offered here is conceptually similar to the one offered by Milgrom and Roberts [1982c] to show that limit pricing may or may not limit entry.

2. The uniform distribution assumption is really a normalization because even if the reservation prices u are distributed according to a distribution function F, we could change variables via $v = F(u)$ and use the fact that v is distributed uniformly on [0, 1].

3. The no-fixed-costs assumption is a relatively innocuous one because fixed costs play no role in the determination of price. One could easily relax it to a positive fixed cost as long as the fixed cost is less than the contributions either type of monopolist generates.

4. The proof is as follows. If $(x - p_1) \geq (x - p_2)/(1 + r)$, then $rx \geq (1 + r)p_1 - p_2$, and because $y > x$, $ry > (1 + r)p_1 - p_2$. Rearranging the terms of the last inequality, we get $y - p_1 > (y - p_2)/(1 + r)$.

5. The reason for the "more than twice" should become clear from the following example. Let [0, 2] represent the time interval under examination. Suppose date 0 denotes the start of the first period (when the price for the first period is announced), date 1 represents the end of the first period and the start of the second period (when the second-period price is announced), and date 2 represents the end of the second period and the end of the time interval. Clearly, the time between price announcements is one here. Suppose the interpurchase time is two (which is not more than twice the time between price announcements). Then, if consumers buy in the first period at date 0, they will return to the market at date 2 when the lower second-price is still in force. This will destroy price discrimination, as the argument in the text shows.

6. It is not always true, however, that the best precommitment policy with far-sighted consumers is to charge the one-period optimal price in both periods. Stokey [1979] suggests examples where some price discrimination is optimal even with far-sighted consumers.

7. This is obtained as follows. The marginal consumer who buys in the first period is $x^* = [2p_1(1 + r) - c_1]/(1 + 2r)$ (based on x^*'s mistaken posterior perception that the monopolist is type 1; see the previous section) and, based on this, the optimal second-period price for the type-2 monopolist is $(x^* + c_2)/2$. So looking at his total profits at the start of the first period, the type-2 monopolist sees $(p_1 - c_2)[X - x^*(p_1)] + [1/(1 + r)][x^*(p_1) - c_2]^2/4$. Maximizing this with respect to p_1 gives the expression in the text.

8. No claim is being made at this point that the $\bar{p}$ in this proposition is unique. In fact, we show later that there is a continuum of rational expectations equilibria differing only in the location of $\bar{p}$.

9. $\hat{L}^1$ in $k - s$ notation is $[(1 + 2r)^2 + 2rs + (1 + 2r)\sqrt{s(s + 4r)}][2(1 + r)(1 + 4r)]$.

10. $\hat{L}^2$ in $k - s$ notation is $[(1 + 2r)^2(1 + s) - (1 + 2r)\sqrt{s^2 - 4rs(1 - s)}]/[2(1 + r)(1 + 4r)]$.

Part III
Dynamic Pricing Models

Anthony J. Zahorik

T he next three chapters deal with rationales and optimal strategies for systematic movements of prices over time. The first chapter, "Pricing New Products from Birth to Decline: An Expository Review" by Shlomo Kalish, reviews some of the major findings about price changes over the product life cycle, and it presents a model that can be used as a framework for many of these earlier results. The second chapter, "Optimal Pricing and Advertising for New Products with Repeat Purchases" by George E. Monahan and Kofi O. Nti, provides an expanded analysis of some of the special cases described in Kalish's chapter by exploring pricing and advertising strategies for new nondurable products. The third chapter, "A Model of Discounting for Repeat Sales" by Chakravarthi Narasimhan, examines systematic price movements for mature nondurables, namely the periodic use of discounts by marketers to spur sales.

In chapter 6, Kalish does not presume to provide a complete review of the literature of life-cycle pricing, but rather presents the major patterns that have emerged from previous studies and provides some intuitive understanding as to why those results should hold.

For a single period, we understand well the nature of the optimal prices that an industry's firm should charge—namely, the prices that simultaneously set marginal revenues equal to marginal costs for all firms (regardless of whether the industry is a monopoly, an oligopoly, or one of monopolist competition). The factors that determine the price levels of the solution, or the firm's pricing environment, are (1) the structure of the demand function, (2) the cost structures that determine marginal costs, and (3) the number and type of competing firms.

The problem of determining price levels becomes more complex when multiple periods are considered. Not only can exogenous factors change the marketer's environment over time, but the firm's own actions in one period can have effects on all three of the preceding factors in other periods. Therefore, the objective function itself must change; one can no longer myopically optimize price within each period, but rather, optimal prices (and other marketing variables) must simultaneously be determined that will maximize discounted cash flows for all periods within the planning horizon.

The linkages that cause events in one period to affect the demand structure in other periods include both "demand learning effects" and "demand negative effects." The former are uncertainty-reducing factors such as consumption experience and word-of-mouth that tend to increase future sales; the latter include factors such as market saturation that tend to suppress future sales. A firm's cost structure is also linked to events in other periods through the experience curve and by economies of scale. The competitive environment is affected across periods when a low price is used to decrease the threat of entry. Each of these factors has an influence on the path a firm's optimal price will take over time; under various assumptions, these influences can be in opposite directions. Kalish's goal in chapter 6 is to lay out the assumptions under which each of these competing factors is dominant in order to provide insights about the conditions under which various pricing policies are optimal.

To incorporate these factors into a dynamic model, Kalish begins with the monopolist's problem, later building toward a model of oligopolist pricing with threat of entry. A key variable in his monopoly model is a quantity called λ, the present value of selling one additional unit in the current period. The optimal price in a period is determined to be $p^* = [\mu/(\mu + 1)](c - \lambda)$, where c is the marginal unit cost and μ is the price elasticity. When $\lambda = 0$, p^* is identical to the familiar one-period (myopic) solution. Pricing below the myopic price ($\lambda > 0$) is referred to as "penetration pricing" and pricing above ($\lambda < 0$) as "skimming." Therefore, by analyzing the path of λ over time, one can compare the optimal prices in the multiperiod problem to the myopic solution as well as track the level of the optimal price over time. For example, he shows that if demand is a function of price alone (no demand learning), there is no saturation effect, and unit costs decline with experience, then λ is always positive (i.e., prices are always below the myopic price). Moreover, if a zero interest rate is used to discount future cash flows, then λ is monotonically decreasing, meaning that the largest discounts from the myopic price are given at the outset and are steadily reduced. However, this steady reduction in discounts does not imply that prices steadily increase over time. In fact, due to experience-curve effects on cost, the optimal price may actually fall over time. (Intuitively, the model recommends building volume early by offering a discount, so that costs fall rapidly. Prices also fall to match the decrease in costs, but at a slower rate, providing an ever more profitable margin.) A host of diverse factors (including whether the product is a durable or nondurable, and whether consumers inventory products) are also shown to influence the firm's optimal pricing strategy.

The introduction of competition into the model complicates the analysis, but appears not to alter the qualitative nature of the monopoly solutions. The principal effect is one of lowering the level of prices, with the greater the number of competitors, the lower the prices. While closed-form analyses are possible when the number of competitors is fixed or entry of another firm is certain, Kalish's discussion of the literature on strategic entry (i.e., situations in which whether or not to enter a market is itself a decision variable) serves to highlight the lack of sound results in this area. In general, such analyses require the use of game theory, which may still be in too embryonic a state to provide analyses of realistic scenarios.

Finally, chapter 6 reviews the generalities about pricing policies throughout the product life cycle that have emerged in the literature. In the introductory stage, the consensus for repeat-purchase products is a penetration strategy; the generally optimal path for durable goods is a skimming strategy, although there are mitigating factors that can make penetration preferable. (Chapter 7 by Monahan and Nti also analyzes some determining factors in this situation.) The pricing models for mature products tend to assume steady state, with emphasis on intertemporal price discrimination through the sort of cyclical discounts discussed by Narasimhan. Pricing strategies in declining markets are briefly discussed and shown to depend upon industry and demand conditions.

In chapter 7, Monahan and Nti explore optimal pricing and advertising decisions for products in the early stages of the life cycle. The demand curve for the product is separated into two components, a random new-customer-demand function (reflecting customer uncertainty and exogenous factors) and a determinist repeat-purchase–demand function. As such, the model focuses more on nondurable goods than on durables. Both components of the demand function are assumed to be functions of past cumulative sales, current price, and current advertising. The objective function is the total expected discounted profit over an infinite horizon, maximization of which yields characterizations of the optimal advertising and pricing strategies as functions of the cumulative number of triers. The authors' terminology for pricing strategies differs somewhat from that of Kalish, in that *skimming* refers to monotonically decreasing prices (rather than prices higher than myopic), and an "introductory" policy is used to describe a monotonically increasing price.

The chapter explores the two cases of price-elastic and -inelastic new-customer demand. Although marketers generally recommend a skimming strategy for cases where demand is price-inelastic, the authors prove (subject to some explicitly stated conditions) that a skimming strategy is optimal for a frequently purchased product only if the repeat-purchase market is highly price-sensitive. On the other hand, an introductory strategy for such products can be optimal if the repeat purchasers become less price-elastic over time, due, say, to advertising that successfully differentiates the product. When new-customer demand is price-elastic, it is shown that an introductory strategy is optimal.

The authors also provide conditions for the structure of certain models that are sufficient for the existence of optimal solutions.

In chapter 8, Narasimhan addresses pricing strategies for a mature, frequently purchased product sold by a monopolist. As in chapter 6, the demand function is separated into two parts, but in this case consumers are classified as "loyal" (those who will repeat their purchases indefinitely) and "new triers" (consumers who may be induced by discounts and may even rebuy without discounts, but whose number declines over time). It is assumed that when such nonloyal consumers have purchased the product and finally left the system, they are replaced by an equal number of identical consumers, so that the model is in steady state, and the discount policy follows the following cycle: If the marketer's customer base is below a given threshold in size, he will offer a discount, which increases the customer base (by an amount that depends upon the size of the discount). This enlarged customer base then erodes over time at a fixed rate until the threshold is again reached. At that time, the process repeats itself.

Therefore, determining the optimal pricing policy involves solving for the pair of values: T^* (the period of time between discounts) and d^* (the size of the discount), which maximizes total discounted profits over a planning horizon. The relationship of the optimal solutions to a variety of influences—such as the size of the loyal segment (and by inference, the age of maturity of the product), the rate of decay of the customer base, and the firm's discount rate—are determined.

These chapters serve to demonstrate two issues about the state of analysis regarding pricing of products.

1. We are a long way from producing a comprehensive model of price. Each author approaches the problem from very different sets of assumptions and assumes a different set of factors to be salient, be it the cumulative number of products sold or the price elasticity of repeat purchasers. The sets of assumptions underlying most of these models, including many of those reviewed by Kalish, are not comparable, so the analyses cannot be easily compared, nor do they appear to be filling in gaps in an organized taxonomy of product situations. The literature in this area remains a rather disorganized body of special cases.

2. Most of the models are quite simplistic in the way they handle (or avoid) the issue of competition. We still appear to be far from a realistic model of the dynamic effects of price competition, primarily due to the intractability of all but very elementary n-person games.

Nevertheless, the next three chapters show the variety of approaches taken by analysts today to better understand the fundamental factors determining the dynamics of price. Each provides some insight into the systematic movements of prices during a product's life cycle.

6
Pricing New Products from Birth to Decline: An Expository Review

Shlomo Kalish

The objective of this chapter is to provide an expository review of dynamic pricing—why and how prices change over time. It tries to integrate the different factors that affect price dynamics in a unified framework so that some generalizations emerge. It concentrates on situations that arise in the context of new-product introductions.

Several review articles of the mid-1980s deal with issues similar to this chapter's. Kalish and Sen [1986] review models incorporating price in the context of a monopoly. Dolan, Jeuland, and Muller [1986] review diffusion models in a competitive framework. Jorgensen [1985] provides a comprehensive review of dynamic pricing in oligopolies. My approach is different in that I emphasize the generalities that emerge from the literature and try to provide the intuitive reasoning behind the results. I therefore do not provide a comprehensive survey, but instead concentrate on the more insightful papers.[1]

I begin by briefly reviewing the factors that effect pricing in a single-period world. I then classify the different reasons why prices change in a multi-period world. Next, I review in detail a simple model of intertemporal monopolistic pricing. I then insert additional complicating factors and discuss their effect on price dynamics. I conclude the chapter with a discussion of some normative implications.

HOW PRICES ARE SET

A product (or service) has some value to the customers. A profit-seeking firm would do best if it could charge exactly the product's value to each customer. Under this perfect-price-discrimination scenario, the firm will sell to all customers whose valuation of the product exceeds its marginal cost, extracting all the surplus from the productive activity.

The customers, on the other hand, would prefer to pay as little as possible. Obviously the firm typically will not sell at a loss (unless there are externalities). Thus, the lower limit on price is marginal cost.

Where the price will actually be set in this range between the two extremes depends on the relative power of the seller (i.e., the competitive situation), the relative power of the buyers, and the distribution of seller and buyer types. If there is one firm and many buyers (monopoly), then the firm may actually set prices according to each customer's willingness to pay, as just explained. While such pricing policies could be illegal, they are frequently practiced indirectly by product differentiation, quantity discounts, nonlinear pricing, and other methods (Nagle 1987; Maskin and Riley 1984; Moorthy 1984). A few examples of such pricing situations are the leasing-charge practices by computer and copier manufacturers as well as airline tickets, movie tickets, and books.

On the other extreme, where there are many sellers and one buyer (monopsony), price will be set at the average cost. Examples are suppliers to General Motors.

The distribution of customer types is important since it forms the basis for the different methods for price discrimination. Moreover, this distribution determines the form of the aggregate demand for the product. Similarly, the distribution of firm types determines the degree of monopoly power the firm has—i.e., what kind of cost advantages it possesses over the competition in producing the particular product bundle.

Since the subject of this chapter is price dynamics, we focus on the price level of the product rather than the price structure; i.e., we assume the following scenario. The firm has some monopoly power. It faces a heterogeneous market where customers value the product differently and form an aggregate demand curve. The firm charges a single price to all customers at any point in time.

Let P and Q be the price and quantity, respectively. Q is a function of price, prices of alternative products, and other exogenous factors. The firm sets price to maximize profits $\pi = PQ(P) - TC(Q) = R - TC$, where R is revenues, and TC is total cost. Equating the derivative of the profit to zero, we get the well-known pricing rule, $MR = MC$ (marginal cost equals marginal revenue). In other words, price will be set at the point where the additional revenues generated as a result of one more unit produced equal the additional cost.

Rearranging the preceding terms, we get the following equation that relates price to marginal cost: $P = [\mu/(\mu + 1)]MC$, where μ is the elasticity of demand $(\partial Q/\partial P)(P/Q)$, i.e., the percentage change in quantity relative to the percentage change in price. (Note that this elasticity/MC/price relation is an implicit relationship, since the elasticity typically depends on the price level, and the marginal cost depends on the number of units produced.) The insight however, is important, First, it shows that price is determined by the marginal cost (the cost of producing the last unit). Second, it shows that the margin depends on the elasticity of demand. In elastic markets, the margin will be low, and vice versa. For example, if $\mu = -5$, then $P = 1.25MC$. If $\mu = -2$, then $P = 2MC$.

In oligopoly, or monopolistic competition, the rule still applies; however, it has to be satisfied simultaneously for all competitors, since μ is now a function of the actions (prices) of all firms. In this case, the prices that solve $MR = MC$ for all firms simultaneously are Nash equilibrium prices in that no firm can unilaterally improve profits by changing prices. Clearly, the more competitors there are, the higher μ is likely to be, and prices will be lower.

In summary, then, there are three factors that determine the price level: demand for the product, (the distribution of the valuations for the product across customers); the production costs that determine the marginal costs; and the competitive situation (how many and what type of competitors exist).

WHY PRICES CHANGE OVER TIME

The preceding analysis ignores time. In practice, the firm maximizes the present value of cash flows. Thus, if any of these basic factors is changing over time, price is changing too. For example, if production cost is falling over time, then prices follow suit. If the number of competitors increases, then prices fall. If demand increases as a result of income growth, then prices typically increase, and so on.

It is useful to differentiate between two kinds of changes over time: those that are a result of what happened in other periods and those that are not linked to whatever happened in other periods. In the latter case, the changes are exogenous to the system. Thus, the pricing rule in every period will still be the myopic single-period–maximizing price as previously presented. However, due to the changing conditions, the price is changing. Typical examples are unpredictable changes in demand (due, e.g., to weather or taste changes) and in production costs. Prices will indeed change over time, but in each period the firm will maximize immediate profits according to the preceding rule. Since the changes in the demand and cost conditions are unpredictable, the prices will typically follow a random walk. Examples are prices of fruits and vegetables and of various commodities.

If the changes are interlinked, then the price in one period may affect the demand, cost, or competitive situation in future periods. Thus, the price in any single period need not maximize that particular period's profit. For example, the positive "diffusion" effect of a new product results in "penetration pricing," where initial profits are sacrificed in order to gain rapid market acceptance and thus stimulate demand. Similarly, the well-known experience-curve cost decline causes the firm to price below the myopic price in order to stimulate demand and thus reduce future production cost, allowing the overall net present value of profits to be higher (Robinson and Lakhani 1975; Dolan and Jeuland 1981; Spence 1981; Kalish 1983a, 1985; Wernerfelt 1985; Kalish and Sen 1986; Dockner and Jorgensen 1987).

Price today may affect the competitive situation in the future. Thus, the firm may want to price at a lower level in order to decrease the probability of future competitive entry (limit pricing).

Note that even if there is no interaction directly in terms of cost and demand, if the changes are predictable, then there is a possible interaction via inventorying. The firm will typically increase inventory in anticipation of future higher demand if its marginal cost function is increasing, and vice versa. Similarly, anticipating consumers will accumulate inventory or delay purchases if prices are changing in a predictable way. These factors tend to smooth prices over time. (See, e.g., Phlips 1983; Amihud and Mendelson 1983a, b.) Inventory decisions are not modeled here; however, they are mentioned where relevant.

Another aspect that I do not review here is the use of dynamic pricing in order to obtain information about the demand curve where there is uncertainty. This area of research, while important, is still in its infancy. (See Braden and Oren 1987; Lazear 1986.)

The following sections classify the different factors that cause conditions to be interlinked across periods.

Changes in Demand

Changes in aggregate demand are classified into changes that are a result of factors varying with time versus those that are a result of some state variables changes (i.e., they relate to what has been done in the past). As argued, the latter are the more interesting changes from a marketing-policy-making perspective.

Endogenous Changes in Demand

We classify endogenous changes into two types. The first, which we term learning effect in demand, includes all the factors that affect future demand positively. The second are factors that have negative effects on future demand.

Demand-Learning Effects

Information Effects. When risk-averse customers are not familiar with the product, its value is lower due to uncertainty about the product. As uncertainty decreases, the product's expected value typically increases. This phenomenon is particularly dominant in a new-product situation. In such cases, information that reduces uncertainty spreads mostly by word of mouth from current users, but also by advertising, salespeople, and public information sources (Kalish 1985).

When the product is of a repeat-purchase type, the uncertainty can be reduced by trying the product. Then, on the average, the value of the product increases over time (Schmalensee 1982; Jeuland 1981). Similarly, the value of the brand or company name increases. This leads to the well-known phenomenon of brand loyalty. Thus, for goods where the actual performance is the expected performance, the value of the good increases as more people adopt the product and as time passes. This typically results in increasing demand for a given price (for repeat-purchase goods).

A related aspect of information diffusion is awareness of the product. Clearly, unless customers know about the product, they can not "demand" it. Awareness is generated, among other things, by word-of-mouth communications. Thus, the more customers there are early on, the faster awareness will be spread (Dodson and Muller 1978; Kalish 1985).

Network Effects. For some goods, the value of the good depends directly on how many people already own/adopt the product. The classic example is a network, where the value of being a member depends on who else is a member and typically increases in the number of subscribers. This phenomenon also applies in nonnetwork goods—durable goods in particular—since the quality and price of service typically improve with the number of users. Network effects are very similar to the informational effects in that they cause demand to increase as more people adopt the innovation. This results in similar pricing practices (Dhebar and Oren 1985).

Other Positive Effects. There are a variety of other phenomena that have positive effect on future demand. They include brand loyalty, habit formation, the carry-over effect of market share, reputation, and imitation effects (Bass 1969, 1980). While some of these phenomena can be explained as informational effects, since they are so prevalent in marketing, we list them specifically.

Demand-Negative Effects

Durable Goods—Saturation Effects. Every customer that purchases a durable good is out of the market for a substantial period. Thus, as the market gets saturated, the demand for the goods decreases. Demand is also affected by expectations of price changes. If price is expected to decline, many customers will delay purchase, and vice versa (Stokey 1981).

Social/Snob Effects. For some goods, the value of the good decreases over time just because it is not new (e.g., fashion items). A related phenomenon is the so-called snob effect, where the value of the good decreases with the number of users.

Exogenous Changes in Demand

Changes in Income. The value of a product to the customer depends not only on his taste, but also on his budget. As his economic situation changes, so does the value of the product to him. For example, if the opportunity cost of his time increases, then the value of a time-saving product such as a microwave oven increases; thus, he his more likely to purchase. In the aggregate, this is manifested by an increase in demand if overall income increases, and vice versa.

Economic Conditions. Changes in economic conditions have an effect on income as just described. However, in addition, uncertainty about the future tends to have a major effect on the demand for high-ticket items, as people are reluctant to make obligations if they are uncertain about future income.

Changes in Taste. The taste of the individuals may change over time as well. This, however, cannot typically be predicted well.

Other Exogenous Factors. Other factors include seasonality, random shocks, environmental changes, and changes in the laws. To the extent that they can be predicted, they cause interperiod links via inventory. Otherwise, the pricing rules are the same as the myopic ones, where in every period marginal revenue equals marginal cost.

Changes in Costs

Production costs change over time as well. They can change as a result of exogenous unpredicted factors, in which case there will not be any interperiod effects (except for inventorying policy when changes are predictable).

More interesting are the endogenous cost changes. Many studies have been published about the experience curve—the phenomenon of production cost declining with cumulative experience in manufacturing. (See, e.g., Yelle [1979] and the references therein.) The sources of the cost decline are numerous—e.g., learning by doing and technological advancement. (See Alchian [1959]; Arrow [1961].)

It is important to point out the difference between experience curve and economies of scale. If economies of scale are present and if the industry is growing, the marginal production cost will decline over the years as volume increases. However, this is quite different than experience-curve cost decline as there is no benefit of increasing production in one period toward decreasing costs in future periods (Devinney 1987).

Changes in Competitive Conditions

The third factor that affects price is the competitive situation. The competitive situation affects pricing in two ways. First, the more competitors there are, the lower the price typically is, even in the single-period model. Thus, as more competitors enter the market, prices fall.

However, even if the firm is a monopoly, it will typically set price taking into account the possibility of a future entrant. The firm may know of a sure entry (Eliashberg and Jeuland 1986) or it may want to affect the possibility of entry by using price (Milgrom and Roberts 1982a). This can be done as a pure signaling device or in combination with other intertemporal factors, such as the experience curve and building market reputation.

A GENERAL FRAMEWORK FOR DYNAMIC PRICING

In what follows, I develop the mathematical description of the pricing problem under dynamic conditions. Our point of departure is a generalization of the monopolist problem as suggested in Kalish [1983a]. In order to simplify the analysis, we collapse all the factors that affect the demand via experience with the product into one factor—the cumulative sales of the product. This cumulative experience has either a positive or negative effect on future demand as just explained. Similarly, cumulative experience is used to model cost. In addition, I model the effects of exogenous factors on cost and demand.

A General Formulation of the Pricing Problem—Monopoly

Let $x(t)$ be the cumulative experience at time t, i.e., the total volume produced by that time. The sales rate is then $s(t) = dx(t)/dt = \dot{x}$. This sales rate is a function of price, cumulative experience, and exogenous factors. We write:

$$\dot{x} = f(x(t), p(t), E(t)) \qquad (1)$$

where $p(t)$ is the product's price, and $E(t)$ is the effect of exogenous factors such as economic conditions and random noise. We assume that demand increases as price decreases ($f_p < 0$). The derivative of demand with respect to cumulative production would typically be positive for repeat-purchase goods (the effects of experience and uncertainty reduction for good products, as previously explained), whereas in the case of durable goods, it will eventually be negative, once the saturation effect overcomes the information/imitation effect. However, early on it could be positive. The effects of the exogenous variables are clearly unrestricted.[2]

Production cost is assumed to be decreasing with cumulative experience. Here we assume a general functional form as follows: $c = c(x(t), t)$, where the derivative of c with respect both to experience and time is negative. This models the effect of experience and technical progress on reducing cost over time.

The monopolist wishes to maximize profits over the planning horizon $(0, T)$:

$$\pi = \int_0^T e^{-rt}(p - c)s\, dt$$

s.t. $\dot{x} = s = f(x(t), p(t), E(t)), x(0) = x_0.$

x_0 is the initial output level and r is the discount rate.

We incorporate the constraint into the objective function by forming the current-value Hamiltonian:[3]

$$H = e^{-rt}(p - c + \lambda)s \qquad (1)$$

where λ is the shadow price of the constraint, i.e., the current value of one additional unit produced on the objective function, which follows the following differential equation:

$$\dot{\lambda} = r\lambda - \frac{\partial H}{\partial x}; \lambda(T) = 0. \qquad (2)$$

The maximum principle states that the solution to this problem maximizes the Hamiltonian H at each point in time, with $x(t)$ and $\lambda(t)$ given equations (1) and (2), respectively.

Assuming regularity conditions on the demand function (see Kalish [1983a]), an optimal price exists and is given by the first-order condition:

$$\frac{\partial H}{\partial p} = 0$$

Taking the derivative and rearranging, we get:

$$p^* = \mu/(\mu + 1)(c - \lambda) \qquad (3)$$

i.e., price is related to marginal cost in a way similar to the single-period optimization, except that in this case marginal cost is adjusted to the effect of the additional unit on future profits, λ. If λ is positive, then price is below the myopic level, and vice versa. If current sales have a positive effect on future profits, then we invest now by lowering price and giving up profits in return for future higher profits, and likewise for learning cost.

We adopt the notion suggested by Dolan and Jeuland [1981] and call pricing below and above the myopic price "penetration pricing" and "skimming," respectively.

From (3), it is apparent that at the end of the planning horizon, the price converges to the myopic price since $\lambda(T) = 0$. This is not surprising, since there is no need to invest in future periods. To see what happens at other times, we need to find the sign and magnitude of λ. From (2), after some algebra using (3), we get:

$$\dot{\lambda} = r\lambda - \frac{\partial H}{\partial x} = r\lambda + c_x f + \frac{f_x p}{\mu}; \qquad \lambda(T) = 0$$

which has the solution:

$$\lambda(t) = \int_t^T \left(-c_x f - \frac{f_x p}{\mu} \right) e^{-r(\tau - t)} d\tau \qquad (4)$$

We see that λ is the accumulation of the future cost decline as a result of the additional unit produced (the first term) plus the effect on revenues of that additional unit. The first term is positive, since cost declines with experience. Thus, if the second is positive, then λ is positive, which means that price is always below the myopic level.[4] Moreover, λ will typically be declining over time in this case (clear if $r = 0$), which means that the difference between optimal and myopic price is maximum early on and decreasing.

Thus, for example, if this is a repeat-purchase type of good with performance as expected, then the penetration price cut given early on would be the highest. If there is no experience-curve cost decline, this will result in a low introductory price that increases to the steady state price.

On the other hand, if there is no learning-curve cost decline, and the effect of additional units on future demand is negative ($f_x < 0$), then λ is negative, meaning prices higher than myopic profit maximizing would apply. This is typically the case for a durable good if the information/imitation effects are not strong.

A second question of interest is what happens to the price path over time. Is it increasing, decreasing, or mixed? This will be affected by the changes in cost, demand, and the "investment in the future," λ. To do this, we take the time derivative of the optimal price in (3). Since it is the solution of $\partial H/\partial p = 0$, we can use the implicit function theorem: $dp/dt = -\partial^2 H/\partial p \partial t /(\partial^2 H/\partial p^2)$. The numerator is negative by assumption of regularity. Thus, the sign of price derivative is the same as the sign of $\partial^2 H/\partial p\,\partial t$. Doing this and rearranging we get:

$$\text{sign}(\dot{p}) = \text{sign}\left[-r\lambda - 2\,\frac{f_x f}{f_p} + \frac{f_{xp} f^2}{f_p^2} + c_t - p\,\frac{\partial}{\partial t}\left(\frac{1}{\mu}\right)\right] \tag{5}$$

Thus, price direction is determined by several factors. First is the interest rate—the larger it is, the more money is wanted now. In cases where λ is positive (i.e., learning curve and demand learning), it means investing less in the future and higher prices now. This creates a pressure for declining prices. The second term is the effect of experience on demand. If it is positive ($f_x >$ 0), then this term is positive; i.e., it means price is lower now and increasing, in order to stimulate future demand. The third term is the second-order effect of price change on demand, and will typically not change the effect of the second term. The last two terms are the effect of exogenous time shifts on cost and demand. The direction of cost change clearly influences price to change in the same direction. Likewise, if elasticity is increasing in time, price is decreasing.

It is interesting to note that cost changes via learning curve do not affect price changes directly. They enter indirectly via λ. Indeed, when $r = 0$, cost enters the pricing formula only through the cost at the end of the planning period, which is the relevant marginal cost (Spence 1981). We turn now to analyze several typical cases that arise in reality.

The Learning-Curve Effect

Consider the effect of the learning curve alone. Assume demand is a function of price alone and that unit cost declines with experience ($c_x < 0$). It is clear from (4) that $\lambda(t)$ is positive for all t. Moreover, for zero interest rate, it is monotonically decreasing. Thus, the discount relative to the myopic price given early on is the highest, and it is decreasing over time. The price path over time, however, is monotonically decreasing, as can be seen from equation (5), which in this case becomes:

$$\text{sign}(\dot{p}) = \text{sign}(-r\lambda + c_t) \tag{6}$$

That is, the price declines with experience (through λ), and through direct time-related cost decrease. In the extreme case where the interest rate is zero (and there is no exogenous cost decline), price is constant for the whole period. In the other extreme case, where the discount rate is very high, price will be close to the myopic one, i.e., closely following the cost decline over time.

Clarke et al. [1982] have investigated a different cost function, where in addition to the variable cost that we model here, there is a fixed cost every period. The fixed cost decreases with experience, but the marginal cost stays constant. Indeed, under these conditions, λ is positive as well. However, since the marginal cost is constant, the price is low at introduction and increasing. Clearly, if we have a combination of decrease both in fixed and variable cost, then the time path may take different directions depending on the parameters of the problem.

The Demand-Learning Effect

Consider next demand learning alone. There are several phenomena just explained that cause the demand for the product to increase as there is more experience with it, including word-of-mouth communications, reduction of uncertainty due to experience, network effects, and habit formation. We look at the effect of these factors alone, assuming that cost is constant and that there are no negative saturation effects. Here, again λ is positive for the whole period. This means that here too price is always below the myopic price. For *zero* interest rate, λ is monotonically decreasing. Since cost is constant, price path over time will be monotonically increasing, as can be seen from (5), which in this case becomes:

$$\text{sign}(\dot{p}) = \text{sign}\left[-2\,\frac{f_x f}{f_p} + \frac{f_{xp} f^2}{f_p^2} - p\,\frac{\partial}{\partial t}\left(\frac{1}{\mu}\right) \right] \tag{7}$$

Thus, price is increasing over time due to learning in demand, and is shifting with the exogenous changes in demand elasticity over time. It is easy to verify that if the demand function has a multiplicative form, i.e., $f = g(x, t)h(p)$, then (7) simplifies considerably, and we get the following result. For the zero-interest case, price is increasing if and only if $g_x > 0$. Thus, as long as there is a positive learning effect on demand, price is increasing and vice versa. (See Kalish [1983a] for additional details where r is positive.)

In a typical repeat-purchase–good situation, this scenario is applicable. There, most of the demand learning is done in the early stages of the new-product introduction. Indeed, we see that in many such cases, price is low at the beginning (directly or indirectly) and increasing over time to the steady state price.[5]

Durable Goods

Durable goods are goods that have a long lifetime. Thus, the effect of each unit sold on future demand is negative, since there is one less customer in the market ($f_x < 0$). If we abstract from learning in both demand and cost, then it is clear that λ is negative—as can readily be seen from (4). Thus, in this case, price will be above the price that maximizes immediate revenues. Over time, then, in the zero-interest case, price will be monotonically decreasing.

The logic here is that the firm charges a high price initially to sell to those willing to pay a high price for the product. Once this segment has bought, price can be reduced to reach the next segment, and so forth. Thus, the firm is using time to discriminate between the customers and increase profits.

In the preceding demand specification, I implicitly assume that consumers are myopic in that they take only today's price into account when making decisions. Clearly, in the case of durable goods, consumers are forming expectations about future price moves and react accordingly. That is, some will buy early, since the value of the product to them is high enough so that they are not willing to wait for the price reduction. Others, however, may decide to delay purchase, since the savings on price are at least as high as the cost of the utility lost while waiting.

Stokey [1981], Conlisk et al. [1984], and Narasimhan [1987] model the case of durable goods where consumers do form expectations. The existence of expecting consumers limits the firm from making dramatic price cuts over time; however, the qualitative nature of the solution is similar. Price is decreasing monotonically over time. While all customers know that this is happening, some prefer to pay more and use the products immediately, while the less intense customers wait for price to fall.

If there is an infusion of new customers into the market every period, this may lead to a cyclical pricing policy. After the market has been cleared of all consumers that have waited for the low price, the whole cycle begins again.

Combining the Effects

Demand learning and cost learning have similar effects in that both cause λ to be positive; i.e., the value of a present additional unit on future profits is positive, and the firm therefore forgoes profits early on by reducing prices in order to stimulate demand, reduce costs, and make more money later. This can be seen in equation (1). Moreover, for a zero-interest rate, it is obvious that λ is monotonically decreasing. Thus, the profit margin over time is monotonically increasing. It could even be negative early on.

The time path of price, however, depends on the modified cost, $c - \lambda$, as in (1). Since cost is decreasing with experience, and λ is also typically decreasing, the price-path direction is not generally the same. In a typical situation, most of the demand learning occurs early on. This results in a pattern of low and increasing prices at introduction, followed by declining prices along the cost curve later on.

Time changes in cost and demand will have immediate effects on price changes, in addition to the experience-based changes already noted. Thus, seasonal increase in demand will cause a price-increase pressure, as will a seasonal increase in costs.

In the case of durable goods, however, both margins and prices decline over time as just explained. If we combine this with learning on the cost side, it has the effect of decreasing early margins somewhat in order to stimulate later sales; however, price is still monotonically decreasing (Kalish 1983a). If, however, there is demand learning, then early margins are further decreased, and it is possible to have a low introductory price that increases later on, before price proceeds to decrease over time (Kalish 1985; Horsky 1987).

The existence of "strategic" customers who have foresight about future prices in the case of durable goods has an effect of mitigating price changes over time, since drastic changes in prices will cause consumers to alter their timing of purchases. Thus, I conjecture that the qualitative nature of the preceding results still hold, while magnitude of price change is reduced. In this case, if there is a flow of new customers entering the market every period, a cyclical pricing pattern may be optimal where every so often a "sale" is announced, and the customers who have waited since they were not willing to purchase at the higher prices buy (Narasimhan 1987).

Summary of Monopoly Dynamic Pricing

We have seen that the single-period pricing rule of equating marginal revenue to marginal cost has to be modified if there are factors interlinking the different periods. If the effects of producing more units this period on future profits is positive, then the firm has an incentive to reduce prices today in order to increase future profits. This is equivalent to any kind of investment decision, where cash is forgone today in expectation of future positive cash flow.

We have identified two such factors—cost learning and learning in demand. Learning causes cost to be lower with more experience, and it causes demand to be higher. Thus, both these factors cause the firm to reduce prices early on relative to the myopic prices. On the other hand, for durable goods there is the opposite pressure—the firm prefers to charge more to early customers, and it reduces the margin as it progresses down the demand curve. The combination of these pressures in any particular situation determines the shape of the price path.

As in any investment decision, the discount rate plays a major role here. The higher the interest rate, the more myopic the pricing strategy will be. Thus, for high discount rates, prices will follow costs more closely. On the other hand, low discount rates will allow for more aggressive strategies, where at the extreme we can see products priced below marginal costs early on.

One of the factors that determines the discount rate is the inherent risk in the new product. Clearly, the higher the risk, the higher the discount rate is. In our context, one of the major factors that determines the risk is to what extent the "asset" being created is of private value. Learning on the cost side can be copied by the competitors. Similarly, learning on the demand side could have spillovers to competitors. In what follows, I shall elaborate on these and other issues regarding competition.

The effects of changes in demand and cost that are related to time directly (such as changes in economic conditions, seasonality, and random changes) have been shown to cause changes in prices as well in the expected direction. These changes in our framework do not have interperiod implications for pricing. Note, however, that we have not considered inventorying. The possibility to build inventory tends to interlink time periods even when the changes are related to calendar times. Anticipating changes in demand and costs leads to building of inventories on both the producers' and customers' sides. This, like customers with expectations, has an effect of mitigating price changes over time (Phlips 1983).

Oligopoly Pricing—No Entry

As stated in the chapter introduction, price is changing due to changes in any one of the three basic factors of cost, demand, and competitive situation. We have seen how price is changing as a result of cost and demand shifts in the monopoly case. Before we review how changes in the competitive structure affect pricing, we examine whether the results obtained earlier still hold in the context of an oligopoly whose structure does not change.

Formulation of the Oligopoly Problem

A straightforward generalization of the monopoly model is to allow sales of one firm to depend also on prices of competing firms and their cumulative experiences as follows. (This analysis follows Dockner and Jorgensen [1987], who have introduced the following in a slightly different model.)

$$\dot{x}_i = f_i(x_1(t), x_2(t), \dots, x_n(t), p_1(t), p_2(t), \dots,$$

$$p_n(t), E(t)) \qquad \text{for } i = 1, \dots n \tag{8}$$

where the usual assumptions about demand function hold, namely, $\partial f_i/\partial p_i < 0$, $\partial f_i/\partial p_j \geqq 0$. The effect of own experience, x_i, on demand is similar to the monopoly case, whereas the effect of competitors' experience on the firm's demand is typically negative, unless there is strong product-class market learning; i.e., the competing brands' penetration stimulates demand for the competitors as well.

We assume cost is declining with own experience and to some extent with industry experience, $c_i = c_i(x_i, \Sigma x_j, t)$, where $\partial c_i/\partial x_i < \partial c_i/\partial \Sigma x_j < 0$; i.e., direct learning is stronger than indirect learning.

Each firm wishes to maximize the present value of cash flow, namely:

$$\text{Max} \quad \pi = \int_0^T e^{-rt}(p_i - c_i)s_i dt \quad \text{subject to constraint 8.} \quad (9)$$

Open-Loop Nash Equilibrium Analysis

Suppose a firm knows the price path of all its competitors. Its problem then is completely equivalent to the monopolist optimal control as in the preceding section and can be solved by the same methods.

An open-loop Nash equilibrium is a set of solutions that satisfy this optimization problem for the n firms simultaneously. If each firm chooses this price path, then no firm can improve its profit by deviating unilaterally from its price path. While this equilibrium concept has some limitations, it serves as a useful first cut at the problem, while maintaining analytical tractability.[6]

Assuming regularity conditions on the demand functions so that there exists an internal price that maximizes the Hamiltonian, we get (in a way similar to the section on the monopoly pricing problem):

$$p_i = \frac{\mu_{ii}}{\mu_{ii} + 1}(c_i - \lambda_{ii}) - \frac{\displaystyle\sum_{j \neq i} \lambda_{ij}\mu_{ji}}{\mu_{ii} + 1} \quad (10)$$

where μ_{ii} is the own-brand elasticity, and $\mu_{ji} = (\partial f_j/\partial p_i)(p_i/f_i)$ (i.e., the change in competitor j's sales relative to i's sales as a result of a relative price change by i).

Optimal Prices in Comparison with Myopic Competition

The first term on the right-hand side of (10) is identical to the monopoly case; i.e., the difference between the myopic price is via λ_{ii}. As before, if more output today has a positive effect on future profit than price today will be lower than when considering currents profits only.

The second term of (10) corrects the price due to the effect of i's price on the competitors' sales, which in turn influence i's profits in the future, as measured by λ_{ij}. Since $\mu_{ji} > 0$ and $\mu_{ii} + 1 < 0$, the sign for the whole term is determined by the signs of the λ_{ij}s, i.e., the effect of additional unit sold by j on i's future profits. In most cases, this is negative. For durable goods λ_{ij} is clearly negative, since the competitor both occupies a "slot" in the market and increases its market and cost-learning effect. But even for repeat-purchase goods, in most cases, if the competition sells more, it hurts firm i since the competition improves its cost and market position. Thus, the price is lowered even more in this case in order to make it more difficult for the competitor to gain a foothold in the marketplace.

For repeat-purchase goods where there are strong spillovers from competitors to i, either in demand or in cost learning, then it is possible that λ_{ij}s are positive, in which case price is adjusted upward.

In sum, then, it seems that in the oligopolist situation, the qualitative analysis of pricing is similar to the monopoly case, except that in most cases, prices are even more aggressive, in order to make it difficult for the competition to gain advantage through experience.

Price Paths over Time

In a manner similar to the analysis of the monopolist case, several special cases can be generalized to the oligopoly framework. Dockner and Jorgensen [1987] show the following results:

1. If there is no learning/saturation in demand (i.e., demand does not depend on xs) and there is experience-curve cost decline, then price is monotonic, decreasing over time for $r > 0$, and constant for $r = 0$.

This result is a generalization of the monopoly case. Indeed, here too prices are below the myopic competition due to cost learning, and margins are increasing over time, however not enough to cause price to actually increase over time. At the extreme, where $r = 0$, price is constant. (See Spence [1981] and Fudenberg and Tirole [1983a] for similar results.)

2. If demand has only self-learning effects and it is multiplicative with price ($f_i = k_i(x_i)q_i(p_1, \ldots, p_n)$), then for the zero discount rate, prices are increasing (decreasing) if $k_i' > 0$ (< 0) for all i.

This is also a generalization of the monopoly result. It is important to note that all k_i are positive or negative for the particular time in question. This is typical for a repeat-purchase good where prices are monotonically increasing from introduction to the steady state. Similarly, for durable goods, after the initial market-learning effects have subsided, prices are monotonically decreasing.

Dockner and Jorgensen [1987] show that if the price part itself $q_i(p_1, \ldots, p_n)$ is multiplicatively separable, then the preceding result holds for every firm on its own; i.e., price is increasing if and only if $k_i' > 0$.

3. If market learning is shared equally by all brands, and the learning effects and price effects are multiplicatively separable, then for the zero discount rate, prices are increasing for all if and only if demand learning is positive and vice versa. (See Dockner and Jorgensen [1987] for additional details and other results.)

The modeling framework shown here includes several previous papers as special cases, including Dockner [1985], Thompson and Teng [1984], and Erickson [1983]. Wernerfelt [1985] uses a similar open-loop Nash equilibrium to investigate the implications of the learning curve in a duopoly. His results are consistent with what is obtained here; i.e., prices are monotonically decreasing. In another paper, Wernerfelt [1986] investigates the effects of a general specification of learning curve and brand loyalty on prices. Rao and Bass [1985] also use open-loop Nash equilibrium in a model with homogeneous goods and diffusion.

Discussion

To summarize the case of a fixed oligopoly, we see that many of the qualitative and quantitative results do carry over from the monopoly case to the competitive case. Clearly, price levels here will, in general, be lower than in the monopoly case. However, with regard to the issue of how much to invest in terms of demand and cost of learning, the qualitative factors are similar. Moreover, in this case, the firm needs to also take into account the indirect effect of its prices on its future profits through the effect on competition. We have seen that this factor tends to strengthen the penetration pricing argument unless there are strong spillover effects.

The Competitive Market: The Future-Entry Problem

How do changes in the competitive conditions affect prices? Here, again, we can distinguish between two situations: (1) the entries are exogenous and have nothing to do with the actions of the current competitors and (2) the entrant threat of entry is a strategic one; i.e., the entrant evaluates the incumbents and enters if he foresees that he can make profits after entry.

Exogenous Entry

Exogenous entry means that the new competitor(s) will enter in the future, regardless of the incumbent's action. The entry time is either deterministically known or there is some probability distribution about entry time.

The entry of competition clearly has the direct effect of increasing price elasticity for any single firm, thus reducing prices. Therefore, even without any learning/saturation effects on demand or cost, price will typically fall as more competitors enter the industry.

The more interesting question is how learning and saturation affect the incumbent pricing prior to entry. On an intuitive level, the incumbent would be more aggressive in his pricing strategy prior to entry if there were no spillover in market and cost learning. The reason for this is that the incumbent is put in a better position to compete in the postentry period. Moreover, in the durable-goods case, the incumbent wishes to fill more "slots" and thus make them unavailable to the competition.

Conceptual general models such as in the preceding section can be specified, where the entry times for the different competitors are given by t_2, t_3, and so on. This has not been done yet in a general framework; however, several papers have done this for special cases. I discuss these next and report whether the results support the preceding intuitive argument.

Spence [1981] models the effects of the learning curve alone, when firms enter over time exogenously. The goods are assumed to be homogeneous, and there is no learning/saturation on demand. Prices are determined by the marketplace, given the aggregate production of all firms. Since there is no discounting in this model, price and output are constant in the monopoly case, and piece-wise constant in the sequential entry case. (These results are consistent with those of the preceding sections.)

Spence [1981] confirms (through numerical simulations) that the incumbent will be more aggressive in the face of future competition and price lower in the pre-entry period as compared with the no-entry case. He also concludes from the simulations that the advantage to the incumbent is highest for a moderate cost-learning decline rate, the reason being that, for fast cost-decline rates, all competitors achieve the low cost quickly. Spence also explores the difference between open- and closed-loop equilibria in the context of a simplified two-period model. He suggests that the more realistic closed-loop equilibria result in even more aggressive pricing on the part of the incumbent and a lower number of firms in the industry. Finally, he explores the issues of spillover in learning-curve advantages. The results confirm the logic here as well; i.e., when spillovers occur, the incumbent will be less aggressive early on, and there will be more entry into the industry.

Spence's modeling framework is also used by Bass and Rao [1983] and Fudenberg and Tirole [1983b]. The latter compare closed- and open-loop equilibria in a two-period model. Both confirm the directional results obtained by Spence. Spence also comments on a particular form of demand learning and suggests that its effect is equivalent to cost learning.

Eliashberg and Jeuland [1986] introduce a monopolist facing a sure entry at some future time. The good is a durable type; however, there is no learning on either cost or demand. The monopolist computes the postentry open-loop equilibrium prices and uses these results to decide on pricing in the pre-entry period. Eliashberg and Jeuland find that: (1) the incumbent will indeed reduce his prices in the pre-entry period relative to the no-entry case (assuming the same planning horizon), (2) nevertheless, the monopolist still prices higher than follows from the immediate maximization of profits, and (3) prices decrease monotonically over time, with an abrupt fall after entry. In a later extension (see Dolan, Jeuland, and Muller, [1986 p. 130]), Eliashberg and Jeuland incorporate a more strategically oriented entrant who has a fixed cost of entering and who does so only if he foresees making profits. In this case, the incumbent will typically be more aggressive in order to deter entry, particularly if (1) time of potential entry is later, (2) fixed cost of entry is larger, and (3) product differentiation of a potential entrant is lower.

Strategic Entry

A firm that is considering entering a given market should take into account the strategic implications of entering; i.e., it should picture the postentry possible scenarios and figure if the expected value of profits is positive. This is clearly a difficult problem to model due to the complexity involved. In addition to obtaining information about the market and cost function of the current players, the potential entrant has to estimate the likely reaction of the incumbent. Assuming rational behavior by the incumbent is the typical rule; however, rationality here depends on the gaming framework. For example, if there are more potential entrants in the future, it may be rational for the incumbent to react with predatory pricing, and thus develop such a reputation in order to deter further entries.

While, to my knowledge, there is no work that deals directly with the issues of demand and cost learning in the context of strategic entry, there are several publications that deal with related issues. These issues are discussed in Jorgensen [1986] and in Dolan, Jeuland, and Muller [1986]. They will be summarized briefly here.

Recent work on entry focused on the notion of "barriers to entry," which was promoted by Bain [1956]. Bain's argument was that the monopolist, by choosing the appropriate price or output level, leaves too little room for an entrant and thus creates barriers to entry. The entrant takes prices and output as given when making entry decisions. Friedman [1979] points out that preentry output and prices are irrelevant for postentry prices—i.e., the monopolist's "signal" that his price will stay the same is not a credible threat, since this is not in his best interest. Several early models of entry, e.g., Kamien and Schwartz [1981], suffer from this naive assumption; they assume that entry is probabilistic, where the probability is a function of price of the monopolist.

In recent years, several papers have been published about the entry problem, taking a strategic view of it (usually based on game-theory approach). Kreps and Wilson [1982] and Milgrom and Roberts [1982a] introduce the idea of incomplete information. The entrant does not know what the incumbent's cost is and therefore has to infer it from his price. While fully aware that the incumbent is using price to signal his cost, the entrant cannot predict the incumbent's cost with certainty. Thus, limit pricing can be used to deter entry, even though both sides behave rationally.

In a different paper, Milgrom and Roberts [1982b] show how another entry-deterrence action, predatory response, can be rational. The idea is that the incumbent is willing to lose in the short run or the current market in order to develop a reputation that will deter entrants in the future or in other markets. (See also Kreps and Wilson 1982a.)

Another line of research, which is more closely related to our topic here, is the issue of commitments. Spence [1977b, 1979] and Fudenberg and Tirole

[1983b] show that irreversible capital commitments that reduce marginal cost can act as an entry deterrent. By making such a commitment first, the incumbent creates a situation where he can credibly threaten entrants with predatory pricing if an entry occurs due to his low marginal cost and the irrelevance of the capital investments once they are made.

This advantage of being first and creating a capital stock provides a relative advantage in marginal cost or demand, and it is clearly relevant to our case of cost and demand learning. While formal models of this type of entry deterrence still wait to be developed, it seems that threat of entry would act as an additional factor to aggressively price the products early on in order to achieve cost and market advantages and thus deter entry. Spillover in either type of asset could reduce this effect. Also, technological development can nullify cost and market advantages. This will, therefore, have the reverse effect.

IMPLICATIONS FOR PRICING IN PRACTICE

We have reviewed a vast body of literature that deals with various aspects of product pricing over time. In what follows, we try to summarize what generalities emerge in the context of specific pricing situations.

Pricing Pioneering Products

Dean [1950a] in a classic article discusses pricing of pioneering products in a qualitative way. In this chapter, we see that many of the issues that he raises are clarified with the new research. Moreover, additional insights are obtained by the refinement in the models. These points are summarized next. (See also Nagle [1987, chapter 6].)

Dean defines a pioneering product as one that incorporates a major innovation. Thus, a new product in an existing product category is not considered to be pioneering. The line of distinction is not black and white—there is a continuum. However, in both cases, the product must have some uniqueness for at least for a segment of the market in order to sell. (The uniqueness could be a cost advantage that translates into a lower price; however, this is of less interest here.) Therefore, the firm has some ability to set prices in these cases. Monopoly pricing is therefore the base pricing method that we consider in this case; i.e., the firm should price a pioneering product according to its value to the customers, not according to its cost.

If the firm can discriminate among customers, the cost is relevant only as a measure of the floor price. If the product has to be sold to all at a single price, then marginal cost and demand elasticity determine the price that maximizes the short-term profits as previously explained. The major difficulty is to estimate the demand function for the product, preferably on an individual or segment basis. Estimation of such demand functions can be done in various ways, including by an experiment (e.g., Nevin 1974), by market survey (e.g., conjoint analysis), by econometric methods (Baumol 1977), or by computing the product's value in use in the case of business customers.[7]

If the product is indeed a major innovation (as perceived by the market), then clearly there is a lot of uncertainty in the marketplace as to its value since its uses are not clear. This is particularly true if the product requires major changes in the way business is done (for business customers) or in the way the product is used (for consumers). For example, the first microcomputers (e.g., Apple) required customers to use computers quite differently than larger computers had been used previously. For such products, quantifying the demand function is clearly not easy, nor is it easy to predict the cost function. Moreover, in cases of major innovation, the firm has to educate the market as to the usefulness of the pioneering product. The value of this education may very well spill over to other future competitors. (For example, IBM/PC entered the market at a time when the market had already been educated about microcomputers.) On the other extreme, the investment in promoting a new product in an existing product category will typically be retained by the firm, since the product value is already known to customers, and the only issue is the performance of the new entrant. A second major distinction is that between durable and repeat-purchase products. I shall comment on each of these situations shortly.

Repeat-Purchase Goods

Consider first the case where there is no spillover in market learning and cost learning and there is no substantial adoption cost to the customer. This situation is typical where there is either patent protection for the new product or the product is second to market; it is also typical in most consumer and some industrial applications.[8]

In these circumstances, uncertainty about the product can be resolved relatively quickly by trying the product. Therefore, in many cases, a penetration pricing strategy is called for. Note, however, that this strategy can be implemented with nonprice instruments. In many cases where there is lack of information, price is taken as an indication of quality. (See Nagle [1987].) This leads to a market that is inelastic in the early stages of the product introduction. It is more efficient in these cases to induce trial by promotional devices; (e.g., free samples, coupons). However, even in these cases, it still makes sense to have a lower price at introduction, since early adopters have an effect on future potential adopters as well. And while price may not be effective in inducing trial, it is certainly important when deciding on adoption. Later in the product life cycle, as uncertainty and other information effects in the marketplace dissolve, price increases to the normal level or declines with cost over time if there are cost-experience effects.

Consider the other extreme where there is complete sharing of cost and market experience generated by the entrant. In this case, the monopoly-planning horizon of the pioneer is shortened and ends by the time competition enters. Thus, investment in market education and cost reduction will be reduced. While the same pattern of pricing is maintained, as we have just seen, the intensity is lower.

In summary, for repeat-purchase goods, penetration pricing should be used. This, in many cases, should be supplemented by other marketing activities, such as price promotions to induce trial and advertising to educate customers. The intensity of the penetration strategy is dependent on the following factors:

the innovativeness of the product (more uncertainty),

the rate of expected cost decline,

the degree of patent or other protection spillover,

the distance of the expected competitive entry, and

the strategy of the entrant's entry decision.

Durable/Capital Goods

This category of goods is more complex since (1) the customer is "locking" himself to the product for a substantial period of time, (2) there is typically a large sum of money involved, and (3) this type of good typically imposes a high switching cost on the customer over and above the purchase price.

Consider first the case where there is protection from competition, e.g., by patents. The base line here is that if the customers are myopic (i.e., they have no foresight), the firm can price discriminate over time by targeting the product to the most intense customers—those that are willing to pay the most—at the high price. Once this segment is saturated, price is reduced to attract the next segment, and so on. This is the classic skimming pricing strategy. If, however, customers do have foresight, then the ability of the firm to price discriminate over time is severely limited. Price reduction over time will have to be mild enough to make it worthwhile for the intended segment to buy right away and use the product, rather than wait and save on a lower purchase price.

In any given situation, the ability of the firm to skim over time depends on how myopic the customers are in their decisions as well as on the distribution of customer intensities and the interest rate. Business customers, for example, are more strategic when bying high-ticket items. Indeed, in this case, we see that leasing/renting is often used as the contractual arrangement, which protects the firm from future price reductions (Coase).

Even in this simple case with no competition, the firm may wish to deviate from the skimming pricing strategy since the problem of uncertainty on the customer side is more severe here due to the higher risks involved and the limited ability to try the product. The more pioneering the product is, the higher the uncertainty, and the larger the switching cost for the customers. Moreover, due to these difficulties, it is well known that word-of-mouth information has an important role in reducing uncertainty and influencing prospective buyers (see Nagle [1987].) In this case, the firm has to resort to penetration pricing. Since it is typically inefficient in such cases to induce trials by other methods, and since warranties do not solve the problem of switching costs to the customers, low pricing is an effective device in stimulating early adopters. Of course, this has to be combined with an advertising and communications campaign to educate users.

Consider the next other extreme case where there is no protection from competition. Unlike repeat-purchase goods, there is always some private value to investing in early penetration, since every customer "slot" that is taken is unavailable to the competition. This is particularly true for products where the supplies and other services associated with the durable good are supplied by the firm that makes the good. The value of every installed system is then high. Therefore, if competition is expected, the penetration-pricing argument is strengthened, since the firm wants to fill more slots before the competition enters. In the case of strategic competition, this may serve to deter entry altogether. On the other hand, here too, if the customers have foresight, they may choose to wait for the competition, and thus the effectiveness of the penetration strategy is reduced. Likewise, the entrant may announce his intention of entry in advance in order to influence the customers' purchase behavior.[9]

In summary, then, the basic pricing strategy for a durable type of good is skimming. This strategy is mitigated and can actually revert to penetration pricing with the following factors: (1) the more strategic and patient the customers are, (2) the more pioneering the product is, (3) the more unknown the company is, (4) the higher the rate of cost decline is, (5) the higher the value of future revenues of services from an installed system is, (6) the more serious the threat of entry is, particularly if it is strategic, and (7) the more patent protection or the less spillover there is in cost and market learning.

Pricing Mature Products

Mature products are characterized by the fact that typically market-information effects have been well diffused. Customers are well aware of the product and its performance. There is little demand learning left, except for new customers that are entering the market. Thus, there is little incentive to invest in demand learning.

While learning-cost improvement is typically more dramatic early on in the product life cycle, it may still be significant for mature product. Competition in this case is relatively stable with little threat of new entrants.

Since the three factors that affect pricing stabilize, price level stabilizes as well. The emphasis in pricing turns to price structure; i.e., the nature of quantity discount price schedule, discount and so on. I review here only the temporal aspect of price structure.

Seasonal Demand and Sales Promotions. Seasonal items represent an opportunity for intertemporal price discrimination. Demand elasticity typically shifts over time from high to low to high again. Where there is no seasonality, occasional sales promotions serve as a price-discrimination tool; i.e., in a way similar to durable-goods cyclical pricing, customers who are willing to pay little wait for a sale. Every so often, a sale is announced, and they are cleared. Then the price changes to the higher level for those who are willing to pay more. Using coupons can have a similar effect (Narasimhan 1985).

Durable-Goods Effects: In durable goods, a cyclical pricing pattern is often used as a price-discrimination device. Low-elasticity customers are paying the high price. Those who are not willing to pay the high price wait until a sale is announced, and the cycle begins again. (See Conlisk et al. 1984).

Fashion Goods. A similar pattern is observed in fashion products, where the goods are introduced at high prices, which are then reduced over time. This pattern is strengthened in cases where there is an overestimation of demand, resulting in too much inventory.

Pricing in Declining Markets

Declining markets are mature markets that experience decreases in demand either due to replacement by new technologies or by decreasing size of the target markets. The former case is more severe, since products' prices have to be reduced in order to compete with the new technology. Clearly, the firms that have higher marginal costs and lower market demand are the first to be forced out. However (since such situations give rise to too much production capacity), if many firms have economies of scale in production, this may lead to cut-throat price competition, where all competitors lose money, before exit occurs.

Once there is exit, however, prices typically rise, as the intensity of competition decreases, and cost increases due to lack of investments in production.

CONCLUSION

This chapter has reviewed intertemporal pricing of products over the life cycle. It has shown how learning in demand and cost, saturation effect, and competition affect pricing over time. The basic principle of equating marginal cost to marginal revenue is modified to take into account present actions on future profit.

Positive effects of present sales on the future, which are typical to a new-product situation, give rise to penetration pricing (pricing below the immediate profit-maximizing price). This is typically even more aggressively done if there is competition existing or forthcoming or if there is even a threat of such, and there is little spillover in cost and market learning across brands.

For durable goods, there is an opposite pressure of intertemporal price discrimination, leading to a skimming pricing strategy. However, even here strong market and cost learning, particularly if coupled with future competition, may lead to a penetration strategy.

Uncertainty is an inherent phenomena associated with new products. Little attention has been given to uncertainty in the literature surveyed. This seems to be a promising direction for future research. (See, e.g., Roberts and Urban [1988]; Eliashberg and Chatterjee [1986].)

Modeling the competitive framework is another area where there is a lot to be done. Most of the work surveyed assumes a common-knowledge determinist framework, where all players know everything about everyone (except, sometimes, the customers, who are considered myopic), and an open-loop equilibrium is sought. A more realistic description of reality, where there is uncertainty about the competitors' cost and demand and asymmetry of information, is called for. Closed-loop equilibria strategies, while more difficult to obtain, would provide a more realistic description of actual behavior. Inclusion of the customers in the game, particularly where large-ticket items are concerned, is also called for.

Notes

1. See also review articles by Rao [1984] on pricing in marketing, by Mahajan and Peterson [1985] on diffusion models, and by Moorthy [1985] on game theory in marketing.

2. Note that our model does not allow for inventorying here. Thus, production equals sales.

3. See Arrow and Kurz [1970] for example.

4. Note that this comparison is done locally. That is, given the same experience and exogenous variable levels, price is below the price that would maximize revenues.

5. This result generalizes similar results obtained by Robinson and Lakhani [1975], Dolan and Jeuland [1981], Bass and Bultez [1982], Jeuland and Dolan [1982], Feichtinger [1982], Jorgensen [1983], and Kalish [1983a] for more restricted models.

6. A closed-loop equilibrium is one where the price path is defined in terms of the positions of the other competitors, rather than in terms of time, as in open-loop equilibrium. Closed-loop is more realistic in that if for some reason there are deviations by some firms, then it is no longer optimal to hold to the original price path. See Dolan, Jeuland, and Muller [1986], Jorgensen [1987], and Kamien and Schwartz [1981] for discussions; see Fudenberg and Tirole [1983b] for an application in the learning-curve context. Note, however, that in repeated games, the issue of whether unique equilibrium exists is not at all trivial. Even in simple games such as the repeated prisoner's dilemma, there are infinitely many strategies that are at equilibrium, while their realization could be widely different under small deviations by some players.

7. Dean recommends using controlled experiments whenever possible. He also discusses various other techniques to estimate product value to the customers.

8. In many industrial applications, incorporating the new material in a product requires a major adjustment cost. Thus, the adoption of such a product resembles durable goods adoption and is therefore discussed there.

9. When IBM introduced the IBM/PC, it used a skimming strategy. There was little threat of a serious near-future entry, and uncertainty in the marketplace was relatively low, since Apple has already educated the market as to the value of microcomputers. Moreover, the IBM brand name served to reduce uncertainty about service and support. When Apple later introduced the Macintosh, it adopted a penetration strategy. The Macintosh was priced aggressively to selected early influential users (particularly university staff and students) as it was a major innovation and the threat of a competitive response from IBM and other manufacturers was real. This strategy succeeded well where the unique concept of the Macintosh was recognized to be superior by at least part of the market. While IBM has not entered with a direct response, it has announced its intention of introducing a new operating system that resembles the Macintosh. By so announcing, it tries to influence prospective buyers to wait before making a purchase decision.

7

Optimal Pricing and Advertising for New Products with Repeat Purchases

George E. Monahan
Kofi O. Nti

P rice and advertising (promotion) play a crucial role in channeling a new product to its eventual success or failure in the marketplace. Together they help overcome the resistance of inertia of people who have never tried the product and simultaneously stimulate repeat purchases by previous clients. It is reasonable to assume that because of uncertainties regarding attributes of the product, new customers may react differently to both price and advertising than do customers for whom these uncertainties have been resolved. The total market for the product therefore consists of two segments—those who have tried the product at least once and those who have never tried the product. Tension may develop concerning the primary target of price and advertising policies. Should price and advertising policies be targeted at new customers or at previous clients? In this chapter, we examine the direct impact of both price and advertising as well as the interaction effects of price, advertising, and maturity of the product on the demand for the product in each of the two market segments. The objective is to identify conditions that give rise to various forms of advertising and pricing policies.

The structure of pricing and advertising policies are discussed extensively in the marketing literature. New products are often said to be priced according to either "introductory" or "skimming" pricing policies. A pricing policy is introductory if the price level increases with the number of adopters; it is skimming if prices decrease with the number of adopters. Such policies are advocated when a market can be meaningfully segmented. A skimming policy attempts to tap the least price-sensitive of the new customers in the early stages of the product's life cycle, whereas an introductory policy tries to tap the most price-sensitive customers during this stage.

The authors gratefully acknowledge the helpful comments on earlier drafts of this chapter received from Gary Lilien and William Blozan.

It is not clear what conditions give rise to skimming or penetration pricing policies given a market segmented into repeat purchasers and new customers. The interaction of price with advertising further confounds the analysis. The form of optimal marketing-mix decisions as a function of the product's market penetration hinges delicately on the relative effectiveness of price and advertising on the demand functions in each of the segments, as well as on the dynamics of this effectiveness as the product penetrates the market. In this chapter, we study the interactions between price, advertising, and a measure of the product's market penetration on demand in two market segments. The ramifications of these interactions on the form of optimal pricing and advertising strategies are specified as functions of the product's market penetration.

An infinite-horizon, stochastic, dynamic model of optimal advertising and pricing is developed for new products in the early stages of the product's life cycle, where marketing-mix decisions jointly affect the potentially conflicting goals of acquiring new customers and servicing established customers. We assume that total single-period demand for a product can be disaggregated into two parts. The first component of single-period sales arises from new customers, who will each try a single unit of the product for the first time. This component, termed *new-customer demand*, is assumed to be random. The randomness of demand in this segment is intended to capture the effects of consumer uncertainty regarding attributes of the product that can only be determined after it has been purchased and used. This is in the spirit of economic models dealing with "experience goods" (see Nelson [1970, 1974]; Schmalensee [1982]), where product quality, for example, can only (perhaps partially) be determined after the product is purchased and consumed. See Kotowitz and Mathewson [1979] for a discussion of "persuasive" advertising directed toward experience goods.

The second component of single-period demand arises from repeat purchases by previous customers, who are assumed to have resolved all of their uncertainties regarding the quality or usefulness of the product. (Therefore, the model is not directly applicable to credence goods, defined by Darby and Karni [1973] as goods such as professional services and auto repairs where uncertainty regarding attributes of the product may remain even after consumption.) These customers are termed *triers;* the collection of all customers who have *ever* tried the product is called the *trier pool.*

The number of triers is a central element of the model developed in the next section. We use the size of the trier pool as a measure of the penetration of the product in the market. In addition to advertising and pricing decisions, the trier pool influences demand in each of the market segments but does so in different ways. New-customer demand is influenced by the number of triers, capturing word-of-mouth effects. Repeat-purchase demand is generated from the pool of triers; therefore, the size of the trier pool influences the level of repeat purchases.

Since new demand is random and represents additions to the trier pool, the size of the trier pool evolves randomly over time. At the beginning of any period, the firm observes the current number of triers. Based upon this information, advertising and pricing decisions are made. Since these decisions depend upon the number of triers, the random evolution of the trier pool makes the determination of optimal prices and advertising expenditures quite complex. Here we specify optimal advertising expenditures and prices (at the beginning of an infinite planning horizon) for every possible size of the trier pool. Therefore, at the beginning of any period within the planning horizon, the optimal actions of the firm are determined once the size of the trier pool is observed.

There are numerous mathematical models in the literature that deal with either optimal advertising or pricing, but few consider the joint problem. See, for example, the survey articles by Little [1979] and Sethi [1977] dealing with advertising models. For an excellent overview of recent pricing models, see chapter 12 of Lilien and Kotler [1983]. The relatively few papers that consider both optimal advertising and pricing include the Bass-type diffusion models of Kalish [1983b, c] and Thompson and Teng [1984] and Markov decision process (MDP) models of Albright and Winston [1979]. While the model developed here is an MDP, it incorporates several attributes typically found in diffusion models; we consider, for example, word-of-mouth effects, repeat purchases, and a market segmented on the basis of consumers' experience with the product. Unlike the typical diffusion model, however, we explicitly consider random new-customer demand. Rather than expressing optimal decisions as functions of time alone, here advertising and pricing policies specify optimal actions as a function a stochastically varying measure of the product's penetration of the market. An additional distinction between the model developed here and (usual) diffusion models centers on the manner in which the market is segmented. We do not explicitly consider individual customers moving through various stages of awareness and loyalty. Instead, we specify *aggregate* customer response to marketing-mix decisions in the form of demand functions specified for each of the two market segments. We do not, however, consider the effect of market saturation typically found in durable-good diffusion models.

We now give an overview of the remainder of the chapter. The optimization model is presented in the next section, following a discussion of both the new-customer and repeat-purchase market segments. In the first part of the subsequent section, there is a discussion of the variety of possible interactions between price, advertising, and the measure of market penetration. In the second part, the monotonicity of both pricing and advertising strategies are established. We show that the direction of monotonicity of the optimal pricing strategy is primarily driven by the interaction between price and market penetration in the repeat-purchase demand function. In particular, in theorem 1, we give conditions under which a skimming pricing policy can be optimal when new demand is perfectly price-inelastic. In theorem 2, we demonstrate that the price inelasticity in the new-demand market is not sufficient for the optimality of a skimming pricing policy. In fact, we give conditions that guarantee the optimality of an introductory pricing strategy for this case. In theorem 3, we establish the optimality of introductory pricing policies when new-product demand is elastic. In all cases, we show that optimal advertising decreases as the product penetrates the market. Concluding remarks appear in the final section.

The proofs of all of the results in this chapter are given in appendixes, which also contain supporting details that are somewhat technical in nature. For notational convenience, the partial derivative of a function is denoted by subscript(s); for example, the partial derivative of $f(x, y)$ with respect to x if f_x, and the cross-partial derivative is denoted f_{xy}. Also, for expositional convenience, the terms *increasing* and *decreasing* are used for *nondecreasing* and *nonincreasing*, respectively.

The Model

The modeling of demand in the two market segments just discussed is presented in the next two subsections: *New-Customer Demand* and *Repeat-Purchase Demand*. We will require that the demand functions share certain general properties. It must be emphasized, however, that there are distinct qualitative differences in the implications of these assumptions on the demand in each of the segments. These differences will be pointed out in the sequel. We assume that productive capacity is such that demand for the product is equivalent to sales in each period.

New-Customer Demand

Let $\mu(s, a, p)$ denote the total single-period new-customer market potential given that the number of triers, advertising, and price are s, a, and p, respectively. This specification of new market potential is a generalization of Bass [1980], Feichtinger [1982], Dolan and Jeuland [1981], Kalish [1983a], and others. Bass's market potential is $N - s$, where N is the total market size; Feichtinger, allowing N to be price-sensitive, uses $N(p) - s$; Dolan and Jeuland use the multiplicative for $(N - s)p$; Kalish considers the form $f(p, s)$. In these models, the level of market penetration s is usually measured by cumulative sales. Penetration, however, can be measured by other attributes of experience, such as time of introduction, reputation, or the size of the trier pool, as we do here.

What proportion of potential customers will actually purchase a new product? This fundamental problem can be addressed either by describing an inter-active process converting potentials into actuals or by estimating the conver-sion rate directly. Diffusion-type models use an epidemiological process to differentiate between innovative and imitative adopters. Here we do not specify any microdynamics of conversion; instead, we assume that a *random proportion* of potential new customers will actually purchase the product each period. Randomness in the conversion from potential customers to triers of the product is intended to model the impact of uncertainties associated with at-tributes of the product that can only be resolved by using the product.

We assume that each new customer purchases one unit of the product at the time of the initial purchase so that in each period, new-customer sales and the number of new customers are equivalent. In light of the initial consumer uncertainty regarding attributes of the product (as discussed earlier), this assumption seems quite reasonable. Examples of such experience goods in-clude magazine subscriptions, health club and health maintenance organiza-tion (HMO) memberships, banking services, and passion fruit.

Let D_t be the random variable denoting sales to new customers in period t. Then

$$D_t = Z_t \cdot \mu(s, a, p), t \in I_+ \equiv \{1, 2, \ldots\}, \tag{1}$$

where Z_t is the random proportion of conversions. We will assume that $\{Z_t, t = 1, 2, \ldots\}$ are independent, identically distributed nonnegative random variables, each with mean of 1. We denote the generic random variable by Z. The assumption that the mean of Z is 1 implies that *expected* new-customer de-mand in period t is simply the market potential in that period; i.e., $E[D_t] = \mu(s, a, p)$, where E denotes expectation. There is no added conceptual dif-ficulty if the mean of Z is not 1—the notation, however, becomes more clut-tered.

Note that our specification of new-customer demand precludes seasonal sales effects since the right side of (1) is independent of time t. The multipli-cative form of new-customer demand presumes that uncertainty in single-period sales does not depend on advertising or pricing decisions and is not influenced by the number of triers. Instead, the uncertainty arises from non-price and nonadvertising factors regarding inherent characteristics of the prod-uct. The multiplicative form of the new-customer demand is quite robust and has been used extensively in stochastic optimization models; see, for example, an early application in an inventory context by Karlin and Carr [1962] and a more recent application in an advertising context by Monahan [1983].

Note also that the specification of new-customer demand given in (1) is a stochastic generalization of new-customer demand for diffusion type models; formally, define $\mu(s, a, p) = (\alpha + \gamma s)f(s, p)$, where $\alpha + \gamma s$ describes the imi-tative and innovative processes driving adoption of the produce, and $f(s, p)$ is the new-customer market potential as specified, for example, by Kalish [1983a].

Different mathematical properties of $\mu(s, a, p)$ are required to describe various market phenomena. Issues such as word-of-mouth effects, saturation, price sensitivity, and the effectiveness of advertising can be modeled by postulating an appropriate shape for $\mu(s, a, p)$. In the diffusion-models literature, for example, new demand as a function of market penetration is assumed to increase initially and then decrease eventually. That particular specification is typically applicable to durable goods for which there is a fixed, finite total market size. The finiteness of the total market size is the characteristic that gives rise to the eventual dampening of market penetration on new-customer sales.

The focus of our model is on new products in the early stages of their life cycles, where the potential market for the product is always large relative to the number of triers. Here we assume an arbitrarily large potential market, which implies that the acquisition of new customers in any period does not significantly affect the generation of new customers in subsequent periods. Accordingly, we assume that μ is an increasing function of s, indicating the positive effects of word-of-mouth. (See Mahajan and Muller [1979] and Horsky and Simon [1983], which demonstrate the positive effect of word-of-mouth on new-product sales.) Our assumption that μ is increasing in s precludes saturation effects but avoids the problem of arbitrarily fixing the potential market size over an infinite planning horizon. Factors such as exogenous additions to the potential customer market make the prior determination of a fixed market size difficult to justify. (Bass [1980] and Bass and Bultez [1983] have developed diffusion models of pricing that also ignore saturation.)

Although we assume that the potential new-customer market each period is positively correlated with the size of the pool (positive word-of-mouth effects), we require, naturally, that the size of the new-customer market be bounded. In particular, we assume that the new-customer market potential is a bounded, concave function of s; i.e., that the rate of increase in new-customer market potential diminishes as the size of the trier pool becomes larger, i.e., μ is a concave function of s. (See figure 7–1.)

Advertising influences expected new sales in a natural way: increases in the level of advertising expenditure increase the market potential but at a diminishing rate. Explicitly, μ is an increasing, concave function of a. The market potential also has the usual downward-sloping property as a function of price. We assume, as does Feichtinger [1982], that μ is a concave function of p. This implies that there is a maximum price beyond which there is no market for the product.

In summary, new-customer sales each period are a random multiple of the market potential. The potential market μ depends on the size of the trier pool, the level of advertising, and the selling price p; μ is increasing in s and a, is

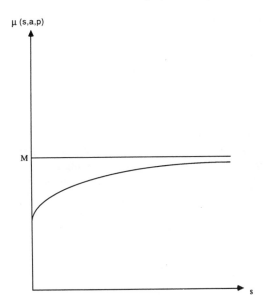

Figure 7–1. Potential New-Customer Market as a Function of the Size of the Trier Pool

decreasing in p, and is concave in each of these variables. To simplify the resulting optimization problem, we will actually use the slightly stronger condition that μ be jointly concave in s, a, and p.

Repeat-Purchase Demand

Repeat-purchase demand is specified by a deterministic demand function q that depends upon s, a, and p. Triers have experienced the product at least once and have resolved their uncertainty regarding the characteristics of the product. In each period, aggregate repeat demand is generated from the pool of triers. For a given level of price and advertising, a larger pool of triers tends to generate higher repeat-purchase demand; i.e., q is increasing in s. While there is a positive correlation between the aggregate level of repeat demand and the size of the trier pool, we do not require that each trier ever repurchase the product in subsequent periods.

The behavior of *individual* triers in the pool is influenced by price and advertising. For example, in some periods, certain individuals may not repurchase the product because the current selling price is relatively high. Other triers may never repurchase the product at any specified price due to dissatisfaction in the trial period. In aggregate, however, the level of repurchases in any period does not diminish as the size of the trier pool increases.

As in the new-demand case, we also assume that repeat-purchase aggregate demand is increasing in advertising, is decreasing in price, and is jointly concave in s, a, and p. This specification includes Jeuland and Dolan [1982], where repeat-purchase demand is $sp^{-\eta}$.

The Optimization Problem

For $t \epsilon I_+ \equiv \{1, 2, \ldots\}$ let S_{t-1} denote the size of the trier pool at the beginning of period t. Let S_1 denote the initial size of the trier pool (which may be zero). Then S_t depends upon S_{t-1} in the following manner: $S_t = S_{t-1} + Z \cdot \mu(S_{t-1}, a_{t-1}, p_{t-1})$, where a_{t-1} and p_{t-1} are the advertising expenditures and price in period $t - 1$, respectively. Let $c > 0$ denote the production cost per unit. We assume that this marginal manufacturing cost remains constant over the planning horizon; thus precluding, for example, learning effects as in Kalish [1983a]. Total discounted (random) profit over an infinite planning horizon can be written in terms of S_t as follows:

$$B = \sum_{t=1}^{\infty} \beta^{t-1} g(S_t, a_t, p_t),$$

where $0 \leq \beta < 1$ is the single-period discount factor and

$$g(s, a, p) = (p - c)[q(s, a, p) + Z \cdot \mu(s, a, p)] - a$$

is the single-period total revenue less advertising expenditures and production costs. The objective of the decision maker is to choose levels of advertising expenditures and prices in each period so as to maximize the expected value of B; that is, the problem is:

$$\underset{a_t \epsilon A,\, p_t \epsilon P}{\text{MAX}} \sum_{t=1}^{\infty} \beta^{t-1} E[g(S_t, a_t, p_t)], \qquad (2)$$

where $A \equiv [0, \bar{a}]$ and $P \equiv [\underline{p}, \bar{p}]$ and $\underline{p} \geq c$. The restriction that a_t and p_t belong to the sets A and P, respectively, bounds the decision set. The requirement that the lowest feasible price be at least the marginal cost of production is not very restrictive for the class of repeat-purchase products of interest here. For these products, production costs may be small relative to advertising and promotion costs. This restriction does *not* require that the firm sell the product at a price above the *total* marginal cost of the product (defined to be the sum of the manufacturing cost per unit and the advertising cost per unit). Therefore, selling the product at an initial loss early in the planning horizon with the goal of quickly acquiring a large number of triers and reaping added benefits later is permitted. For examples of other dynamic pricing models that impose a similar restriction on the choice of price, see Deshmukh and Winston [1977] and Eliashberg and Steinberg [1984].

Let

$$G(s, a, p) = (p - c)[q(s, a, p) + \mu(s, a, p)] - a \qquad (3)$$

denote expected one-period profit.

Let $V(s)$ denote the optimal expected infinite-horizon profit when the firm has s customers who have previously purchased their product. Using standard dynamic-programming arguments, it can be shown that $V(\cdot)$ satisfies the following functional equation:

$$V(s) = \underset{a \in A, \, p \in P}{\text{MAX}} J(s, a, p), \qquad (4)$$

where

$$J(s, a, p) = G(s, a, p) + \beta E\{V[s + Z \cdot \mu(s, a, p)]\}, \qquad (5)$$

for $S \in R_+ \equiv (0, \infty)$. The first term represents one-period expected profit given the firm currently has s triers and chooses a as the level of advertising and p as the current-period price. The last terms represent the optimal expected profits that can be earned from the next period onward, where $s + Z \cdot \mu(s, a, p)$ denotes the new level of triers.

The model specified by (4) and (5) is an infinite-horizon Markov decision process. The state of the process is s, the size of the trier pool. The evolution of the states is random since the size of the trier pool is augmented each period by D_t, the random sales to new customers. Note that *total* sales in each period is also random and depends upon the size of the trier pool as well as the decisions made in that period, namely the level of advertising (a) and the selling price (p). Since D_t, given in (1) also depends upon these decisions, the random evolution of the states is controlled. Since the distribution of D_t depends only upon s and the decisions in period t, the process is history-independent.

We have chosen to formulate the problem as an infinite-horizon model, not for analytical tractability, but for modeling reasonableness. All of the results developed in this chapter hold for *any finite planning horizon* if we assume a zero "salvage value" at the end of the horizon. Therefore, our results can be applied in cases where saturation effects in the potential new-customer market are of concern if end effects are ignored as they are in the finite-planning-horizon diffusion models of Kalish [1983a], Jeuland and Dolan [1982], and others. In particular, the results could be used when, under any reasonable advertising and pricing policy, the length of the planning horizon spans the growth stages of the product life cycle. Given the random evolution of the state of the decision process developed here, the choice of a finite planning horizon becomes somewhat arbitrary and requires the careful specification of what happens at the end of the horizon. These complications are avoided in the infinite horizon model. Instead of specifying a fixed time at which the decision process ends, the discount factor implicitly reduces the significance of rewards and costs incurred in distant periods.

The following example illustrates the structure of the model specified in (4) and (5). A health maintenance organization is beginning operation in a large city. Typically, these firms formulate promotion and pricing strategies on a month-to-month basis over some start-up period that may extend over three or more years. Each month, the potential number of new customers is specified by the function μ. Because the potential enrollees are not certain about the quality of health care available at the HMO, not all will enroll. The actual number of new enrollees in month t is the random variable $\mu(s, a, p) \cdot Z$. It is expected that, because of promotional activity, the potential number of new customers who may join the HMO each month (perhaps over the next few years) will not decline given reasonable pricing and advertising strategies. While planners acknowledge the fact that new enrollments will eventually decline, they are not certain when such a decline will take place. For planning purposes, a possible decline ten or twenty years from now will not have any bearing on the decisions made in the first few years.

Each month, new customers are enrolled in the HMO. Records are kept of everyone who has ever enrolled. Of all the people who have enrolled, some will use the HMO in subsequent time periods and some will not. If the number of enrollees is s, the number of people who will use the HMO for a second or greater time in any month is specified by the demand function $q(s, \ldots)$. In summary, total monthly demand for the services of the HMO is random and is affected by both price and the level of advertising. The planners' task is to develop a profit-maximizing pricing and advertising strategy that balances the potentially conflicting goals of acquiring new enrollees and stimulating current clients to continue their patronage.

Let $a(s)$ and $p(s)$ denote the (least) optimal levels of advertising and price, respectively, when there are s triers. One objective of this chapter is to determine how changes in s influence both $a(s)$ and $p(s)$. Another objective is to determine qualitative characteristics of the optimal expected profit function, $V(\cdot)$. To this end, it is convenient to define *finite-horizon* analogs of (4) and (5); then, the methodology for deriving characteristics for elements of the infinite-horizon model entails showing that these qualities hold for any finite-planning horizon and that the infinite-horizon model, as the limiting case, inherits these properties.

Let $V^n(s)$ denote the optimal expected discounted profits when the firm has s triers and there are n periods *remaining* in the planning horizon. Again, using standard dynamic programming arguments, it can be shown that the functions $\{V^1(\cdot), V^2(\cdot), ...\}$ satisfy the recursions:

$$V^n(s) = \underset{a \, \epsilon \, A, \, p \, \epsilon \, P}{\text{MAX}} J^n(s, a, p), \tag{6}$$

where

$$J^n(s, a, p) = (p - c)[q(s, a, p) + \mu(s, a, p)] - a \tag{7}$$
$$+ \beta E\{V^{n-1}(s + Z \cdot \mu(s, a, p))\},$$

for $s \, \epsilon \, R_+$, $n \, \epsilon \, I_+$; let $V^0(s) \equiv 0$.

Let $a_n(s)$ and $p_n(s)$ denote the least values of $a \, \epsilon \, A$ and $p \, \epsilon \, P$, respectively, that jointly maximize $J^n(s, a, p)$.

The first result establishes that the infinite-horizon optimal-expected-profit function is increasing and concave in the number of triers and reflects the intuitively appealing notion that additional triers are beneficial but that the benefit diminishes as the pool of triers increases in size.

Proposition 1. For $s \, \epsilon \, R_+$,

(1) $p(s)$ and $a(s)$ exist,

(2) $V(\cdot)$ is increasing on R_+, and

(3) $V(\cdot)$ is concave on R_+.

These properties are fundamental in the development of qualitative characteristics of the optimal decisions given in the next section.

Optimal Pricing and Advertising Strategies

In this section, we characterize optimal advertising and pricing strategies as a function of the number of triers. Two cases are considered. We identify conditions that ensure that an "introductory" pricing policy is optimal; that is, the optimal pricing strategy is monotonically increasing as a function of the number of triers. We also establish conditions that ensure that a skimming pricing policy is optimal; i.e., as the number of triers increases, it is optimal to diminish price. In either of these two cases, we show that optimal advertising expenditures are monotonically decreasing in the number of triers. It is optimal to diminish advertising expenditures as new customers are acquired.

Since our goal is to examine the dependence of optimal prices and advertising levels on the size of the trier pool, it is necessary to comment on the nature of the interaction between s, a, and p in the underlying demand functions. In general, the impact of the number of triers on the effectiveness of both advertising expenditures and price in each segment of the market will differ. We explore these interactions next.

Interaction Effects

In our model, the size of the trier pool is always small relative to the total market. This suggests that in the new-demand segment, the *marginal* effectiveness of a dollar increase in both price and advertising does not change when the size of the trier pool changes. Formally, $\mu_{as} = 0$ and $\mu_{ps} = 0$. Note that these conditions only relate to the *interaction* between s, on the one hand, and a and p on the other: (1) interactions between a and p are not necessarily negligible and (2) new-customer market potential is still sensitive to each of the variables s, a, and p as described earlier.

In contrast, the size of the trier pool is a significant factor influencing the effectiveness of price and advertising in the repeat-purchase market segment. In particular, as the size of the trier pool increases, the marginal repeat sales generated by a dollar of advertising declines. Although an increase in the level of advertising expenditures increases repeat-purchase sales, the rate of the increase diminishes as the size of the trier pool increases. Formally, $q_{as} \leq 0$. In other words, word-of-mouth effects substitute for advertising in the repeat-purchase market. As the number of people who have tried the product increases, personal recommendations carry more weight than advertising. The case where q_{as} is positive corresponds to the situation where consumers base their repeat-purchase decisions more on advertising exposure than on their own experience with the product. This is difficult to justify for consumers in the aggregate. This case also corresponds to the situation where a dollar of advertising spread over a larger pool generates proportionately more repeat sales; this is also difficult to justify. Hence, the demand function describing aggregate consumer response cannot have q_{as} positive.

The impact of price changes on repeat-purchase sales depends upon the nature of the product, the size of the trier pool, and the type of advertising consumers are exposed to. Simon [1979] provided empirical evidence on the variation of price elasticity over the product life cycle. Simon's analysis gives support to the conclusion that the magnitude of price elasticity decreases in the introductory and growth stages and then declines further during the decline stage of the life cycle. Simon also discusses earlier views and evidence supporting the alternative situation where price elasticity increases in the early stages and then declines as the product matures. The latter evidence might occur, for example, if early adopters are less price-sensitive than later adopters. The discussion in Simon is applicable here since the size of the trier pool is our measure of the maturity of the product. Therefore, the price elasticity of repeat-purchase demand may increase or decrease as the size of the trier pool increases.

The behavior of price elasticity as the number of triers increases will also depend on the type of advertising made for the product. Farris and Albion [1980] note that advertising can either help to differentiate a product or inform consumers about product characteristics. The former type of advertising can establish brand loyalty or entry barriers. In this case, repeat-purchase customers may become less sensitive to price changes as the product becomes more established. In other words, the price elasticity of repeat-purchase demand decreases as the number of triers increases; i.e., $q_{ps} \geq 0$.

In figure 7–2, repeat-purchase demand functions are graphed as a function of price for two levels of the size of the trier pool, s_1, and s_2, where $s_1 < s_2$, under the assumption that price elasticity decreases as the number of triers increases.

An increase in price elasticity might be expected if advertising informs consumers about product attributes and value. Consumers develop expectations about the value of the product and therefore react unfavorably to price increases. This view is similar to Jeuland and Dolan's [1982] suggestion that the price at which consumers initially purchase a product may serve as a reference point against which future prices are compared. Therefore, future price increases may be detrimental to repeat-purchase sales. Another factor that may

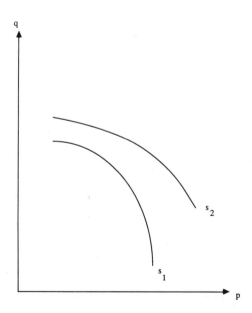

Figure 7–2. Decreasing Price Sensitivity

contribute to an increase in price elasticity is the impact of competition. A new product may have few substitutes initially, but substitutes may become available as the product develops (as the number of triers increases). If these substitution effects are strong, then repeat-purchase demand will become more price-elastic as the number of triers increases. Under any of the conditions discussed in this paragraph, $q_{ps} \leq 0$. Typical repeat-purchase demand functions depicting the increase in price sensitivity are given in figure 7–3 for two sizes of the trier pool, s_1 and s_2, where $s_1 < s_2$.

In the remainder of this section, we examine the ramifications of the interactions discussed here on optimal pricing and advertising strategies.

Price-Inelastic New-Customer Demand

In this subsection, we study the form of optimal advertising and pricing strategies when new-trier demand is price-inelastic. A *skimming* pricing strategy is often suggested when new demand is relatively insensitive to price; that is, prices should be decreased as the product penetrates the market. Initially, relatively high prices are set for a new product for which there may be substitutes. As the product penetrates the market, prices are adjusted downward, perhaps as a deterrent to potential entrants. Consider the extreme case where new-trier demand is perfectly price-inelastic; i.e., μ is independent of p. Since the size of the new-demand market segment is always large rela-

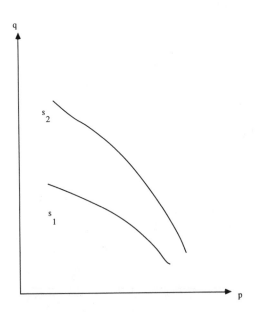

Figure 7–3. Increasing Price Sensitivity

tive to the trier pool, it would appear that if new demand is insensitive to price, a skimming pricing policy would be optimal. This is not necessarily so. The form of the pricing policy depends in a crucial way on the price sensitivity of repeat-purchase demand as the product penetrates the market.

The first theorem establishes the intuitive result that if repeat-purchase demand becomes more price-elastic as the product penetrates the market, a skimming pricing policy can, in fact, be optimal. In contrast, we show in theorem 2 that an *introductory* pricing policy can be optimal even when demand in the (arbitrarily large) new-trier segment is perfectly price-inelastic; that is, it may be optimal for the firm to raise prices as the product penetrates the market. The managerial implications of these results point to the importance of the role of repeat-purchase demand in formulating pricing policies.

The first result, which establishes the optimality of a skimming pricing policy, requires an additional hypothesis regarding the net impact of a price increase on total single-period demand. In particular, we assume that

$$- (p - c) \, q_{ps}(s, a, p) \geq q_s(s, a, p) + \mu_s(s, a) \tag{8}$$

for $s \in R_+$, $a \in A$, and $p \in P$. This condition is best interpreted using figure 7–4. The level of advertising remains fixed at a. When the size of the trier pool is s, a unit increase in price reduces repeat sales by an amount denoted by L_1 in figure 7–4. With price fixed at p, an increase in the size of the pool from s to $s + 1$ results in additional repeat- and new-customer sales denoted by G in the figure. Finally, the loss due to a price increase when the size of the pool is $s + 1$ is denoted by L_2. The condition given in (8) requires that L_2 exceed G. The net impact of increases in both price and the size of the trier pool is negative; i.e., the detrimental effects of a price increase outweigh the positive effects associated with the acquisition of a new customer.

It may appear that the net detrimental effect associated with price increases given in (8) necessarily implies the optimality of a skimming pricing policy. Note, however, that (8) does not incorporate the direct positive effects associated with an increase in advertising. In general, the interaction of price, advertising, and the number of triers in two market segments makes the determination of the form of optimal advertising and pricing policies quite difficult. The set of assumptions given in the next result, however, are sufficient for the optimality of diminishing both price and advertising as new customers are acquired.

Theorem 1. If q is linearly separable in a and p, μ is independent of p, $q_{ps} \leq 0$, and (8) holds, then $a(s)$ and $p(s)$ are decreasing functions of s.

The conditions given in theorem 1 are worth reiterating. While new demand is perfectly price-inelastic, the price elasticity of repeat-purchase

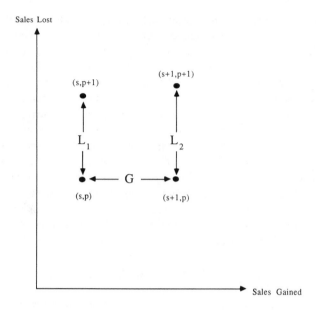

Figure 7-4. Effects of Increases in *s* and *p*

demand increases with the number of triers. As noted earlier, the form of advertising might be responsible for the increasing price-elasticity of repeat-purchase demand. Intuitively, what theorem 1 requires is that the price elasticity of repeat-purchase demand dominates the price insensitivity of new customers. This relationship between price elasticities in the two market segments—coupled with hypothesis (8), which ensures that positive word-of-mouth effects do not compensate for price increases—makes a skimming pricing policy optimal. The conditions outlined in theorem 1 provide insightful guidelines for the development of marketing strategy: if repeat purchases are expected to be an important part of sales for a new product, then a skimming pricing strategy can be justified only if the repeat-purchase market-price sensitivity is the dominant factor.

The following example shows that the hypotheses of theorem 1 hold for a rich class of demand functions. The demand functions specified next are log linear in *p* and *s* and are empirically robust in econometric estimation.

Example 1. Let $q(s, a, p) = K_1(\bar{p} + 1 - p)^\delta (s + 1)^\gamma + K_2 a^\alpha$, where $\alpha, \delta, \gamma \geq 0$ and $0 \leq \gamma + \delta \leq 1$, and $\alpha \leq 1$. Let $\mu(s, a) = w_1(s) + w_2(a)$, where $w_i(\cdot)$ are increasing concave functions, $i = 1, 2$. Note that q is multiplicatively separable in *p* and *s*, it has constant price and advertising elasticity, and $q_{ps} < 0$. It can be shown that condition (8), applied to this example, implies that the pricing strategy be of the form of a modified markup, where the optimal price must exceed the marginal cost c by at least a fixed amount.

As we pointed out in the beginning of this subsection, q_{ps} plays a central role in determining optimal pricing policies. Theorem 2 will show that if $q_{ps} \geq 0$, then an *introductory* pricing policy may be optimal even if new-product demand in an arbitrarily large potential market is perfectly price-inelastic. This result requires an assumption, similar in spirit to (8), regarding the interaction between price and advertising. Specifically, we require that

$$- (p - c) q_{ap}(s, a, p) \geq \mu_a(s, a) + q_a(s, a, p), \qquad (9)$$

for $s \in R_+$, $p \in P$, and $a \in A$. As in the development of (8), the condition given by (9) is depicted in figure 7–5.

L_1 and L_2 represent sales lost due to a price increase when the levels of advertising are a and $a + 1$, respectively. G represents the increase in sales resulting from increasing advertising from a and $a + 1$. Condition (9) is equivalent to requiring that L_2 exceed G. Here, the detrimental effects of a price increase outweigh the positive effects associated with an increase in advertising. It can be shown that (9) also implies that the price elasticity of

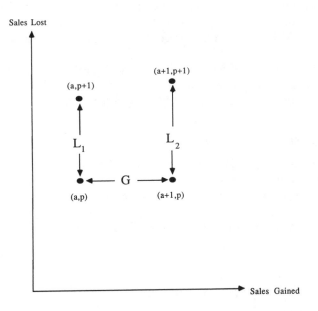

Figure 7–5. Effects of Increases in a and p

repeat-purchase demand must be greater than 1; therefore demand in this segment is price-elastic.

Theorem 2. If $q_{ps} \geq 0$, μ is independent of p, and (9) holds, then $a(s)$ is decreasing in s and $p(s)$ is increasing in s.

In theorem 2, the new-demand market is perfectly price-inelastic while the price elasticity of repeat purchasers decreases in the number of triers. The decreasing price elasticity of repeat purchasers is the dominant factor only if the positive effects of advertising cannot compensate for the detrimental effects of price increases, as noted by condition (9). It is interesting to note that the form of advertising implicit in condition (9) is precisely the type that helps to differentiate the product or to raise entry barriers. The conditions outlined in theorem 2 also provide useful guidelines in the development of marketing strategy: if repeat purchases are expected to be a significant portion of sales for a new product, then an introductory pricing strategy should be pursued only if the accompanying advertising helps to differentiate the product.

As in example 1, the hypotheses of theorem 2 also hold for an empirically rich class of demand functions.

Example 2. Let $q(s, a, p)$ be as it is in example 1, with a and s interchanged; i.e., $q(s, a, p) = K_1(\bar{p} + 1 - p)^\delta(a + 1)^\gamma + K_2 s^\alpha$, where the parameters α, δ, and γ satisfy the conditions in example 1. The μ function is the same as it is in example 1. Again, it can be shown that condition (9) implies that price exceed unit cost by some fixed margin.

The assumption that new-customer demand is perfectly price-inelastic is relaxed in the next subsection. Additional hypotheses are presented that also yield the optimality of an introductory pricing policy.

Price-Elastic New-Customer Demand

In this subsection, we relax the restriction that μ be the independent of p. We do, however, require that expected new-customer demand be independent of advertising; that is, in this subsection $\mu(s, a, p) = \mu(s, p)$. This assumption implies that potential customers are aware of the product's existence. Advertising is directed toward the repeat-purchase market. Kotowitz and Mathewson [1979] refer to this as "persuasive" advertising.

Theorem 3. If $q_{ps} \geq 0$, μ is independent of a, and (9) holds, then $a(s)$ is decreasing in s and $p(s)$ is increasing in s.

But note that for the pure price version of the model where q is also independent of a, condition (9) holds trivially. Therefore, an introductory pricing policy is optimal for a pure pricing model when $q_{ps} \geq 0$ and the demand functions have the standard monotonicity and concavity properties.

Theorem 3, which is similar to theorem 2, also advocates an introductory pricing strategy when the decreasing price elasticity of repeat customers is the dominant factor. In contrast to theorem 2, theorem 3 identifies a situation where an introductory pricing strategy is optimal even when new customers are extremely sensitive to price increases. Instead, they rely on word-of-mouth effects or personal recommendations of experienced buyers. The marketing strategy in theorem 3 is to use advertising to differentiate the product and let word-of-mouth effects stimulate new demand. This strategy initially sets low prices to increase the size of the trier population and then increases prices as the price sensitivity of repeat purchasers decreases.

The following example demonstrates a class of functions that satisfy the hypotheses of theorem 3.

Example 3. Let $q(s, a, p)$ be as it is in example 2. Let $\mu(s, p) = w_1(s) + w_3(p)$, where w_3 is a decreasing, concave function of p.

Theorem 3 can be related to several models of new-product pricing in the literature, especially the diffusion models of Mahajan and Peterson [1978], Feichtinger [1982], Kalish [1983a], and Jeuland and Dolan [1982]. These papers use the methods of optimal control theory to establish structured pricing policies over time. With the exception of Feichtinger, papers in this genre rarely discuss or verify sufficiency conditions. These sufficiency conditions, however, are needed to ensure that solutions that satisfy the first order necessary conditions of Pontryagin are in fact optimal. It appears that at least joint concavity of the Hamiltonian in the state and control variables is required. (See, for example, Seierstad and Sydsaeter [1977]). It is our conjecture that a careful analysis of the sufficiency issue would require that explicit conditions be placed on the basic elements of the market models described in those papers. In particular, certain specifications of demand functions may not be suitable for the optimal control methodology. We use Feichtinger's model to explore these issues.

Feichtinger develops a Bass-type diffusion model of new-product pricing with no repeat purchases. In our notation, he specifies new-customer sales as $\mu(s, p) = (\alpha + \gamma s)[g(p) - s]$, where α and γ are parameters, $g(p)$ is a concave function denoting market potential when the selling price is p, and s is the number of triers. He shows that the optimal price increases over time. For this model, Feichtinger can only establish sufficiency when $\alpha = 0$ and when the restriction $s < g(p)$ is ignored. Feichtinger's analysis shows that this specific functional form may not be technically satisfactory for a diffusion model with innovators. We can, however, apply our theorem 3 to Feichtinger's model when $\alpha \neq 0$, provided some minor conditions are satisfied. As we noted following theorem 3, an introductory pricing policy is optimal in a model with no advertising if μ is jointly concave in s and p and is increasing in s. In Feichtinger's model, this is true for $\gamma^2 g_p^2 + 2\gamma(\alpha + \gamma s)g_{pp} \geq 0$. Additionally, μ is increasing in s when $2\gamma s < \alpha - g$; i.e., where the market potential is much greater than the number of triers. In particular, Feichtinger's specification used in our context has an optimal introductory pricing policy when new demand is linear and downward-sloping in price.

Conclusion

A stochastic, dynamic model of optimal advertising and pricing was developed for new products where repeat purchases are a significant portion of demand. Optimal advertising policies were shown to be decreasing in the number of triers. An important feature of the model is the specification of two sources of demand for the firm's product—those who have tried the product previously and those who haven't. Demand in each of these segments depends upon price, advertising, and the size of the trier pool. The impact of interactions between these factors within each market segment as well as between market segments on pricing and advertising strategies is developed. We showed in theorem 1 and 2 that either a skimming or an introductory pricing policy could be optimal when the potential market for the product is perfectly price-inelastic. A crucial factor in determining which form of the pricing strategy prevails is the sensitivity of price elasticity in the repeat-purchase market to the number of triers. Theorem 3 established the optimality of introductory pricing when new-customer demand is not perfectly price-inelastic.

Several strategic implications of the theorems were discussed. When new-customer demand is not price-sensitive, introductory pricing is appropriate if advertising in the repeat-purchase market helps differentiate the product, whereas a skimming pricing policy is optimal if the repeat-purchase market is price-sensitive. If new-customer demand is also very sensitive to price, introductory pricing is still optimal if the repeat-purchase demand becomes less price-sensitive as the product matures.

Another contribution of this chapter is that we identify explicit conditions on basic elements of a market model that are sufficient for the optimality of well-structured marketing-mix policies. Some of the analyses and insights developed here may serve as a first step in a more general investigation of pricing and advertising that explicitly considers the possibility of entrants and competition.

Appendix 7A-1
Proofs of the Results

The preponderance of the results in this chapter are the parametric analyses of solutions to maximization problems. The proofs of results such as theorems 1, 2, and 3 could be obtained by using standard techniques in differential calculus if we could show, for example, that the optimal strategies are differentiable with respect to s. While this might be done, drawing on results in Blume, Easley, and O'Hara [1982], for instance, it will be much more convenient to use the powerful theory of lattice programming. For an exposition of this theory, see Topkis [1978] of Heyman and Sobel [1984, chapter VIII]. The principal definitions and results used here are also discussed in Albright and Winston [1979].

If $f:R_+^3 \to R$ is twice-differentiable, then $f(\cdot, \cdot, \cdot)$ is *supermodular* on R_+^3 if and only if $f_{xy}(x, y, z) \geq 0$, and $f_{xz}(x, y, z) \geq 0$, and $f_{yz}(x, y, z) \geq$ for all $(x, y, z) \in R_+^3$; see, e.g., Ross [1983, proposition 4.2]. Let $y(x)$ and $z(x)$ denote the least values of y and z, respectively, that jointly maximize $f(x, \cdot, \cdot)$ for a given $x \in R_+$, on a compact subset of R_+^2. If f is supermodular on R_+^3, then $y(x)$ and $z(x)$ exist and are each nondecreasing in x; see, e.g., Heyman and Sobel [1984, chapter VIII, corollary 4.1]. Furthermore, if $g(x, y, z) = f(x, -y, z)$ and $g(\cdot, \cdot, \cdot)$ is supermodular on R_+^3, then $y(x)$ is nonincreasing on R_+ and $z(x)$ is nondecreasing on R_+.

Appropriately signing expressions (I), (II), and (III) in appendix 7A-3 establishes the supermodularity of $J^n(\cdot, \cdot, \cdot)$. The monotonicity of both $p(s)$ and $a(s)$ in s stated in theorems 1, 2, and 3 then follows from the discussion given here.

We sketch the procedures for establishing the fact that the infinite-horizon problem inherits the properties established for finite-horizon problems. The proof that $V(s)$ is the (point-wise) limit of $V^n(s)$ for $s \in R_+, n \in I_+$ is standard and is omitted. A result in Sobel [1971, lemma 3] as applied in Monahan [1983, lemma 1] can be used to verify that any sequence of $\{a_n(s), p_n(s))\}_{n=1}^{\infty}$ that converges, converges to $a(s)$ and $p(s)$. The infinite-horizon optimal strategies therefore possess the qualitative characteristics established for the finite-horizon problem.

Appendix 7A-2
Proof of Proposition 1

T
o prove that the three components of proposition 1 hold, we will prove that analogous results hold for finite-horizon problems, where the horizon is any length. Standard results, discussed in the appendix 7A-1, demonstrate that the finite-horizon value functions $V^n(\cdot)$ converge to the infinite-horizon value function $V(\cdot)$ and that any sequence of optimal prices and optimal level of advertising expenditures that converge as the planning horizon increases, converge to the optimal infinite-horizon price and advertising levels. This implies that the infinite-horizon value function and optimal decision variables inherit the properties established for their finite-horizon counterpart.

Therefore, to prove that parts (1)–(3) in proposition 1 hold, it suffices to prove by induction on n, the number of periods remaining in the planning horizon, that for any $n \in I_+$,

(0)'. $J^n(s, a, p)$ is concave on R^3_+,

(1)'. $a_n(s)$ and $p_n(s)$ exist,

(2)'. $V^n(\cdot)$ is continuous and increasing on R_+, and

(3)'. $V^n(\cdot)$ is concave on R_+,

where $V^n(\cdot)$ and $J^n(\cdot, \cdot, \cdot)$ are defined in (6) and (7), respectively.

Since $V^0(s) = J^0(s, a, p) = 0$ for any $(s, a, p) \in R^3_+$, conditions (0)' through (3)' hold trivially for $n = 0$. Assume that (0)' through (3)' hold for some $n = k - 1 \geq 1$. The proof will be complete when we show they also hold at $n = k$.

Since $J^k(s, \cdot, \cdot)$ is continuous on the compact set $C \equiv A \times P$, $a_k(s)$ and $p_k(s)$ exist, so condition (1)' holds at $n = k$. By the induction hypothesis, $V^{k-1}(s)$ is increasing in s. Since μ is increasing in s, $E\{V^{k-1}[s + Z \cdot \mu(s, a, p)]\}$ is also increasing in s. Similarly, it follows that $J^k(s, a, p)$ is increasing in s for any $(a, p) \in C$. Assume that $s_1 < s_2$ for $(s_1, s_2) \in R^2_+$. Then

$$V^k(s_2) = J^k[s_2, a_k(s_2) \cdot p_k(s_2)] \geq J^k[s_2, a_k(s_1), p_k(s_1)]$$

$$\geq J^k[s_1, a_k(s_1), p_k(s_1)] = V^k(s_1).$$

The first inequality follows from the definition of $a_k(s)$ and $p_k(s)$, while the second follows since $J^k(\cdot, a, p)$ is increasing. Therefore condition (2)' holds for $n = k$. The crucial step in proving the concavity of $J^k(s, a, p)$ on R^3_+ is showing that $E\{V^{k-1}[s + Z \cdot \mu(s, a, p)]\}$ is concave on R^3_+. We will establish this result and sketch the remaining details.

Choose any $z \in R^3_+$. For any $(s_1, a_1, p_1) \in R^3_+$, and $(s_2, a_2, p_2) \in R^3_+$, and $\lambda \in (0, 1)$, let $(\tilde{s}, \tilde{a}, \tilde{p}) = \lambda \cdot (s_1, a_1, p_1) + (1 + \lambda) \cdot (s_2, a_2, p_2)$. Since, by assumption, $\mu(\cdot, \cdot, \cdot)$ is concave on R^3_+ and $V^{k-1}(\cdot)$ is increasing by the induction hypothesis, it follows that

$$V^{k-1}[\tilde{s} + z \cdot \mu(\tilde{s}, \tilde{a}, \tilde{p})] \geq V^{k-1}\{\lambda \cdot [s_1 + z \cdot \mu(s_1, a_1, p_1)]$$

$$+ (1 - \lambda) \cdot [s_2 + z \cdot \mu(s_2, a_2, p_2)]\}$$

$$\geq \lambda \cdot V^{k-1}[s_1 + z \cdot \mu(s_1, a_1, p_1)] +$$

$$(1 - \lambda) \cdot V^{k-1}[s_2 + z \cdot \mu(s_2, a_2, p_2)].$$

Since this is true for all $z \geq 0$, it follows that $E\{V^{k-1}[s + Z \cdot \mu(s, a, p)]\}$ is concave on R^3_+, and (0)' holds for $n - k$. Since C is a convex set and $J^k(\cdot, \cdot, \cdot)$ is concave on R^3_+, it follows that

$$\lambda V^k(s_1) + (1 - \lambda)V^k(s_2) = \lambda J^k[s_1, a_k(s_1), P_k(s_1)] +$$

$$(1 - \lambda)J^k[s_2, a_k(s_2), p_k(s_2)] \leq J^k(\lambda s_1 +$$

$$(1 - \lambda)s_2, \lambda a_k(s_1) + (1 - \lambda)a_k(s_2),$$

$$\lambda p_k(s_1) + (1 - \lambda)p_k(s_2)] \leq V^k[\lambda s_1 +$$

$$(1 - \lambda)s_2].$$

Thus $V^k(s)$ is concave, proving condition (3)' for $n = k$.

Appendix 7A-3
Proofs of Theorems 1, 2, and 3

$\mathbf{I}$ n light of the remarks prefacing the proof of proposition 1 and the discussion in appendix 7A-1, the monotonicity of the optimal policy can be established by appropriately signing the cross-partial derivatives of $J^n(s, a, p)$, here labeled I, II, and III:

  I. $J_{ps}^n(s,\, a,\, p)$

 II. $J_{as}^n(s,\, a,\, p)$

III. $J_{ap}^n(s,\, a,\, p)$

Proof of Theorem 1

By assumption, μ is independent of p so that $J_{ps}^n(s,\, a,\, p) = G_{ps}(s,\, a,\, p) = (p - c)q_{ps}(s,\, a,\, p) + q_s(s,\, a,\, p) + \mu_s(s,\, a) \geq 0$, where the inequality follows from (8). Since μ is independent of p, and q is linearly separable in a and p, $J_{ap}^n(s,\, a,\, p) = \mu_a(s,\, a) + q_a(s,\, a,\, p) \geq 0$, where the inequality follows from the assumption that demand in each market segment increases with increases in advertising. Finally,

$$J_{as}^n(s,\, a,\, p) = (p -)q_{as}(s,\, a,\, p) \tag{A1}$$
$$+ \beta E\{V_{ss}^{n-1}[s + Z \cdot \mu(s,\, a)] \cdot Z \cdot \mu(s,\, a)$$
$$\cdot [1 + Z \cdot \mu_s(s,\, a)]\}$$

is negative, since the first term on right side of the equality is negative by the assumption in "Interaction Effects" that $q_{as} \leq 0$ and the second term in the sum is negative. (This follows from the concavity of V^n, the positivity of Z, and the fact that μ is increasing in s.) Since $J_{ps}^n \geq 0$, $J_{as}^n \leq 0$ and $J_{ap}^n \geq 0$, $J^n(s, -a, -p)$ is supermodular on $R_+ \times C$, from which it follows, based upon the discussion in appendix 7A-1, that $a(s)$ and $p(s)$ are each decreasing in s.

Proof of Theorem 2

By assumption, $q_{ps} \geq 0$, $q_s \geq 0$, and $\mu_s \geq 0$. Therefore, $J_{ps}^n(s, a, p) = (p - c)q_{ps}(s, a, p) + q_s(s, a, p) + \mu_s(s, a) \geq 0$. Next, $J_{ap}^n(s, a, p) = (p - c)q_{ap}(s, a, p) + \mu_a(s, a) + q_a(s, a, p) \leq 0$ by (9). Finally, $J_{as}^n(s, a, p)$, which satisfies equation (A1), is negative, using the arguments given in the proof of theorem 1. Then $J_{ps}^n \geq 0$, $J_{as}^n \leq 0$, and $J_{ap}^n \leq 0$ imply that $J^n(s, -a, p)$ is supermodular on $R_+ \times C$, from which it follows that a(s) is decreasing in s and p(s) is increasing in s.

Proof of Theorem 3

By assumption, μ is independent of a so that $J_{ps}^n(s, a, p) = (p - c)q_{ps}(s, a, p) + \mu_s(s, p) + q_s(s, a, p) + \beta E\{V_{ss}^{n-1}[s + Z \cdot \mu(s, p)] \cdot [1 + Z \cdot \mu_s(s, p)] \cdot Z \cdot \mu_p(s, p)\} \geq 0$, since each term in the sum is positive. The first term is positive by the hypothesis that $q_{ps} \geq 0$, the next terms (q_s and μ_s) are positive by the discussion in "New-Customer Demand" and "Repeat-Purchase Demand," and the last term is positive by the concavity of V^{n-1}, the positivity of Z, and the fact that μ is increasing in s and is decreasing in p. As in the proof of theorem 1, $J_{ap}^n(s, a, p) \leq 0$ follows from (9). Finally, $J_{as}^n(s, a, p) = (p - c)q_{as} \leq 0$ follows from the discussion in "Interaction Effects". Then $J_{ps} \geq 0$, $J_{ap} \leq 0$, and $J_{as} \leq 0$ implies that $J^n(s, -a, p)$ is supermodular on $R_+ \times C$. It follows from the discussion in appendix 7A–1 that a(s) is decreasing and that p(s) is increasing in s.

8
A Model of Discounting for Repeat Sales

Chakravarthi Narasimhan

Consider a firm selling a single product. If the demand in any period does not depend on the price set in earlier periods or the demand in earlier periods, the firm then essentially sets the same price.[1] But suppose that consumers, having bought the product today, repeat-purchase the product in the next period with some probability greater than zero; then, setting the same price every period may not be optimal. Such a scenario might arise, for example, in the frequently purchased nondurables category where close substitutes are available to a product or the consumer simply forgoes consumption in a period. The objective of this chapter is to analyze the pricing strategies of firms faced with such a demand structure. Specifically, it will be assumed that some consumers who have not tried the product can be induced to buy the product this period through a price reduction and in subsequent periods the sales from these "new triers" decline due to attrition in the repeat-purchase. Thus, one may expect the price to vary over time. This chapter studies the price dynamics associated with this kind of dealing activity.

In the marketing literature, many authors have studied the incentives for firms to change their prices. Blattberg et al. [1981] and Jeuland and Narasimhan [1985] construct models of retailer and consumer and argue that a firm will discount its price periodically as a means of transferring its inventory cost to a segment of consumers (Blattberg et al.) or as a means of price discriminating (Jeuland and Narasimhan). Narasimhan [1984] argues that the practice of discounting through cents-off coupons is to price discriminate between consumers with high time costs and low time costs. Narasimhan [1988] shows that when firms are faced with brand-loyal segments and brand switchers, price dealing may occur. The research on new-product–diffusion phenomena (see, e.g., Dolan and Jeuland [1981]) shows that a firm may vary its price over time due to cost or demand dynamics. In contrast to all these works, this chapter focuses on repeat purchases. The purpose here is to construct a stylized model that can explain repeated price discounts that are commonly observed in the consumer nondurables market. Note that the issue addressed in this chapter is not that of gradual falling of prices overtime. What is being addressed is the phenomenon of temporary price cuts that occur between periods of regular (i.e., higher) prices.

The phenomenon of price discounting to encourage nonbuyers to buy the product today, in the hope that they will repeat-purchase the product in subsequent periods, is well recognized by marketing managers. New products may be introduced with heavy promotions (price discounts), distribution of free samples, small trial sizes, and so on. However, the nature of the optimal discount to be provided and how it is affected by the demand parameters have not been studied very much. One major exception is the work of Spatt [1981]; a brief description of his work is provided next.

Spatt considers a monopoly with a fixed market size. He assumes that sales decay at a constant rate. The repeat purchasers are willing to pay more than nonrepeaters and he models the price dynamics under this scenario, where the firm maximizes the net present value of future returns. He shows that the optimal strategy is to provide a discount at regular intervals and derives several properties of the decision variable (time between discounting). In this chapter, his work is extended in two key dimensions. First, Spatt assumed that the only decision variable is the timing of the discount. In his model, the discount given is a constant and the entire set of consumers buys the product. This assumption will be relaxed. Next, the existence of a "loyal" segment that repeat-purchases indefinitely will be assumed. The modeling of such a segment should be appealing to marketing researchers, since there are some crucial trade-offs that are affected by the size of this segment.

The rest of the chapter is organized as follows. In the next section, a very simple model of a monopolist is presented and the monopolist's optimal strategy is examined. This basic model is then generalized to a continuous time version to illustrate the optimal values of the decision variables and their dependence on model parameters. Finally, directions for further work in both theoretical and empirical dimensions are identified.

The Model

In this section, two different models to capture the dynamics involved when consumers repeat-purchase a product are considered. First, a simple model with a discrete time interval and a restrictive repeat-purchase process is examined. The optimality conditions for a firm to offer a discount to encourage repeat sales are then derived. The basic model is then extended to accommodate a general repeat-purchase structure.

Assumptions:

(A-1)   The market consists of a single firm manufacturing and selling a product. The marginal cost of the product is c and there are no other costs. There are N number of consumers assumed exogenous to the model.

(A-2)   Consumers desire at most one unit per time period.[2]

(A-3)   Consumers are divided into two segments. A set I consists of "loyal" consumers who repeat-purchase the brand forever and are willing to pay a maximum price of $v > c$. The "nonloyal" segment consists of $(N - I)$ consumers who do not purchase the product at the price v. Further, the number of consumers from the nonloyal segment who will purchase the product when a discount $d > 0$ is offered $= (N - I)$ $\alpha(d)$ where α is a contact function. We assume $0 \leq \alpha(d) \leq 1, \alpha'(d)$ > 0, and $\alpha''(d) < 0$.

(A-4)   When a consumer from the nonloyal segment purchases the product, he repurchases the product next period at the price v with a probability p, but not thereafter. The repeat-purchase probability is independent of the discount given in the current period.[3]

(A-5)   Consumers are fully informed about the discount.

(A-6)   The firm faces a one-period time-invariant interest rate of r. Let

Π_0 = present value of the profits over two periods when the firm does not discount.

$\Pi(d)$ = present value of the profits over two periods when the firm offers a discount of d in the current period.

Then

$$\Pi_0 = I(v - c)\left(1 + \frac{1}{1 + r}\right) \tag{1}$$

and

$$\Pi(d) = I(v - c)\left(1 + \frac{1}{1 + r}\right) - Id + (N - I) \tag{2}$$

$$\times \ \alpha(d)\left[(v - c - d) + \frac{p(v - c)}{1 + r}\right]$$

$$= \Pi_0 - Id + (N - I)\alpha(d)\left[(v - c - d) + \frac{p(v - c)}{1 + r}\right].$$

(A–7) We assume that

$$(N - I)\alpha(d)(v - c - d) < (N - I)\alpha(d) \left(v - c - d + \frac{p(v - c)}{1 + r}\right).$$

That is, the loss from discounting to the loyal consumers (Id) must be less than the net discounted gain and is more than the current-period profit from these new triers. What it means is that if consumers from the nonloyal segment do not repeat-purchase, the firm has no incentive to offer a discount. Intuitively, this means that the number of loyal consumers should not be too small relative to the rest of the market.

Given the profit function in (2), it is straightforward to derive the first-order and second-order conditions.

$$\frac{\partial \Pi}{\partial d} = 0 = -I + (N - I)\alpha'(d)\left[(v - c - d) + \frac{p(v - c)}{1 + r}\right] - (N - I)\alpha(d) \quad (3)$$

and

$$\frac{\partial^2 \Pi}{\partial d^2} = \Delta = (N - I)\alpha''(d)\left[(v - c - d) + \frac{p(v - c)}{1 + r}\right] \quad (4)$$

$$- 2(N - I)\alpha'(d) < 0$$

Note that (4) holds because of (A–3)

It is difficult to get a closed-form expression for d from (3) without explicitly parameterizing $\alpha(d)$. However, given that our interest is in understanding the influence of the model parameters, p, r, v, c, and N on the optimal value of the decision variable, it is not necessary that we derive a closed-form expression for the optimal value of d. From (3), we can say that the optimal value of d, viz. d^*, will be a function of v, c, p, r, N, and I. To see how d^* changes with respect to changes in these parameters, totally differentiate (3) with respect to each one of them and use (4) to obtain

$$\frac{dd^*}{dp} = \frac{(N - I)\alpha'(d^*)(v - c)}{\Delta(1 + r)} > 0 \quad (5)$$

$$\frac{dd^*}{dr} = \frac{(N - I)\alpha'(d^*)p(v - c)}{\Delta(1 + r)^2} < 0 \quad (6)$$

$$\frac{dd^*}{dv} = - \frac{(N - I)\alpha'(d^*)}{\Delta} > 0 \quad (7)$$

$$\frac{\mathrm{d}d^\star}{\mathrm{d}c} = \frac{(N-I)\alpha'(d^\star)}{\Delta} < 0 \tag{8}$$

$$\frac{\mathrm{d}d^\star}{\mathrm{d}I} = \frac{1}{\Delta}\left\{1 + \alpha'(d^\star)\left[(v - c - d^\star) + \frac{p}{1+r}(v-c)\right] - \alpha(d^\star)\right\} \tag{9}$$

$$= \frac{N}{\Delta(N-I)} < 0$$

$$\frac{\mathrm{d}d^\star}{\mathrm{d}N} = \frac{1}{\Delta}\left\{\alpha(d^\star) - \alpha'(d^\star)\left[(v - c - d^\star) + \frac{p}{1+r}(v-c)\right]\right\} \tag{10}$$

$$= \frac{1}{\Delta}\left[\frac{-I}{N+I}\right] > 0.$$

Further note that

$$\frac{\mathrm{d}\Pi(d^\star)}{\mathrm{d}p} = \frac{(N-I)\alpha(d^\star)(v-c)}{(1+r)} > 0$$

by the envelope theorem.

Equations (5) through (10) have the following implications:

From (5), the optimal discount offered will be greater, the greater the repeat-purchase probability.

From (6), the discount offered will be smaller, the greater the interest rate.

From (7) and (8), the discount will be larger, the larger the margin on the item.

From (10), a shift in the potential number of consumers increases the optimal discount.

All these implications should agree with one's intuition. If the repeat-purchase probability increases, the present value of the profit stream increases $[\mathrm{d}\Pi(d^\star)/\mathrm{d}p > 0]$ and, therefore, the firm will be willing to sacrifice to a greater extent the current-period profits. (This is the cost side—viz., loss resulting from discounting to loyal consumers.) If the loyal segment increases, then the "cost" of giving a discount in the current period increases and, there-fore, the optimal discount decreases. Exactly the opposite argument holds for an exogenous shift in the market size. The empirical implications of these will be discussed in the last section of this chapter.

Next, suppose that in the model, one assumes that the nonloyal segment consisting of $(N - I)$ consumers buy with a probability q the product at its regular price. How will the discounting policy differ? First, as a justification for the preceding assumption, note that the notion of "impulse buying" is prevalent in the marketing literature. According to this notion, some consumers buy a product that they do not purchase on a regular basis when no change in the price or any other marketing variable has been observed. Thus, the probability q can be interpreted as the impulse-buying probability of the nonloyal segment. Under this assumption, equation (2) becomes

$$\Pi(d) = I\left(1 + \frac{1}{1 + r}\right)(v - c) - Id + (N - I)(1 - q) \tag{2'}$$

$$\alpha(d)(v - c - d) + (N - I)q(v - c - d)$$

$$+ (N - I)q\frac{(v - c)}{(1 + r)} + (N - I)\frac{(1 - q)\alpha(d)}{(1 + r)}p(v - c)$$

$$= \Pi_0' - [I + (N - I)q]d + (N - I)(1 - q)\alpha(d)$$

$$\left[(v - c - d) + p\frac{(v - c)}{(1 + r)}\right]$$

where

$$\Pi_0' = I\left(1 + \frac{1}{1 + r}\right)(v - c) + (N - I)q\left(1 + \frac{1}{1 + r}\right)(v - c).$$

Analogous to equation (3), we will now have,

$$\frac{\partial \Pi}{\partial d} = [I + (N - I)q] + (N - I)(1 - q)\alpha'(d)\left[(v - c - d) + p\frac{(v - c)}{(1 + r)}\right] \tag{3'}$$

$$- (N - I)(1 - q)\alpha(d) = 0$$

and

$$\frac{\partial d^*}{\partial d} = \frac{1}{\Delta}\left\{(N - I) + (N - I)\alpha'(d^*)\left[(v - c - d^*) + \right.\right.$$

$$\left.\left. p\frac{(v - c)}{(1 + r)}\right] - (N - I)q(d^*)\right\} < 0.$$

That is, as the impulse-buying probability increases, the optimal discount decreases. In fact, it is easy to see from (2') that the profit to the firm increases as q increases, and a critical q^* exists such that for $q > q^*$, the firm may decide not to discount at all. Intuitively, if the net profit from repeat purchases is less than from "random" (impulse) purchases, the firm has no incentive to discount.

As a further extension, one can think of the following process to occur. On buying at a discount, the nonloyal consumers become loyal (forever) with some probability. Similarly, the loyal consumers may become nonloyal with some small probability. If the *net* increase to the loyal segment is positive, then it is clear that the effect is similar to the increase of I over time. Thus, over time, the firm may build its loyal base by discounting; after some time, when the loyal base becomes large enough, the firm will stop offering discounts.

So far, a very restrictive structure for the repeat-purchase process has been assumed. Consumers having bought today, repeat-purchase with a probability α for one more period. If one assumes that after two periods, a fresh set of customers who are unaware of the product's attributes are introduced into the system, the discounting process will repeat indefinitely; i.e., the firm will discount every two periods. This intuition is followed in the generalization of the preceding simple model by casting it in a continuous framework.

Continuous-Time Model

In this section, the basic model is reformulated and extended by relaxing some of the earlier assumptions. It is assumed that the time interval between purchases is small enough for the problem to be cast in a continuous-time framework.

Assumptions. Retain the assumptions (A–1) and (A–2), drop (A–3) through (A–7), and instead add the following assumptions (A–8) through (A–11).

(A–8) When consumers from the nonloyal pool purchase the product and exit from the system, they are replaced by an identical number of consumers with similar characteristics.

This assumption requires some clarification. One can think of a situation in which consumers enter and exit from the market. If all consumers enter the marketplace in the first period, then it is clear that the monopolist will offer a discount in the first period and never after that. However, this assumption of no infusion of new consumers is unrealistic. In the real world, consumers become aware of the product and some try it. Some of these consumers who never tried the product may forget about its appeal and might become aware of the product sometime in the future. Still other consumers may try it once, become nonusers for some time, and then repeat the product. Due to changes in life cycle, there may be an infusion of potential customers every period. Thus, the number of consumers who have not tried the product but who are potential consumers is affected by a large number of factors. One can then say that the total number of consumers in the system (those currently purchasing and potential purchasers) is governed by some stochastic process. This may very well be. But modeling this more "realistic" behavior while complicating the model has very little payoff unless one can hypothesize an appropriate stochastic process and predict how certain observable factors affect the parameters of such a process. Thus, while assumption (A-7) is somewhat unrealistic, it is made for tractability; in the discussion section this will be further analyzed.

The reader might have guessed by now that the assumption of continuous infusion of "new" consumers into the system is the one that drives the results of the chapter. The repeated nature of discounting is indeed driven by assumption (A-8), but the comparative static results are governed by the balancing of the effect of different parameters on the decision variables.

(A-9) The firm discounts its profit in continuous time with the instantaneous interest rate i assumed constant.

(A-10) The purchases from the nonloyal segment conditional on a purchase in the current period decays exponentially at a constant rate δ. Thus, if x consumers from the nonloyal segment buy today, then t periods later, the number of consumers from this segment will be $x e^{-\delta t}$.

(A-11) The function $\alpha(d)$ is reformulated as follows. The instantaneous number of consumers that are buying from the firm when a discount d is in effect is given by $N\alpha(d)$. This formulation has the following implications. Consider some point in time t when the firm has $B > I$ number consumers. ($B - I$ = number of nonloyal consumers left over from the last period.) If the firm gives a discount of d, its clientele the instant after the discount is $N\alpha(d)$. Therefore, the instant after the discount, it has $[N\alpha(d) - I]$ nonloyal consumers. Thus, the *incremental* nonloyal consumers it obtains after the discount = $[N\alpha(d) - B]$. But since the total number of consumers in the system is a constant, what this means is that the *incremental* number of nonloyal consumers the firm obtains is a decreasing function of current customer base B.

One could think of $\alpha(d_0)$ as the probability that a randomly chosen nonloyal consumer will have a cost of trial less than or equal to d_0. It is then obvious that $\text{Prob}[d < d_0 \,|\, d > d']$ is a decreasing function of d'.[4] (See figure 8-1).

Proofs. Given these assumptions, let us now examine the discounting policy of the firm in an infinite-horizon environment by assuming the just-mentioned repeat-purchase structure.

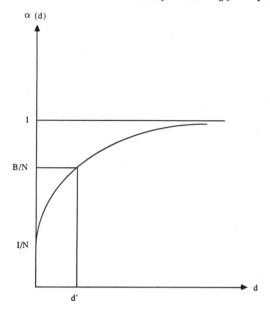

Figure 8-1. Nature of the Contact Function $\alpha(d)$

First note that if the firm never discounts its price, then the present value of its profits over the time horizon is given by

$$\Pi_0 = \int_0^\infty (v - c) e^{-it} dt = \frac{I(v - c)}{i}. \tag{11}$$

Suppose if the current customer base is $B > I$ (I being the number of loyal consumers), then the present value of the profit streams is given by

$$\Pi = (v - c) \int_0^\infty (B - I) e^{-(\delta + i)t} dt + \frac{I(v - c)}{i} \tag{12}$$

$$= \frac{(B - I)(v - c)}{(\delta + i)} + I\frac{(v - c)}{i}.$$

Note that in (12), the first term represents the contribution from nonloyal consumers. If $\delta = \infty$ (i.e., instantaneous decay of the repeat-purchases), then (12) reduces to (11).

If the firm decides to give a discount d when the current customer base is B, then the present value of the profit stream is given by

$$\Pi = (v - c)\int_0^\infty [N\alpha(d) - I]e^{-(\delta + I)}dt + I\frac{(v - c)}{i} - N\alpha(d)d \qquad (13)$$

$$= \frac{[N\alpha(d) - I]}{(\delta + i)}(v - c) + I\frac{(v - c)}{i} - N\alpha(d)d.$$

The first two terms in (13) represent the discounted value of the profits and the last term represents the total cost of discounting. Note that the cost of discounting is independent of the current customer base since the total number of consumers buying from the firm at that instant is $N\alpha(d)$.

Therefore, the firm will give a discount when its customer base is B if

$$\frac{[N\alpha(d) - B]}{(\delta + i)}(v - c) - N\alpha(d)d > 0. \qquad (14)$$

Inequality (14) implies that $N\alpha(d) > B$. This is obvious since in the instant after discounting, the number of consumers must be greater than the instant before. The firm's problem is to

$$\max_d \quad N\alpha(d)\left[\frac{(v - c)}{(\delta + i)} - d\right] \qquad (15)$$

s.t. $d > d'$ and given that $N\alpha(d') = B$.

Let d_0 represent the optimal value of d for the unconstrained maximization of the problem in (15) and let $B_0 = N\alpha(d_0)$. The maximum value of the objective function (call it V^*) is given by

$$V^* = N\alpha(d_0)\left[\frac{(v - c)}{(\delta + i)} - d_0\right].$$

Note that the objective function given in (15) is strictly concave with a unique maximum in the range where the function is positive. (See figure 8–2.) Thus, the solution to (15) is either d_0 (interior maximum) or d' (corner solution). If an interior maximum exists, i.e., $d^* = d_0 > d'$, then it is obvious that $B < B_0$. If a corner solution exists, then $d^* = d'$ and $B > B_0$. But if $d^* = d'$, then combining (14) and (15), we see that (14) is violated and therefore the firm will not discount. We have, therefore, proved the following lemma.

Lemma:

Under the preceding assumptions, the firm will never discount when its current customer base is $B > B_0$.

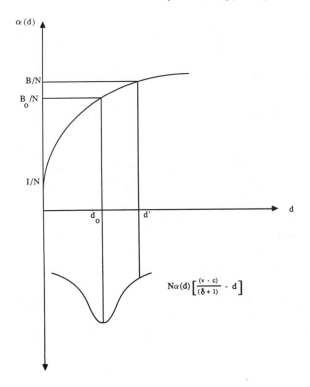

Figure 8-2. Optimal Discount and Critical Customer Base

Corollaries:

(a) The firm will discount once (if it discounts at all) when $\delta = 0$.

(b) The firm may either not discount or discount every period (i.e., set a lower price) when $\delta = \infty$.

Proof of (a)

If the current customer base $B > B_0$, then $B > B_0$ for all future periods and therefore the firm will never discount. If $B < B_0$, the firm will offer a discount $= d_0$ and its customer base after discount will be $N\alpha(d_0) > B_0$. Hence, for all future periods, the customer base will never be less than or equal to B_0 and the firm will never offer a discount again.

Proof of (b)

If $\delta = \infty$, the present value of the profits when discount d is offered is given by

$$[N\alpha(d) - I](v - c - d) + I\frac{(v - c)}{i} - Id$$

For discounting to be optimal, we should have

$$[N\alpha(d) - I](v - c - d) + I\frac{(v - c)}{i} - Id > I\frac{(v - c)}{i}$$

i.e., discount if

$$N\alpha(d)(v - c - d) > I(v - c). \qquad (16)$$

If (16) holds, the firm will discount every period; i.e., it will have a permanent low price. If (16) fails to hold, the firm will never discount.

What we have shown through the preceding arguments is that for some customer base below B_0, it is optimal for the firm to discount. As we will demonstrate next, there is some optimal time to *wait* before a discount is given. To see this formally, let the customer base at time 0 be $B < B_0$, where $B_0 = N\alpha(d_0)$. Assume that the firm plans to discount and denote t as the time at which it discounts. The profit function is

$$\Pi = (v - c)\int_0^t (B - I)e^{-(\delta + i)\tau}d\tau + \frac{I(v - i)}{i} - e^{-it}B_0d_0$$

$$+ (v - c)\int_t^{\infty}(B_0 - I)e^{-(\delta + i)\tau}d\tau$$

i.e.,

$$\Pi = \frac{(v - c)}{(\delta + i)}(B - I)[1 - e^{-(\delta + i)t}] + \frac{I(v - c)}{i} - e^{-it}B_0d_0 +$$

$$\frac{(v - c)}{(\delta + i)}(B_0 - I)e^{-(\delta + i)t}$$

The optimal time to discount is then given by $\partial\Pi/\partial t = 0$; i.e.,

$$(v - c)e^{-\delta t^*}(B_0 - B) = iB_0d_0$$

or

$$t^* = -\frac{1}{\delta}\ln\left[\frac{iB_0d_0}{(v - c)(B_0 - B)}\right].$$

Thus, the preceding analysis shows that even when $B < B_0$, there is an optimal waiting time before the firm decides to give a discount; the customer base at that time will be $B^* = B e^{-\delta t^*}$. The intuition behind this is the following. By waiting for one more period, the firm postpones giving the discount and thereby reducing (in present-value terms) the cost of discounting. However, by waiting one more period, the firm forgoes the incremental profit from $(B_0 - B)$ consumers over the one-period time shift. The optimal t^* balances these two forces.

So far, what we have established is that given the structure of repeat purchases, when the customer base drops to some value, it is optimal for the firm to give a discount. Assuming stationarity, it is then obvious that the process has to repeat itself. That is, the firm will discount periodically, giving the same discount. A firm with foresight (i.e., one that knows that it has to give periodic discounts) will then take this into account and determine both the magnitude and the periodicity of the discount optimally. Thus, in contrast to the myopic case just discussed for pedagogical reasons, the optimal discount with foresight will be different depending in particular on the periodicity of the discount. These arguments are more formally developed next. The dynamics of the customer base is illustrated in figure 8–3.

To describe the firm's optimal policy, one should characterize the optimal (T^*, d^*) pair. That is the period between successive promotions and the

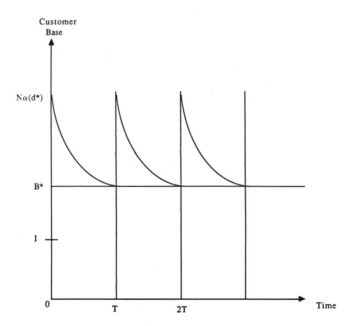

Figure 8–3. Dynamics of the Sales Pattern in Continuous Time

amount of discount that is given. The objective is to explore the nature of dependence of (T^*, d^*) on the model parameters, viz., I, δ, i, and $(v - c)$.

To determine the optimal time interval between discounts, write down the present value of the profits of the firm as a function of the discounting interval. The dynamics are very similar to the machine-replacement problem and the structure and the analysis has some resemblance to Spatt [1981]. Let the present value of the returns over a discounting cycle of length T with the discount d be given by $\Pi(T, d)$. Then,

$$\Pi(T, d) = (v - c)\int_0^T [N\alpha(d) - I]e^{-(\delta + i)t}dt + I(v - c)\int_0^T e^{-it}dt -$$

$$N\delta(d)de^{-iT} + \Pi(T, d)e^{-iT}.$$

The first term represents the profits from the purchases of nonloyal consumers, the second term represents the profits from the loyal consumers, the third term represents the end-of-period cost of discounting, and the last term represents the profits from the next cycle.[5]

The profit function can be rewritten as

$$\Pi(T, d) = (v - c)\frac{[N\alpha(d) - I](1 - e^{-(\delta + i)T})}{(1 - e^{-iT})(\delta + i)} + I\frac{(v - c)}{i} - \frac{N\alpha(d)de^{-it}}{(1 - e^{-iT})} \quad (17)$$

The firm determines (T^*, d^*) by setting $\partial\Pi/\partial T = \partial\Pi/\partial d = 0$.

$$\frac{\partial\Pi}{\partial T} = (1 - e^{-iT})\{(V - c)[N\alpha(d) - I]e^{-(\delta + i)T} + id\,N\delta(d)e^{iT}\} \quad (18)$$

$$- ie^{-iT}\left\{\frac{(v - c)[N\alpha(d) - I]}{(\delta + i)}(1 - e^{-(\delta + i)T}) - N\alpha(d)de^{-iT}\right\} = 0.$$

As detailed in appendix 8A–1, this can be simplifed as

$$x^{y + 1} - (y + 1)x + yk = 0 \quad (19)$$

where

$$y = i/\delta \quad (20)$$

$$x = e^{-\delta T} \quad (21)$$

$$k = 1 - \frac{dN\alpha(d)(\delta + i)}{(v - c)[N\alpha(d) - I]} \quad (22)$$

Note that $y > 0$, $0 < x < 1$, and $0 < k < 1$. If $k < 0$, a solution to (19) does not exist. The conditions under which k will be negative depend on the magnitude of the loyal base (I) and the optimal d^* to be given.

Consider (19) as a polynomial in x and write

$$f(x) = x^{y+1} - (y+1)x + yk = 0$$

$$f'(x) = (y+1)(x^y + 1) < 0$$

and

$$f''(x) = y(y+1)x^{y-1} > 0.$$

Therefore, f is a monotonically decreasing function in x and strictly convex. Further, $f(0) = yk > 0$ (assuming k is nonnegative) and $f(1) = -y(1 - k) < 0$. Therefore, $f(x^*) = 0$ for some x^* such that $0 < x^* < 1$ and, further, this x^* is unique. The optimal T^* is then found through (21) by $T^* = -1/\delta \ln x^*$.

to find the optimal d^*, we differentiate (17) with respect to d and set it equal to zero.

$$\frac{\partial \Pi}{\partial d} = \frac{(v-c)}{(\delta + i)} \alpha'(d)(1 - e^{-(\delta + i)T}) - \alpha'(d)de^{-iT} \tag{23}$$

$$- \alpha(d)e^{-iT} = 0.$$

This can be simplified as

$$\alpha'(d)(a - d) = \alpha(d) \tag{24}$$

where

$$a = \frac{(v-c)}{(\delta + i)}e^{-iT}(1 - e^{-(\delta + i)T}).$$

Note that a feasible solution d^* to (24) should satisfy $d^* < a$. To prove the uniqueness of such a d^*, note that the left-hand side of (24) is a monotonically decreasing function of d, while the right-hand side a monotonically increasing function; therefore, if a solution exists, it is unique. To show existence, note that for $d \geq a$, $\partial \Pi / \partial d < 0$ (from (23)). Therefore, if for some d, such that $0 < d < a$ if $\partial \Pi / \partial d > 0$, then existence is guaranteed. By the mean value theorem, $\alpha'(x)(a - d) = \alpha(a) - \alpha(d)$ for $d < x < a$.

Since α is strictly concave, this implies

$$\alpha'(d)(a - d) > \alpha(a) - \alpha(d).$$

Therefore, if a d_0 exists such that $\alpha(a) > 2\alpha(d_0)$, then existence of a d that satisfies (24) is assured. If, for example, $I = 0$ (i.e., there are no loyal consumers), then $\alpha(a) = 0$ and existence is automatically guaranteed. Therefore, unless the loyal base is too large, existence does not seem to be a problem.

The second-order condition for a maximum requires that the Hessian of the objective function be negative definite. Specifically, we require that $\partial^2\Pi/\partial T^2, \partial^2\Pi/\partial d^2 < 0$ and $(\partial^2\Pi/\partial T^2)(\partial^2\Pi/\partial d^2) - (\partial^2\Pi/\partial T\partial d) < 0$. From (18) and (23), it is easy to show that $\partial^2\Pi/\partial T^2, \partial^2\Pi/\partial d^2 < 0$ whenever the first-order conditions hold. However, to show that the Hessian is negative definite is complicated and it will be assumed that the Hessian is negative definite whenever the first-order conditions hold so that the first-order conditions are both necessary and sufficient.

One can now compute the customer base that triggers a discount. This is given by

$$B^* = I + [N\alpha(d^*) - I]e^{-\delta T^*}. \tag{25}$$

Assume for a moment that $\alpha(0) = I/N$, while $\alpha(d_0) = 1$ and $\alpha(d) = 0$ otherwise. That is, the firm either gives a discount of d_0 or does not discount. In this case, the only decision variable is T. Certain comparative statistics can be computed in this case. From (19),

$$\frac{dx^*}{dd_0} = \frac{y}{f''(x^*)}\left(-\frac{\partial k}{\partial d_0}\right) \tag{26}$$

from (22) it is obvious that $\partial k/\partial d_0 < 0$. Therefore, $\partial K^*/\partial d_0 < 0$. This implies that $dT^*/dd_0 > 0$.[6] That is, if the cost of augmenting the current customer base increases, the firm will offer a discount less frequently. Similarly, letting $g = v - c$

$$\frac{dT^*}{dg} = -\frac{\partial x^*}{\partial g} = -\frac{y}{f''(x^*)}\left(-\frac{\partial k}{\partial g}\right) < 0.$$

That is, if the unit contribution increases (perhaps due to a decrease in cost), the firm will offer the discount at a greater frequency.

Similarly, one can derive $dT^*/d\delta$ as follows:

$$\frac{dT^*}{d\delta} = \frac{1}{\delta^2}\left[\ln x^* - \frac{\delta}{x^*}\frac{dx^*}{d\delta}\right]$$

Assuming $\delta = i$, from (17) $x^* = 1 - \sqrt{1 - k}$ so that

$$\frac{dT^*}{d\delta} = \frac{-1}{2\delta}\sqrt{1 - k} = \frac{-1}{2\delta}(1 - x)$$

$$\therefore \quad \frac{dT^*}{d\delta} = \frac{1}{\delta^2}\left[\ln x^* + \frac{(1 - x)}{2x}\right]$$

for small values of δ, we find k and x are close to 1. Therefore, the bracketed term is dominated by $\ln x$, which is negative ($0 < x < 1$). For large values of δ, we find k and x tend toward 0 and the bracketed term is dominated by $1/x$, which is positive. Thus, T^* is nonmonotonic with respect to δ. For small values of δ, T^* decreases with δ whereas for large values of δ, T^* increases with δ. An intuitive explanation for this comparative static is the following. When δ is small (i.e., when the customer base decays slowly), an increase in δ means that the firm loses customers faster and therefore discounts more often (i.e., T decreases), but above certain critical δ, it is no longer profitable to discount since consumers leave the firm at a greater rate. Since the cost of discounting is the same (note that d is constant), the firm would rather wait to get the benefit of repeat purchases and then discount again, thereby increasing T^*.

However, deriving comparative statics in general is difficult because of the nonlinearities involved. Simulation is performed to derive them. The details are explained next.

Comparative Statics through Simulation

The purpose of the simulation is to solve for the optimal T^* and d^*, using equations (19) and (24), and to derive the properties of the optimal values. Specifically, the interest is to find how T^* and d^* vary with respect to the parameters $(v - c)$, i, δ, and I. However, in the simulation model it is assumed that $\delta = i$ so that equation (19) is a quadratic and the value of T^* can be explicitly calculated. The ranges for the parameter values and the step sizes are:

$(v - c = g \in (1, 5)$ in steps of 1

$\delta = i \in (.05, 0.5)$ in steps of 0.05

$N = 10,000$ fixed

$I \in (0, 9000)$ in steps of 1,000

$\alpha(d) = \dfrac{I}{N} + \left(\dfrac{N - I}{N}\right)(1 - e^{\gamma d}) \quad \gamma \in (5, 6.8)$ in steps of 0.2

so that $\alpha(0) = I/N$ and $\alpha(\infty) = 1$. α is continuous, differentiable, and concave everywhere.

Note that, $\partial\alpha'(d)/\partial\gamma = e^{-\gamma d}(1 - \gamma^2) \lessgtr 0$ as $\gamma \gtrless 1$. $\partial\alpha'(d)/\partial\gamma$ is a measure of how difficult it is to attract consumers with a discount as the parameter γ is varied. Thus, for $\gamma > 1$, an increase in γ means that the marginal number of consumers the firm will be able to attract decreases at a given discount level.

The results of the simulation are given in table 8–1. In the table, the effects of changes in model parameters g, δ, I and, γ on T^*, d^*, B^*, Π^* are given where B^* is the optimal customer base that triggers the discounting. B^* is given by $[N\alpha(d^*) - I]e^{-\delta T^*} + I$. From table 8–1, it can be seen that the effect of an increase in δ on d^* and T^* is ambiguous. The simulation results reveal that d^* and T^* decrease with δ for small values of δ but at large values of δ, d^* and T^* increase, consistent with earlier predictions.

Empirical Implications

1. As the share of loyal buyers increases, the firm should discount less often $(dT^*/dI > 0)$.

2. A product with greater share of loyal purchases should offer shallow discounts $(dd^*/dI < 0)$.

3. Over the life of a product, one would expect that the product will develop its loyal franchise gradually. Therefore, the model would predict that new brands would discount more often than established brands.

4. By similar arguments, one would expect new brands to offer deeper discounts than older, more established brands.

5. The customer base that triggers discounting will depend inversely on the decay rate (δ) and interest rate (i).

Table 8–1
Comparative Statics from Simulation

Parameters	d^*	T^*	Π^*	B^*
$g = (v - c)$	+	+	+	+
$i = \delta$	−, +	−, +	−	−
I	−	+	+	+
γ	−	+	+	+

Notes: Entries are the signs of partial derivatives of the column values with respect to the row parameters.

B^* refers to customer base that triggers discounting and is given by $B^* = [N\alpha(d^*) - I]e^{-\delta T^*} + I$.

6. The optimal customer base that triggers the discount increases with growth in the loyal franchise.

7. Across different brands in a product class with different retention rates of repeat purchases (i.e., δ), the discounting period should first decrease and then increase with δ.

Limitations, Conclusions, and Further Directions

In this chapter, a model of a single firm was considered when the firm is faced with consumers who are willing to repeat purchase at an increased price conditional on the fact that they make their first purchase at a lower price to compensate for their cost of trial. Several assumptions were made in the development of the model. These are discussed next.

The assumption that consumers buy only one unit is certainly restrictive. But there does not seem to be an easy way out of this without enormously complicating the model. One can assume that conditioned on trial, the demand curves of those who bought at a lower price are the same as the demand curves of the loyal segment (those who buy indefinitely). This means one has to model the trial and repeat purchases separately. Incorporating this might lead to further insights.

The assumption that the total number of consumers in the system is constant (i.e., equal numbers of new consumers and those who leave) is unpalatable. As argued earlier, the number of consumers is likely to follow a stochastic process with the changes in every period depending on a lot of factors. While the payoffs of relaxing this assumption are not clear, certainly from a modeling point of view this seems to be a useful exercise. Further, if the number of consumers in the nonloyal pool exit from the market without trying the product, then the incentive for the firm to give a discount is even greater, since the number of consumers available in the pool next period may be less.

Several other assumptions are also worth reiterating. We assumed that (1) consumers do not inventory the product, (2) the repeat-purchase rate is independent of the discount given, and (3) the firm is a monopolist. Clearly, if all consumers are identical in their inventorying aspects, this should not pose any problem. Modeling a heterogeneous population in terms of inventorying behavior can be an important extension to the work presented here. Next, the assumption that the aggregate decay rate is independent of discount (δ is independent of d in this chapter) can be relaxed by making δ a function of d. While this might be somewhat more realistic, the payoff is not clear. Finally, this chapter addressed the strategies of a single firm. Suppose now there are several firms competing noncooperatively for the consumer purchases. How would the discounting strategy be different from the one proposed in this chapter? The problem is somewhat similar to the tree-cutting problem discussed in the game theoretic literature and one has to worry about such issues as the existence of an equilibrium to the game. This is left for future research.

Notes

1. Due to "learning" effects on the cost side, the price in successive periods will also be affected independent of any dynamics on the demand side. However, such effects are ignored in this chapter.

2. This assumption is obviously restrictive. If one assumes that consumers have identical demand curves, then it will be difficult to argue why the nonloyal consumers do not buy at the regular price. If the consumers have different demand curves, then it may be that discounting occurs to price discriminate between loyal and nonloyal consumers. Such effects are excluded to focus on repeat-purchases.

3. This is a crucial assumption that will be carried through the rest of the chapter. We assume that, regardless of the price paid today, the probability of repeat-purchase in the next period is the same. Thus, in the continuous-time version of the model in the next section, we assume that the decay curves for different values of the discount are parallel to one another.

4. If x is a continuous random variable, then $(\partial/\partial x_0)\int_{x_0}^{x_1} f(\alpha)d\alpha < 0$.

5. Note that we are ignoring any fixed cost of promotion. The implications of this chapter are not affected by this omission. Only the absolute level of profit will decline.

6. Note that $N\alpha(d_0)$ is a constant.

Appendix 8A–1:
Proof of Equation (19)

We start with equation (18) in the text

$$(1 - e^{-iT})\{(v - c)[N\alpha(d) - I]e^{-(\delta + i)T} + id\,N\alpha(d)e^{-iT}\}$$

$$- ie^{-iT}\{(v - c)\frac{[N\alpha(d) - I]}{(\delta + i)}(1 - e^{-(\delta + i)T}) - N\alpha(d)de^{-iT}\} = 0$$

dividing by e^{-iT}

$$(1 - e^{-iT})\{(v - c)[N\alpha(d) - I]e^{-\delta T}\} + id\,N\alpha(d)$$

$$- i(v - c)\frac{[N\alpha(d) - I]}{(\delta + i)}(1 - e^{-(\delta + i)T}) = 0 \qquad \text{(A–1)}$$

i.e.,

$$(1 - e^{-iT})e^{-\delta T} - \frac{i}{(\delta + i)}(1 - e^{-(\delta + i)T}) + \frac{id\,N\alpha(d)}{(v - c)[N\alpha(d) - I]} = 0 \quad \text{(A–2)}$$

Set $y = i/\delta$ and $x = e^{-\delta T}$. Then,

$$(\delta + i) = \delta(y + 1)$$

and

$$x^{y + 1} = e^{-\delta T}e^{-iT} = e^{-(\delta + i)T}.$$

Let $k = -\{d\,N\alpha(d)(\delta + i)\}/\{(v - c)[N\alpha(d) - I]\} + 1.$

Making these substitutions, one gets

$$(\delta + i)(x - x^{y+1}) + ix^{y+1} - ik = 0 \qquad \text{(A-3)}$$

This reduces to

$$\delta x^{y+1} - (i + \delta)x + ik = 0. \qquad \text{(A-4)}$$

Dividing by δ,

$$x^{y+1} - (y + 1)x + yk = 0$$

which is equation (19) in the text.

Part IV
Competitive Behavior

Brian T. Ratchford

I n the traditional marketing literature, one sees discussions of penetration versus skimming pricing strategies, administered versus conventional channels and their consequences for channel conflict, of end prices, loss leaders, and price lining. Traditionally, about all one gets in the way of guidance in considering these policies is a list of pros and cons and a vague set of conjectures about what will or will not work in a given setting. Rigorous explanations of why these policies may or may not work are notably lacking.

One reason for this lack of explanation is the complexity of the environment in which the marketing manager seeks to implement the preceding policies. One simply could not build a model that captures all the possible facets of new product, channel, or product-line pricing problems. But, if one is willing to assume away all but the bare essentials of the problem and to proceed from there with an analytical model, one can get very valuable insights into the forces that will make one or the other pricing policy viable. This is the traditional approach of the theoretical economist, an approach that has been increasingly applied to problems of competitive pricing by marketing scholars since around 1980. The three chapters in part IV are very much in this tradition.

In chapter 9, Rao deals with new-product pricing, specifically addressing the viability of skimming (starting high and gradually reducing the price) versus penetration (starting low) pricing strategies. This is the area of pricing strategy that has received perhaps the most theoretical scrutiny. But, until the early 1980s, work in this area has ignored the behavior of actual or potential competitors. Rather, it has sought to characterize the dynamic pricing policy of a monopolist in the presence of learning on the cost side and diffusion on the demand side. (Dolan and Jeuland [1981] is a representative example.) A well-established result that emerges from this literature is that a penetration strategy becomes attractive when diffusion and/or learning are strong.

More recent work has focused on pricing in competitive settings where diffusion and learning may be present (Rao and Bass [1985] is a good example; Eliashberg and Chatterjee [1985] provide a comprehensive review) or in which an innovative firm is faced with the possibility of entry by a competitor. The latter is the domain of Rao's chapter here.

Rao uses sophisticated game-theoretic concepts to address an issue that has been prominent in the industrial-organization literature for many years—whether a monopolist faced with potential entry will deliberately lower price to deter entry. An important feature of Rao's model is that it allows entry to be determined endogenously. Rather than being treated as a given, entry timing is allowed to depend on the strategy of the initial entrant in the market. Given this very reasonable feature of his model, Rao does get the result that low initial prices to deter entry are optimal. If entry later becomes inevitable no matter what the initial firm does, it will raise its prices beyond the entry-deterring level to exploit whatever is left of its monopoly. Thus, we get an alternative rationale for the strategy of a low initial price followed by a higher price. Elsewhere in the literature, it has been shown that when interpersonal communication stimulates demand (diffusion is important), a low initial price can help to promote the product, after which one might increase the price to exploit demand when diffusion builds it to a peak. (See, e.g., Dolan and Jeuland [1981]). Here it has been shown that a low initial price might be used to deter entry, after which one might increase the price when entry deterrence no longer becomes possible.

While Rao considers pricing strategies at the same (horizontal) level of competition, Shugan and Jeuland in chapter 10 consider vertical-pricing issues within the channel of distribution. In doing so, they explicitly recognize the fundamental conflict over how to divide channel profits between different members of the channel. The Shugan-Jeuland chapter is representative of a body of theoretical literature on channel relations, which, though perhaps smaller than that on horizontal competition just discussed, is no less important. Examples of other significant work in this area are McGuire and Staelin [1983a], Jeuland and Shugan [1983a,b], and Coughlan [1985]. Readers who are tired of a steady dose of game theory and attendant mathematics may be interested in Rubin [1978], who provides a nonquantitative but economically sound discussion of the rationale for pricing structures observed in franchise arrangements.

In chapter 10, Shugan and Jeuland argue that vertically integrated channels are, all things being equal, more profitable in total and, as a consequence, the more enduring type of channel arrangement. Intuitively, this is because the struggle of the nonintegrated members to maximize their profits leads to myopic decisions, resulting in too high a price and too small an output. Coordination is required to maximize joint profits.

As a possible exception to their argument that vertical channels are more profitable, Jeuland and Shugan argue that a nonintegrated (leader-follower) channel can be more profitable in a highly competitive market when both channels follow this mode of behavior. Intuitively, this is because the leader-follower channels create a closer to monopolist price than would otherwise be the case. The result is the same as if the channels had colluded to raise prices. In this case, adding a layer to the channel provides a buffer from competition. In the absence of collusion, however, Shugan and Jeuland argue that this equilibrium is unstable—one channel can increase its profits by integrating and undercutting the other's price.

When the channels are not competitive, vertical integration is best. In this case, there is no gain from setting a collusive price because each channel already has a monopoly. In the final section of chapter 10, Shugan and Jeuland point out that intrabrand competition may have to be limited to give retailers an adequate incentive to handle a manufacturer's product (or, in general, to offer essential services, such as displays and selling effort). They propose that this may be done through offering different models across retailers. Other, possibly illegal, alternatives are resale-price maintenance and exclusive territories.

While Shugan and Jeuland argue that vertical integration is best, their analysis begs the question of how this is to be achieved in practice. There are a host of possibilities of coordinating mechanisms ranging from ownership of one's own retail outlets, to franchises, to the the use of various pricing mechanisms such as quantity discounts (Jeuland and Shugan 1983a,b). An interesting paper on the subject of achieving vertical agreements in channels is Norton [1987].

While chapters 9 and 10 discuss pricing under horizontal and vertical competition, chapter 11 by Saghafi discusses pricing under a third type of competition, competition arising from one's own products. Since virtually every firm in existence sells more than one product, it is perhaps surprising that, as Saghafi points out, product-line pricing has not received a great deal of theoretical or empirical research. As with other areas of pricing, a possible explanation is the complexity of the decision.

Dating back at least to Hicks [1935], the theory of product-line pricing has been treated in various places in the economics and marketing literatures. (Preston [1963] is particularly interesting.) However, Saghafi presents a very thorough treatment of the subject in terms of general shapes of demand and cost functions. Moreover, he extends this to objectives other than profit maximization. A basic result of this analysis is that one must adjust prices to take account of demand interdependence—under profit maximization, substitutes are priced higher and complements are priced lower than if the interdependence were ignored. Indeed, the latter can be priced on the inelastic portion of the demand curve or even below unit cost.

While the chapters in this part are theoretical, they are worthy of careful examination by empirically minded readers. Indeed, the only real way of verifying whether the highly simplified models presented here really do capture the essential aspects of the problems being addressed is to subject them to empirical testing. Chapters 9 and 10 in particular have a number of potentially testable implications. For example, Rao's chapter suggests that a critical determinant of whether a skimming versus penetration pricing strategy will be adopted is whether a low price can affect the rate of entry. While it obviously would be difficult to determine whether the last condition holds, a creative researcher might be able to develop a persuasive test of this hypothesis using historical data or in the laboratory. Similarly, Shugan and Jeuland's chapter suggests that administered channels are more likely when products are highly differentiated, but that conventional channels might be used to buffer competition between commodity products. They also suggest that there should be a drift toward administered channels over time in a given industry. Finally, one might hypothesize from Shugan and Jeuland that manufacturers are more likely to strive to limit intrabrand competition for their products through product differentiation or other means particularly if the retailers have high fixed costs of selling the manufacturer's products. Many other hypotheses could likely be gleaned from the chapters in part IV. The point is that the implications of the work presented here can and should be tested empirically.

9

Strategic Pricing of Durables under Competition

Ram C. Rao

P enetration pricing is a strategic alternative discussed in marketing text-
books (Kotler 1984) and among managers. It can be thought of as the
strategy of choosing low initial prices and corresponding high initial
output rates so as to penetrate the market (i.e., reach a large number of potential consumers). There are at least three scenarios that would render penetration pricing optimal. First, if future cost advantages accrue from increased
cumulative production as a result of learning-curve effects, initial prices would
be lower than those warranted by myopic considerations that ignore the effects
of current actions on future costs (Dolan and Jeuland 1981). Second, if the
adoption of a new product becomes rapid as the size of the population of consumers who have already adopted it increases, due to the imitation effect suggested by Bass [1969], a low initial price would hasten the diffusion of a product, thereby bringing forward future cash flows (Kalish 1983a).[1] A third
possibility is that low initial prices could be used to affect entry by potential
competitors in a favorable way for an existing firm. This last aspect has not
been studied as extensively as the other two scenarios that favor penetration
pricing.

This chapter formally examines the role of penetration pricing as a strategy to affect competitor entry. In their study of the pricing strategies of a
monopolist prior to entry of another competitor whose time of entry is known,
Eliashberg and Jeuland [1986] conclude "entry deterrence strategy can be
more profitable than the strategy that does not attempt to prevent entry. This
deterrence strategy is credible because it is based on the irreversible penetration of the market" (p. 32, footnote 13). Thus, they hint at a monopolist's
pricing strategy designed to affect entry. Because the entry timing of the competitor in their model is fixed, the strategic aspects of penetration pricing are
not fully developed by them. This chapter will, therefore, examine a duopoly
in which entry timing is chosen by the second firm endogenously in the model
(as opposed to exogenously specified entry). This is an important feature of

the model. As in Eliashberg and Jeuland, interest here is in a market for consumer durables, with analysis focusing on first purchase.

Another crucial feature of the model is the definition of an appropriate equilibrium. Specifically, two equilibrium concepts—both of which assume noncooperative profit-maximizing behavior by the two firms—will be focused upon. Under the first equilibrium concept, called simple strategy, the second firm chooses a time to enter and a postentry pricing strategy. The first firm chooses a preentry pricing strategy and a postentry pricing strategy. The postentry pricing strategies constitute a Nash equilibrium in light of preentry strategies. Moreover, the preentry pricing strategy of firm 1 and the entry timing of firm 2 constitute a Nash equilibrium in light of postentry strategies. This equilibrium is perfectly plausible and in a sense represents a natural way of extending the Eliashberg-Jeuland ideas to make entry time endogenous. But it has a drawback. On closer examination, we can see that this game has only two stages: a preentry stage and a postentry stage. In the preentry stage, firm 2 is committed to its entry timing regardless of what firm 1 does in the time interval prior to actual entry. If entry *is* the irreversible commitment of firm 2, in the language of Spence [1979], then firm 1 need not take time of entry as given until entry by 2 has actually occurred. As Rao and Rutenberg [1979] have pointed out, sophisticated firms should recognize this and act upon it: firm 1 should not take time of entry as given but only take the manner in which entry timing is chosen as given. The exact specification of the rules by which entry timing is determined can be achieved by viewing the preentry stage as not one but several stages. To keep the decision simple, suppose firm 2 can choose to enter or not at specified discrete intervals of time. Each interval is then a stage in the entry game. At each stage, firm 1 chooses its price and firm 2 takes its decision to enter or not enter, in Nash fashion. This multistage game can be cast as a backward induction dynamic program in the manner of Rao and Rutenberg [1979]. Following Kreps and Wilson [1982b], let us denote the equilibrium generated in this fashion a sequential equilibrium. It is well known that for entry problems, the Rao-Rutenberg equilibrium is subgame-perfect and inherits all the consequential desirable properties. (See also Fudenberg and Tirole [1985].)

The main results of this chapter consist of contrasting the two equilibrium concepts given that entry is endogenous. With the simple strategies equilibrium, the basic pattern of price in the preentry period is one of continuous decline. This is a consequence of the monopolist practicing price discrimination by lowering the price gradually. This particular price behavior is also observed in Kalish [1983a] and Rao [1986a]. Eliashberg and Jeuland [1986] also find declining prices in the monopoly period, but their result does not follow from price discrimination since price does not affect demand in their model, only the rate of diffusion. For their case, prices decline because to achieve a given penetration at the end of a certain period, the monopolist finds it optimal to charge high initial prices since market potential is large. Turning now to the sequential equilibrium, a major difference is seen. Through a numerical example, it is demonstrated that prices in the preentry period can actually increase. This occurs solely to affect entry by rivals. By charging low initial prices (i.e., penetration pricing), the monopolist leaves a smaller fraction of the market for the second firm, which then is in no hurry to enter. Once the market for firm 2 becomes less attractive, firm 1 can charge a higher price.

The rest of the chapter is organized as follows. The next section presents the basic model and derives the duopoly pricing strategies in the postentry period. In addition, the monopolist's pricing behavior in the preentry period is derived parametric to the entry time. The subsequent major section takes up equilibrium entry timing by examining the two solution concepts and contrasting them through a numerical example. The last section provides concluding comments.

Dynamic Pricing under Foreseen Entry

The model examined here is a variant of the one studied by Eliashberg and Jeuland [1986]; it is different from theirs in two ways. First, a duopolist marketing undifferentiated products is studied. This keeps the exposition simple and does not affect any of the arguments pertaining to competition and consequences out of that. The second difference is more crucial and materially affects competition. Whereas Eliashberg and Jeuland prespecify the timing of entry of the second firm, it is treated endogenously here. The situation under investigation then is the following. Firm 1 enters the market at time 0 and must choose its strategy prior to entry by the second firm. Firm 2 chooses the time to enter the market in light of the strategy chosen by firm 1 prior to entry and correctly anticipating firm 1's strategy after entry. In addition, firm 2 chooses its own strategy after entry. Finally, firm 1 in choosing its preentry strategy correctly anticipates firm 2's choice of entry timing. One way to think of this is to visualize two stages: preentry and postentry. Preentry equilibrium is sustained by postentry equilibrium, which of course depends on the former. Thus, the equilibrium is of the subgame perfect variety. The particular equilibrium concept invoked here satisfies Bellman's principle of optimality; it is also often referred to as a feedback equilibrium and is sequentially rational. (See, for example, Kydland [1975], and Kreps and Wilson [1982b].)

The Model

The market under consideration is for durable products that are bought only once by a given consumer. Thus, as the cumulative buyer population grows, the remaining market potential declines, ceteris paribus. The market potential is assumed to be a function of price with the usual downward-sloping property. Denote x_t to be the size of the population that has bought the product by time t and p_t to be the price at t. Let $g(p)$ denote the market potential corresponding to price p. This means that if the price were held constant at p, eventually we expect the total adopter population to be $g(p)$. Effective market potential at time t, M_t, is then given by (suppressing t to facilitate exposition)

$$M = g(p) - x \tag{1}$$

The instantaneous demand q_t at time t is then assumed to be[2]

$$q_t = \alpha[g(p) - x] \tag{2}$$

where α can be thought of as a diffusion coefficient. Equation (2) is the familiar model of partial adjustments (see Nerlove [1958]). Since the market is one for durables, focusing only on first purchase, we have $\dot{x} = q_t$, so that (2) becomes

$$\dot{x} = \alpha[g(p) - x] \tag{3}$$

Since our interest is in a market of undifferentiated products, both firms, after entry of the second firm, are required to choose the same price. Following Rao and Bass [1985], the price competition is modeled by supposing that each firm treats q_t as its decision variable. Denote $T_E \geq 0$ as the time at which firm 2 enters, with firm 1 entering at time 0.

Postentry Price Path

Characterized first is the behavior of price for $t \geq T_E$. This problem has been studied by Rao and Bass [1985] and the exposition will be brief. For illustrative purposes, assume $g(p)$ to be linear in p, so that (3) reduces to

$$\dot{x} = \alpha(a - bp - x), \qquad a, b > 0$$

which leads to the inverse demand function

$$p = A - Bx - D\dot{x} \tag{4}$$

where $A = a/b$, $B = 1/b$, $D = 1/\alpha b$. The cumulative-buyer population $x = x_1 + x_2$ where x_i denotes the cumulative buyer population of firm i. Let c denote the constant marginal cost of each of the firms. The maximizing problems faced by the duopolists are, assuming a zero discount rate,

$$\max_{y_i} \int_{T_E}^{\infty} (A - Bx_1 - Bx_2 - Dy_1 - Dy_2 - c) y_i \, dt \tag{5}$$

subject to

$$\dot{x}_i = y_i \tag{6}$$

$$x_1 (T_E) = x_E \tag{7}$$

$$x_2 (T_E) = 0 \tag{8}$$

Denote π_i to be the maximum profit of firm i resulting from the maximization of the preceding problems with y_i being chosen in Nash noncooperative fashion. Such an equilibrium is ordinarily an open-loop equilibrium, but for the problem at hand the open-loop equilibrium turns out to be a feedback equilibrium also. The optimal y_i^* is given by

$$y_i^* = (\alpha/6)(a - bc - x)$$

(See equation (A-15) in appendix 9A-1.) An alternative characterization of the output path as a function of time is

$$y_{i_t}^* = (a - bc - x_E) \exp \left[-\alpha(t - T_E)/3 \right]/6 \tag{9}$$

This shows that output rate decreases monotonically and exponentially. Moreover, from equation (A-16) in appendix 9A-1, we obtain

$$\pi_i^* = (1/6b)(a - bc - x_E)^2 \tag{10}$$

Finally, the price path can be seen to satisfy the following equation (equation (A-17) in appendix 9A-1):

$$\dot{p} = -(2\alpha/9b)(a - bc - x) \tag{11}$$

Solving it and using (A-13) from appendix 9A-1, we find

$$p_t = c + (2/3b)(a - bc - x_E) \exp(-\alpha(t - T_E)/3), \quad t \geq T_E \tag{12}$$

An alternative way to look at the price path is to see the behavior of p parametric to x. From appendix 9A-1, equation (A-18), we have

$$dp/dx = -2B/3 \tag{13}$$

The behavior of prices is best understood from figure 9-1, which shows the inverse demand function for $\dot{x} = \epsilon > 0$ and displays (13) graphically. The

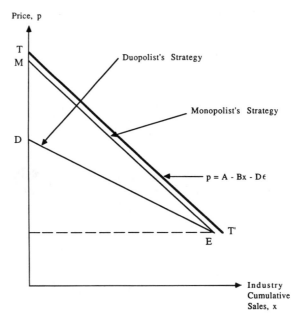

Figure 9-1. Feedback Pricing Strategies of a Monopolist and Duopolist

straight line ME represents a monopolist's optimal pricing policy with ME approaching TT' arbitrarily closely. The duopolists' pricing strategy is given by DE with E arbitrarily close to T'. Thus, we see that competition will induce lower prices everywhere and the price decline in $p - x$ space is smaller relative to the case of the monopolist. Since the price-path behavior is independent of α in the $p - x$ space, we find, as in (11), that as α increases, price declines faster over time. Using the same arguments, we see why output rate $y^\star$ is decreasing in α in equation (9). Turning now to equation (10), we find that the optimal profits are independent of α. In other words, the duopolists adjust their outputs and prices depending on α, but always so as to obtain the same profits regardless of α. On the other hand, industry profits for a duopoly are $(1/3b)(a - bc - x_E)^2$, while profits for a perfectly discriminating monopolist are $(a - bc - x_E)^2/2b$ so that competition has reduced profits by 33 percent. The behavior of output, prices, and profits with respect to the other parameters, a, b, and c is as expected.

Preentry Price Path

Let us now turn our attention to the preentry price behavior. Before T_E, firm 1 is a monopolist and must choose an output rate y_1 so as to maximize its profits. This problem can be written as

$$V_1 = \max_{y_1} \int_0^{T_E} (A - Bx_1 - Dy_1 - c) y_1 \, dt + \pi_1(x_E) \tag{14}$$

subject to

$$\dot{x}_1 = y_1 \tag{15}$$

$$\pi_1(x_E) = (1/6b)(a - bc - x_E)^2 \tag{16}$$

$$x_1(0) = 0 \tag{17}$$

In order to solve this problem, it is necessary to know the value of T_E. There are two ways of thinking about this. Firm 1 can take T_E as given and solve for y_{1_t}, $t \in [0, T_E)$ and examine if the assumed T_E would be an equilibrium choice for firm 2 given its strategy y_1. Alternatively, firm 1 can pick an output path sequentially at each instant t depending on whether or not 2 has entered. Given this sequential decision making by firm 1, firm 2 may decide at each instant whether or not it should enter. It would of course be possible to define an equilibrium using this sequential approach. Such an equilibrium would be subgame perfect. The next section will contrast the two equilibria. Here, T_E is assumed to be known and the optimal strategy for firm 1 is derived in the manner of Eliashberg and Jeuland [1986].

To solve equations (14) through (17) for a given T_E, it is easier to examine the following fixed-end-point problem:

$$\pi^B = \max_{y_1} \int_0^{T_E} (A - Bx_1 - Dy_1 - c) y_1 \, dt \tag{18}$$

subject to

$$\dot{x}_1 = y_1 \tag{19}$$

$$x_1(0) = 0, \quad x_1(0) = x_E \tag{20}$$

From Rao [1986a], the optimal solution has the following properties:

$$y_1^* = x_E / T_E \tag{21}$$

$$dp/dx = -B \tag{22}$$

$$\pi^B = (1/b)\{(a - bc) x_E - (x_E^2/2)[1 + (2/\alpha T_E)]\} \tag{23}$$

The optimal policy for the monopolist is to produce at a constant rate over $(0, T_E)$. The price path in the $p - x$ space is a straight line parallel to the demand curve. Finally, from (23), we see that as αT_E increases, the monopolist is able to maximally price-discriminate for a given x_E, thereby increasing his profits. Since π^B has now been obtained as a function of x_E

alone, it is trivial to solve for x_E in (14) to (19) by maximizing $\left[\pi^B + \pi_1(x_E)\right]$ with respect to x_E and then choosing $y_1{}^*$ in accordance with (21). Performing this, we find the solution to (14) to (19) to be

$$y_1^*(T_E) = \alpha(a - bc)/(3 + \alpha T_E) \tag{24}$$

Thus the preentry output rate is inversely proportional to T_E. In other words, if entry by firm 2 is anticipated to be late, firm 1's preentry output rate is decreased. Moreover, as α increases, the optimal output rate is higher.

Competition and Entry Timing

We can now proceed to investigate the central issue of this chapter: pricing in the face of entry. To do this, a Nash equilibrium in simple strategies prior to entry will be examined first. Firm 1 chooses $y_1^*\,(T_E)$ with an implied x_E and firm 2 chooses T_E. The equilibrium is described by the pair (y_1^*, T_E).

Equilibrium in Simple Strategies

From the prior section, we know that

$$y_1^*(T_E) = \alpha(a - bc)/(3 + \alpha T_E) \tag{25}$$

Firm 2's problem is one of maximizing its profits $\pi_2(x_E)$ given by equation (10) less costs of entry. Assume that, ceteris paribus, it is less expensive for firm 2 to enter if entry is delayed. This is consistent with the idea that hastening entry by compressing the interval over which investment for entry is carried out is costly. So firm 2 is assumed to choose T_E so as to maximize its value V_2 given by

$$V_2(T_E) = \max_{T_E} \left[-F(T_E) + (1/6b)(a - bc - x_E)^2\right] \tag{26}$$

subject to

$$x_E = \alpha T_E(a - bc)/(3 + \alpha T_E) \tag{27}$$

where $F(T_E)$ is the cost of entry. This cost is assumed to be decreasing and convex in T_E. A necessary condition for solving firm 2's problem is then

$$-F'(T_E) - (\alpha/b)(a - bc - x_E)(a - bc)/(3 + \alpha T_E)^2 = 0 \tag{28}$$

The Nash equilibrium for this problem is then the solution to (25) and (28) with $x_E = T_E y_1^*(T_E)$.

To see the ideas clearly, consider a numerical example with the following values:

$$a = b = 1, \quad c = 0, \quad \alpha = 1$$

Further assume that entry can take place only at integer values of T_E and

$$F_0 = \infty$$
$$F_1 = f = 0.4$$
$$F_k = 0, k \geq 2$$

With these parameters, firm 2's entry strategies are to enter at $T_E = 1$ or 2. Any further delay does not reduce entry costs. Firm 1's strategies are $y_1^*(1)$ and $y_1^*(2)$ since we require that for optimality, equation (25) be satisfied. The profits under the four scenarios are displayed in figure 9–2. It is easy to see that for this problem, $T_E = 1$ is a dominant strategy for firm 2 and corresponding to that, firm 1's best strategy is to choose an output rate of $y_1^* = 0.25$. The values of the two firms are respectively 0.25 and 0.05375.

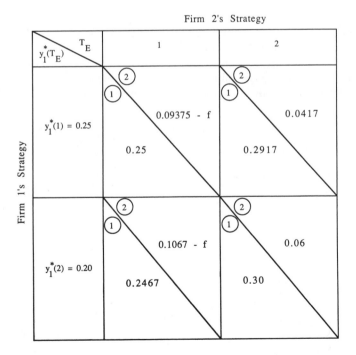

Figure 9–2. Nash Equilibrium in Simple Strategies

There is an important feature of this equilibrium, which is that firm 2 has adopted $T_E = 1$, no matter what. We could ask the question, what if firm 1 chose an output level greater than 0.25? Would it still pay firm 2 to enter at $T_E = 1$? And, if not, could firm 1 take advantage of this? It is this idea of sophisticated thinking on the part of both firms (firm 2 cannot be really commited to $T_E = 1$ no matter what y_1^* is and firm 1 is aware of this) that leads to the sequential equilibrium concept to which we now turn.

Sequential Equilibrium

The best way to understand sequential equilibrium in the context of entry is to visualize entry prevention. Two questions can be asked. Can firm 1 adopt a preentry pricing strategy that would prevent entry at some T_E? Will such a strategy be superior for firm 1 relative to allowing entry at T_E? If the answer to both questions is yes, then it is obvious that T_E is not a candidate for entry under equilibrium. At first glance, this may suggest that firm 1 has unlimited opportunity to deter entry. Such is not the case. For the numerical example considered in the previous section, we find that entry cannot be prevented beyond period 2. The real question is whether firm 1 should find a choice of entry timing by firm 2 credible. If not, firm 1 should devise its strategies with the knowledge that firm 2 will intelligently choose its strategy conditioned on what firm 1 has done. This particular concept has been used by Rao and Rutenberg [1979] in the context of entry in a growing market and by Spence [1979] in studying investment in growing markets.

To illustrate the sequential equilibrium, let us return to the numerical example. Let $v_{it}(x_t)$ be the value of firm i from period t on given that x_t is the cumulative sales of firm i up to t. Since we know that entry will occur surely at $t = 2$, we can use backward induction by focusing on $t = 2$ first and then on $t = 1$.

$t = 2$

$$v_{12}(x_2) = v_{22}(x_2) = (1 - x_2)^2/6 \qquad (29)$$

$t = 1$

$$v_{21}(x_1) = \max \begin{cases} [(1 - x_1)^2/6] - 0.4 & \text{if firm 2 enters} \\ \\ v_{22}(x_1 + y_1^*(x_1)) & \text{if firm 2 does not enter} \end{cases} \qquad (30)$$

$$v_{11}(x_1) = \max \begin{cases} (1 - x_1)^2/6 & \text{if firm 2 enters} \\ \\ \max_{y_1} \int_1^2 (1 - x - y_1)y_1\,dt + v_{12}(x_2) & \text{if firm 2 does not enter} \\ \\ \text{subject to} \quad \dot{x} = y_1, \quad x(1) = x_1 \end{cases} \qquad (31)$$

Solving the optimal control problem in (31), we find that $y_1^* = (1 - x_1)/4$ and firm 1's profits are higher when firm 2 does not enter. Specifically,

$$v_{11}(x_1) = \begin{cases} (1 - x_1)^2/6 & \text{if firm 2 enters} \\ \\ (1 - x_1)^2/4 & \text{if firm 2 does not enter} \end{cases} \tag{32}$$

Now turning to firm 2, substituting for y_1^* in (30), we obtain

$$v_{21}(x_1) = \max \begin{cases} \left[(1 - x_1)^2/6\right] - 0.4 & \text{if firm 2 enters} \\ \\ (1 - x_1)^2 9/16 & \text{if firm 2 does not enter} \end{cases} \tag{33}$$

It is easy to see from (33) that firm 2 does not enter if $x_1 > 0.2593439$. Corresponding to this critical value of x_1, firm 1's output rate in period 2 is $y_1^* = (1 - x_1)/4 = 0.185164$, which results in $x_2 = 0.4445079$. Finally, we find at $t = 0$ the following situation obtains:

$t = 0$

$$v_{20}(0) = \begin{cases} \left[(1 - x_1)^2/6\right] - 0.4 & \text{if } x_1 < 0.2593439 \\ \\ (1 - x_2)^2 - 0.4 & \text{otherwise} \end{cases} \tag{34}$$

$$v_{10}(0) = \max_{y_1} \int_0^1 (1 - x - y_1)y_1 dt + v_{11}(x_1) \tag{35}$$

subject to $\dot{x} = y_1, \quad x(0) = 0$

Solving (35), we find that

$$v_{10}(0) = 0.2955979 \text{ and } y_1 = 0.2593439, \quad t \in (0, 1)$$

In other words, firm 1's output rate is sufficiently higher than that corresponding to the equilibrium in simple strategies ($y_1 = 0.25$, in the prior section) to delay firm 2's entry. This leads to higher profits for it. The full equilibrium can now be described as follows:

Interval	Outputs under Sequential Equilibrium	
	Firm 1	Firm 2
$t \in (0,1)$	0.2593	0
$t \in (0,2)$	0.1852	0
$t \in (2,\infty)$	$.0926 \exp(- (t - T_E)/3)$	$.0926 \exp(- (t - T_E)/3)$
		(from equation 9)

This can be contrasted with the equilibrium in simple strategies, which yields:

Interval	Outputs under Equilibrium in Simple Strategies	
	Firm 1	Firm 2
$t \in (0,1)$	0.25	0
$t \in (1,\infty)$	$0.125 \exp(-t/3)$	$0.125 \exp(-t/3)$

There are several points we can note about the sequential equilibrium. The time path of industry output is displayed in figure 9–3. Initial output rate is larger relative to simple equilibrium. Moreover, calculations show that firm 1 obtains sales from 44 percent of the eventual market prior to entry, while under the simple equilibrium it obtains 25 percent. The eventual share of total sales for firm 1 under sequential equilibrium is 72.2 percent, while in the simple equilibrium it is 62.5 percent. Finally, firm 1's output rate is declining in the preentry period for the sequential equilibrium. In contrast, if firm 2 were committed to $T_E = 2$, we know that firm 1 would have held a constant output rate of 0.3 over $t \in (0, 2)$.

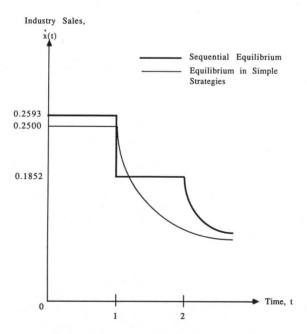

Figure 9–3. Industry Sales over Time

Price Paths under Alternative Equilibria

For the duopoly period, we know from equation (12) that price follows the path

$$p_t = (2/3)(1 - x_E) \exp(-(t - T_E)/3), \quad t \geq T_E \quad (36)$$

In the preentry period, we have two possible cases, one the equilibrium in simple strategies and the other the sequential equilibrium. Each will be examined in turn.

For the numerical example at hand, in the first case the output rate is $y_1 = 0.25$ for $t \in (0,1)$ and $T_E = 1$. Thus, the price path is

$$p_t = 1 - 0.25t - 0.25$$

or

$$p_t = 1 - 0.25(1 + t), \quad t \in (0,1) \quad (37)$$

In the second case, $T_E = 2$ and the output rate is $y_1^* = 0.2593$, $t \in (0,1)$, and $y_1^* = 0.1852$, $t \in (1,2)$. The price path then is given by

$$p_t = \begin{cases} 1 - 0.2593(1 + t) & t \in (0,1) \\ 0.7407 - 0.1852t & t \in (1,2) \end{cases} \quad (38)$$

Combining (36) through (38), we obtain figure 9–4, which displays the price path over time for the two equilibria. Figure 9–4a corresponds to the case of equilibrium in simple strategies while figure 9–4b is for the case of sequential equilibrium. In both cases, we find that there is no discontinuity of the price path at the time of entry. This is because industry output, as seen in figure 9–3, is continuous in time. This is in contrast to the result of Eliashberg and Jeuland [1986], who find a discontinuity in the price path. The reason for this difference is that focus here is on undifferentiated products, whereas Eliashberg and Jeuland are dealing with differentiated products. On the other hand, firm 1's output shows a discontinuity at $T_E(= 2)$ as seen in figure 9–3.

The more interesting feature in this model is seen in figure 9–4. At $t = 1$, *there is a discontinuity in price and the price is increasing.* This corresponds to the discontinuity in industry output in figure 9–3. The reason for this is that over $t \in (0,1)$, firm 1's output rate is driven by considerations of competition: firm 1's choice is designed to delay entry by firm 2. Since 2 can only enter at $t = 2$ once $t > 1$, firm 1 feels free to cut back on its output in $t \in (1,2)$ and allow prices to increase. *Thus we have here a case of penetration pricing arising specifically out of competitive considerations with a view to delay rival entry.* All prior studies on dynamic pricing have shown the optimality of penetration pricing

a. Equilibrium In Simple Strategies

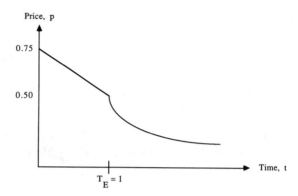

b. Sequential Equilibrium

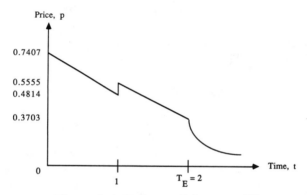

Figure 9-4. Industry Price over Time

for diffusion purposes (i.e., charge a low price to speed the adoption of a product; then increase price). (See, for example, Kalish [1983a].) While conventional wisdom would argue for low initial prices to deter entry, to my knowledge there exists no formal model that demonstrates the optimality of increasing prices over time from the point of view of competition.

Conclusion

This chapter has analyzed the strategic pricing decision of a firm facing entry in a durable-goods market characterized by eventual saturation. Demand diffuses at a constant rate and the market potential is assumed to be a function of price. Within this market, the preentry pricing strategy of a monopolist has been characterized when the entry of a second firm is treated endogenously. Equilibrium outcomes have also been examined under two alternative equilibria for the entry-timing problem: an equilibrium in simple strategies and a sequential equilibrium. The key result obtained is that penetration strategy is indeed optimal for a sophisticated monopolist: one who views the entry problem as a sequential game. Such a monopolist will start off with high output rates and decrease them. The decreased output may actually result in price increasing during the preentry period. Thus a monopolist may delay rival entry by starting off with a low price and increasing it later.

The concepts of sequential equilibrium and subgame perfectness are becoming increasingly popular. This chapter has demonstrated their usefulness in the context of preentry pricing strategies. They have great potential for yielding sharp results for many marketing problems involving competition.

Notes

1. See also Clarke, Darrough, and Heineke [1982], Feichtinger and Dockner [1985], and Jorgensen [1983].

2. Consumers are assumed to be myopic, so they do not anticipate future price declines. For a model of consumers with expectations, see Stokey [1981].

Appendix 9A-1

Consider the duopoly described by equations (5)-(8), with symmetric firms. Let $T_E = 0$ with $x(T_E) = x_0$. Then the maximizing problem of firm i, $i = 1,2$ is

$$\max_{y_i} \int_0^\infty (p - c) y_i \, dt \qquad \text{(A-1)}$$

subject to

$$\dot{x}_i = y_i \qquad \text{(A-2)}$$

$$p = A - Bx_1 - Bx_2 - Dy_1 - Dy_2 \qquad \text{(A-3)}$$

with $x = x_1 + x_2$, $y = y_1 + y_2$, and $x(0) = x_0$. The Hamiltonian for firm i is then given by

$$H_i = (p - c) y_i + \lambda_i y_i + \mu_i y_j, \quad j = 3 - i \qquad \text{(A-4)}$$

A necessary condition for optimality then is

$$\partial H_i / \partial y_i = 0$$

which yields

$$\lambda_i = -A + Bx_1 + Bx_2 + 2Dy_i + Dy_j + c \qquad \text{(A-5)}$$

Differentiating (A-5) with respect to t we obtain

$$\dot{\lambda}_i = B\dot{x}_1 + B\dot{x}_2 + 2D\dot{y}_i + D\dot{y}_j \qquad \text{A(-6)}$$

Now, from the adjoint equation for i, we have

$$\dot{\lambda}_i = -\partial H_i / \partial x_i = B\dot{x}_i \qquad \text{(A-7)}$$

Putting (A-7) in (A-6) yields,

$$B\dot{x}_j + 2D\dot{y}_i + D\dot{y}_j = 0 \qquad \text{(A-8)}$$

Exploiting symmetry, $x_1 = x_2$ and $y_1 = y_2$ so that we have

$$B\dot{x} + 3D\dot{y} = 0$$

or

$$\dot{y} + (B/3D)\,\dot{x} = 0 \qquad \text{(A-9)}$$

Denote $\gamma = -(B/3D) = -\alpha/3 < 0$. Then the solution to (A-9) is given by

$$y = K \exp(\gamma\, t) \qquad \text{(A-10)}$$

K being the constant of integration. From the transversality condition, we require that $\lim_{t \to \infty} \lambda = 0$, so that we have in (A-5)

$$Bx(\infty) + (3D/2)\, y(\infty) = A - x_0 - c \qquad \text{(A-11)}$$

Using (A-10), we find

$$y(\infty) = 0 \text{ and}$$
$$x(\infty) = x_0 + K\int_0^\infty \exp(\gamma\, t)\, dt$$
$$= x_0 - (K/\gamma)$$

Substituting for $x(\infty)$ and $y(\infty)$ in (A-11) yields

$$-(K/\gamma) = A/B - c/B - x_0 = (a - bc - x_0) \qquad \text{(A-12)}$$

To obtain x_t, we can now integrate (A-10) and use (A-12) to substitute for K. This leads to

$$x(t) = x_0 + K\int_0^\infty \exp(\gamma u)\, du$$

or

$$x(t) = x_0 + (a - bc - x_0)\left[1 - \exp(\gamma t)\right] \qquad \text{(A-13)}$$

The profits of firm i can now be computed as one half of the industry profits. Combining (A-1), (A-10), and (A-13), we find this to be

$$\pi_i = (1/2)\int_0^\infty (A - Bx - Dy - c)\, y dt \qquad \text{(A-14)}$$

First differentiate (A–13) with respect to t to get

$$y = \dot{x} = -\gamma(a - bc - x) \tag{A-15}$$

So (A–14) reduces to

$$\pi_i = (1/3b) \int_{x_0}^{x(\infty)} (a - bc - x)\, dx$$

or

$$\pi_i = (a - bc - x_0)^2/6b \tag{A-16}$$

To obtain the price-path dynamics, we note that

$$\dot{p} = -B\dot{x} - D\dot{y}$$

or

$$\dot{p} = -(2\,\alpha/9b)(a - bc - x) < 0 \qquad (\because a - bc \geq x) \tag{A-17}$$

An alternative way of writing (A–17) is to evaluate p as a function of x. We find

$$\dot{p} = -(2B/3)\,\dot{x}$$

or

$$dp/dx = -2B/3 \tag{A-18}$$

Appendix 9A–2:
Glossary of Technical Terms

Expression	Definition
t	Time
q_t	Total industry sales at t
y_{i_t}	Output of firm i, $i = 1,2$, at t
y_t	$y_{1_t} + y_{2_t}$
x_{i_t}	Cumulative output of firm i at t
x_t	$x_{1_t} + x_{2_t}$
p_t	Price at t
$g(p)$	Demand function
M_{px_t}	Potential market at price p and cumulative output x_t
$\dot{x}_{i_t}$	y_{i_t}
T_E	Time firm 2 enters
X_E	Cumulative output at T_E
a, b	Parameters of demand function
A, B, D	Parameters of inverse demand function
V_i	Sum of discounted profits of i over $(0, \infty)$
v_{ij}	Value of firm i at time j
α	Diffusion coefficient
π_i	Profits of firm i over (T_E, ∞)
π^B	Profits of firm 1 over $(0, T_E)$
c	Marginal cost

10
Competitive Pricing Behavior in Distribution Systems

Steven M. Shugan
Abel P. Jeuland

C ompetition is a major force shaping the institution of channels of distribution. Researchers and practitioners in the distribution area usually distinguish between horizontal-channel competition and channel-system competition. (See Kotler [1980, p. 551]). Horizontal competition refers to competition at the same channel level. For example, wholesalers are in horizontal competition. System competition refers to competition between different channels. System competition can occur between different types of channels. Stern [1982, p. 71] calls this form of competition "intertype competition."

These concepts of competition are useful for better understanding within channel relationships, such as channel cooperation and channel coordination. Channel members (e.g., manufacturers, wholesalers, retailers, dealers, and manufacturer representatives) often seek cooperation. Jeuland and Shugan [1983b] show that cooperation can increase channel profitability because channel cooperation leads to a coordination of channel decision making. Jeuland and Shugan [1983b] also discuss different mechanisms used by channel members to achieve coordination. Such mechanisms are important because channels do not easily achieve coordination. For example, a manufacturer may often disagree with its own dealers. Behavioral scientists, as well as researchers with a sociological orientation, call these disagreements "within-channel competition" or "channel conflict." Vertical-channel conflict can destroy coordination and lead a channel away from maximum profits.

Behavioral science approaches and sociological approaches continue to contribute to the channel literature. These traditional approaches have greatly influenced research in the area of channels of distribution and, particularly, research on channel competition. A few papers have deviated from this tradition and employed a multivariate statistical approach.[1] This approach seeks to uncover significant factors affecting distribution decisions. Until recently, the quantitative modeling research approach of theory building has been very notably absent. It is not the purpose of this chapter to explore the reasons underlying this absence. Instead, as quantitative marketing modelers, we will attempt to partially remedy this situation. We believe that there is a great benefit derived from employing different research approaches in the important area of channel research. Within this vast area of research there are many problems. And different approaches may be applicable to different problems.

In the past few years, several model-oriented papers have helped develop the economics of channels of distribution. These papers include Doraiswamy, McGuire, and Staelin [1979], McGuire and Staelin [1983a,b], Zusman and Etgar [1981], Jeuland and Shugan [1983a,b, 1988], Coughlan [1985], and Pasternack [1985]. This research in marketing is complemented by work in economics that continues to investigate the area of channels and, particularly, the area of vertical integration. The economic theory of agency is proving to be a very potent approach to analyzing multimember institutions such as channels of distribution.

The objective of this chapter is to draw some of the general principles and concepts that emerge from the marketing articles just cited and that deal with the simple economics paradigm of profit maximization. More specifically, we operationalize the concept of competition as a reaction function and study two basic sets of influences on the nature of the reaction function of the channel: first, within-channel interactions; and, second, between-channels interactions. The first case of within-channel interactions deals with the vertical dimension of the channel. For this case, we address the issue of durability of channel structure. Then, the equilibrium between competing channels with the same or different structures is derived. The equilibrium implications result from the joint effect of within-channel interactions and horizontal competition. We confirm the link uncovered by McGuire and Staelin between equilibrium profitability and both the vertical dimension of the channel (channel structure) and the horizontal dimension of product differentiation, even though some of our assumptions differ from theirs. Coughlan generalizes McGuire and Staelin's work to include a more general demand function and multiple middlemen. She argues that middlemen can be used to shield the manufacturer from competition by decreasing the reactivity of the channel. She also examines some of the institutional arrangements we discuss in this chapter. Finally, we extend the model by incorporating fixed costs and show their influence on the specific problem of intrabrand competition.

Our chapter is thus organized as follows. The next section develops the different reaction functions corresponding to different channel arrangements: coordinated, leader-follower, or conventional channels. The subsequent major section addresses the stability of these different channel arrangements, a question not considered by McGuire and Staelin or by Coughlan. Coordination is found to be a stable arrangement, a finding that may explain the emergence of vertical marketing systems as the dominant form of channels of distribution. The following section discusses the equilibrium implications—what the market price is—of different channel arrangements and different degrees of product substitutability. The relationships between channel reactions and equilibrium prices and profits are discussed. The section after that introduces fixed costs in the analysis and shows their critical importance in one example: intrabrand competition. The final section gives our conclusion and tries to foresee future research on channel competition in the modeling area.

Operationalizing the Notion of Channel Competition: Channel Reaction as a Function of Channel Structure

The notion of competition should capture a firm's reaction to its environment and, in particular, to the other firms in the same market. This partial definition of competition appears to be generally applicable and, thus, applicable in the channel area. Consequently, we begin by operationalizing the notion of a reaction function in the context of channels of distribution. For example, we expect that a vertically integrated channel does not react in the same way as a conventional channel (i.e., a channel comprised of independent buyers and resellers). Because many types of decisions (e.g. advertising, shelf space, and margins) are made by resellers, many different types of reaction functions could be defined. For example, we could define advertising reaction functions or margin (price) reaction functions. However, at this early stage of research, it is not productive to investigate too many phenomena at once. For this reason, this chapter will deal with only one type of reseller decision—the margin (or price) decision. We do not wish to imply that margin decisions are more important than advertising decisions, shelf-space decisions, or other reseller-support decisions. We merely seek a research strategy aimed at developing a simple yet general framework. We hope that future research will provide additional complexities and realism. Ultimately, our framework should predict how the structure of the channel affects retail prices. We start by studying reaction functions because particular channel arrangements, (e.g., vertically integrated, conventional, leader-follower) will imply specific within-channel reaction functions. For example, an independent wholesaler may react differently to a manufacturer's price increase than a franchise will react to its manufacturing franchisor. We expect that the price to the end buyer will be a function of the intermediate within-channel margin-reaction functions.

To formalize resellers' pricing decision making, we first specify the demand conditions. We follow McGuire and Staelin [1983b] in postulating a duopolist model of demand for two differentiated products:

$$q_i = a - bp_i + \gamma p_j \qquad i,j = 1,2 \qquad j \neq i \tag{1}$$

where q_i is the demand for product i sold through reseller i at price p_i given that the price of the other product is p_j. The parameters of the demand equation satisfy $a > 0$, $b > \gamma > 0$. The condition $b > \gamma$ is necessary for the demand function to be well behaved. For example, if both products are available at the same price p, $q_i = q_j = q = a - (b - \gamma)p$ and is decreasing with price if and only if $b > \gamma$. γ measures the effect of the other product's price on the product demand and thus operationalizes the degree of substitutability between the two products.[2] The closer γ is to b, the greater is the substitutability between the products. This measure of substitutability is used by Coughlan [1985]. She shows that substitutability can be defined with a more general demand function.

We select a two-product market rather than a more general situation of multiple products and multiple resellers in order to keep the model simple. We believe that a two-product market is sufficiently rich to be a useful first step toward modeling more complex and, possibly, more realistic situations. However, realism is not totally compromised because, in many local markets, competition often means competition between two different outlets and two products or product lines. Figure 10–1 illustrates the economic scenario under investigation.

Also, following McGuire and Staelin, we assume that the manufacturer and reseller profit functions are respectively given by

$$\pi_i = w_i q_i \qquad i = 1,2 \tag{2}$$

and

$$\pi_i = m_i q_i = (p_i - w_i) q_i \qquad i = 1,2 \tag{3}$$

where w_i is the wholesale price for product i (the price that manufacturer i charges reseller i) and m_i is reseller i's margin. p_i is the price paid by the buyer to the reseller.[3] Because total channel profits are $\Pi_i + \pi_i = p_i q_i$, if one also assumes zero marginal costs for the reseller, the relation between price, p_i, and manufacturer and reseller decision variables, w_i and m_i, is given by

$$p_i = w_i + m_i \tag{4}$$

Equation (4) shows that the price is the immediate consequence of the separate margin decisions, w_i and m_i, of the manufacturer and the reseller.[4] We assume that the channel members (manufacturers and resellers) seek to maximize their own profit functions. We also assume that no cooperation exists at any horizontal level. It is indeed illegal for two manufacturers to cooperate and also for two resellers (wholesalers or retailers) to cooperate. In addition, we limit our investigation to the situation where the manufacturer and reseller of one channel cannot observe the relationship between manufacturer and reseller of the competing channel. As a result, noncooperative behavior of one channel implies that only the price of the other channel is taken as given. For example, manufacturer 1 maximizes his profits Π_1, taking p_2 as given. We thus differ

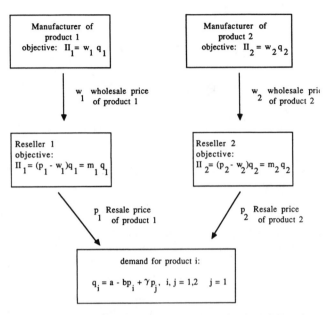

Figure 10-1. Distribution of Two Differentiated Products

from McGuire and Staelin [1983b], who allow manufacturer 1 to maximize his profits Π_1, given w_2.

Reaction Function of the Conventional Channel (C)

We first assume that the relationship in the channel is symmetric and that all channel members display equal degrees of sophistication. We define as conventional the symmetric arrangement where the manufacturer and the reseller independently maximize their own profit, assuming no degree of control over the other partner's decision. In other words, the conventional manufacturer-reseller channel is the situation where manufacturer and reseller independently choose their own margin, taking the other's margin as given:[5]

$$
\text{Conventional channel}
\begin{cases}
\textit{Manufacturer:} \quad \max_{w_i} \Pi_i \quad \Big|\; m_i, p_j \qquad i, j = 1,2 \quad j \neq i \quad (5) \\[2em]
\textit{Reseller:} \quad \max_{m_i} \Pi_i \quad \Big|\; w_i, p_j \qquad i, j = 1,2 \quad j \neq i \quad (6)
\end{cases}
$$

It is easy to derive from optimization (5), i.e., $\partial\Pi_i/\partial w_i|_{m_i,p_j} = 0$, the following condition

$$w_i = \frac{a - bm_i + \gamma p_j}{b} \qquad i, j = 1,2 \quad j \neq i \tag{7}$$

and from optimization (6), i.e., $\partial\pi_i/\partial m_i|_{w_i,p_j} = 0$, the condition

$$m_i = \frac{a - bw_i + \gamma p_j}{2b} \qquad i, j = 1,2 \quad j \neq i \tag{8}$$

Equations (7) and (8) are within-channel reaction functions. Equation (7) represents the manufacturer's wholesale price, w_i, as affected by reseller i's margin m_i. Equation (8) represents the retailer's margin as a function of the manufacturer's wholesale price. In addition, both w_i and m_i are functions of the price, p_j, charged by the competing channel. In other words, decision rules (7) and (8) reflect both within-channel division of the total profit margin between manufacturer and reseller, and horizontal competition between the two channels. If the price of the other channel, p_j, is increased, the two channel members find that they should increase their own margins w_i and m_i. However, if reseller i increases m_i, the manufacturer finds that he must decrease his margin w_i (and reciprocally). This means that the pressure to compete with the other channel makes each partner partially compensate for the actions of the other channel member. It would be useful to investigate the class of demand functions for which this result holds.

We derive the reaction of the conventional channel that results from the interplay of the just-mentioned manufacturer and reseller decision rules, i.e., the functional form that links p_i to p_j. Using equation (4), we obtain

$$p_i = \frac{2}{3b}(a + \gamma p_j) \tag{9}$$

As explained earlier, the size of parameter γ in relation to b is a measure of substitutability between the two products. Hence, we expect that channel price reaction should be increasing in γ and decreasing in b. Coughlan [1985] also shows that channel reactivity and channel-member reactivity depend on substitutability.

Reaction of the Leader-Follower Channel (LF)

This situation corresponds to the departure from the symmetry of the conventional arrangement and assumes that the manufacturer is more sophisticated than the reseller. The reseller is still assumed to maximize his profit independently given p_j and w_i. However, the manufacturer realizes the existence of the reaction function of his reseller—that is, $m_i(w_i, p_j)$—given by equation (8). He factors this internal reaction function into his own decision rule. We, therefore, denote the manufacturer as the leader.

Leader-
follower
channel $\left\{ \begin{array}{} \textit{Manufacturer:} \quad \max \quad \Pi_i \\[1em] \text{Leader} \quad w_i \\[1em] \textit{Reseller:} \quad \max \quad \Pi_i \\[1em] \text{Follower} \quad m_i \end{array} \right.$

	$i, j = 1,2 \quad j \neq i$	
$m_i(w_i, p_j), p_j$		
	$i, j = 1,2 \quad j \neq i$	
w_i, p_j		

The optimization problem of the manufacturer (leader) follows.

$$\max_{w_i} \quad w_i q_i = \max_{w_i} \quad w_i[a - b(w_i + m_i) + \gamma p_j]$$

where m_i is the function given by equation (8). The new decision rule of the manufacturer follows.

$$w_i = \frac{a + \gamma p_j}{2b} \tag{10}$$

Equation (10) shows that, given the same price of the competing channel, p_j, the more sophisticated manufacturer wants a larger margin than the manufacturer who does not take his reseller's decision into account (because $a - bm_i + \gamma p_j < a + \gamma p_j$). As a consequence, the reseller receives a smaller margin. Combining equations (8) and (10) gives the reaction function of the leader-follower channel arrangement:

$$p_i = \frac{3}{4b}(a + \gamma p_j) \tag{11}$$

Contrasting equations (9) and (11) illustrates that the LF channel (leader-follower) responds with a higher price than the C channel $[(3/4) > (2/3)]$. The higher price is caused by the manufacturer demanding a larger margin and the reseller not completely compensating for this increase. The higher price of the C channel is quite significant. The higher price implies that the structure of the channel (C versus LF) does have an influence on the way the channel competes.

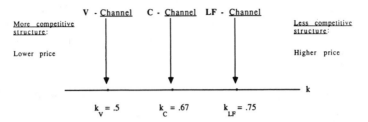

Figure 10-2. Channel Price Reaction, p_s, to Price of Other Channel, p_j, as a Function of Channel Structure $S(S = V, C, or LF)$ $p_s = k_s(a + \gamma p_j)/b$

Reaction of the Vertical System (V)

Another important channel arrangement is the situation where manufacturer and reseller coordinate their decisions. This case corresponds to the maximization of total channel profits, i.e., $(w_i + m_i)q_i = p_i(a - bp_i + \gamma p_j)$ given the competitive channel price. Given the price charged by the competing channel, p_j, the vertical channel reacts according to the following function.

$$p_i = \frac{a + \gamma p_j}{2b} \tag{12}$$

As a consequence, the V-type channel (vertical system or coordinated system) responds with a lower price than the C channel and the LF channel. Figure 10-2 summarizes our findings. We find the V-type channel to be the most competitive. The existence of within-channel reaction functions, given respectively by (7) and (8) for the C channel and (8) for the LF channel, make these channels less responsive to the outside environment. In other words, these channel arrangements are less competitive. In order to survive, the LF and C channels must have some compensating advantage (for example, lower marginal costs.)

Having established the competitiveness of different channel structures, we might ask which structure is more enduring. For example, is the more competitive V-type structure more or less stable than the less competitive LF and C structures?

Are Certain Channel Structures More Enduring?

Given our premise of channel members seeking profit maximization, the last question can be rephrased as follows: "Can channel profits be increased by switching from one channel arrangement to another?[6]

This question is straightforward to answer. Given the price of the competing channel p_j, the profit-maximizing reaction is, by definition, the V-type reaction, because the V-type channel maximizes total channel profits. In other words, V-arrangement profits can always be divided between manufacturer and reseller in such a way that both are more profitable than they would be under the LF-profit division or the C-profit division. In fact, at any given price p_j of the competing channel, one can easily quantify the gain by switching from the C or LF structures to the V arrangement. Given the best response of equation (12) to the price p_j charged by the competing channel, maximum achievable profits are

$$\pi_V = \Pi_i + \pi_i = p_i q_i = \frac{(a + \gamma p_j)^2}{4b} \tag{13}$$

In contrast, the C-channel—with a response function given by equation (9)— would only achieve

$$\pi_C = \frac{2(a + \gamma p_j)^2}{9b} \tag{14}$$

i.e., 83 percent of maximum achievable profits. The LF channel—with a response function given by equation (11)—would achieve

$$\pi_{LF} = \frac{3(a + \gamma p_j)^2}{16b} \tag{15}$$

i.e., 75 percent of maximum achievable profits. These results are quite intuitive. As the price is increased from the V price to the C price or the LF price (see figure 10-2), the higher channel margin (profit per unit sold) does not compensate for the decline in volume sold. Total channel profits, therefore, decline and channel members are worse off than they would be with an appropriate division of coordinated channel profits.

The implication of this finding is that vertical systems (or coordinated systems) may be more enduring than other channel arrangements. Channel-of-distribution specialists have indeed acknowledged the predominance of vertical marketing systems or systems acting as vertically integrated systems. Obviously, if different channel arrangements had widely different cost structures, cost advantages might favor an otherwise less profitable (lower-revenue) channel arrangement. It is beyond the scope of this chapter to address the complex issue of cost/structure interactions. Our model would need to incorporate many variables in order to satisfactorily address these cost interactions. For example, costs are generally related to the amount of information possessed by each channel member. The present research effort has at least highlighted the importance of these issues and should encourage future research.

Equilibrium of Duopolist Distribution: What Are the Market Prices?

The preceding two sections have dealt with the profit-maximizing behavior of channel members and the role of channel structure. The vertical system offers the best response in terms of generating revenues. If the costs of channel coordination or integration are not significantly larger than the costs of other channel arrangements, then vertical (or coordinated) systems are more profitable and thus more enduring. This result is consistent with the actual observation of vertical (or coordinated) systems being the dominant form of distribution, at least in the United States.

The profit maximizing behavior of the economic agents (as described in the previous sections) cause specific market prices. The equilibrium market prices result from the interplay of the economic agents' decisions rules (as specified by equations (9), (11), or (12) depending upon the channel arrangement). The market equilibrium is, by definition, the consequence of the economic agents' decisions and thus is not foreseen by them. Rules (9) and (11) lead to unstable or nonenduring equilibria because any channel moving from decision (9) or (11) to (12) would increase profits. In duopolist distribution, the equilibrium resulting from a V-channel competing against a V-channel is stable, while the others are not. However, these other equilibria (conditional equilibria), although unstable, may be of interest because their equilibrium point is very profitable. Table 10–1 summarizes the different possible equilibria (some being conditional equilibria): V/V is the duopolist structure where two vertical systems compete, C/C where both channels are conventional, C/LF where one channel is conventional and the other a leader-follower arrangement, and so on. The mathematical derivations are not difficult and have therefore been omitted. The V/V structure, for example, has an equilibrium price that is obtained by simultaneously solving $p_i = (a + \gamma p_j)/2b$, $i, j = 1,2$ $j \neq i$. The resulting equilibrium prices are $p_1^* = p_2^* = a/(2b - \gamma)$. The resulting channel profits are $\Pi_1^* + \pi_1^* = \Pi_2^* + \pi_2^* = a^2 b/(2b - \gamma)^2$. Because a vertical system does not specify the division of total channel profits, Π_i^* and π_i^* are indeterminate. The other arrangements, C and LF, implicitly divide channel profits between the manufacturer and the reseller. The resulting profits are reported in table 10–1.

Table 10–1 also implies a rank ordering for the equilibrium price across different channel arrangements. Table 10–2 presents that rank ordering. The reaction functions, for each channel form, can be written as $p_i = k_i(a + \gamma p_j)/b$. The k_i coefficients for V, C, and LF channels are respectively $k_V = .5$, $k_C = .67$, and $k_{LF} = .75$ for channels 1 and 2 ($i = 1,2$). For the scenario of two colluding channels (the benchmark that defines the maximum profits achievable in the duopolist market), the implied reaction functions are $p_i = (a + 2\gamma p_j)/2b$ (see footnotes b and c to table 10–1), which means that

Channel Structures Channel 1 / Channel 2	Reaction Functions $P_1(P_2)$	$P_2(P_1)$	Equilibrium Prices P_1^*	P_2^*	Equilibrium Profits Π_1^*	$\Pi_1^* + \Pi_1^*$	Π_2^*	Π_2^*	$\Pi_1^* + \Pi_2^*$
V/V	$P_1 = \dfrac{a + \gamma p_2}{2b}$	$P_2 = \dfrac{a + \gamma p_1}{2b}$	$P_1^* = \dfrac{a}{2b - \gamma}$		Division of channel profits intermediate	$\dfrac{a^2 b}{(2b-\gamma)^2}$	Same as channel 1	Same as channel 1	Same as channel 1
C/C	$P_1 = \dfrac{2(a + \gamma p_2)}{3b}$	$P_2 = \dfrac{2(a + \gamma p_1)}{3b}$ [a/]	$P_1^* = \dfrac{2a}{3b - 2\gamma}$		$\Pi_{1_1}^* = \dfrac{a^2 b}{(3b-2\gamma)^2}$	$\dfrac{2a^2 b}{(3b-2\gamma)^2}$	Same as channel 1	Same as channel 1	Same as channel 1
C/LF	$P_1 = \dfrac{2(a + \gamma p_2)}{3b}$	$P_2 = \dfrac{3(a + \gamma p_1)}{4b}$	$P_1^* = \dfrac{a(4b+3\gamma)}{3(2b^2-\gamma^2)}$	$P_2^* = \dfrac{a(3b+2\gamma)}{2(2b^2-\gamma^2)}$	$\Pi_{1_1}^* = \dfrac{a^2 b(4b-3\gamma)^2}{36(2b^2-\gamma^2)^2}$	$\dfrac{a^2 b(4b+3\gamma)^2}{18(2b^2-\gamma^2)^2}$	$\dfrac{a^2 b(3b+2\gamma)^2}{18(2b^2-\gamma^2)^2}$	$\dfrac{a^2 b(3b+2\gamma)^2}{36(2b^2-\gamma^2)^2}$	$\dfrac{a^2 b(3b+2\gamma)^2}{12(2b^2-\gamma^2)^2}$
LF/LF	$P_1 = \dfrac{3(a + \gamma p_2)}{4b}$	$P_2 = \dfrac{3(a + \gamma p_1)}{4b}$	$P_1^* = \dfrac{3a}{4b - 3\gamma}$		Division of channel profits indeterminate	$\dfrac{3a^2 b}{(4b-3\gamma)^2}$	Same as channel 1	Same as channel 1	Same as channel 1
V/C	$P_1 = \dfrac{a + \gamma p_2}{2b}$	$P_2 = \dfrac{2(a + \gamma p_1)}{3b}$	$P_1^* = \dfrac{a(3b+2\gamma)}{2(3b^2-\gamma^2)}$	$P_2^* = \dfrac{a(2b+\gamma)}{3b^2 - \gamma^2}$	Division of channel profits indeterminate	$\dfrac{a^2 b(2b+\gamma)^2}{4(3b^2-\gamma^2)^2}$	$\dfrac{a^2 b(2b+\gamma)^2}{4(3b^2-\gamma^2)^2}$	$\pi_2^* = \Pi_2^*$	$\dfrac{a^2 b(2b+\gamma)^2}{2(3b^2-\gamma^2)^2}$
V/LF	$P_1 = \dfrac{a + \gamma p_2}{2b}$	$P_2 = \dfrac{3(a + \gamma p_1)}{4b}$	$P_1^* = \dfrac{a(4b+3\gamma)}{8b^2 - 3\gamma^2}$	$P_2^* = \dfrac{3a(2b+\gamma)}{8b^2 - 3\gamma^2}$	Division of channel profits indeterminate	$\dfrac{a^2 b(4b+3\gamma)^2}{(8b^2-3\gamma^2)^2}$	$\dfrac{2a^2 b(2b+\gamma)^2}{(8b^2-3\gamma^2)^2}$	$\pi_2^* = \dfrac{a^2 b(2b+\gamma)^2}{(8b^2-3\gamma^2)^2}$	$\dfrac{3a^2 b(2b+\gamma)^2}{(8b^2-3\gamma^2)^2}$
"Collusion [b/] Between Vertical Channels"	Does not strictly [c/] apply		$P_1^* = \dfrac{a}{2(b - \gamma)}$		Division of channel profits indeterminate	$\dfrac{a^2}{4(b - \gamma)}$	Same as channel 1	Same as channel 1	Same as channel 1

a/ Obtained by summing equations (7) and (8).

b/ The optimization is $\max\limits_{p_1, p_2} \; [p_1(a - bp_1 + \gamma p_2) + p_2(a - bp_2 + \gamma p_1)]$.

c/ However, given the objective function specified in footnote (b), channel 1's decision rule is
$$\frac{\partial(\Pi_1^* + \pi_1 + \Pi_2 + \pi_2)}{\partial p_1} = 0 \;, \; \text{i.e.,} \quad p_1 = \frac{a + 2\gamma p_1}{2b} \;.$$
This equation can be considered the reaction function corresponding to collusive behavior.

Table 10–1
Retail Price Reaction Functions, Equilibrium Retail Prices and Channel Profits as a Function of the Channel Structure

Table 10-2
Channel Reactions and Equilibrium Prices

Duopolist Channel Scenarios	Collusion with Strong Product Differentiation γ → 0	V/V	V/C	V/LF	C/C	C/LF	LF/LF	Collusion with No Product Differentiation γ → b
Scale of channel reaction k_i:								
Channel 1	→ .5	.5	.5	.5	.67	.67	.75	→ 1
Channel 2	→ .5	.5	.67	.75	.67	.75	.75	→ 1
Average reaction $\bar{k} = (k_1 + k_2)/2$	→ .5	.5	.58	.63	.67	.71	.75	→ 1
Rank order of average equilibrium price $\bar{P}^* = 1/2(P_1^* + P_2^*)$	$\bar{P}_{collusion},\ \gamma \to 0$ <	$\bar{P}_{V/V}$ <	$\bar{P}_{V/C}$ <	$\bar{P}_{V/LF}$ <	$\bar{P}_{C/C}$ <	$\bar{P}_{C/LF}$ <	$\bar{P}_{LF/LF}$ <	$\bar{P}_{collusion},\ \gamma \to b$ very large (mathematically → ∞)
Equilibrium profitability	Maximum profitability under strong differentiation	Intermediate/Profitability						Maximum profitability under no differentiation
Profitability under strong differentiation[1]	.5		.47	.438	.444	.41	.38	
Profitability under no differentiation[1]		2	2.69	3	4	4.81	6	very large (mathematically → ∞)

Note: → means "converges toward."

1. Profits are reported up to the multiplicative constant a^2/b. The numbers reported in the last two rows are comparable within a given row but not across rows.

the k_{iM}s for collusion are not a constant[7]: $k_{iM} = (a + 2\gamma p_j)/(2a + 2\gamma p_j)$ depends both on the particular price currently charged by the other channel as well as the parameters of the model, i.e., a and b. If γ is zero (the case of no product substitutability), $k_{1M} = k_{2M} = .5$, and we achieve the same result as for vertical systems. However, as demonstrated by table 10-1, if product differentiation is weak (γ approaches b), prices charged by the colluding channels are very high because $a/2(b - \gamma)$ approaches infinity. Furthermore, $k_{1M} = k_{2M} = 1$, which is larger than k_{LF}. In sum, rows 2 and 3 of table 10-2 give the reaction coefficients k_i for channels 1 and 2. Row 3 reports the average of these two channel coefficients. Row 4 reports the average of the equilibrum prices of the two competing channels. Finally, the last two rows report total profits ($\Pi_1 + \pi_1 + \Pi_2 + \pi_2$) for the cases of strong differentiation ($\gamma \to 0$) and no product differentiation ($\gamma \to b$). The multiplicative constant a^2/b is not included.

The V/V duopolist scenario is the most profitable equilibrium when there is strong differentiation. This may be one additional argument why vertical marketing systems are so prevalent in the United States. Indeed, in many markets, product differentiation seems to be more the norm than no differentiation.

On the other hand, in situations of commodity marketing, higher prices increase industry profitability. This is why the constrained LF/LF scenario is, at equilibrium, more profitable. However, this arrangement is not stable, as explained earlier. At the equilibrium, the manufacturer receives profits of 2 and the reseller profits of 1 (channel profits are 3 and industry profits are 6). The price is $3a/(4b - \gamma) \to 3a/b$ as $\gamma \to b$. Profits are $\Pi_1 \to 2a^2/b$ and $\pi_1 \to a^2/b$. If at price $p_2 = 3a/b$, channel 1 were to unilaterally reorganize and act as a vertical system, thus charging $p_1 = a + \gamma p_2/2b \to a/2b + (1/2)p_2 = 2a/b < 3a/b$, its profits would increase from $3a^2/b$ to $(a + \gamma p_2)^2/4b \to 4a^2/b$. However, this increased profitability is achieved at the expense of the other channel that would see its profits decrease from $3a^2/b$ to $p_2q_2 = (3a/b)[a - b(3a/b - 2a/b)] = 0$. The situation is thus analogous to the famous prisoner's dilemma: what one competitor gains is more than offset by the losses of the other. As the economic agents comprehend the situation, they may not choose to engage in self-satisfying behavior that will eventually make them worse off. It is for that reason that the non-stable LF/LF equilibrium may be lasting. Table 10-3 shows how total channel profits are divided between the manufacturer and reseller in different equilibria. The instability of the LF/LF equilibrium is further demonstrated by the fact that the C/LF equilibrium leads to higher profits for the reseller of the C channel ($\pi_1 = 1.36$) than if this reseller were a member of a leader-follower channel ($\pi_1 = 1$), while the other channel remains a leader-follower channel. This observation is also true for a strongly differentiated product ($\pi_1 = .11$ versus $\pi_{|1} = .06$).

Table 10-3
Division of Equilibrium Industry Profits between Manufacturers and Resellers as a Function of Product Substitutability and Optimizing Behavior Scenario

Profits up to multiplicative constant a^2/b	V/V	V/C		V/LF		C/C	C/LF		LF/LF	Collusion
		V	C	V	LF		C	LF		
Strong substitutability, $b \sim \gamma$										
Manufacturer	Not defined[1]	Not defined[1]	.56	Not defined[1]	.72	.5	1.36	1.39	2	Not defined[1]
Reseller			.56		.36	.5	1.36	.69	1	
Total	1	$\frac{25}{16} = 1.56$	$\frac{18}{16} = 1.13$	$\frac{49}{25} = 1.96$	$\frac{27}{25} = 1.08$	1	$\frac{49}{18} = 2.72$	$\frac{25}{12} = 2.08$	3	∞
Manufacturer substitutability, $\gamma \sim 0$										
Reseller	Not defined[1]	Not defined[1]	.11	Not defined[1]	.13	.11	.11	.13	.13	Not defined[1]
Reseller			.11		.06	.11	.11	.06	.06	
Total	.25	.25	$\frac{2}{9} = .22$	.25	$\frac{3}{16} = .19$	$\frac{2}{9} = .22$	$\frac{2}{9} = .22$	$\frac{3}{16} = .19$	$\frac{3}{16} = .19$	.25

Optimizing Behavior Scenarios

1. For an integrated channel (V), the division of channel profits is indeterminate.

In summary, we have established that the equilibrium of two vertical systems distributing strongly differentiated products is both stable and most profitable. For the case of commodity-type products, stability is still achieved with vertical systems. However, higher equilibrium profits are not achieved because competition in the distribution of a commodity is characterized by a prisoner's dilemma situation. The self-satisfying profit-maximization behavior of one channel is achieved at the expense of the other channel. After several price cuts, the channel prices converge to an equilibrium where both channels are worse off. It is most likely that competing distributors of a commodity would realize the destructive nature of these price cuts. However, this interpretation is beyond the static model of competition used in this chapter and the model employed by McGuire and Staelin. It requires a model of cooperation.

We conclude this section by noting that, in the gasoline market, strongly differentiated brands (e.g., Amoco and Shell) are distributed through channels that are more vertically coordinated than the independent distributor system handling nondifferentiated lower price brands.

Role of Fixed Costs in Intrabrand Competition

Until now, we have ignored fixed costs. Yet, fixed costs may have a significant role in shaping both horizontal competitive activity and competitive activity within the channel. (Remember that we defined within-channel competition as channel members competing for the largest share possible of channel profits.) It is beyond the scope of the present chapter to completely investigate the role of fixed costs. For this reason, we selectively analyze one specific question, namely whether reseller fixed costs play a role in manufacturers differentiating the products that competing resellers carry. In the language of channels of distribution, this question might be rephrased as "What is the role of fixed costs in determining the level of intrabrand competition?"

Consider the scenarios in figure 10–3. Scenario 1 corresponds to the manufacturer supplying the *same* product to both resellers and thus charging them the same wholesale price, W. This wholesale price is the sum the manufacturer's variable cost, C, and his margin, G. (See the arrows in figure 10–4.) The other scenario corresponds to the manufacturer trying to lower intrabrand competition by introducing product differentiation. Hence, the manufacturer slightly modifies the products (without significant effects on production costs). For example, the manufacturer might introduce different brand names, different packages, and other minor differences in features. We contrast the two scenarios by labeling scenario 1 the national brand strategy and scenario 2 the distributor brand strategy.

The manufacturer makes independent decisions when pricing the two

<table>
<tr><td>

Scenario 1: c Large

No Limit on Intra-Brand Competition
National Brand Strategy

</td><td>

Scenario 2: c Small

Limit on Intra-Brand Competition
Distributor Brand Strategy

</td></tr>
</table>

Manufacturer: $\underset{W}{\text{MAX}}\ (W - C)(q_1 + q_2)\Big|_{m_1, m_2}$

Manufacturer: $\underset{W_1, W_2}{\text{MAX}}\ (W_1 - C)q_1 + (W_2 - C)q_2\Big|_{m_1, m_2}$

Resellers: $\underset{m_i}{\text{MAX}}\ m_i q_i\Big|_{W, p_j}$

Resellers: $\underset{m_i}{\text{MAX}}\ m_i q_i\Big|_{W, p_j}$

Figure 10–3. Intrabrand Competition and Brand Strategy

products to the two resellers. (See the two arrows labeled W_1 and W_2 in figure 10–4.) We postulate our previous demand function, i.e., $q_i = a - bp_i + \gamma(p_j - p_i)$. We consider the measure of product substitutability, γ, to be different in each of the two scenarios. When the products are differentiated (in terms of name, packaging, features, and so on), γ is smaller. In the national brand strategy (no differentiation), the manufacturer maximizes his profits $(W - C)(q_1 + q_2) - F$. In the second case, he maximizes $(W_1 - C)q_1 + (W_2 - C)q_2 - F$. In both situations, the resellers *each* maximize their own profit given by $m_i q_i - f = (p_i - w_i - c)q_i - f$, $i = 1,2$. In order to eliminate effects other than the level of product differentiation, we assume that the retailers have the same fixed and variable costs. We summarize the objective functions below in figure 10–4.

Even though the two optimization problems are conceptually different, the symmetry dictates that $W_1 = W_2$. As a result, the mathematics of the two scenarios are the same. The derivations are straightforward and lead to the following equilibrium decisions and profits

$$W = W_1 = W_2 = C + \left(\frac{a}{b} - TC\right)\frac{b + \gamma}{3b + 2\gamma} \tag{16}$$

$$m_1 = m_2 = \left(\frac{a}{b} - TC\right)\frac{2b + \gamma}{3b + 2\gamma} \tag{17}$$

$$\Pi = \frac{2}{b}\left[\frac{b + \gamma}{3b + 2\gamma}(a - b\,TC)\right]^2 - F \tag{18}$$

$$\pi_i = (b + \gamma)\left(\frac{a - b\,TC}{3b + 2\gamma}\right)^2 - f \tag{19}$$

where $TC = C + c$

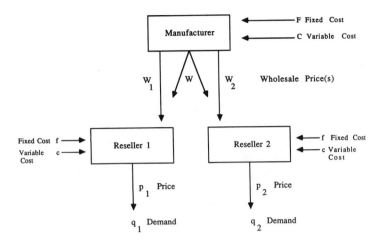

Figure 10-4. Intrabrand Competition

Equation (19) shows that reseller profits π_i depend upon the degree of substitutability γ through the term $(b + \gamma)/(3b + 2\gamma)^2$. It is easy to verify that this term is decreasing in γ. In fact, as γ becomes large and, thus, extreme competition occurs between the two resellers, the gross profits approach zero—i.e., $(b + \gamma)/(3b + 2\gamma)^2 \to 0$ as $\gamma \to \infty$ and $\pi_1 = \pi_2 \to -f$. Given no contribution toward fixed costs, the resellers would obviously drop the product. Hence, the manufacturer may desire a limit on reseller intrabrand competition when the manufacturer needs resellers. In other words, the manufacturer may reduce intrabrand competition to encourage resellers to adopt the product, thereby allowing product availability. Although the manufacturer is interested in increasing competition, because he benefits more from the increased volume than he loses from the lower margin (his profits Π depend upon γ via the term $\{[(b + \gamma)/(3b + 2\gamma)]^2$ that is increasing in $\gamma\}$, there is a limit as to how much intrabrand competition is possible. If the manufacturer wants to keep his resellers profitable and thus ensure distribution for his product in the local market, the manufacturer must ensure reseller profitability.

In summary, intrabrand competition is good for the manufacturers but creates difficulties for the resellers. If store differentiation is not sufficient to limit intrabrand competition, the resellers may request product modifications so as to make direct product substitutability less likely. Strategies other than "product differentiation/distributor brand strategies" solve this manufacturer-reseller conflict. For example, channel coordination between manufacturer and resellers can reduce conflict. It is beyond the scope of this chapter to fully investigate other possibilities. Ultimately, the choice of one strategy versus another (e.g., national brand versus distributor brand) will depend on the increased revenues generated and the costs of implementing each strategy.

Conclusion

We have developed a simple framework where channel competition is operationalized as the set of reaction functions of the competing channels. These reaction functions incorporate the nature of demand (e.g., degree of product differentiation) and the nature of channel structure (i.e., whether the channel is a vertical system or not). This framework has enabled us to address several important questions: (1) What is the relationship between competitiveness and channel structure? (2) What is the stability of a given channel structure? (3) What are the market prices for different scenarios of two competing channels—channels that may or may not have the same structure? (4) What is the profitability resulting from these market prices? (5) What is the role of fixed costs?

Even though this set of questions is rich, the framework is limited. Doing justice to the area of channel management will require significant extensions in a number of dimensions. First, as stated earlier, channel decisions other than price and margin decisions are important. These include advertising and shelf-space. Second, channel members are involved in long-term relationships. As a result, the static framework used in this chapter cannot, by definition, accommodate the multiperiod decision making involved. We believe that competition is a repeated game that may lead to cooperative behavior (Radner 1981). In other words, a multiperiod framework may resolve the gap that we have noted between stability and equilibrium profitability in the situation of low differentiation. Third, channel decisions, like most management decisions, involve uncertainty. The present framework completely ignores this aspect. Channel structure is certainly affected by costs of monitoring one's partners in the channel as well as competing channels' actions.

In summary, the present chapter develops a set of tools that should prove useful in analyzing channels of distribution in greater depth. There is no doubt that marketing productivity will significantly improve in the near future as technological change makes possible the precise monitoring of how channels of distribution function and compete. The managers involved need specific guidelines to analyze the issues. The present research effort may be a step toward developing general, precisely defined concepts that are useful for structuring channel analysis.

In conclusion, pricing decisions in the marketplace cannot be understood without recognizing how pricing decisions are made in practice. And this involves recognizing the role of channels of distribution. The preceding research clearly shows that retail pricing is the complex outcome of margin decisions made by manufacturers and resellers.

As more powerful communications technologies become available, it becomes possible to further coordinate manufacturer and reseller decisions without incurring the costs of vertical integration.[8] Our framework predicts increased competition at the retail price level as a result of increased de facto integration or coordination in the surviving channels.

Notes

1. An example of this approach is Montgomery [1975].

2. Rewriting equation (1) as $q_1 = a - (b + \gamma)p_1 + \gamma(p_j - p_i) = a - \beta p_i + \gamma(p_j - p_i)$ shows that γ measures the effect on the product's demand of the price differential with the other products.

3. Equations (2) and (3) assume that marginal costs for the manufacturer are zero. This simplifying assumption is made because it will not change the nature of our results. Otherwise, if the manufacturer's marginal cost is C, equation (2) becomes $\Pi_i = (w_i - C)q_i = M_i q_i$ where M_i denotes manufacturer margin.

4. With nonzero marginal cost for the reseller, c, equation (4) becomes $p_i = w_i + m_i + c$.

5. The symbol $\mid x$ in equations (5) and (6) means "given x."

6. Coughlan [1985] argues that equilibrium channel profits can be higher when marketing middlemen are used by all sellers than with marketing integration. However, she does not address the stability of this de facto collusion (i.e., both channel members implicitly agreeing to use middlemen).

7. The subscript M means "maximum" since maximum profits are achieved when the two channels collude.

8. A single firm usually does not have expertise and resources to manage effectively both manufacturing and distribution.

11

Optimal Pricing to Maximize Profits and Achieve Market-Share Targets for Single-Product and Multiproduct Companies

Massoud M. Saghafi

I t is no secret anymore to marketing researchers that among the four sacred marketing-mix variables, price needs their most acute, most immediate, and most concerted attention. Constant reminders by prominent scholars in the field and the 1987 call by the American Marketing Association encouraging more research on pricing issues demonstrate this need. The purpose of this chapter is to address two of the most neglected topics in pricing: multiproduct pricing and pricing to attain the targeted market share.

The bulk of the available research on price-determination theories is developed by economists and is primarily based on the neoclassical microeconomic theory. The economic theory of price determination is based on several strong assumptions regarding the nature and behavior of firms. Most of those assumptions have been questioned by marketers as well as by many economists on the grounds of being unrealistic and because they result in theories that cannot be used to develop pricing strategies for real-life applications.

One of the most restrictive assumptions of microeconomists about the behavior of firms is the well-known profit-maximization objective. It is simply "assumed" that firms are profit maximizers where profit is defined as revenue less costs. This assumption has been criticized by economists and marketers alike. Baumol [1967] in his widely cited research suggests that companies in the real world do not necessarily maximize profits. Sales maximization while achieving a target profit level is also a viable objective.

Simon [1959] extensively discussed his very well known satisficing theory. In Simon's opinion, people are not necessarily maximizers or minimizers. They are instead satisficers attempting to achieve a number of objectives at any given time. Human beings satisfice, Simon [1965] declares, because "they have not the wits to maximize."

Lanzillotti [1958] studied the actual pricing objectives and practices of twenty of the largest American corporations, including Alcoa, American Can, Du Pont, G.E., GM, General Foods, Goodyear, Sears, Standard Oil, and Gulf. He found that in setting their prices, fifteen of these corporations had maintaining or increasing market share as their primary or secondary objective. Increasing the rate of return on investment and matching the competition were among the others.[1] Webster [1981] also argues that most marketing managers (who are heavily influential in setting retail prices) have market-share increase as their primary objective. Fruhan [1972] finds similar results. In short, it has been well established that although profits are important, profit maximization is not the only or even the most widely used objective of firms in setting their prices. Joint profit–market-share goals seem more appropriate in reality. Nevertheless, in almost all price-determination theories, marketers assume the profit-maximization objective for firms. Rao [1984] provides a comprehensive survey of this literature.

The profit-maximization assumption automatically implies the marginal cost/marginal revenue equalization for the optimum solution. Saghafi [1987a] derives the pricing strategy in a competitive environment for a firm that has a market-share–stability goal (defined as zero overtime variation in market share). His results are different from the standard profit-maximization rule and suggest a direct relationship between variation in prices of all products in the marketplace. In this chapter, other more realistic objectives of companies will be discussed.

The second simplifying assumption of microeconomists is that each firm produces only one product (or a number of demand-independent products). This assumption, mostly made for the sake of simplicity, totally eliminates issues pertinent to production, pricing, and sales of a product line. Obviously, in real life, most companies produce a product line and not a single good. The product line may consist of a number of substitute or complement products or a set of independent goods. This assumption also ignores the possibility of adding a new product to your existing line.

Most important, many of the optimal-pricing rules that are applicable to the single-product situation are not relevant in a product-line case. For instance, the conventional one-product pricing rule under profit maximization implies that the product must be priced in the elastic segment of the demand. Saghafi [1987b], on the other hand, proves that in a multiproduct situation, depending on the degree of the economies of scale in production and the relative influence of the self- and cross-price elasticities of demand, products can be priced in the inelastic segment of their demand for positive profits.

Several researchers have become aware of the shortcomings of microeconomics in addressing the product-line pricing issues and the ignorance of other disciplines in developing relevant theories to fill the gap. Oxenfeldt [1966], Gabor [1979], Monroe and Della Bitta [1978], and Rao [1984], among others, point out the insufficiency and inapplicability of multiproduct pricing research. Nevertheless, their call for more attention to this subject has, for the most part, been left unanswered. Indeed, Lund, Monroe, and Choudhury [1982], in their annotated bibliography, find only nine articles (among nearly three hundred cited on pricing) that directly or indirectly discuss product-line pricing. In light of this inadequate record, the comment made by Andre Gabor [1979] may have sounded relevant in 1982 or even now: "There is no single rule for product-line pricing."

Multiproduct-pricing literature suffers not only from a shortage of theories but also from the stringent assumptions made in developing those theories. For instance, Monroe and Della Bitta [1978] presented one of the first rigorous product-line–pricing models. Their assumption of linear cost functions, however, results in constant per unit operating costs and eliminates the benefits of economies of scale in production. Saghafi [1987b] illustrates the importance of this issue in multiproduct pricing. Oren, Smith, and Wilson [1984] assume that competitors' prices and products are fixed and that products are only partially substitutable.

Finally, one element of the available literature on product-line–pricing theory (e.g., Monroe and Della Bitta 1978; Oren, Smith, and Wilson 1984; Rao 1984) presupposes simple profit maximization as the behavioral norm of producers. A product-line manager whose primary pricing objective is to achieve target market shares for the products in the line or a manager who wants to increase the total profits earned while achieving target market shares for one or more items in the product line will find little use in unconstrained profit-maximizing–based pricing rules.

Another group of research efforts takes a welfare-oriented approach to multiproduct pricing. Spence [1980], for instance, derives the multiproduct-pricing strategy for a firm whose objective is to maximize the sum of the benefits to consumers (measured by the consumer surplus) and benefits to producers (measured by the earned profit) subject to nonnegativity constraints. Little and Shapiro [1980] develop a similar model in which stores maximize profits subject to a given level of utility for consumers; they arrive at results similar to Spence's. The problem with this group of models (similar to public-good pricing) is that they require the knowledge of subjective consumer utilities to measure the benefits buyers derive from their products.

There is also the conceptual line of research on multiproduct pricing. This area, researched by Dean [1950b], Oxenfeldt [1966], Gabor and Granger [1973], and Monroe and Petroshius [1980], reveals general guidelines for pricing a product line but does not offer any specific and definite rules that can assist in analyzing various aspects of multiproduct pricing.

In this chapter, product-line–pricing strategies under the joint profit-maximization–market-share target objective and for both single-product and multiproduct situations will be formulated. It will be shown that these policies are different from the simple profit-maximization case. Conditions under which optimal pricing strategies are feasible and the importance of price and cost elasticities in determining multiproduct pricing rules are also derived. An example is then presented to illustrate our findings.

The objective of this chapter is exploratory. Therefore, precision and rigor are given priority. To make the results meaningful and manageable, throughout this chapter, all models are constructed in a two-product market framework. To simplify the matter and to economize on space, all notations are given in the appendix at the end of the chapter.

In the next section, optimal pricing strategy for a profit-maximizing firm with a target market-share level is provided. I agree with Lanzillotti [1958] that many pricing strategies are designed to achieve this joint objective. Next, multiproduct-pricing strategies under market-share constraints are discussed. Following Urban [1969], I define market shares as the fraction $US/(US + THEM)$. Following Oxenfeldt [1966] and Gabor [1979], a product line is defined as a set of products in a firm that are demand-interdependent (sales-interdependent).

Pricing for Profit Maximization with a Market-Share Target

This section combines the basic behavioral assumption of microeconomic theory of the firm (profit maximization) with the goal of maintaining market share that is attributed to marketing managers. The purpose is to study the pricing strategies to achieve both of these goals.

This model especially applies to pricing decisions for new entrants when the new-entry product, X, is to achieve a desired market-share level. This is, however, different from the earlier research on new-product pricing by Dean [1973], Gabor and Granger [1970], and Abernathy and Baloff [1973]. Here, an exact pricing rule for both the new product and the product already in the market are presented.

Market share of a product in general is defined as the quantity $US/(US + THEM)$. Let us define US as the dollar sales of product X and $THEM$ as the sales of product Y that competes with X. Then the market share of X can be defined as $S_x = TR_x/(TR_x + TR_y)$. Since X and Y are substitute products, demands for X and Y depend on both prices: $Q_x = Q_x(P_x, P_y)$ and $Q_y = Q_y(P_x, P_y)$.

If the target market share of X is set at $S_x = \bar{S}_x$, then $\bar{S}_x = TR_x/(TR_x + TR_y)$. A profit-maximizing firm that has a market-share target of $\bar{S}_x$ is then facing the following problem:

$$\max_{P_x} \pi_x = P_x Q_x - TC_x \tag{1}$$

subject to:

$$\bar{S}_x = TR_x/(TR_x + TR_y) \tag{2}$$

From (2), we get: $TR_x = S(TR_y)$ where $S = \bar{S}_x/(1 - \bar{S}_x)$. Since $1 - \bar{S}_x = \bar{S}_y$ is the share of the rest of products in the same market, $S = \bar{S}_x/\bar{S}_y$ is the relative market share of X to Y. Substituting for TR_x in (1) and noting that $TC_x = C_x Q_x$, we get:

$$\max_{P_x} \pi_x = SP_y Q_y - C_x Q_x \tag{3}$$

as the unconstrained objective of the firm. Of course, the nonnegativity constraint $\pi_x \geq 0$ must not be violated. If $\pi_x < 0$, X will not even be produced or marketed. Note that to maintain (or achieve) $\bar{S}_x$ level of market share, both price and quantity can be employed as competitive weapons. This implies that $\partial P_i/\partial P_j$ and $\partial Q_i/\partial P_j$ for $(i, j) = (X, Y)$ are nontrivial.

To derive the pricing rule that satisfies (3), we take the derivative of the objective function with respect to P_x and set it equal to zero. After some simple manipulations, we obtain the following:[2]

$$P_x^* = \frac{\eta_x}{\eta_{yx} + (1 + \eta_y)\delta_{yx}} MC_x \tag{4}$$

Interestingly enough, P_x^* is independent of the target market share and only depends on the self-price elasticities of demand, on cross-price elasticities, and on δ_{yx}. Since $\eta_x < 0$, the numerator of (4) is negative. Because X and Y are substitutes, $\eta_{yx} > 0$.

The term $\delta_{yx} = (\partial P_y/\partial P_x)(P_x/P_y)$ may need some explanation. The kinked demand theory of Paul Sweezy [1939] argues that in an oligopolist situation, rivals may not react to a price hike but may match a price cut. This, in the strict sense, implies that if P_x is raised, P_y will not follow it upward. Therefore, $\delta_{yx} = 0$. This, however, implies that $P_x^* = (\eta_x/\eta_{yx})MC_x < 0$. If P_x is cut, P_y will be cut by the same rate, so $\delta_{yx} = 1$. Thus, if firm X perceives firm Y as not willing to follow a price hike, $\delta_{yx} = 0$, the optimum pricing collapses. From (4), it is evident that $P_x^* > 0$ if and only if Y is priced in the elastic segment of its demand. If a drop in P_x causes P_y to fall by exactly the same percentage points, $\delta_{yx} = 1$, X will be marketed ($\pi_x \geq 0$) if and only if $\eta_x - \eta_y - \eta_{yx} - 1 < 0$. Even if contrary to the pure kinked demand theory, all other firms raise their prices when P_x is increased (such as in markets with one or a few large producers) or cut their prices in different proportions, X will still be produced ($\pi_x > 0$) and the optimum-pricing rule (4) is applicable.

Volume Market Shares

If *US*, in the market-share definition, is quantity instead of revenue, $\hat{S}_x = Q_x/(Q_x + Q_y)$. The firm then wants to control S_x portion of the volume market share. Then, following a similar procedure, optimum-pricing strategy for the following system:

$$\text{Max } \pi_x = (P_x - C_x)\,Q_x \,; \text{ subject to } Q_s = SQ_y$$

where $\hat{S} = \hat{S}_x/\hat{S}_y$ can be derived as:

$$P_x^{**} = \frac{\mu_x\eta_x + \eta_{yx} + \eta_y\delta_{yx}}{1 + \eta_{yx} + \eta_y\delta_{yx}}\, C_x \tag{5}$$

Again, $\hat{S}_x$ does not directly appear in the optimum-pricing rule. The optimum markup derived from (5) is: $(\mu_x\eta_x - 1)/(1 + \eta_{yx} + \eta_y\delta_{yx})$. So long as this markup is positive, X will be marketed.

If the price-reaction elasticity, $\delta_{yx} \leq 0$, similar to the revenue market-share maintenance case, no optimum pricing rule will be attainable. If price-reaction elasticity is positive ($\delta_{yx} = 1$ according to the pure kinked demand theory for similar products), then $\mu_x\eta_x < 1$ is the sufficient condition for earning positive profits. Thus, X should be marketed at P_x^{**} to maximize that profit and to maintain the relative market share at $\hat{S}_x/\hat{S}_y$. Again, both profit-oriented (return-oriented) and share-oriented practitioners will be satisfied with this pricing rule.

The condition $\mu_x\eta_y < 1$ is the sufficient condition for production and marketing of X. If μ_x (the cost elasticity of output) is positive, the firm is in the diseconomies-of-scale side of its cost function, but $\mu_x\eta_y < 1$ is guaranteed. Obviously, if $\mu_x = 0$, the firm is most cost-efficient and similar results hold. If $\mu_x < 0$, implying that the firm is in its economies-of-scale side, the constraint $\mu_x\eta_x < 1$ becomes binding.

Let us now summarize the findings of this section. First, it was shown that the optimum-pricing strategy for a company that sells a single product and has the joint profit-maximization–market-share-maintenance goal is feasible. The optimum-pricing rule does not directly depend on the actual level of the market share; it is a function of the self- and cross-price elasticities of all demands and is crucially dependent on the price-reaction elasticity that measures the retaliatory reactions of rivals to changes in prices. If this variable is zero, no pricing strategy can be established to satisfy the firm's joint objectives. This, however, is very unlikely. Price reductions, if not followed (perhaps due to cost differentials, regulations, or management error), especially when products are close substitutes and not highly differentiable (as with gasoline, air travel, and different brands of salt), result in losses of both market share and profits.

We can then conclude that profit maximization and market-share target (or maintaining market share) are, in general, compatible and can be achieved simultaneously. On the other hand, the degree of economies of scale measured by the cost elasticity of output (μ_x) plays an important role in determining if a product should or should not even be produced. The product $\mu_x \eta_x < 1$ was shown to guarantee that X will be produced. Only under unusual reactions of rivals (e.g., when a price increase is countered by rivals with a price reduction or when rivals don't react to price cuts) do we get inconsistency in these multiple objectives. Under the normal circumstances, fortunately, we can keep both economists and marketers satisfied.

Profitability and Target–Market-Share Objectives for Multiproduct Firms

In the previous section, the pricing strategy for a product (or a brand) competing with another product (or brand) was derived. It was assumed that rivals reacted to each other's price variations to preserve or improve their competitive position.

An alternative situation is when a company (or a division or subsidiary) produces two or more products that are substitutes. This situation occurs frequently in real life. For instance, suppose a firm produces Y and decides to introduce a second brand to extend its product line and penetrate other market segments. The new brand, X, is differentiated from Y by price, quality, packaging, and so on. The brand manager for Y now becomes the product-line manager. The desired market share for X is set at S_x by the marketing manager. The product-line price should maximize profits and attain the desired market share.

Another interesting situation that calls for developing this model is when the firm that produces Y decides to merge with one of its competitors. The brand manager for Y will then be placed in the exact same situation as in the newly added product case just explained. Since both product prices are set by a single manager, the price-reaction function in this case is irrelevant; $\delta_{yx} = \delta_{xy} = 0$. We now assume that the overall profit maximization and target market share for each product are simultaneously desired. The problem of the firm in this case becomes:

$$\pi = \pi_x + \pi_y = (P_x - C_x)Q_x + (P_y - C_y)Q_y \tag{6}$$

subject to $TR_x/(TR_x + TR_y) = S_x$

$$S_x = \bar{S}_x, \quad \pi \geq 0$$

The objective of the firm is then to formulate a product-line–pricing strategy that maximizes its profit and achieves the target market share of $\bar{S}_x$ for product X $(1 - \bar{S}_x = \bar{S}_y$ for product $Y)$.

Substituting from the constraint into (6), the unconstrained optimization problem becomes:

$$\underset{P_x, P_y}{\text{Max}} \ \pi = [(1/\bar{S}_x)P_x - C_x]Q_x - C_yQ_y \tag{7}$$

To derive the prices that satisfy (6), we take the derivatives of the profit formation with respect to P_x and P_y and set them equal to zero. The following pricing rules will be derived:

$$P_x^* = [\Gamma\bar{S}_x/(\Gamma + \eta_y)] MC_x \tag{8}$$

$$P_y^* = [\Gamma\bar{S}_y/(\Gamma + \eta_x)] MC_y \tag{9}$$

where $\Gamma = \eta_x\eta_y - \eta_{xy}\eta_{yx}$.

Obviously, (8) and (9) are more general than the standard profit maximization rule for single products. If $\eta_{xy} = \eta_{yx} = 0$ and $\bar{S}_x = 1$ (products are independent and X is the only product in the market), then the typical monopoly pricing of $P_x = [\eta_x/(1 + \eta_x)] MC_x$ will be obtained.

Since $MC_x = (1 + \mu_x)C_x$ and $MC_y = (1 + \mu_y)C_y$, we can rewrite (8) and (9) as:

$$P_x^* = C_x + \left(\frac{[\bar{S}_x(1 + \mu_x) - 1]\Gamma - \eta_y}{\Gamma + \eta_y} \right) C_x \tag{10}$$

and

$$P_y^* = C_y + \left(\frac{[\bar{S}_y(1 + \mu_y) - 1]\Gamma - \eta_x}{\Gamma + \eta_x} \right) C_y \tag{11}$$

The terms in parentheses in (10) and (11) are the optimal markups for products X and Y.[3] If prices P_x^* and P_y^* are charged for products X and Y, the product-line profit is maximized and the market-share targets are achieved or maintained. These markups must be nonnegative. But if $\Gamma < 0$, indicating strong cross-price–elasticity effects, the firm will lose money on both products. This implies that when products are very similar and are very sensitive to price changes of competitors, such that $\eta_{xy}\eta_{yx} > \eta_x\eta_y$ implies $\Gamma < 0$, profit maximization subject to market-share targets cannot be pursued as a viable objective. It might be perceived unreasonable to ascertain that cross-price–elasticity effects being stronger than the self-price–elasticities effects. Nevertheless, theoretically, it is not implausible to hypothesize circumstances that result in exactly that situation.

If $\Gamma + \eta_x > 0$ and $\bar{S}_x < -(\eta_x/\Gamma)$, then producing Y is profitable. If $\Gamma + \eta_y > 0$ and $\bar{S}_x > 1 + (\eta_y/\Gamma)$, then producing X is economical. Finally, if $1 + \eta_y/\Gamma < \bar{S}_x < -(\eta_x/\Gamma)$, then both X and Y in the product line yield profits.

Optimum prices of X and Y depend on a set of self- and cross-price elasticities of demand, their respective desired market shares, their per unit costs, and, finally, the cost elasticities of production (μ_x and μ_y). If X and Y are being produced in the economies-of-scale side of their respective cost functions, then $\mu_x < 0$ and $\mu_y < 0$. If cost per unit of production for X and Y are constant, then $\mu_x = \mu_y = 0$. Otherwise, μ_x and μ_y are both positive.

Quantity-Market-Shares Constraint

If maintaining quantity market share, rather than dollar market share, is desired, then (following a similar procedure) optimum prices for the product line can be derived:

$$P_x^{**} = \frac{\eta_x(1 + \mu_x)}{(1 + \eta_x) + \eta_{xy}} C_x - (\hat{S}_y/\hat{S}_x) \star$$

$$\left[\frac{(\Gamma - \eta_{yx})\mu_y + (1 + \eta_{xy})(\eta_x + \eta_y) - \eta_x}{(1 + \eta_x) + \eta_{xy}} \right] C_y \qquad (12)$$

A similar pricing rule for Y can also be found. Again, if $\hat{S}_y = 0$, $\hat{S}_x = 1$, and $\eta_{xy} = 0$, (12) collapses to the standard profit-maximization solution for one product. In this case, price of X not only depends on the cost of producing X but also on C_y and on the cost efficiency of Y, depicted by the cost elasticity of output (μ_y). Equation (12) is quite different from the optimum-profit-maximization–pricing rule. Note that according to (12), if the relative market share of X to Y is to rise ($\hat{S}_y/\hat{S}_x$ decreasing), P_x should fall and P_y should rise; i.e., $\partial P_x^{**}/\partial(\hat{S}_y/\hat{S}_x) > 0$, which is the term in brackets. From (12), sensitivity of P_x to all of its determinants can be studied.

We can graphically illustrate this problem. Suppose Y is the only product. The hypothetical demand and average-cost schedules for Y are given in panel (a) of figure 11–1. The derived profit function for Y is given in panel (e). Given π_y, P_y' will be optimally charged. Given C_y', $\pi_y = \pi_y'$ level of profits is achieved.

Now suppose another product is added to the line. Then, demand for Y in panel (a) actually becomes $Q_y = Q_y(\bar{P}_x, P_y)$. Panel (c) depicts the demand and average-cost schedules for X, the new product as $Q_x = Q_x(P_x, \bar{P}_y)$, and $C_x = C_x(Q_x)$. Assume that the firm has $\hat{S}_x$ as the target quantity-market share for X. Panel (b) illustrates this constraint.

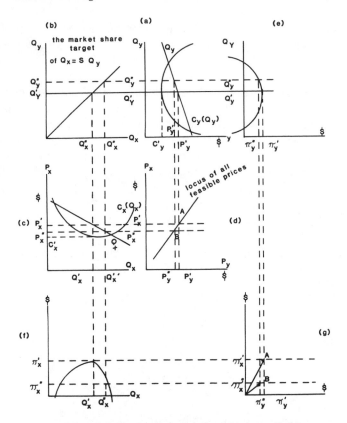

Figure 11-1. Graphic Illustration of the Conclusion of the Quantity-Market-Shares Constraint

If P_y is still set at P_y', then from panel (a), $Q_y = Q_y'$, while from panel (b), $Q_x = Q_x'$, Given Q_x', $P_x = P_x'$, and $C_x = C_x'$, are derived as shown in panel (c). With this information, $\pi_x = \pi_x'$ is obtained as represented in panel (f).

The intersection of P_x' and P_y' is depicted in panel (d) and is denoted as point (A). π_x' and π_y' are transferred from (f) and (e) to panel (g); their intersection is denoted as point (A'). The vector **OA'** is then $\pi' = \pi_x' + \pi_y'$.

If P_y' changes to P_y'', following a similar procedure, points (B) and (B') and the vector **OB'** are obtained. Connecting points A, B, and so on, the locus of all prices P_x and P_y that satisfy the constraint is obtained. The problem is then reduced to finding the one point on that line at which the quantity $\pi^* = \pi_x + \pi_y$ is the largest. This is identical to selecting a vector such as **OA'**, **OB'**, and so on that has the highest value.

Operationalization Issues

Determining the optimum prices derived in this chapter is neither easy nor inexpensive. Nevertheless, it is not an impossible task for researchers. Optimization models of price determination, by nature, result in optimum prices that depend on a set of elasticities as well as on production and marketing costs. Knowledge of these elasticities would lead practitioners to their optimum pricing policies. Estimating the self- and cross-price elasticities of demand, cost elasticity of output and price-reaction elasticities, for the most part, are the only serious obstacles between theory and practice of optimal-price determination. The list of researchers who have successfully implemented this task, for the single-product case, is too long to provide here.

Due to its complexities, empirical studies of product-line pricing are not ample. Some of the most widely recognized research in this area was conducted by Urban [1969]. Urban developed a six-equation general model of product-line decision under the behavioral assumption of constrained profit maximization. Price-sales relationships are modeled exponentially and all elasticities are presumed constant and independent of other variables of the model. Urban then employs the data compiled on a three-good product line (collected from one hundred grocery stores) and applies the mathematical search techniques to estimate the coefficients of his model, including the self- and cross-price elasticities of demand. One of the outcomes of his endeavor is a set of prices for the product line.

Reibstein and Gatignon [1984] follow Urban's modeling approach, but employ ordinary least squares and seemingly unrelated regressions to estimate self- and cross-price elasticities of demand for a product line consisting of different sizes and types of eggs. They also compute the prices of eggs in the line and show that sellers' actual pricing schemes were not consistent with their profit-maximization levels.

Conjoint analysis is another approach that has been used to estimate self- and cross-price elasticities of demand (Mahajan, Green, and Goldberg 1982).

An Example

Elasticity estimates generated in Reibstein and Gatignon's research will be used here to compute the product-line prices with profit-maximization–market-share-target objective. The product in their model, as previously indicated, was eggs: extra large, large, private-label (large), medium, and twenty-pack. All five are close substitutes. Although there are five items in the line, the matrix of estimated self- and cross-price elasticities of demand consisted of only two products for which all elasticities were estimated: private-label (large) and medium. This matrix is:

Table 11–1
Actual Market Data

Product Line	Cost ($/dozen)	Mean Price ($/dozen)	Mean Sales (dozen over 23 weeks)	Mean Revenue (mean price times mean sales)
X	$0.65	$1.00	926	$926
Y	0.59	0.93	129	120

$$\begin{pmatrix} \eta_x & \eta_{xy} \\ \eta_{yx} & \eta_y \end{pmatrix} = \begin{pmatrix} -3.106 & 2.756 \\ 1.996 & -2.144 \end{pmatrix}$$

where X is the large, private-label and Y is the medium-size eggs. Other information about this product line is given in table 11–1. All information is collected over a multiweek period. Averages are presented here. Actual-volume market share of X is: $\hat{S}_x = 0.80$. Obviously, if $P_x \cong P_y$, unless there is some bias against the private-label brand, X, it will overwhelmingly sell as compared to Y (as is the case here).

Suppose, for some reason, X becomes scarce and Y is now ample.[4] The supermarket (or the manufacturer) now wants to increase sales of Y and reduce sales of X. Let us, as an illustration, propose that the decision maker wants to price X and Y such that:

1. The volume market share of X is to drop from 80 percent to 70 percent and that of Y is to rise to 30 percent.
2. Both types of eggs should be profitable.
3. Total profit generated by the line should be as high as possible.

Conditions (1), (2), and (3) imply that the firm wants to solve a problem similar to equation (6) with quantity-market-share targets, $\pi_x > 0$ and $\pi_y > 0$. Solving equation (12) for P_x^{**} we get:

$$P_x^{**} = 11.974 \, (\hat{S}_y / \hat{S}_x) - 3.106 \quad \text{and similarly}$$

$$P_y^{**} = 3.756 \, (\hat{S}_x / \hat{S}_y) - 7.71$$

Obviously, to increase $\hat{S}_x$, P_x must decline and P_y must rise, as is evident from the preceding relations. If $\hat{S}_y = 0.30$, $\hat{S}_x = 0.70$, so $P_x^{**} = \$2.02/\text{dozen}$ and $P_y^{**} = \$1.05/\text{dozen}$.

Comparing these prices to what was actually charged, it is evident that X

(the private label) does not easily lose market share. Its price must double, while the price of its only competitor remains practically the same for a small loss of ten market-share points.

Reibstein and Gatignon derive the optimal price of X and Y under the profit-maximization assumption as P_x = \$.98 and P_y = \$1.08. The latter is near what we found, but the former is obviously far from the price, \$2.02, found previously. Again, note that in Reibstein and Gatignon's model, five types of eggs were competing.

Conclusion and Extensions

In this chapter, I argued that creating pricing strategies to maximize short-run profits in a one-product world, as neoclassical microeconomics formulates, is not really what real-life firms attempt to accomplish. Most companies, instead, have a set of objectives that they try to attain or a set of targets that they hope to achieve.

One step in the direction of generalizing the simple profit-maximization hypothesis for the one-product case is to theorize that maybe maintaining market share or achieving a target market share is another goal of companies. Furthermore, most firms do produce a number of demand-related products called a product line.

With these hypotheses in mind, the optimum pricing strategies for companies that have the joint profit-maximization–market-share-target objective was formulated and an example was presented.

It was shown that this joint objective, although well desired by real-world companies, may not always have a theoretical solution. The relative market-share targets should be set within an acceptable range, price elasticities must have the appropriate signs, economies-of-scale factors must be considered, and cross-price elasticities and price-response elasticities must all have acceptable signs and magnitudes.

An innocent-looking problem of pricing a product line (composed of only two goods in this chapter) becomes a major empirical puzzle to solve. Nevertheless, I believe that under reasonable conditions, an optimum profit-maximizing–market-share-maintenance objective, as desired by many companies, is attainable.

Although I criticized some of the earlier works on product-line pricing because of their strong assumptions, I made a few of my own. Theories of pricing behavior, the present one included, have in general made assumptions about the environment (whether the outcomes are certain or probabilistic); the time dimension (static versus dynamic); the number and nature of the goals and constraints of the firm; and the production process (the number and nature of products, production costs, and technology. Figure 11–2 illustrates

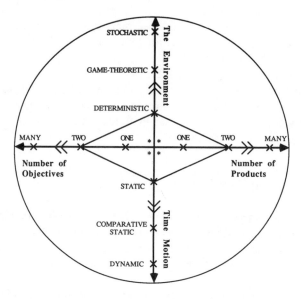

* : Least general
→ : Most general
X : Different possible cases
◇ : The standing of the present chapter
≪ : Next logical direction for extension

Figure 11–2. Standing of the Present Research

the nature of these assumptions and the relative standing of this chapter. Future research should attempt to generalize this approach along all the four specified dimensions. Specifically, more attention should be paid to probabilistic (game–theoretic) and dynamic pricing models.

Notes

1. Lanzillotti receives harsh critical reviews from M.A. Adelman [1959] and Alfred Kahn [1959]. Adelman contends that many firms price low to "prevent competition" and to guarantee continuous patronage even when competitors open shop. Kahn's comments are equivocal. He criticizes Lanzillotti for discarding profit mazimization as the primary objective of companies. Concomitantly, he states "these large corporations typically price to maximize monetary profits—not day by day, to be sure, but to a large extent year by year and certainly over a fairly brief period of years." Kahn calls this a "workable" hypothesis.

It is interesting to note that neither Adelman's competition-deterring pricing behavior nor Kahn's modified profit-maximization objective are as Lanzillotti [1959] points out "the conventional profits maximization or marginal price theory."

2. If the derivative of (2) with respect to P_x is taken, it can be shown that:

$$(1 + \eta_x) = \delta_{yx} + \eta_{yx} \quad \text{implies} \quad \text{from (4):} \quad P_x^* = \frac{\eta_x}{(1 + \eta_x) + \eta_y \delta_{yx}}$$

It is obvious that if $\delta_{yx} = 0$, then (4) is reduced to the simple profit-maximization solution of the neoclassical microeconomics; i.e., if X has 100 percent of the market share, there is no competition, or firms do not react in an oligopolist manner. None of these hypotheses, however, seem realistic.

3. In the unconstrained profit-maximization case, P_x^* and P_y^* are *directly* interdependent (Saghafi 1987b). Even under the market-share–*stability* conditions, direct interdependencies exist (Saghafi 1987a). In (10) and (11), however, P_x and P_y appear only through the elasticity arguments. If, in practice, these elasticities are defined as constant parameters (Urban 1969), then a one-time estimation would transform (10) and (11) into two completely independent models.

4. This example should not be confused with the issue of pricing with scarcity constraints. See Monroe and Zoltners [1979] for an introduction to that subject.

Appendix 11A–1:
Glossary of Technical Terms

Expression	Definition
P_i	Price of product i
Q_i	Quantity of product i demanded
TR_i	Total revenue generated from selling product i
TC_i	Total cost of producing product i
π_i	Profit generated from product i
η_i	Price elasticity of product i where $$\eta_i = (\partial Q_i/\partial P_i)(P_i/Q_i)$$
η_{ij}	Cross-price elasticity of demand for product i with respect to the price of product j, where $$\eta_{ij} = (\partial Q_i/\partial P_j)(P_j/Q_i) \quad i \neq j$$ $$\Gamma = \eta_i\eta_j - \eta_{ij}\eta_{ji} \quad i \neq j$$
μ_i	Cost elasticity of product i, where $$\mu_i = (\partial C_i/\partial Q_i)(Q_i/C_i)$$
S_i	Market share of product i
C_i	Per unit cost of producing product i
MC_i	Marginal cost of producing product i, where $$MC_i = (1 + \mu_i)C_i = (\partial TC_i/\partial Q_i)$$
δ_{ij}	The price-response (reaction) elasticity of i with respect to j, where $$\delta_{ij} = (\partial P_i/\partial P_j)(P_j/P_i)$$
$^-$ or $^\wedge$	Implies a constant value
$\star$ or $\star\star$	Implies an optimal value

Part V
Normative Pricing Models

Timothy M. Devinney

Pricing-strategy research has three primary components: the building of theoretical models to explain observed behavior, the empirical testing of those theoretical models, and the development of normative rules based on the tests of the theoretical models. Prior sections of this book have concentrated heavily on the first component of research in pricing strategy, theoretical model building. In part V, three chapters provide examples of the latter two aspects of pricing-strategy research. Chapter 12 analyzes the empirically observed dynamics of price elasticity over the product life cycle. Chapter 13 investigates the pricing of different products as well as different but related products at different outlets. Chapter 14 provides an explanation of the observed differences in price markups in supermarkets.

It is interesting to note that a large percentage of this book is devoted, not to empirical research or direct observation, but to extentions and developments of pure theory. Later (in chapter 15 by Dolan, Bonoma, and Crittenden and in chapter 16 by Monroe and Mazumdar), the implications of this fact are dealt with more thoroughly; however, this, plus other facts, are telling about the evolving nature of pricing-strategy research and need to be briefly discussed here.

In three other major volumes, we see some interesting evidence on the changes occurring in the area of pricing research or the economics-marketing interface. In 1969, Taylor and Wills compiled *Pricing Strategy.* In that volume, 51 percent of the papers were devoted to either empirically tested models or direct observations and descriptions of current pricing practices. In 1980, the *Journal of Business* published a volume entitled *Interfaces Between Marketing and Economics,* which contained only one empirical research paper (13 percent of the total number of papers). A subsequent volume of the same journal, published in 1984 and entitled *Pricing Strategy,* also contained only one empirical work (although this amounted to 25 percent of the total number of papers if two survey papers are excluded). This casual empiricism would tell us little except that it is confirmed by any cursory examination of the relevant marketing and economics journals. What we find is a declining trend in empirical studies and more of a reliance on theoretical tractability than statistical validity. The three chapters in this part are not meant to stem this decline, but to provide empirical balance to the theoretical works that have preceded them.

In chapter 12, Yoon and Lilien build on the seminal work of Simon [1979] by reexamining the dynamic behavior of price elasticity over the product life cycle. This is a particularly interesting and important subject because, while relatively little is known about the dynamics of price elasticity and how it is affected by other marketing-mix variables, it remains the key component in most all pricing-strategy decisions. Theoretical models, from Marshall [1890] to chapters in this book (see, e.g., chapters 1, 6, and 11), show that optimal pricing strategies are a function of price elasticity. From a practical standpoint, managers clearly recognize that their latitude in pricing decisions is a function of the price sensitivity of their customers. Indeed, this is what professors actually teach them to do!

Simon [1979] empirically observed that price elasticity declined in the early stages of the product life cycle, stabilized, and then rose as the product aged. As Yoon and Lilien note, Simon had a difficult time finding a good empirical definition of the product life cycle. Using a consistent set of products (industrial chemicals) rather than a number of product categories, the authors partially resolve this problem, removing much of the compounding between the effect of the life cycle and its definition. They show that, for the class of products studied, price elasticity is in fact more stable over the product life cycle than previously thought. Price elasticity is initially somewhat stable, declines, and then stabilizes. Yoon and Lilien argue that such a pattern is consistent with the development of a market for a new product where the product improves with time, costs decline, and entry into the industry occurs.

In chapter 13, Shugan examines the role that outlets—in other words, distribution of the product in the marketplace—play in determining price. This is a particularly important piece of research since most models assume that consumers search for products across outlets, rather than searching either for outlets and then products or searching for both simultaneously. Theoretically, Shugan shows that there is a significant difference between the expected price outcomes when consumers search first for outlets and then for products. Since search across outlets is expensive, it pays the retailer to restrict the selection available to consumers. In addition, what is critical in determining the price distribution in the marketplace is whether or not both single- and multiple-brand outlets exist. If both types of outlets are in operation, then multiple-product outlets sell low-quality products more cheaply than single-product outlets, while selling high-quality products at a higher price.

Empirically, Shugan finds support for his arguments. First, few outlets offer the same assortment of brands, purposely attempting to differentiate their product offerings. This implies that most of the traditional assumptions about consumer search are rather limited since most consumer search appears to occur over imperfectly comparable alternatives. Second, there is little relation within an outlet between the number of products and the price margins or between the price of one product in the store and all other prices. Finally, the spread between high-priced and low-priced items in multiple-product outlets is larger than in the market as a whole.

In the final chapter in this part, Nagle and Novak examine the question of the difference in product price-cost margins within the same store. In their theoretical model, they take an approach similar to Shugan's by assuming that shopping within a store is cheaper than shopping across stores. This again leads to the natural implication that consumers will consolidate their purchases at one or a few stores. Using this theoretical base, the authors argue that consumers can actually be viewed, not as purchasers of a single product, but as purchasers of a single product bundle, whose "characteristics" are the individual products. This innocuous-seeming notion has important implications. First, it implies that there is little reason for price-cost margins to be constant within a store. Second, and most important, it is conceivable that these margins could be negative, giving us a much needed explanation for the loss-leader phenomenon.

Nagle and Novak have two explanations for the pattern of price-cost margins they observe empirically. The first is the segmentation hypothesis. The store offers a number of brands to a host of nonidentical customers. Since all a consumer is concerned about is the price of the bundle, the individual product prices will be set such that the likelihood that a primary customer enters the store is as high as possible without losing too much in profits to other customers who view this product as less essential. The second hypothesis argues that customers infer the overall level of prices from those most frequently purchased. This price-awareness hypothesis implies that stores would willingly suffer losses on high-awareness items simply to earn more money on low-awareness items.

The normative implications of these chapters are clear. Yoon and Lilien show the importance of understanding the dynamic evolution of the product category and the marketplace so as to understand the evolution of price elasticity. Shugan shows that consumer-search behavior appears to be different than typically assumed in our theoretical search models. In addition, the differentiation strategies of outlet dealers appear to have a profound effect on the benefits of search and, therefore, the returns to manufacturers. In a similar vein, Nagle and Novak show that for many firms, it pays to view their product offerings not as single products but as characteristics within a bundle being offered to heterogeneous customers.

12

An Exploratory Analysis of the Dynamic Behavior of Price Elasticity over the Product Life Cycle: An Empirical Analysis of Industrial Chemical Products

Gary L. Lilien
Eunsang Yoon

P rice elasticity is one of the central concepts in price theory and pricing research. It is a critical input in many pricing and related marketing decisions, including new-product pricing (Seglin 1963; Kalish and Lilien 1986), brand pricing (Simon 1979), product-line pricing (Urban 1969; Monroe and Della Bitta 1978), retail promotions (Wilkinson, Mason, and Paksay 1982), and advertising (Della Bitta, Monroe, and McGinnis 1981). (For a review of numerous other applications of price elasticity in marketing research, see Monroe and Della Bitta [1978] and Rao [1984].)

Although price elasticity is important to both researchers and practitioners, relatively little is known about its dynamics. Price elasticity is subject to seasonality, may be affected by economic conditions and the stage of the product life cycle, and interacts with other marketing-mix elements and competition. We focus here on the relationship between price eleasticity and time (or stage in the life cycle).

Some authors (Mickwitz 1959; Robertson 1967) argue that price elasticity increases during the early stages of the life cycle and decreases later. Others (Parsons 1975; Simon 1979) contend that price elasticity exhibits a nonlinear decline or a U-shaped behavior over the product life cycle. These differences are critical because marketing decisions are intimately tied to the level and dynamics of price elasticity. For example, for pricing by means of a simple markup to be optimal, price elasticity must be constant over time. New-product–diffusion models develop guidelines for optimal pricing in dynamic environments but assume certain specific dynamic patterns of price elasticity. The assumptions made in these models and these decision rules need to be validated through empirical research on the dynamic behavior of price elasticity.

In the next section, we review the literature on the behavior of price elasticity in a dynamic environment and its implications for pricing decisions. Several important issues in research on price elasticity are discussed in the following section. In the section after that, we perform an empirical analysis with data for thirty-five industrial chemicals and allied products. There we (1) identify the stages of the product life cycle for each product, (2) develop and estimate four price-sales response models, (3) show that price elasticity generally follows a pattern of "stable → decrease → stable" over the product life cycle, and (4) compare these results with past research findings. In the next section, we discuss the managerial and research implications of these findings, particularly for optimal markup pricing rules and for new-product-diffusion models. We conclude with a section on limitations of this research and suggestions for further study.

Literature Review

Price elasticity, defined as the ratio of the percentage change in demand to the percentage change in price, may give a precise answer to the question of whether a firm has set a product's price too high or too low in a (static) market environment. For revenue maximization, the price is too high if the demand elasticity at that price is greater than one, and it is too low if less than one. However, whether this rule is also true for profit maximization depends on the behavior of costs, even in a static environment (Lilien and Kotler 1983). In a dynamic environment, a product's price is subject not only to the other elements of the marketing mix, to cost dynamics, and to competition, but also to external influences including economic conditions and seasonal variation of customer demand. Sales response to price change also depends on these dynamic influences. In the literature, the propositions and empirical findings on the dynamic behavior of price elasticity have been inconclusive.

Mickwitz [1959] speculated that price elasticity increases over the first three stages of the product life cycle (introduction, growth, and maturity) and decreases during the last stage (decline). Lambin [1970] and Kotler [1971] concurred with this argument. Liu and Hanssens [1981], using data for inexpensive gift goods, found that price elasticity increases slightly over time. Empirical research in the diffusion literature (Robertson 1967; Rogers 1983) supports this argument with the finding that early adopters of new products typically have higher incomes and so are less price-sensitive (that is, are more likely to have a higher reservation price) than later adopters.

Parsons [1975] contended that price elasticity exhibits a nonlinear decline over time up to the maturity stage of the life cycle. In his competitive simulation model, Kotler [1965] also assumed that price elasticity decreases over time. Using consumer-products data, Wildt [1976] observed that promotional elasticity decreases over time.

An important empirical study by Simon [1979] focused on the price elasticity of consumer products over the "brand" life cycle. Using time series data of pharmaceuticals, detergents, and cleaners, he found that price elasticity decreases to a minimum at the maturity stage and then increases over the brand life cycle. He also investigated the implication of these changing price elasticities for an optimal brand-price–setting policy. Simon suggests that his findings support a penetration pricing strategy for brands introduced into markets with existing substitutes; that is, marketers should set relatively low markups during the introduction and growth stages, relatively high markups during the maturity stage, and low markups again during the decline stage. One limitation of Simon's work is his lack of an operational definition for life-cycle stages, which makes his work difficult to replicate.

Constant markup pricing, the simplest and most widely employed form of cost-oriented pricing (Kotler 1980), is closely related to the price-elasticity level and its changes over time. Is pricing through a constant markup over cost optimal? Generally, no. Any model that ignores the dynamics of demand elasticity in setting price is not likely to lead to profit maximization. As demand elasticity changes—seasonally, cyclically, or over the product life cycle—the optimum markup changes.

A rigid (constant) markup may lead to optimum profit under special conditions. One set of conditions is that (1) marginal costs are constant for different points on the demand curve and (2) price elasticities are constant over time. If both conditions are met, the optimal markup over the average cost is given by $1/(\eta - 1)$, where η is absolute price elasticity (Seglin 1963). Those two required conditions—constant marginal costs and constant elasticities—roughly characterize many retailing situations, where fairly rigid markups are so widespread. Yet, in many manufacturing situations, these special conditions are less likely to hold, and so fixed-markup pricing is more difficult to justify on a priori grounds. For new-product pricing, the conditions of constant marginal costs and constant price elasticities are even less likely to hold due to more complex interactions in dynamic diffusion environments. Empirical studies (Yoon 1984), however, report that cost- or margin-based (especially constant-markup) pricing is the most frequently employed policy for new industrial-product pricing.

If prices can be changed continuously and costs vary over time, the dynamic extension of the static markup equation is given by:

$$P_t = [\eta_t/(\eta_t - 1)] C_t'$$

where P is the optimal price, η is absolute price elasticity, C' is marginal cost, and t is a time subscript.

In a general new-product–diffusion model, where the sales rate of a new product is a function of both cumulative sales of the product and the product's price, the optimal price can be given as (Kalish 1983a):

$$P_t = [\eta_t/(\eta_t - 1)](C_t' - L_t)$$

where L_t is the shadow price—the marginal impact on cost associated with producing an incremental unit, derived primarily from the experience-curve effect.

In research on new-product pricing, price elasticity is assumed to follow different patterns over time—for example, constant over time (Bass 1980; Jeuland and Dolan 1982), proportional to the price level (Robinson and Lakhani 1975; Kalish and Lilien 1986), or dependent on specific situations (Kalish 1983a; Dolan and Jeuland 1981; Rao and Bass 1985). There has been limited empirical research to justify these assumptions.

Issues in Empirical Research on Price Elasticity

Our research on the behavior of price elasticity over the product life cycle deals with the following issues: (1) data collection, (2) identification of the stages of the product life cycle, (3) specification of sales-response models, parameter estimation, and model validation, and (4) interpretation and application of the results.

Data Collection

To investigate the dynamic behavior of price elasticity, we need time series data long enough to cover more than one life-cycle stage. For many frequently purchased consumer products, weekly or monthly data spanning a few years is sufficient; but for many consumer durables and industrial products, semi-annual or annual data for many years is required. Data should be available not only for the product (or brand) sales but also for the variables that can explain sales changes over time. Explanatory variables include (1) trend variables such as time, GNP, retail sales, or industrial production indexes, (2) marketing-mix variables such as price, advertising expenditures, and other sales-supporting efforts, and (3) competitive variables for brand–life-cycle studies. Data availability often restricts the choice of an appropriate model to very simple formulations. Two other problems that frequently occur in such analyses are changes in the ratio of product quality to relative value over time and the lack of variation in the price level.

Identification of the Stages of the Product Life Cycle

Empirical evidence on the existence and pattern of the product life cycle is quite uneven. In a literature review, Rink and Swan [1979] identify twelve types of product–life-cycle patterns. For example, Cox [1967], in his study of

754 ethical drug products, found that the most typical form of the product life cycle was a cycle-recycle pattern, and Buzzell [1966] reports a scalloped life-cycle pattern representing a succession of life cycles based on the discovery of new product characteristics, new uses, or new markets.

Besides these differences in shape, there are clearly differences in cycle lengths. Rink and Swan [1979] report on twelve studies of consumer non-durables, nine of consumer durables, and four of industrial products; they suggest that empirical research is insufficient to lead to generalizable conclusions within and across these product groups. Research results are likely to depend on the level of product aggregation; Thorelli and Burnett [1981] report in their study of 1,148 PIMS industrial products that product classes tend to have longer life cycles than brands.

Another difficulty is that many strategic, market-structure, and performance variables change over the product life cycle. Studies by Harrell and Taylor [1981] and Thorelli and Burnett [1981] conclude that sales growth rates are only one aspect of the product life cycle. Elements such as market innovation and market concentration as well as the influence of replacement sales also affect the structure of the life cycle. The problems of phase change and phase length are compounded by the widely held belief that life cycles are becoming shorter (Qualls, Olshavsky, and Michaels 1981).

These variations in definition and the unevenness of empirical findings imply that we cannot definitely determine the current stage of any brand's or product's life cycle. However, for an ex post empirical analysis, the sales-growth-rate history can be used as a major variable identifying phase changes of the life cycle.

Specification of Sales-Response Models and Parameter Estimation

An important issue in model specification is whether the model parameters can be assumed to be stationary. Constant-parameter models assume that model coefficients do not change during the specified time frame and that dynamic changes in sales response are explained by adding a trend to the model. (See Taylor [1975] for a review on the price elasticity of the demand for electricity and Rao [1984] for a review on price modeling in marketing.)

Wildt and Winer [1983] argue that time-varying coefficient models are more appropriate for many situations characterized by changing market environments. They refer to Simon's [1979] model as an example of a systematic parameter-variation approach where price and lagged sales effects are functions of time. They cite Liu and Hanssens [1981] as an example of a stochastic random-variation approach that relates sales and prices for an inexpensive-brand gift item. Wildt and Winer [1983] also review a variety of econometric and marketing models that use the time-varying–parameter approach, but most of these relate sales to advertising effort rather than to price.

The variable-parameter approach is undoubtedly a more realistic representation of many dynamic market situations. But because several models may fit the data equally well, the findings may be due to the particular functional forms used (Shoemaker 1986). So applying that approach requires careful model evaluation, validation, and testing.

Timing of sales response in terms of leads and lags has also been an important element in structuring price-sales response models. A one-period lag has frequently been employed in previous studies (Parsons 1975; Simon 1979). A leading effect, representing price-change expectations on sales, should be considered when price changes are announced in advance of their implementation.

To select and validate a model, we should test several life-cycle patterns against the empirical data. In addition, choosing a model should entail several other criteria. Since price elasticity ranges between limits, model validation should include an assessment of whether the estimated elasticity values are reasonable. Other general validation procedures include goodness-of-fit tests, error-structure tests (particularly, for serial correlation), and statistical significance tests.

Interpretation and Application of the Empirical Results

The behavior of price elasticity over the product life cycle can be used in drawing managerial implications for pricing decisions in a dynamic environment. In particular, markup pricing can be evaluated on its consistency with the product objectives (for example, profit maximization) over the life cycle. Similar tests can be performed with pricing policies for new products.

In the following section, we report the results of our exploratory analysis with a data base of industrial chemicals and allied products.

An Empirical Analysis of Industrial Chemical Products

Data

For this analysis, we selected thirty-five industrial chemicals and allied products from *Chemical Economics Handbook* published by Stanford Research Institute [1975]. Our selection criteria were that the product should have consistent annual data over time for sales volume and average unit price, and that the time series should be long enough to cover at least two phases of the product life cycle.

To remove annual fluctuations, we smoothed the sales-volume data into three-year moving averages. This smoothing removes lags in the purchase decision, contract, order, and shipment processes as well as the effect of short-term economic fluctuations. Price data were also smoothed over three years to account for lead or lag effects of the announcement and implementation of price changes. Price was then deflated using the Producer Price Index of the U.S. Department of Commerce to remove inflation effects and to account for the effect of price competition with substitute chemical products.

Identification of Product–Life–Cycle Phases

The trend of sales volume was used as the basic criterion for identifying the product–life–cycle phases of each chemical product. The early slow sales build-up period is referred to as the "introduction" phase and the following rapid sales build-up period as the "growth" phase. The stationary sales period following the growth phase is the "maturity" phase. The late declining sales period is the "decline" phase.

We applied the stage-boundary criterion of plus or minus 5 percent in real sales growth rates suggested by Polli and Cook [1969]. The introduction stage was defined as that time period when the annual sales growth rates were less than 5 percent. The growth stage was defined as that time period when the annual sales growth rates were maintained at higher than 5 percent. The maturity stage was defined as that time period when the sales growth slowed down to less than 5 percent and stayed between plus 5 and minus 5 percent. The decline stage was defined as that time period when the sales decreased more than 5 percent annually. In the actual stage-identification process, we disregarded temporary ups and downs in the sales growth rates. The first line of each series in appendix 12A-1 summarizes the trends of sales volume (and price in real terms) and the corresponding life-cycle periods for each of thirty-five chemical products.

In appendix 12A-1, the slow sales-growth trend during the initial stage of the life cycle and the stable sales trend during the maturity stage are indicated by S: the increasing and declining sales trends are indicated by I and D, respectively. However, since eleven out of the thirty-five products we studied did not follow the pattern of transition from growth to maturity, we allowed two modified life-cycle patterns, that is, growth1 (early growth) → maturity → growth2 (late growth) (a type of cycle-recycle pattern (Cox 1967)), and growth1 → growth2 → maturity (a scalloped life-cycle pattern (Buzzell 1966)). Typically, the average sales growth rates for the growth1 phase are two to three times higher than those for the growth2 phase. In the appendix, If indicates a relatively high sales growth, and Is refers to a relatively lower sales growth during the same growth stage of the life cycle. We also observe that in four out of thirty-five products, growth is directly followed by decline.

The transition from one phase to another in the product life cycle was confirmed by the behavior of trends in the product (real) price as well as in sales. As shown in appendix 12A-1, sales and price trends are consistent for different phases of the product life cycle. (Price trends I and D refer to increasing and decreasing trends, respectively, and S indicates a stable price trend.) Introduction is characterized by a stable or slowly growing sales trend and a decreasing price trend. Only one out of eleven series with an identified introduction stage shows an increasing price trend during that stage (styrene). The growth stage (and growth1 phase in the cycle-recycle pattern) is characterized by increasing sales matched with decreasing price. Out of thirty-five products, we see five exceptions that show increasing or stable price trends during the growth stage (organic accelerators, carbon tetra-chloride, synthetic medicinals, synthetic tanning, and titanium dioxide).

During growth2 phase in the cycle-recycle pattern (table 12A–1-C), increasing sales trends are matched with decreasing price trends in eleven out of seventeen cases. Apparently, a recycle in an industrial chemical product's life is often due to a lowering of product prices. Process innovations, higher competition among sellers, and learning-curve effects could be major reasons for these price reductions. Maturity is characterized by either increasing or stable price trends in eight out of eleven cases (table 12A–1-B), and the decline stage by decreasing sales matched with decreasing prices in three out of four cases (table 12A–1-E). Thus, it appears that prices generally decline during the product life cycle except during the mature phase. During a growth2 phase, prices appear to resume their declining trends, although it is impossible to determine causality here without further investigation of each product market.

The boundary year dividing the life-cycle phases was generally included in both phases (except for barbituric acid, cellulose ethers, and ethyl acetate, where inclusion in both phases made the boundary unclear). This overlapping of the boundary year is consistent with the analysis as sales volume and price were smoothed over three years.

Models and Estimation of Price Elasticity

To estimate price elasticity, we start with the conceptual model in figure 12–1, suggesting that demand for an industrial input product is determined by the output demand level (demand for products for which this product is an input or ingredient), the input substitution strength (how well the product is able to withstand substitutes or can substitute for others), and the diffusion effect. Since an industrial product is purchased to use in producing output products (derived demand), the demand for the output products determines the need for the input industrial product and its substitutes. Given that need, an industrial product competes with other substitutes. The value-in-use of the input product is one major influence on product selection; therefore, the "competitive price level" of the product is a major determinant of its substitution strength (Uradnisheck 1978; Forbis and Mehta 1981).

In a dynamic environment, the demand for an industrial product follows

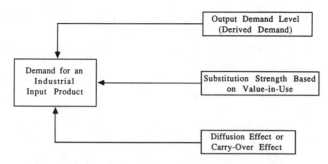

Figure 12–1. Determinants of Demand for Industrial Input Products

a diffusion process known as "imitative buying." Input demand is also subject to "carry-over effects" because the adoption of a new industrial product may involve fixed costs, while changing products may involve switching costs and uncertainty. Both imitative buying and carry-over effects are closely related to the cumulative sales level of that product, which is a measure of "diffusion effect."

A mathematical form that captures these effects, at least locally, is:

$$SALES = a\ CUM^b\ IPI^c\ PRICE^d \quad \text{or}$$

$$\log(SALES) = a + b\log(CUM) + c\log(IPI) + d\log(PRICE)$$

(1)

where $SALES$ = three-year average (smoothed) sales

CUM = cumulative sales to date

IPI = industrial production index for chemicals and allied products

$PRICE$ = three-year average price in real terms; that is, unit sales value/producers price index for chemicals and allied products

a = constant

b = elasticity measure of diffusion effect

c = elasticity measure of output demand level

d = price elasticity, or elasticity measure of substitution strength

A major factor in the choice of equation (1) is that it is a flexible, constant-elasticity–model form that, at least locally, should provide a reasonably reliable measure of price elasticity. When estimating the model in equation (1), however, we observed high multicollinearity between the two explanatory variables, *CUM* and *IPI*. These two variables increase over time and are related to carry-over effects in a theoretical sense. Either variable seems to do a reasonable job for the carry-over and diffusion effects. Therefore, we employed the following two simplified models for estimating the price elasticities of industrial chemical products:

Model 1 (diffusion effect–price model):

$$\log(SALES) = a + b \log(CUM) + d \log(PRICE) \qquad (2)$$

Model 2 (output demand level–price model):

$$\log(SALES) = a + c \log(IPI) + d \log(PRICE) \qquad (3)$$

In order to test the reliability of the price elasticity estimated with models in equations (2) and (3), we also estimated the following two modified-form models:

Model 3 (modified diffusion effect–price model):

$$\log(SALES) = a + b \, CUM + d \, PRICE \qquad (4)$$

Model 4 (modified output demand level–price model):

$$\log(SALES) = a + c \, IPI + d \, PRICE \qquad (5)$$

The Dynamic Behavior of Price Elasticity: Findings

The estimates of price elasticity along with the levels of fit for the thirty-five industrial chemical products are compared in appendix 12A-1 across different phases of the product life cycle, using the four models in equations (2) through (5). As an example of how to read the appendix, consider acetone in table 12A-1-A. Both model 1 and model 2 show that the price elasticity for acetone was higher during the introduction stage of its life cycle than during the growth stage (-2.48 versus 0.16 with model 1 and -1.81 versus 0.13 with model 2 in appendix table 12A-1-A). For antibiotics, model 1 estimated a higher level of price elasticity in the growth stage than in the maturity stage (-1.23 versus -0.17 in appendix 12A-1-B), whereas model 2 estimated relatively low price elasticity for both stages (-0.98 versus -0.22). For alkydres resins, model 1 shows that price elasticity was higher during growth1 phase than during growth2 phase (-1.77 versus -0.77 in appendix 12A-1-C), but model 2 estimated a positive price elasticity for growth1 phase and relatively lower price elasticity for growth2 phase (1.36 versus −0.72). Other cases can be interpreted similarly.

Table 12-1 summarizes the directions of shift in the level of the price elasticity over the product–life-cycle phases from appendix 12A-1. The results from model 1 show that, when we compare the estimate of price elasticity for the growth stage with that for the introduction stage, the directions of change

Table 12-1
Proportional Changes of Price-Elasticity Level over Product Life Cycle

Comparison	Introduction versus Growth1	Growth1 versus Maturity1	Growth1 versus Growth2	Growth2 versus Maturity2	Growth1 versus Decline
Model 1:					
Upward shift	4/11	2/11	0	0	0
Stable/indeterminate	4/11	5/11	8/17	2/2	3/4
Downward shift	3/11	4/11	9/17	0	1/4
Significance level for sign test[1]	0.637	0.344	0.004	—	0.500
Model 2:					
Upward shift	1/11	1/11	0	0	0
Stable/indeterminate	6/11	5/11	8/17	2/2	4/4
Downward shift	4/11	5/11	9/17	0	0
Significance level for sign test[1]	0.188	0.109	0.002	—	—
Model 3:					
Upward shift	5/11	2/11	3/17	0	1/4
Stable/indeterminate	4/11	4/11	5/17	2/2	0
Downward shift	2/11	5/11	9/17	0	3/4
Significance level for sign test[1]	0.227	0.227	0.073	—	0.313
Model 4:					
Upward shift	3/11	2/11	1/17	0	2/4
Stable/indeterminate	3/11	4/11	5/17	2/2	0
Downward shift	5/11	5/11	11/17	0	2/4
Significance level for sign test[1]	0.363	0.277	0.003	—	0.688

Note: The denominator is the number of series compared and the numerator is the number of series that show the relevant shifts between the compared life-cycle stages.

[1] The sign test is performed to test the hypothesis: the probability of upward shift is equal to the probability of downward shift. Therefore, the significance level is for the rejection of that null hypothesis in the two-tailed test (Conover 1980, pp. 122-128).

are almost equally distributed among "upward shift," "stable or indeterminate," and "downward shift" (4, 4, and 3 out of 11 cases for each direction). The results from model 2 more frequently demonstrate a "stable or indeterminate" pattern (6 out of 11) and show "upward shift" less frequently (1 out of 11). A comparison of maturity phase with the growth phase shows that the frequency for "upward shift" is low, but the frequencies of "stable or indeterminate" and "downward shift" are much higher (2/11 versus 5/11 versus 4/11 for model 1 and 1/11 versus 5/11 versus 5/11 for model 2).

The comparison of growth2 phase with growth1 phase of the product life cycle clearly shows more cases of "stable or indeterminate" and "downward shift," but no cases of "upward shift" (0 versus 8/17 versus 9/17 for both model 1 and model 2). Maturity2, observed for two products, was compared with growth2; price elasticity remained "stable or indeterminate" (0 versus 2/2 versus 0) for both model 1 and model 2. When decline was compared to growth, price elasticity was "stable or indeterminate" (0 versus 3/4 versus 1/4 for model 1 and 0 versus 4/4 versus 0 for model 2). These observations on the dynamic behavior of price elasticity are confirmed by the results for the two modified models, model 3 and model 4 in table 12–1.

Sign tests on the shifts of the level of price elasticity between different life-cycle phases show that the null hypothesis (the likelihood of upward shift is equal to the likelihood of downward shift) is rejected between growth1 and growth2 at 0.10 significance level for all four models (by two-tailed tests as suggested by Conover [1980]). The same null hypothesis is not rejected for the other comparisons.

We can check the reliability of these findings on the frequency distribution of the directional change of the price-elasticity level by comparing the results for different model specifications. In table 12–1 we observe that 7 out of 11 products are classified in the same way by both model 1 and model 2; that 3 products classified as "upward shift" by model 1 are classified as "stable or indeterminate" by model 2; and that 1 product classified as "stable or indeterminate" by model 1 is classified as "downward shift" by model 2. Similarly, we find that for the growth-to-maturity stages, 5 out of 11 products are differently classified (by models 1 and 2); 9 out of 17 products for growth1-to-growth2 phases; and 1 out of 4 products for the growth-to-decline stages. Among these inconsistent classifications, however, one product (barbituric acid) is reclassified from "upward shift" to "downward shift"; all others are from "upward shift" or "downward shift" to "stable or indeterminate" or vice versa. Therefore, it appears that the differences between the results of models 1 and 2 (and, similarly, of the modified models 3 and 4) are not particularly important in developing qualitative insights about the general pattern of shift in the level of price elasticity over the product life cycle.

A parametric test also confirms the dynamic behavior of the price elasticity. Pairwise comparisons of the price elasticities between growth1 as the base

Table 12–2
Pairwise Comparison of Price Elasticity between Product-Life-Cycle Phases

Model–	Growth1 versus Introduction		Growth1 versus Maturity1		Growth1 versus Growth2		Growth1 versus Decline	
	D	s(D)	D	s(D)	D	s(D)	D	s(D)
Model 1	−0.35	0.91	0.11	0.58	1.14*	0.48	0.42	0.69
Model 2	0.42	0.81	0.06	0.46	0.85*	0.41	0.40	0.58
Model 3	1.59*	0.66	0.17	0.49	1.15*	0.62	1.27	1.42
Model 4	0.29	0.68	0.07	0.48	1.72*	0.60	0.40	0.99
Number of observations	11		11		17		4	
T-statistic (two-tailed, 0.10 level)	1.81		1.81		1.75		2.35	

Note: Growth phase is used as the base of the comparison because of the comparability in terms of the numbers of paired phases.

D : mean difference between compared life-cycle stages.

$s(D)$: standard deviation of mean difference, D.

* : statistically significant at $\alpha = .10$.

1. Model 1: Diffusion-effect–price model in equation (2).
   Model 2: Demand-level–price model in equation (3).
   Model 3: Modified-diffusion-effect–price model in equation (4).
   Model 4: Modified-demand-level–price model in equation (5).

and each of the other phases of the product life cycle are shown in table 12–2. The levels of the price elasticity are different between growth1 and growth2 phases at 10 percent significance level for all four models. The other pairs do not show any significant difference for any model except in the comparison between introduction and growth stages for model 3.

Table 12–3 aggregates the frequencies of shifts in the level of price elasticity across the four models in table 12–1. It suggests that price elasticity generally follows a pattern of "stable → decrease → stable/decrease → stable/decrease" over the product life cycle. We can summarize our observations as:

The level of price elasticity tends to be lower during the later stages of the product life cycle (maturity and decline) than during the earlier stages (introduction and growth).

There is no clear tendency of shift in the level of the price elasticity between the introduction and the growth stages.

Table 12-3
Behavior of Price Elasticity over the Product Life Cycle

Comparison over Stages of the Product Life Cycle	Introduction ⟶	Growth1 ⟶	Growth2 ⟶	Maturity[1]	Decline
Upward shift	13	4	7	1	
Stable/indeterminate	17	26	26	7	
Downward shift	14	38	19	6	
Interpretation	Stable	Decrease	Stable/decrease	Stable/decrease	

Note: Frequencies of shifts were aggregated across the four models in table 12-1.
1. Frequencies over growth1 ⟶ maturity1 and over growth2 ⟶ maturity2 were aggregated.

Over the later two stages of the product life cycle (maturity and decline), price elasticity shows a tendency to be stable.

If the sales of an industrial chemical or allied product follow a cycle-recycle pattern of product life cycle, the price elasticity is lower during the "late growth phase" than during the "early growth phase."

Comparison with Past Research Findings

No comparable study has been reported on the dynamic behavior of price elasticity over the product life cycle. (See table 12-4.) Neither Mickwitz [1959] nor Parsons [1975] provided empirical reports for their propositions. The empirical studies by Wildt [1976] and Liu and Hanssens [1981] were on the behavior of the price elasticity over physical time rather than over the product life cycle. Moreover, past research on the price-elasticity behavior over time or stages of the life cycle focused on consumer products, whereas our empirical research deals with industrial products. Only Simon's [1979] study gives a picture of the dynamic behavior of the price elasticity over product–life-cycle stages, but it is on brand–sales-growth pattern rather than on the industry-sales pattern.

For the early stages of the life cycle (introduction-to-growth), Simon's findings indicate a decline in price elasticity, whereas our results suggest that price elasticity is more likely to remain stable. For the growth-to-maturity stages of the life cycle, both studies found that price elasticity decreases. For the maturity-to-decline stages, price elasticity increases (or stays stable in some product classes) in Simon's research, whereas it is stable in our results.

Table 12–4
Research on Dynamic Behavior of Price Elasticity

Reference	Product	Stage of Product Life Cycle			
		Intro ⟶	Growth ⟶	Maturity ⟶	Decline
Mickwitz[1] [1959]		Increase	Increase	Increase	Decrease
Parsons[1] [1975]		Decrease	Decrease	Decrease	
Wildt [1976]	Consumer products	(Promotion elasticity decreases over time)			
Simon[2] [1979]	Pharmaceuticals, detergents	Decrease Decrease	Decrease Decrease	Stable Increase	
Liu and Hanssens [1981]	Inexpensive gift items	(Increases over time)			
Lilien and Yoon (this chapter)	Industrial chemicals	Stable	Decrease/ Stable	Stable/ Decrease	

1. No empirical support was provided for these propositions.
2. Simon's [1979] study was on the brand life cycle rather than product life cycle.

Implications and Applications

The behavior of price elasticity over the early stages of the product life cycle reflects the market situation faced by a new-product innovation. During the introduction-to-growth stages of the life cycle, we may observe (1) innovative buyers who are less sensitive to a price change (Rogers 1983) and early adopters who recognize the economic benefits of the new product through previous buyers and users; (2) a declining price trend reflecting cost dynamics or an increasing price trend due to market-penetration policy and production-capacity constraints; (3) improvement of the product's quality; and (4) entries of competitive firms (Kotler 1980).

Increasing price sensitivity, decreasing price trend, quality improvement, and greater competition will influence the level of the price elasticity in a positive direction. Price elasticity will increase or shift up over time in such market situations. Faster diffusion of the economic benefits of the new product (high value-in-use, for example), increasing price trend, and high fixed costs for adopting the new product will influence the level of the price elasticity in a negative direction. Price elasticity will decline or shift down over time in such situations. However, it is not easy to identify each of these influences separately through empirical analysis. Our finding that there was no clear likelihood of shift in the level of the price elasticity during the early stages of the product life cycle may mean that negative influences on price elasticity tend to offset positive influences.

The shift down or the decreasing trend of the level of the price elasticity during the growth-to-maturity stages of the life cycle reflects the dominance of the negative influences over the positive influences. In particular, the diffusion of the new product's value-in-use might be a major factor that induces major adopters (Rogers 1983) to be relatively less sensitive to price. Price elasticity's recovery of a stable tendency during the maturity-to-decline stage of the life cycle could result from the introduction of substitute products and the increased competition that typically pushes the product's price downward.

What are the managerial implications of these findings? One implication is that a simple markup rule (Seglin [1963] for a short-term rule and Kalish [1983a] for a dynamic rule) is justifiable during the early stages of the product life cycle. As the life cycle passes its growth stage and moves to the maturity phase, a higher markup may generate greater profit for the industry as a whole.

Another application of the results of this exploratory analysis will be validating the assumptions on the price behavior that are made in the new-product–diffusion models. Our finding of no clear likelihood of change in the level of the price elasticity during the introduction-to-growth phases of the product life cycle indicates that, when new product models deal with the diffusion of industrial (particularly, chemical) products, we could reasonably assume that the price elasticity is stable. Other assumptions, like increasing or decreasing price elasticity, may need special explanations.

Conclusion

This research has several limitations in the data base, model, and estimation procedure. The sample size of thirty-five chemicals and allied products is not large enough to draw a conclusive observation on the dynamic behavior of the price elasticity in the chemical industry. Empirical studies with larger sample data and variables are expected to confirm or modify the findings of our study.

A high statistical fit of a model to data does not mean that the model is correctly specified. We need to validate our models by adding other relevant explanatory variables in future studies. In the regression analysis, we found nonrandom error structures for several chemical products, which indicates the existence of serial correlation, suggesting a need for more sophisticated estimation procedures.

Further study will need to expand the data base and validate the model specifications and estimation procedures through an extensive sensitivity analysis. It should also confirm the validity of the three-way categorization of the directional shifts of the price elasticity.

Appendix 12A-1:
Product–Life-Cycle Phases and Price Elasticity of Sales for Industrial Chemical Products

Table 12A-1-A
Introduction versus Growth

| Product | Trend | | Stage of Product Life Cycle | | | | | |
	Sales	Price	Introduction	R^2	Growth	R^2	Maturity/Decline	R^2
Acetone	S I	D D	1947–57		1957–71			
Model 1			H (−2.48*)	.80	N (0.16)	.99		
Model 2			H (−1.81**)	.75	N (0.13)	.99		
Model 3			H (−1.28)	.74	L (−0.66)	.97		
Model 4			H (−0.99)	.75	L (−0.31)	.99		
Methyl chloride	S I	D D	1950–58		1958–69			
Model 1			H (−7.33*)	.89	N (−0.62)	.99		
Model 2			H (−2.35*)	.62	N (−0.27)	.99		
Model 3			H (−2.13)	.67	L (−1.48)	.99		
Model 4			H (−1.81)	.58	L (−0.49)	.99		
Ethylene oxide	S I	D D	1956–63		1963–70			
Model 1			H (−2.44**)	.93	P (1.98**)	.98		
Model 2			H (−2.46**)	.82	P (0.66**)	.99		
Model 3			H (−2.69)	.80	H (−4.80)	.97		
Model 4			H (−1.76)	.76	P (2.26)	.99		
Polyvinyl chloride	S I	D D	1956–64		1964–72			
Model 1			N (0.01)	.99	H (−2.93*)	.99		
Model 2			P (1.97**)	.96	H (−2.92*)	.99		
Model 3			N (−0.07)	.81	H (−2.74)	.99		
Model 4			P (0.66)	.87	H (−2.54)	.99		
Ethyl acetate	S I	D D	1945–57		1957–71			
Model 1			N (−0.10)	.15	L (−0.39***)	.98		
Model 2			P (1.00*)	.61	L (−0.50*)	.98		
Model 3			P (1.09)	.49	N (0.27)	.98		
Model 4			P (0.90)	.71	N (0.15)	.99		

			1949–58			1958–72			*(Maturity)* 1956–69	
Ethylene glycol	S I	D D								
Model 1			N (0.41)	.23	L (−0.57***)	.98				
Model 2			P (1.58**)	.59	L (−0.90*)	.98				
Model 3			P (2.08)	.68	H (−1.09)	.97				
Model 4			P (2.03)	.81	N (−0.39)	.97				
			1950–57			1957–71				
Dodecyl mercaptans	S I	Df Ds								
Model 1			N (−0.62)	.06	L (−0.58**)	.88				
Model 2			N (2.81)	.31	N (−0.46)	.86				
Model 3			N (0.28)	.02	N (−0.23)	.87				
Model 4			P (1.14)	.21	N (−0.07)	.86				
			1956–63			1963–72				
Propionic acid	S I	D D								
Model 1			N (0.10)	.96	N (−1.54)	.89				
Model 2			P (0.90**)	.99	N (−0.31)	.91				
Model 3			P (1.49)	.98	H (−1.56)	.90				
Model 4			P (1.52)	.98	H (−1.01)	.91				
			1941–47			1947–56			1956–69	
Carbon tetrachloride	S If Is	D I D								
Model 1			N (1.11)	.91	P (0.75*)	.99	P (0.35*)	.99		
Model 2			L (−0.76**)	.91	P (0.79***)	.98	P (0.57**)	.99		
Model 3			H (−4.36)	.87	P (1.48)	.98	P (1.25)	.99		
Model 4			L (−0.81)	.91	P (1.36)	.98	P (1.44)	.99		
			1946–54			1954–70				
Styrene	S I	I D								
Model 1			P (1.65*)	.69	N (−0.06)	.98				
Model 2			H (−2.30***)	.65	N (−0.29)	.97				
Model 3			P (1.41)	.51	N (−0.84)	.97				
Model 4			H (−1.35)	.59	N (−0.81)	.97				
			1948–56			1956–63			*(Decline)* 1963–69	
Rosin esters and adducts	S I D	D I D								
Model 1			P (0.30**)	.40	N (−1.74)	.93	N (−3.13)	.56		
Model 2			N (0.62)	.36	N (−1.39)	.93	N (−2.48)	.51		
Model 3			P (0.50)	.36	H (−1.51)	.94	H (−3.55)	.64		
Model 4			N (0.65)	.41	H (−1.29)	.95	H (−3.00)	.60		

For notes, see page 286.

Table 12A–1–B
Growth versus Maturity

| | Trend | | Stage of Product Life Cycle | | | | | |
Product	Sales	Price	Growth1	R^2	Maturity	R^2	Growth2	R^2
Antibiotics	I S	Df Ds	1952–63		1963–68			
Model 1			H (−1.23**)	.98	L (−0.17**)	.69		
Model 2			L (−0.98*)	.99	L (−0.22**)	.78		
Model 3			L (−0.95)	.99	L (−0.25)	.46		
Model 4			L (−0.76)	.99	L (−0.33)	.63		
Ethylene dichloride	I S	D D	1949–60		1960–67			
Model 1			H (−3.80*)	.92	N (−0.27)	.64		
Model 2			H (−3.21*)	.93	N (−0.56)	.60		
Model 3			H (−1.46)	.95	N (−0.50)	.63		
Model 4			H (−2.28)	.94	N (−0.75)	.58		
Alkydres resins	I S I	D S D	1946–54		1954–61		1961–69	
Model 1			H (−1.77**)	.83	N (0.15)	.31	L (−0.77*)	.97
Model 2			P (1.36*)	.97	N (0.10)	.26	L (−0.72*)	.98
Model 3			L (−0.39)	.84	N (0.10)	.28	L (−0.80)	.97
Model 4			P (0.81)	.96	N (0.10)	.25	L (−0.78)	.97
Synthetic dyes	I S I	D I I	1941–47		1947–57		1957–68	
Model 1			H (−(1.05*))	.97	N (−0.17)	.95	L (−0.23*)	.99
Model 2			H (−1.01*)	.98	L (−0.44**)	.94	L (−0.49*)	.99
Model 3			H (−1.18)	.98	L (−0.41)	.94	L (−0.31)	.98
Model 4			H (−1.06)	.98	L (−0.58)	.92	L (−0.66)	.97
Antioxidants	I S I	D I S	1937–48		1948–58		1958–70	
Model 1			N (−0.03)	.92	H (−3.92*)	.75	P (4.05*)	.94
Model 2			N (−0.16)	.98	H (−3.50*)	.74	P (3.08*)	.96
Model 3			N (−0.29)	.68	H (−4.20)	.59	P (5.62)	.91
Model 4			N (−0.04)	.98	H (−3.98)	.59	P (4.80)	.93

		1938-46		1946-67	
Barbituric acid	I S D D				
Model 1		N (−0.66)	.96	L (−0.79*)	.67
Model 2		H (−1.56*)	.97	L (−0.71*)	.51
Model 3		H (−2.66)	.86	L (−0.65)	.47
Model 4		H (−1.93)	.97	N (−0.38)	.51

		1942-55		1955-69	
Synthetic tanning	I S If Is				
Model 1		N (0.24)	.35	N (−0.18)	.03
Model 2		L (−0.79*)	.86	N (−0.92)	.33
Model 3		N (−0.29)	.66	L (−0.92)	.20
Model 4		L (−0.48)	.84	H (−1.02)	.59

		1938-46		1946-53		1953-63	
Sodium salicylate	I S I D I S						
Model 1		N (−0.09)	.99	N (0.17)	.71	P (1.27*)	.99
Model 2		L (−0.89*)	.96	N (0.03)	.75	P (0.86*)	.99
Model 3		H (−1.59)	.97	N (0.15)	.71	N (−0.04)	.99
Model 4		H (−1.42)	.97	N (0.03)	.74	L (−0.74)	.99

		1940-48		1948-61		1961-70	
Organic accelerators	I S I D I D						
Model 1		P (0.62*)	.93	N (0.92)	.95	N (−0.27)	.99
Model 2		N (0.21)	.79	N (0.85)	.95	N (0.33)	.99
Model 3		P (0.77)	.80	P (1.49)	.94	L (−0.90)	.99
Model 4		N (0.15)	.78	P (1.56)	.95	N (−0.25)	.99

		1933-42		1942-49		1949-69	
Synthetic medicinals	I S I I I D						
Model 1		P (1.58*)	.93	N (−0.31)	.22	P (0.12***)	.99
Model 2		P (0.67**)	.98	N (−0.08)	.43	P (0.26*)	.99
Model 3		P (0.90)	.97	N (−0.09)	.15	N (0.16)	.92
Model 4		P (0.52)	.99	N (−0.09)	.45	N (−0.23)	.89

		1947-56		1956-69	
Carbon tetrachloride	S If Is D I D				
Model 1		P (0.75*)	.99	P (0.35*)	.99
Model 2		P (0.798***)	.98	P (0.57*)	.99
Model 3		P (1.48)	.98	P (1.25)	.99
Model 4		P (1.36)	.98	P (1.44)	.99

For notes, see page 286.

Table 12A-1-C
Growth1 Phase versus Growth2 Phase

Product	Trend		Stage of Product Life Cycle					
	Sales	Price	Growth1	R^2	Maturity1	R^2	Growth2	R^2
Alkydres resins	I S I	D S D	1946–54		1954–61		1961–69	
Model 1			H (−1.77**)	.83	N (0.15)	.31	L (−0.77*)	.97
Model 2			P (1.36*)	.97	N (0.10)	.26	L (−0.72*)	.98
Model 3			L (−0.39)	.84	N (0.10)	.28	L (−0.80)	.97
Model 4			P (0.81)	.96	N (0.10)	.25	L (−0.78)	.97
Synthetic dyes	I S I	D I I	1941–47		1947–57		1957–	
Model 1			H (−1.05*)	.97	N (−0.17)	.96	L (−0.23*)	.99
Model 2			H (−1.01*)	.98	L (−0.44**)	.94	L (−0.49*)	.99
Model 3			H (−1.18)	.98	L (−0.41)	.94	L (−0.31)	.98
Model 4			H (−1.06)	.98	L (−0.58)	.92	L (−0.66)	.97
Coumarone resins	If Is	D I	1950–57				1957–69	
Model 1			H (−1.31*)	.98			N (−0.29)	.80
Model 2			H (−1.01**)	.98			N (−0.07)	.78
Model 3			H (−1.43)	.94			N (−0.06)	.79
Model 4			H (−1.20)	.97			N (−0.09)	.76
Phenolic resins	Is If	D D	1961–66				1966–72	
Model 1			H (−1.14**)	.98			N (−1.10)	.94
Model 2			N (−1.23)	.93			N (−0.62)	.98
Model 3			N (−0.39)	.97			P (0.51)	.96
Model 4			H (−2.47)	.93			P (0.56)	.99
Titanium dioxide	If Is	S D	1955–64				1964–76	
Model 1			H (−3.25**)	.92			N (0.00)	.90
Model 2			L (−0.96*)	.99			N (0.30)	.95
Model 3			H (−1.12)	.99			N (−0.17)	.88
Model 4			N (−0.49)	.97			N (0.39)	.94

			1955–62	R^2	1962–69	R^2
Chloroform	If Is	D D				
Model 1			H (−2.57**)	.97	P (1.58***)	.98
Model 2			N (−0.07)	.99	P (1.42*)	.99
Model 3			L (−0.66)	.99	H (−4.34)	.94
Model 4			N (−0.49)	.99	P (1.73)	.95
			1953–62		1962–71	
Mono-, di-triethanomines	If Is	D D				
Model 1			H (−2.09*)	.99	P (0.38*)	.99
Model 2			H (−2.68**)	.99	N (0.10)	.99
Model 3			H (−4.18)	.98	L (−0.75)	.95
Model 4			H (−3.89)	.98	N (0.42)	.98
			1938–48		1948–63	
Salicylic acid	Is Is	D I				
Model 1			L (−0.57***)	.91	N (−0.87)	.87
Model 2			H (1.16)	.98	N (−0.90)	.91
Model 3			N (−0.38)	.94	P (17.49)	.93
Model 4			N (−0.32)	.96	P (15.92)	.92
			1956–64		1964–71	
Polyethylene resins	If Is	D D				
Model 1			L (−0.92*)	.99	N (−0.34)	.99
Model 2			N (1.16)	.98	N (−0.68)	.99
Model 3			H (−3.60)	.99	L (−0.75)	.99
Model 4			H (−3.17)	.98	N (−0.26)	.99
			1952–60		1960–72	
Polyvinyl acetate	If Is	D D				
Model 1			L (0.16*)	.99	L (−0.51*)	.99
Model 2			H (−1.83*)	.99	L (−0.53**)	.99
Model 3			H (−3.23)	.99	L (−0.63)	.95
Model 4			H (−2.46)	.99	N (−0.26)	.98
			1951–60		1961–71	
Cellulose ethers	If Is	D D				
Model 1			N (−1.32)	.98	N (0.25)	.94
Model 2			N (−1.41)	.99	N (1.21)	.93
Model 3			H (−2.21)	.94	N (−0.25)	.98
Model 4			H (−2.04)	.96	P (1.09)	.97

Table 12A–1–C (Continued)

Product	Trend Sales	Price	Growth1	R²	Maturity1	R²	Growth2	R²
Epoxy resins	If Is	D D	1956-64				1964-72	
Model 1			N (−1.23)	.97			L (−0.24)	.96
Model 2			H (−2.31**)	.99			N (−0.44)	.96
Model 3			H (−5.14)	.97			H (−1.65)	.94
Model 4			H (−3.85)	.98			H (−1.26)	.95
Carbon disulfide	I I	D D	1942-48				1948-56	
Model 1			N (−0.07)	.98			P (1.04*)	.99
Model 2			H (−1.08**)	.65			N (−1.00)	.99
Model 3			N (0.47)	.97	P (1.27)	.99	N (−0.19)	.56
Model 4			H (−1.15)	.64	P (1.21)	.99	N (−0.20)	.59
Antioxidants	I S I	D I S	1937-48		1948-58		1958-70	
Model 1			N (−0.03)	.92	H (−3.92*)	.75	P (4.05*)	.94
Model 2			N (−0.16)	.98	H (−3.50*)	.74	P (3.08*)	.96
Model 3			N (−0.29)	.68	H (−4.20)	.59	P (5.62)	.91
Model 4			N (−0.04)	.98	H (−3.98)	.59	P (4.80)	.93
Sodium salicylate	I D I	D I S	1938-46		1946-53		1953-63	
Model 1			N (−0.09)	.99	N (0.17)	.71	P (1.27*)	.99
Model 2			L (−0.89*)	.96	N (0.03)	.75	P (0.86*)	.99
Model 3			H (−1.59)	.97	N (0.15)	.71	N (−0.04)	.99
Model 4			H (−1.42)	.97	N (0.03)	.75	L (−0.74)	.99
Organic accelerators	I S I	D I D	1940-48		1948-61		1961-70	
Model 1			P (0.62*)	.93	N (0.92)	.95	N (−0.27)	.99
Model 2			N (0.21)	.79	N (0.85)	.95	N (0.33)	.99
Model 3			P (0.77)	.80	P (1.49)	.94	L (−0.90)	.99
Model 4			N (0.15)	.78	P (1.56)	.95	N (−0.25)	.99

Synthetic medicinals	I S I	I I D	1933-42	R^2	1942-49	R^2	1949-69	R^2
Model 1			P (1.58*)	.93	N (-0.31)	.22	P (0.12***)	.99
Model 2			P (0.67**)	.98	N (-0.08)	.43	P (0.26*)	.99
Model 3			P (0.90)	.97	N (-0.09)	.15	N (0.16)	.92
Model 4			P (0.52)	.99	N (-0.09)	.45	N (-0.23)	.89

For notes, see page 286.

Table 12A-1-D
Growth2 Phase versus Maturity 2 Phase

	Trend		Stage of Product Life Cycle					
Product	Sales	Price	Growth1	R^2	Growth2	R^2	Maturity2	R^2
Salicylic acid	If Is	S D I S	1938-48		1948-63		1963-68	
Model 1			L (-0.57***)	.91	N (-0.87)	.87	P (19.34*)	.91
Model 2			H (-1.09*)	.87	N (-0.90)	.91	P (19.03*)	.93
Model 3			N (-0.38)	.94			P (17.49)	.93
Model 4			N (-0.32)	.96			P (15.92)	.92
Carbon disulfide	I I S	D I D	1942-48		1948-56		1956-69	
Model 1			N (-0.07)	.98	P (1.04*)	.99	N (-0.20)	.53
Model 2			H (-1.08**)	.65	N (-1.00)	.99	N (-0.10)	.60
Model 3			N (0.47)	.97	P (1.27)	.99	N (-0.19)	.56
Model 4			H (-1.15)	.64	P (1.21)	.99	N (-0.20)	.59

For notes, see page 286.

Table 12A-1-E
Growth versus Decline

Product	Trend		Stage of Product Life Cycle					
	Sales	Price	Introduction	R²	Growth	R²	Decline	R²
Ethyl chloride	I D	D D			1955–66		1966–72	
Model 1					H (−1.80*)	.97	N (−0.09)	.82
Model 2					N (−0.92)	.90	N (0.01)	.84
Model 3					L (−0.92)	.88	N (−0.21)	.86
Model 4					N (−0.42)	.85	N (0.00)	.85
Dodecyl benzene	I D	D I			1952–67		1967–72	
Model 1					N (0.13)	.96	N (0.82)	.93
Model 2					N (−0.50)	.89	N (−0.12)	.89
Model 3					H (−1.12)	.88	N (0.47)	.93
Model 4					H (−1.33)	.88	N (−0.38)	.89
Potassium phosphates	I D	D D			1961–66		1966–71	
Model 1					N (−0.54)	.98	N (0.12)	.88
Model 2					N (−1.74)	.98	N (−0.36)	.93
Model 3					H (−3.00)	.97	L (−0.80)	.94
Model 4					H (−2.50)	.97	N (−0.41)	.95
Rosin esters and adducts	S I D	D I D	1948–56		1956–63		1963–69	
Model 1			P (0.30**)	.40	N (−1.74)	.93	N (−3.13)	.56
Model 2			N (0.62)	.36	N (−1.39)	.93	N (−2.48)	.51
Model 3			P (0.50)	.36	H (−1.51)	.94	H (−3.55)	.64
Model 4			N (0.65)	.41	H (−1.29)	.95	H (−3.00)	.60

Notes: For each chemical product, the sales trend, the price trend, and the period of each of the identified product-life-cycle phases are shown in the first row.

For sales and price trends, the following indicators are used:

I: Increasing   If: Increasing fast   Is: Increasing slowly
D: Decreasing   Df: Decreasing fast   Ds: Decreasing slowly
S: Stable

For each model, an elasticity indicator, price-elasticity estimate, and a level of model fit are shown for each identified product–life-cycle phase.

The elasticity indicators for model 1 and model 2 are:

H: price elasticity is statistically significant at at least the 15 percent level and is greater than 1.0.
L: price elasticity is statistically significant but is less than 1.0.
N: price elasticity is statistically not significant.
P: price elasticity is positive, probably due to model misspecifications or missing variables.

The elasticity indicators for model 3 and model 4 are:

H: price elasticity is greater than 1.0.
L: price elasticity is less than 1.0, but greater than 0.5.
N: price elasticity is between (−) 0.5 and positive 0.5.
P: price elasticity is positive and greater than 0.5.

The price-elasticity estimate is:

  ⋆ Statistically significant at the 5 percent level
 ⋆⋆ Statistically significant at the 10 percent level
⋆⋆⋆ Statistically significant at the 15 percent level

The level of model fit is given by the R^2 value for each model where:

Model 1: $\log(SALES) = a + b \log(CUM) + d \log(PRICE)$

Model 2: $\log(SALES) = a + c \log(IPI) + d \log(PRICE)$

Model 3: $\log(SALES) = a + b\, CUM + d\, PRICE$

Model 4: $\log(SALES) = a + c\, IPI + d\, PRICE$

where CUM = cumulative $SALES$

     IPI = an economic trend variable; that is, the industrial production index for chemicals and allied products

13
Pricing When Different Outlets Offer Different Assortments of Brands

Steven M. Shugan

Pricing research continues to be an important part of the marketing literature (Rao 1984). Research in pricing has studied product pricing by manufacturers (Monroe and Della Bitta 1978), the affects of distribution members on manufacturer price setting (Baligh and Richartz 1967; Coughlan 1983; Jeuland and Shugan 1983a; McGuire and Staelin 1983a), defensive pricing (Hauser and Shugan 1983), and the pricing of a manufacturer's product line (Oren, Smith, and Wilson 1984; Shugan and Balachandran 1976). This past research has not considered situations where manufacturers sell their products through different outlets at different prices. This form of price discrimination is often precluded by legal restrictions on pricing. Nevertheless, even if manufacturers sell their products to different outlets at the same price, these outlets may still resell these manufacturers' products at different prices. As a consequence, shoppers often find the same product sold through different outlets at different prices.

This idea of price dispersion across outlets is not new to the literature. In fact, the behavior of shoppers searching to find lower prices has been well studied. Since Stigler's [1961] seminal paper, much research has concentrated on how a shopper searches for a given product across outlets in order to obtain a lower price (Nagle 1984; Nelson 1978; Wilde 1979, 1980). This research, however, has not considered the different assortments of products carried by different outlets. Yet, product assortment does vary across outlets (Stern and El-Ansary 1982; Pintel and Diamond 1977). Some outlets offer a large assortment of product categories (e.g., lawn mowers, cameras, tools), while other outlets offer few product categories. Even within product categories, some outlets offer a narrow assortment of products (e.g., only a few brands of cameras), while other outlets offer a wide assortment of products (e.g., many brands and models of cameras).

The author is very grateful to Thomas Nagle for his extensive comments on an earlier draft of this chapter.

The economic search literature has not considered variation in product assortment for a good reason. Variation in product assortment is not important when shoppers first choose a product and then choose an outlet to obtain that product. In this chapter, I argue that consumers shop for outlets in addition to products. Although these decisions can occur independently, outlet and product decisions do influence each other. Product search can be costly! Outlets seldom carry all available products (Levitt 1980; Pintel and Diamond 1977) and shoppers' decisions are sometimes based on an entire shopping basket of products rather than one product. Once the outlet selection is made, the shopper is temporarily restricted to those products carried by the selected outlet. For example, if a shopper chooses to purchase a lawn mower from K-Mart, that shopper will purchase from the products carried by K-Mart. In this chapter, we explore sequential behavior when shoppers first choose the outlet and then choose the product. We allow a consumer to shop at other outlets only after the consumer shops within the outlet. This outlet shopping behavior is found to lead to different pricing implications than when consumers search for one product across different outlets.

I argue that when shoppers sequentially choose an outlet and then a product, the product's price will depend on the width of an outlet's product line. I show that outlets offering a wide product line should offer their highest-priced products at higher prices than outlets offering a narrower product line. I also show that outlets offering a wide product line should offer lower-priced products at lower prices than outlets offering a narrower product line.

I begin by stating my assumptions in the next section. The subsequent section considers outlets that carry one product in a specific product category. Actual outlets are seldom limited to one product (Urban and Hauser 1980). Hence, this analysis is extended to dual-product outlets and multiproduct outlets in the following sections. The section after that provides an example while the following one tests our hypothesis against competing explanations for price variation across outlets. Our empirical results, which are summarized in the final section, provide support for the chapter's theoretical arguments.

Our Assumptions

We can state the key assumption of this chapter as follows:

Assumption 1: Shoppers shop within an outlet before shopping across outlets.

Our key assumption hypothesizes the following scenario for consumer shopping behavior. First, shoppers choose an outlet. That choice may or may not be related to the product category under study. Next, consumers shop for products in different product categories within that outlet. For each product category, the shopper searches within the outlet for the most preferred product within the product category given that outlet's prices. Upon finding that product, the shopper can either purchase the product or leave the outlet without buying a product in that category.

Note that the effect of this sequential outlet-product decision may be partially offset by shoppers who simultaneously choose the product and the outlet or by shoppers who first choose the product and then the outlet. I suspect that in few product categories will shoppers simultaneously choose the outlet and the product. Such a decision requires shoppers to have information both about which products each outlet carries and about the prices of those products. Rarely would shoppers have such complete information. However, for some product categories, shoppers might be more likely to choose the product and then shop across outlets. This behavior should be found when the expected savings from shopping across outlets would be greater than the transaction cost of shopping. Hence, for high-priced products (e.g., automobiles, refrigerators) where prices have substantial variation across outlets, shoppers may select a product and then search across outlets until a sufficiently low price is found. However, I still expect my shopping hypothesis to be true for a large number of product categories.

In addition to my shopping hypothesis, I require several other conditions. I limit this study to product categories and outlets for which the following conditions hold. The section *Empirical Findings* examines issues of validity.

Assumption 2: Products within the product line can be ranked from the highest-priced product to lowest-price product.

This condition assumes that a product line exists. If products could not be ranked according to some criterion, we would have a product space rather than a product line. One example of a product line that satisfies this condition is the Canon Camera line. This line consists of a series of camera models starting with the bottom-of-the-line Snappy 20, followed by several other models (the Snappy 50, AV-1, AE-1, and A-1) and concluding with the top-of-the-line F-1.[1] Shoppers can upgrade or downgrade depending on their preferences. In this example, the shopper who wants more quality and features than the AE-1 offers would upgrade to the A-1. On the other hand, the shopper who wants to spend less than the price of the AE-1 would downgrade to the AV-1. For lack of a better name, we refer to products at the bottom of the line as low-end products. Low-end products often are of lower quality or have fewer features than high-end products. Moreover, within a particular outlet, high-end products command a higher price than low-end products. The terms, low-end and high-end are relative terms. Indeed, the low-end product at one outlet may be the high-end product at another outlet.

Assumption 3: Shoppers who buy lower-priced products are, on average, more price-sensitive (have greater absolute price elasticity of demand) than shoppers who buy higher-priced products.

This assumption is also quite common and can be shown to follow from other reasonable assumptions about shopper behavior. (For example, see Oren, Smith, and Wilson [1984]; Shugan [1984].) Generally, shoppers who are willing to pay more for quality will buy higher-quality products.

Although the following assumption is not necessary, it is a sufficient condition that simplifies our analysis.

Assumption 4: On any particular shopping trip, shoppers buy no more than one product from any particular product category.

This standard assumption in marketing is known as the quantal-choice problem. This is not a key assumption in our analysis and is only required to simplify the development. Because we use an aggregate model, it is possible to allow a shopper to make multiple purchases by modeling that shopper as two shoppers. We now use these assumptions to derive the profit function of a single-product outlet.

Single-Product Outlets

Before considering more complex situations, which are covered in the next section, we begin our analysis by considering the expected behavior of a shopper who enters an outlet that carries only one product in a specific product line. This outlet might be a mass merchandiser who carries many product categories (e.g., lawn mowers, cameras, tools) but a limited assortment in each product category. In this situation, the shopper enters the outlet and thereafter observes which product is carried by the outlet and the price of that product. The shopper then must decide whether to purchase the product or try another outlet where a superior value might be found. In this case, the shopper does not know the price of the product until the outlet is entered.

This situation has been well studied. The shopper should consider the price of the given product at this outlet and the distribution of prices for that product across outlets. The shopper must then decide whether additional search across outlets is worthwhile. Some shoppers will decide that additional search is not worthwhile; these shoppers will purchase the product. Other shoppers will decide that additional search is indeed worthwhile and these shoppers will not purchase the product. The decision will depend on, among other factors, the value of the shopper's time (as determined by income and number of children needing attention, for example), the shoppers' resources for search (e.g., means of transit, mobility), the cost of additional search, and the distribution of prices in the market (Blattberg and Sen 1974).

In general, a shopper purchases a product if the price of the product is less than some price, r, where the value of r often depends on the previously mentioned variables (McCall 1965); Rothschild 1973). The price r is called the shopper's reservation price. Shoppers usually have different reservation prices and some number of shoppers will have a reservation price that exceeds the price of the product. We denote that number as $v(p_j)$. (Note that $dv(p_j)/dp_j < 0$.) We can now express the profits of the single-product outlet with equation (1).

$$Y_j = (p_j - c_j)(1 - M_j)v(p_j) - F_j \qquad (1)$$

Y_j = profit from product j^2

p_j = price of product j

c_j = variable cost of product j

M_j = fraction of shoppers who do not visit the outlet because the product assortment is too limited

$v(p_j)$ = number of total shoppers who would purchase at price p_j

F_j = fixed cost of carrying product j.

Equation (1) represents the profits of an outlet that carries one product. That product might be a high-price high-end product or a low-price low-end product. We denote the low-end product with an L and the high-end product with an H. The next section considers an outlet that chooses to carry both a high-end product and a low-end product.

Dual-Product Outlets

Suppose an outlet currently carries a relatively low-end product, L. Then, that outlet's profits are given by equation (1) where $j = L$. If the outlet decides to add a more expensive high-end product, say product H, the high-end product draws some shoppers from the low-end product. However, the shoppers drawn to the higher-priced product from the lower-priced product are likely to be less price-sensitive than the shoppers who continue to purchase the low-end product L.

We capture this effect by partitioning the outlet's customers into two segments, segments 1 and 2, respectively. The second segment consists of shoppers who are less price-sensitive (i.e., have a smaller absolute price elasticity of demand) than the shoppers in the first segment. Hence, in the case of the single-product outlet, the number of shoppers who purchase product L is the number of shoppers in the first segment who buy product L plus the number of shoppers in the second segment who buy product L.

When a higher-end product is offered, a fraction of the less price-sensitive shoppers in segment 2, denoted $k(p_L, p_H)$, prefer the high-end product at price p_H to the low-end product at p_L. Equation (2) shows the number of shoppers who purchase product L when product H is also offered.

$$v(p_L, p_H) = v_1(p_L) + [1 - k(p_L, p_H)]v_2(p_L) \qquad (2)$$

where $v(p_L, p_H)$ = the number of shoppers who purchase product L at price p_L when product H is offered at price p_H

$v_i(p_L)$ = the number of shoppers in segment i who would purchase product L at price p_L if product H were not available

$k(p_L, p_H)$ = the percentage of shoppers in segment 2 who prefer product H at price p_H to product L at price p_L

Equation (2) shows that a fraction, $k(p_L, p_H)$, of segment-2 consumers prefer the high-end product at price p_H to the low-end product at p_L. Of those shoppers, some $w(p_L, p_H)$ will actually buy product 2, as shown in equation (3).

$$w(p_L, p_H) = k(p_L, p_H)w_2(p_H) \qquad (3)$$

where $w_2(p_H)$ = the number of shoppers in segment 2 who would purchase product H at price p_H if product L were not available

$w(p_L, p_H)$ = the number of shoppers who will purchase product H at price p_H when product L is priced at p_L

Note that equations (2) and (3) make two implicit but almost innocuous assumptions. First, we implicitly assume that $w_2(p_H)$ is not a function of p_L. This assumption is not very restrictive because most dependencies of $w_2(p_H)$ on p_L can be captured by redefining $k(p_L, p_H)$ to include those dependencies. Second, we have assumed that none of the more price-sensitive shoppers in segment 1 purchase the higher-priced product. This assumption merely requires that we only include shoppers in segment 1 who have reservation prices for product H that are below the relevant range of prices for product H. Moreover, even if we allowed some members of segment 1 to purchase product H, the conclusions that we would derive would remain unaltered, provided that more segment shoppers purchase product H.

Given equations (2) and (3), we can express the profits of the dual-product outlet as shown in equation (4).

$$Y_{LH} = (p_L - c_L)(1 - M_{LH})v(p_L, p_H)$$

$$= (p_H - c_H)(1 - M_{LH})w(p_L, p_H) - F_{LH} \tag{4}$$

where Y_{LH} is the profit of an outlet carrying both product L and product H.[3]

When the dual-product outlet maximizes profits given by equation (1), the optimal prices, $\hat{p}_L$ and $\hat{p}_H$ satisfy condition (5).

$$[v_1(p_L) + (p_L - c_L)v_1'(p_L) + v_2(p_L) + (p_L - c_L)v_2'(p_L)] +$$

the single-product–outlet condition

$$k(p_L, p_H)[-v_2(p_L) - (p_L - c_L)v_2'(p_L)] +$$

the segmentation effect

$$\left[(\partial k(p_L, p_H)/\partial p_L)((p_H - c_H)w_2(p_H) - (p_L - c_L)v_2(p_L))\right] = 0 \tag{5}$$

the trade-up effect

where $v_j'(p_j) = dv_j(p_j)/dp_j$ and $j = L, H$.

Equation (5) has three terms in brackets. The first term represents the condition for maximizing the profits of a single-product outlet. If the first term equals zero (at the optimal prices, $\hat{p}_L$ and $\hat{p}_H$), then the dual-product outlet would price the low-end product at the same price as the single-product outlet. If the first term is negative, the dual-product outlet would set a higher price for the low-end product than the single-product outlet. If the first term is positive, the dual-product outlet would set a lower price for the low-end product than the single product outlet.

The sign of the first term depends on the other bracketed terms. We call the first of these other terms the *segmentation effect*. The second term is the *trade-up effect*. When the high-end product is offered, some of the less price-sensitive shoppers prefer the high-end product over the low-end product. The segmentation effect represents the increase in price sensitivity of the shoppers who consider the low-end product. It is possible to show that the segmentation effect is always negative. Hence, if the trade-up effect were negative, the segmentation effect would cause the first term in equation (5) to be positive and the dual-product outlet would offer the low-end product at a lower price than the single-product outlet.

The trade-up effect is proportional to the difference in profits between the low-end product and the high-end product, i.e., the difference in profits caused by segment 2. A positive trade-up effect means that the outlet wants segment-2 customers to trade up from the low-end product to the high-end product. The trade-up effect is usually positive because shoppers in segment 2, who buy the high-end product, are less price-sensitive than shoppers who buy the low-end product. Furthermore, the fixed costs associated with carrying a high-end product often require higher absolute margins for high-end products. These costs come from more expensive decor, higher carrying costs, better-trained personnel, and superior locations in higher-rent areas than outlets carrying low-priced products. Outlets carrying lower-priced products can often save on such expenses, allowing them to maintain lower fixed costs. If a dual-product outlet could not recover these added costs from the high-end product, the outlet would become a single-product outlet and not offer the high-end product.

We see that the trade-up effect usually works in the opposite direction as the segmentation effect. The trade-up effect causes the dual-product outlet to raise the price of the low-end product to induce shoppers to trade up from the low-end product to the higher-margin high-end product. If the trade-up effect dominates the segmentation effect, the dual-product outlet will offer the low-end product at a higher price than the single-product outlet. However, to account for this fact, we make the following assumption.

Assumption 5: The segmentation effect dominates the trade-up effect.

We make this assumption because, in most markets, we would not expect the trade-up effect to be extremely large. If the trade-up effect were very large, the outlet would be obtaining a much higher profit from segment 2 purchases of the high-end product than segment 2 purchases of the low-end product; because shoppers in segment 2 vastly prefer high-end products to low-end products. However, if this were true, the outlet would have the incentive to offer an even higher-end product. In fact, the outlet would continue to add higher-end products until the added profits from the high-end products were no longer greater than the profits lost from shoppers trading up. In other words, the outlet has the incentive to offer additional high-end products until the trade-up effect is near zero. In the next section, I argue that by offering even higher-end products, outlets draw segment-2 shoppers from the current high-end product, further diminishing the trade-up effect. At this point, I summarize my conclusions with theorem 1.

Theorem 1: Assumptions 1 through 5 imply the following:

A. If the low-priced product at a dual-product outlet is also carried by a single-product outlet, then the dual-product outlet will price that product at a lower price than the single-product outlet.

    B. If the high-priced product at a dual-product outlet is also carried by a single-product outlet, then the dual-product outlet will price that product at a higher price than the single-product outlet.

This theorem indicates that when shoppers sequentially choose the outlet and then the product, the sequential nature of this process affects outlets' pricing decisions. Theorem 1 has the following corollaries for the product line under study.

Corollary 1: A dual-product outlet will have a larger variability in prices within the outlet than the variability in prices existing across single-product outlets.

This corollary is caused by some outlets carrying a more limited product assortment than that available in the market. Hence, an outlet only carrying product H has the incentive to lower the price of H, thereby attracting shoppers who would prefer product L if L were available. Outlets offering product L, in addition to product H, need not make this reduction in the price of product H. Similarly, an outlet offering only product L raises the price of product L, thereby reacting to price-insensitive shoppers who are buying product L because product H is not available.

Corollary 2 also follows from theorem 1.

Corollary 2: Assuming that outlets face the same cost, c_j:

    a. A dual-product outlet will receive a larger per-unit margin on the outlet's high-priced product than the single-product outlet.

    b. A dual-product outlet will receive a smaller per-unit margin on the outlet's high-priced product than the single-product outlet.

    c. A dual-product outlet will receive a larger per-unit margin on the outlet's high-priced product than its low-priced product.

This corollary is caused by the shoppers who buy the high-end product being more sensitive to price than the shoppers who buy the low-end product.

    In summary, the price of the low-end product at a single-product outlet should be higher than the price of the same product at a dual-product outlet when the latter outlet also carries a high-end product. From equation (5), we know the optimal price for product L at the single-product outlet does not depend on the number of shoppers who enter the outlet $(1 - M_j)$, nor does it depend on the fraction of shoppers in segment 2 who would prefer a high-end product (the function $k(p_L, p_H)$). Hence, the single-product outlet would price product L at a lower price than the dual-product outlet regardless of the number of shoppers entering the outlet and the preferences of shoppers in segment 2. Hence, our conclusions are valid even if outlets with high-end products attract more shoppers who prefer high-end products. However, it is also possible that outlets carrying high-end products discourage patronage by price-sensitive shoppers (i.e., shoppers in segment 1).

We consider this situation by assuming that a fraction of the shoppers in segment 1 do not patronize outlets carrying high-end products. We denote that fraction as z where z is a function of the assortment of high-end products and $0 \leq z \leq 1$. We examine the effects of $z \neq 1$ in the next section.

Multiproduct Outlets

If an outlet offers higher-end products than product H, some shoppers will purchase the higher-end products instead of product H. We capture this effect by allowing a fraction, $h(\underline{p})$, of the less price-sensitive segment to prefer higher-end products to product H. The fraction $h(\underline{p})$ is a function of the prices of these higher-end products and the price of product H; denoted $\underline{p}$ where $\underline{p} = (p_L, p_H)$. The fraction of shoppers who buy higher-end products increases as the prices of higher-end products decrease. Hence, $\partial h(\underline{p})/\partial p_E < 0$ for any higher-end product E. Finally, the fraction of consumers who buy higher-end products decreases as the price of product H decreases; i.e., $\partial h(\underline{p})/\partial p_H > 0$.

As noted previously, the addition of higher-end products may discourage more price-sensitive shoppers from shopping at the outlet. In this case, the number of segment-1 shoppers may decrease relative to the number of segment-2 shoppers. Hence, we allow segment-1 shoppers to decrease by a fraction, z, where $0 \leq z \leq 1$. The condition necessary to set p_L to maximize the profits of a multiproduct outlet can now be obtained. That condition would be the same condition as equation (5) except for the addition of two new terms. We call these new terms the image effect and the multiproduct effect. These new terms are shown in equation (6).

$$\underbrace{\left[\partial k(p_L, p_H)/\partial p_L\right]\left[1 - h(\underline{p})\right]\left[(p_H - c_H)w(p_H)\right]}_{\text{multiproduct effect}} +$$

$$\underbrace{\left[- z\right]\left[v_1(p_L) + (p_L - c_L)v_1'(p_L)\right]}_{\text{the image effect}} \tag{6}$$

The *multiproduct effect* is positive while the *image effect* is negative. The multiproduct effect acts the same way on product H as product H acts on product L. Hence, as the presence of a high-end product tended to decrease the price of the low-end product, the presence of very high-end products tends to decrease the price of product H.

The image effect is the result of price-sensitive shoppers not shopping at an outlet because that outlet carries high-end products. Perhaps the shopper perceives the high-end outlet as an expensive place to shop. The image effect works in the opposite direction as the multiproduct effect. The image effect raises the price of low-end products. Nevertheless, the image effect should be small for the same reason that the trade-up effect should be small. If the image effect were very large, then outlets that only carried product L would have many more individuals in segment 1 than outlets that carried both product L and high-end products. Then, the outlets carrying product L would have the incentive to offer even lower-end products than product L. The result would be a trading-down of shoppers from product L to lower-end products until the number of segment-1 shoppers buying product L at both outlets would approach each other and z would approach unity. To summarize, we make assumption 6.

Assumption 6: The multiproduct effect dominates the image effect.

Hence, we obtain the same conclusion for the multiproduct outlet that we obtained for the dual-product outlet, and theorem 1 generalizes to theorem 2.

Theorem 2: If an outlet carries all the products of another outlet except some product T, given asumptions 1 through 6, the following are true:

A. All products priced higher than product T will be priced higher at the outlet carrying product T.

B. All products priced lower than product T will be priced lower at the outlet not carrying product T.

Figure 13–1 illustrates theorem 2. The figure shows an arbitrary distribution of shopper sensitivities to price. If all three products (L, H, and X) are offered, product L will capture the shoppers with the highest sensitivity to price while product X will capture shoppers with the lowest sensitivity to price. However, if product X is not offered, product H will attract some of the less price-sensitive shoppers who would buy product X. Hence, the price of product H should be increased. However, if product X is offered, but H is not, product X's price must be lower while product L's price must be raised in order to attract shoppers in the midrange of price sensitivity.

We close this section with some corollaries to theorem 2.

Corollary 1: If the lowest-priced product at a multiproduct outlet is also carried by a single-product outlet, the single-product outlet will price the product at a higher price than the multiproduct outlet.

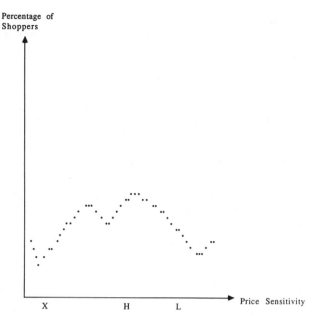

Figure 13-1. Illustration of Theorem 2

Corollary 2: If the highest-priced product at a multiproduct outlet is also carried by a single-product outlet, the single-product outlet will price the product at a lower price than the multiproduct outlet.

Corollary 3: Consider the product line (1, 2, 3, 4, 5, ...) where the first product is the lowest-end product. If one outlet carries products $(1, 2, \ldots, \mathcal{J})$ and a second outlet carries products $(\mathcal{J} - N, \mathcal{J} - N + 1, \ldots, \mathcal{J}, \mathcal{J} + 1, \ldots, \mathcal{J} + M)$, then all products carried by both outlets will have a higher price at the first outlet. (Of course, $N < \mathcal{J}$ and $M \geq 0$.)

An Example

We now provide an example of how the depth and breadth of product lines affect prices within the line. Figure 13-2 shows a market with four outlets denoted 1, 2, 3, and 4, respectively) and seven products (denoted *A* through *G*). The products are ordered according to their places in the product line, where *A* is at the highest end. The columns represent the outlets; the rows represent the products. An *X* in a given column and row indicates that the

	1	2	3	4
A	X			
B	X	X		
C	X	X	X	
D			X	
E			X	X
F				X
G				X

Figure 13–2. Examples of Product Lines

product in that row is offered by the outlet in the corresponding column. For example, outlet 1 carries models *A, B,* and *C.* Our theory implies that products *B* and *C* have their lowest prices at outlet 1. Product *C* then has its highest price at outlet 3, while product *E* would have its lowest price at outlet 3.

We now investigate the empirical validity of our theoretical implications.

Empirical Findings

This section describes some preliminary findings based on price data collected within the Chicago metropolitan area. Data were collected at sixty-five different outlets located in suburban shopping malls, large department stores, small retailers near shopping malls, and the downtown area. Nearly all of the data were collected during a two-day interval although the downtown data were collected on a third day. Hence, prices were not likely to change during the data-collection period.

Pricing data were collected in thirteen different product categories. I chose categories that were readily comparable. In many cases, I found that outlets within a given area did not carry the same models of a brand. Therefore, I needed to limit the analysis to items carried by more than one outlet. Even here, few outlets carried identical brands, so sample sizes were small and conclusions must be considered preliminary. The product categories, items, item abbreviations, and sample sizes are given in table 13–1.

Some of the product categories (basketballs, calculators, cameras, coffee makers, film, sandwich grills, infant seats, and steam irons) had clearly defined brand lines. Other categories (alkaline batteries, hard-cover books, and stereo records) had no lines, while the remaining categories (toys and video

Table 13-1
Items Used in the Study

Item Abbreviation	Product Category	Items on Which Prices Were Collected	Sample Size
BAS1	Basketballs	Spalding Official Magic Johnson Ball	8
BAS2	(BAS)	Spalding Official Kareem Abdul Jabbar Ball	2
BAT1	Alkaline batteries	Duracell C-size battery	31
BAT2	(BAT)	Duracell AA-size battery	26
BOO1	Hard-cover books	*In Search of Excellence*	13
BOO2	(BOO)	*Megatrends*	13
CAL1	Calculators	Texas Instruments model 55-II	9
CAL2	(CAL)	Texas Instruments model 35	10
CAM1	Cameras (CAM)	Canon AE-1 program with FD 1.8 lens without case	14
CAM2		Canon Snappy 20 camera	11
COF1	Coffee makers	Norelco Dial-a-Brew 12-cup model HB-5193	5
COF2	(COF)	Norelco Dial-a-Brew 10-cup model HB-5185	5
FIL1	Film	Kodak Kodacolor C135-24 35mm film	20
FIL2	(FIL)	Kodak 1000 2GCZ 35mm film	20
GRIL	Sandwich grills	Oster Hot 'n Toasty Sandwich Grill #713-06	6
INFA	Infant seats (INFA)	Kolcraft Tot-Rider	9
REC1	Stereo records	*Synchronicity* (Hugh Padghant and the Policy)	16
REC2	(REC)	*Flashdance*	16
STE1	Steam irons	General Electric model F320HR in white	4
STE2	(STE)	Hamilton Beach model 750 in white[a]	2
TOY1	Toys	Stomper and Stomper 4×4 toy trucks and cars	15
TOY2	(TOY)	Stomper and Stomper semi toy trucks	8
VID1	Video games	Atari E.T. video game for the Atari 2600	17
VID2	(VID)	Atari DEFENDER video game for the Atari 5200	14

[a] This item was found at only two outlets and, therefore, was not used in the analysis. Many other items were found at only one outlet. These items are not listed.

games) had weakly defined lines. Remember, our theory only applies to a line of products having a definite price ordering regardless of the outlet or the outlet's assortment. However, a line can be created with different brand names by adopting a low-end model of one brand and a high-end model of another brand.

There were several data-collection problems. The most notable problem was the reluctance of small retailers to provide extensive price information for all of their products. Hence, I was somewhat limited as to the amount of information I could collect from any particular outlet. For each outlet and for each of the items in table 13–1, I observed the following: (1) the item price (e.g., the price of the Canon Snappy 20, Canon AE-1, and Canon A-1), (2) the number of brand names in that product category that were carried by the outlet (e.g., Canon, Nikon, Pentax), (3) the highest-priced and lowest-priced products with the same brand name as the item (e.g., the highest-priced and lowest-priced Canon cameras), (4) the highest-priced and lowest-priced products in the same product category as the item (e.g., the highest-priced and lowest-priced cameras at the outlet), and (5) whether or not the item was on price promotion (i.e., whether the store noted the item price as a sale price).

My theory suggests that an item should have a lower price in an outlet where that item is at the low end of the outlet's product line than in an outlet where the item is at the high end of the product line. In other words, I expect B_H in equation (7) to be positive but B_L in equation (7) to be negative.

$$P_{jk} = A_j + B_{Hj} D_{jHk} + B_{Lj} D_{jLk} + e_{jk} \qquad (7)$$

where P_{jk} = the price of item j at store k

$$D_{jHk} = \begin{cases} 1 \text{ if item } j \text{ is the highest-priced model of the brand at store } k \\ 0 \text{ otherwise} \end{cases}$$

$$D_{jLk} = \begin{cases} 1 \text{ if item } j \text{ is the lowest-priced model of the brand at store } k \\ 0 \text{ otherwise} \end{cases}$$

e_{jk} = an error term

A_j, B_{Hj}, B_{Lj} are constants.

Although the significance levels are not overly impressive because of the small sample sizes (seldom were all items found at all outlets), the signs of the mean differences are very consistent.[6] In eight out of nine cases, the lowest-priced model in the outlet was lower in price than the average market price for that model. Moreover, in nine out of nine cases, the highest-priced model in the oulet was higher in price than the average market price for that model. These results involve averaging all items in the category (adjusting for mean differences). Table 13–3 shows the results for individual items.

The individual-item analysis shown in table 13–3 is quite consistent with the total-product-category results shown in table 13–2. Twenty-three out of twenty-eight observations are consistent with my theory. However, there are alternative hypotheses.

Table 13-2
Effect of Lowest-End and Highest-End Models on Product-Category Price

Category	B (lowest)	Standard Error	t	B (highest)	Standard Error	t
BAS	-4.8333E+00	1.5914E+02	-0.030	1.0517E+02	1.5914E+02	0.661
BAT	-5.6516E-01	1.3637E+01	-0.041	3.0979E+01	1.5438E+01	2.007
CAL	-3.1660E+02	3.3129E+02	-0.956	4.9998E+02	3.1838E+02	1.570
CAM	-9.0965E+02	3.8150E+03	-0.238	9.2745E+02	2.0127E+03	0.461
COF	-5.8976E+02	5.6194E+02	-1.050	5.8051E+02	4.2289E+02	1.373
FIL	-1.4146E+01	1.9094E+01	-0.741	6.3020E+01	2.3503E+01	2.681
STE	-7.0000E+02	5.0000E+02	-1.400	1.6520E+03	4.3301E+02	3.815
TOY	5.7810E+00	7.7815E+01	0.074	5.3035E+01	5.4936E+01	0.965
VID	-4.9464E+02	2.3068E+02	-2.144	1.1296E+03	2.5661E+02	4.402

Table 13-3
Effect of Lowest-End and Highest-End Models on Item Price

Category	B (lowest)	Standard Error	t	B (highest)	Standard Error	t
BAS1	-4.8333E+00	1.7362E+02	-0.028	1.0517E+02	1.7362E+02	0.606
BAS2	-1.2770E+00	2.0669E+01	-0.062	3.5723E+01	2.0669E+01	1.728
BAT2	-9.8095E+00	2.1425E+01	-0.458	8.0000E+00	3.1688E+01	0.252
CAL1	3.1080E+02	3.6638E+02	0.848	3.4720E+02	3.6638E+02	0.948
CAL2	-9.1714E+01	4.4840E+02	0.205	6.6286E+01	3.3630E+02	0.197
CAM1				1.3677E+03	3.1113E+03	0.440
CAM2	-7.9433E+02	4.7416E+02	-1.675	-2.2567E+02	4.7416E+02	-0.476
COF1				7.5283E+02	4.2932E+02	1.754
COF2	3.0400E+02	4.0000E+02	0.760	-5.9900E+02	4.0000E+02	-1.498
FIL2	-6.6644E+01	4.0889E+01	-1.630	5.9308E+01	2.9348E+01	2.021
STE1	-7.0000E+02	5.0000E+02	-1.400	1.6520E+03	4.3301E+02	3.815
TOY1	-8.7000E+01	6.7054E+01	-1.297	3.5250E+01	4.5690E+01	0.772
TOY2	2.0000E+02	1.9364E+02	1.033	6.6167E+01	1.4789E+02	0.447
VID1	-2.9676E+02	2.5771E+02	-1.151	1.9646E+03	3.3742E+02	5.822
VID2	-6.8370E+02	3.0573E+02	-2.236	4.3891E+02	2.7769E+02	1.581

Table 13–4
Correlation of Item Prices within the Outlet

Category	Correlation
BAS	−0.027635
BAT	0.025820
BOO	0.028125
CAL	0.000914
CAM	0.000355
FIL	0.007964
REC	0.006684
TOY	−0.001627
VID	−0.011196

Perhaps prices vary across outlets because some outlets are high-priced and others are low-priced (Salop and Stiglitz 1977). Perhaps high-price outlets offer more services (including a better shopping atmosphere) and command a higher price than outlets offering fewer services. To test this hypothesis, I computed the correlation of prices within each category as shown in table 13–4. No strong positive correlation was present. (Fifty percent were negative.)

There is still another fact contradicting the service hypothesis. We find low-end items are less expensive at outlets offering higher-end brands. We would expect the opposite if outlets offering higher-end brands had higher percent markups resulting from additional services.

Perhaps outlets providing a better assortment lower the search cost of shoppers and can, therefore, price their products at a higher price. This possibility can also lead to price variation across outlets. To test this alternative hypothesis, we regress the number of models on the item price. The results are shown in table 13–5.

Table 13–5 shows no clear positive correlation between item price and the number of models of the item's brand carried by the outlet. In fact, fourteen out of twenty-one cases show a negative correlation. We can also check the relationship between item price and the number of brands carried by the outlet. (See table 13–6.) Although table 13–6 makes a slightly better case for a positive relationship between brand assortment and item prices, the results are not convincing.

Still another alternative hypothesis exists. Perhaps both prices and product assortments are random. We do exclude this possibility when we require a product line because prices in the line must be ordered and, therefore, not random. Nevertheless, if prices are random, then the average price of the outlet may reflect the average price in the market. We check this alternative

Table 13-5
Effect of Number of Models on Item Prices

Category	B (models)	Standard Error	t
BAS1	−2.2438E+01	1.4661E+01	−1.530
BAT1	−5.3974E−01	3.9866E+00	−0.135
BAT2	−1.2815E+00	2.6740E+00	−0.479
BOO1	1.8510E+01	4.3860E+01	0.422
BOO2	3.5113E+00	3.3599E+01	0.105
CAL1	−7.1644E+01	6.5075E+01	−1.101
CAL2	−5.3671E+01	6.0431E+01	−0.888
CAM1	−8.4534E+02	9.6438E+02	−0.877
CAM2	−2.5194E+01	1.1305E+02	−0.223
COF1	−3.8565E+02	1.9119E+02	−2.017
COF2	−2.1250E+00	9.5747E+01	−0.022
FIL1	6.0961E−01	1.8348E+00	0.332
FIL2	−1.7460E+00	4.4247E+00	−0.395
GRIL	7.4180E+02	4.8698E+02	1.523
REC1	1.2679E+01	3.1697E+01	0.400
REC2	9.9333E+00	2.5553E+01	0.389
STE1	−2.6040E+02	8.6023E+01	−3.027
TOY1	−2.6117E+00	3.9951E+00	−0.654
TOY2	−9.9900E+01	3.0375E+01	−3.289
VID1	−4.7248E−01	1.5858E+01	−0.030
VID2	1.1703E+01	1.9194E+01	0.610

hypothesis by computing the mean difference between items when they are the lowest-priced model, the highest-priced model, and neither. We find results inconsistent with the random hypothesis. Across brands, line influence becomes weaker rather than stronger. (See table 13-7.)

Table 13-7 shows that ten out of thirty-nine observations are inconsistent with the random hypothesis. Although I would not dismiss the random hypothesis, the data more strongly support the product-line theory because we do observe more consistency of the lowest-end and highest-end product effect when product lines are present.

Finally, this section concludes by analyzing another interesting issue. I checked to determine whether stated price promotions (sales) actually result in lower prices than the average market price. Table 13-8 shows that for most items, sales do result in lower prices. Moreover, in every product category, the overall average effect of a stated price promotion was a lower average price across all items in the category.

The data are consistent with my product-line theory. However, there is another, perhaps even more important finding. The difficulties of my data-collection effort indicate the impracticality of sequentially searching across

Table 13-6
Effect of Number of Brands on Item Prices

Category	B (brands)	Standard Error	t
BAS1	$-1.1115E+01$	$4.5744E+01$	-0.243
BAT1	$-4.4650E+01$	$1.6524E+01$	-2.702
BAT2	$-5.6923E+00$	$1.3460E+01$	-0.423
BOO1	$1.8510E+01$	$4.3860E+01$	0.422
BOO2	$3.5113E+00$	$3.3599E+01$	0.105
CAL1	$-7.1714E+00$	$7.6239E+01$	-0.094
CAL2	$-1.7923E+01$	$6.0921E+01$	-0.294
CAM1	$-5.2402E+02$	$8.3285E+02$	-0.629
CAM2	$2.4827E+02$	$6.4552E+01$	3.846
COF1	$2.8371E+02$	$5.1334E+01$	5.527
COF2	$2.0165E+02$	$7.4705E+01$	2.699
FIL1	$-1.5521E+00$	$6.9244E+00$	-0.224
FIL2	$1.7912E+01$	$2.8739E+01$	0.623
GRIL	$-1.2257E+02$	$1.5296E+02$	-0.801
INFA	$-4.5302E+01$	$1.6057E+01$	-2.821
REC1	$1.2579E+01$	$3.1697E+01$	0.400
REC2	$9.9333E+00$	$2.5553E+01$	0.389
STE1	$1.8218E+01$	$5.9908E+02$	0.304
TOY1	$-4.1000E-01$	$1.1624E+02$	-0.353
VID1	$5.7616E+01$	$9.4705E+01$	0.608
VID2	$5.2693E+01$	$5.8347E+01$	0.903

outlets to find a given brand at the lowest price. Seldom, if ever, do outlets offer identical products. In fact, only with difficulty could I find any products offered at a sufficient number of outlets to make meaningful statements about price comparisons. As expected (Eaton and Brander 1984; Levitt 1980), outlets found ways to differentiate every product. Outlets carrying the same brand of merchandise very often carry different models. Brand-name cameras are often bundled with private-label accessories (cases, flashes, and so on) and sold only as a kit. Some outlets sold batteries only in packs of four, while other outlets sold batteries in packs of two. Even records were differentiated by selling records to store-club members at a different price than to nonmembers. Joining the club required paying a fee that was only worthwhile if other purchases were to be made. In some cases, prices actually varied within the outlet depending on the location within the outlet. It is not realistic to assume that shoppers search across outlets making only price comparisons. Such almost effortless search behavior is almost nonexistent except possibly in supermarkets and for high-priced items. Shoppers must make difficult and simultaneous quality comparisons on a large number of attributes in addition to making price comparisons. (See Shugan [1983] for further discussion on this point.)

Table 13-7
Effect of Lowest-End and Highest-End Brands on Item Prices

Category	B (lowest)	Standard Error	t	B (highest)	Standard Error	t
BAT1	1.6939E+00	2.1458E+01	0.079	3.6494E+01	2.1458E+01	0.701
BAT2	4.0632E+00	1.7506E+01	0.232	1.9800E+01	2.9140E+01	0.679
BOO1	-2.3667E+01	1.8113E+02	-0.131			
BOO2	1.5300E+02	2.5368E+02	0.603			
CAL1				4.6820E+02	2.6557E+02	1.763
CAM1				-3.4004E+02	2.5986E+03	-0.131
CAM2	-2.0425E+02	4.0696E+02	-0.502	-2.6425E+02	5.4599E+02	-0.484
COF1	-7.5467E+02	4.2824E+02	-1.762			
COF2	6.3433E+02	1.1215E+02	5.656			
FIL1	1.2208E+01	1.3566E+01	0.900			
FIL2	-7.0721E+01	4.1988E+01	-1.684	5.1803E+01	3.0604E+01	1.693
GRIL	4.0300E+02	4.8888E+02	0.824	3.2100E+02	6.1839E+02	0.519
INFA	-5.0957E+02	1.7335E+02	-2.940			
REC1	-2.1400E+01	4.5129E+01	-0.474			
REC2	-6.1000E+01	8.0383E+01	-0.759	-9.7500E+00	3.8915E+01	-0.251
STE1	-1.3347E+03	6.9723E+02	-1.914			
TOY1	-6.0667E+01	3.5452E+01	-1.711	9.1033E+01	3.7519E+01	2.426
TOY2	1.0711E+02	7.9097E+01	1.354	2.0761E+02	7.9097E+01	2.625
VID1	-7.1930E+02	3.6782E+02	-1.956	1.6592E+03	5.2018E+02	3.190
VID2				3.4840E+02	3.1239E+02	1.115

Table 13-8
Effect of Stated Sale Price on Actual Price

Category	B (sale)	Standard Error	t
BAT1	1.2767E+01	5.2236E+01	0.244
BAT2	−2.5680E+01	3.4733E+01	−0.739
BOO1	−5.6836E+02	1.8266E+02	−3.112
BOO2	−4.7364E+02	1.2597E+02	−3.760
CAM2	2.8433E+02	3.8110E+02	0.746
COF1	−5.3333E+00	6.1092E+02	−0.009
FIL1	−3.6895E+01	2.9935E+01	−1.232
REC1	4.3700E+01	4.1958E+01	1.042
REC2	−7.5032E+01	3.1815E+01	−2.358
TOY1	−9.2583E+01	4.6590E+01	−1.987
VID1	−9.1204E+02	5.0836E+02	−1.794
VID2	−6.3808E+02	4.0989E+02	−1.557
BATT	−8.3455E+00	3.5153E+01	−0.237
BOO	−5.2100E+02	1.4927E+02	−3.490
CAM	−1.0948E+04	7.1206E+03	−1.537
COF	−9.4190E+01	3.3575E+02	−0.281
FIL	−9.7410E+01	8.2845E+01	−1.176
REC	−4.8839E+01	4.0624E+01	−1.202
TOY	−2.5207E+02	1.3415E+02	−1.879
VID	−1.0152E+03	4.6006E+02	−2.207

Conclusion

This chapter developed a theory based on the hypothesis that consumers search for products within an outlet before searching across outlets. When shopping within outlets, shoppers temporarily limit their purchases to those brands and models carried by the particular outlet. The outlet responds by pricing its products according to the magnitude of several effects. First, the outlet would like to shift shopper purchases from lower-priced products at a higher-percentage margin than higher-priced products, so shoppers will trade up to higher-priced products. I argue, however, that this effect is dominated by another opposing effect. The second effect, called the segmentation effect, results from most outlets having more limited product assortments than are available in the entire market. As a result, outlets compensate for their more limited assortment by making their product lines appeal to a wider range of shoppers. Outlets can sell to consumers with different price sensitivities by lowering the price of their lowest-priced products (which are purchased by their most price-sensitive shoppers) and raising the price of their highest-priced products (which are purchased by their least price-sensitive shoppers). I argue that this segmentation effect often dominates the trade-up effect because product assortments, which maximize outlet profits, decrease trade-up effects.

In addition to furnishing empirical evidence for my hypothesis, I provide several other empirical findings:

1. I found that outlets seldom, if ever, offer identical products. In fact, only with difficulty could I find any products offered at a sufficient number of outlets to make meaningful statements about price comparisons. Outlets found ways to differentiate every product. Outlets carrying the same brand of merchandise very often carry different models. Brand-name cameras are often bundled with private-label accessories (cases, flashes, and so on) and sold only as a kit. Shoppers must make difficult and simultaneous quality comparisons on a large number of attributes in addition to making price comparisons.

2. My data are inconsistent with the hypothesis that retailers use the same percentage markup for all products in a product category. I found that higher-priced products often have a higher percentage markup than lower-priced products.

3. When outlets identify an item's price as a "sale price," the price is usually below the average price available at other outlets.

4. Item prices are not usually correlated with either the number of other models of the branded item or the number of other brands carried by the outlet. Outlets with large assortments of products price neither higher nor lower than outlets with smaller assortments of products.

5. The price of one item within the outlet is not significantly correlated with the price of other items within the same outlet. In other words, if the price of one item in an outlet is above the average market price, the price of other items in that outlet are not necessarily above the average market price. The services provided by an outlet do not seem to adequately account for price differences across outlets (or, at least, the cost of those services are not equally reflected in the price of every product in the outlet).

Note

1. Although the Canon Camera line can be ranked from low end to high end, for simplicity, we have not mentioned all camera models in the Canon line.

14
The Roles of Segmentation and Awareness in Explaining Variations in Price Markups

Thomas T. Nagle
Kenneth Novak

There once was a popular myth that retailers set prices by applying standard markups to the wholesale costs of their products. While the standard markup might vary somewhat across product categories to reflect differences in handling costs, retailers supposedly set prices with little regard for differences in demand. In the early 1960s, Robert Holdren [1960], Ralph Cassady [1962], and Lee Preston [1963] each independently debunked that myth with empirical studies showing that grocery price markups[1] customarily ranged, within the same store, from over 50 percent at the high end to negative values at the low end. Moreover, they observed variations in markups not only across product categories, but also across brands within the same category. The extent of the variation in markups was too large to be explained adequately by cost differences alone (Cassady 1962, pp. 119–23).

Each of those authors argued that a major reason why stores charged different markups was that the effect of a price on a store's total patronage varies across products. Low prices for some products "pull" customers into a store, while the prices for other products apparently have little effect on the number of buyers who shop there. The loss leader, for example, selling at a price below even the wholesale product cost, cannot be explained without reference to such product line interactions in demand. Retail grocery pricing, they concluded, is not mechanical, but is the result of a deliberate strategic attempt to take low unit profits where they will have the greatest effect on store patronage, while taking higher profits on products whose pricing seems not to affect store patronage.

The authors gratefully acknowledge the helpful comments received from Gary Russell, Timothy Devinney, and seminar participants at the University of Chicago and Boston University. The authors also wish to thank the University of Chicago for financial support.

Our discussions with executives of four different chains and reports by other authors (Holdren 1960, p. 73; Preston 1963, p. 40) indicate that grocery retailers generally do not know why the prices of some products affect store patronage more than do the prices of other products. They are practical men and women who simply set prices based on "what works," as revealed over time by their own and their competitors' experience. They know what products they must price at low levels to retain patronage and what products they can price at high levels without endangering that patronage, but they do not know why. That knowledge would nevertheless be useful to them. With it, they could avoid costly experimentation with new products and could adjust their pricing strategies more quickly to changing market conditions.

Why the prices of different products affect store patronage differently is still unknown. It is a question often asked and frequently conjectured about. Until now, however, it is a question that no one has tried to answer empirically. In this chapter, we combine sales and pricing data from a major supermarket chain with survey data on product usage to test two hypotheses. One explains the differences in markups as a response to differences in the way customers use the prices of particular products to evaluate a store's overall price level. The other explains the variations as an attempt to price differently to segments of buyers with different price sensitivities. We find that both hypotheses can partially explain why supermarkets find it profitable to price otherwise similar products differently. They may also explain variations in pricing at other retail stores (e.g., drug, hardware, clothing, sporting goods) where customers make multiple purchases from broad product lines.

Formulating Alternative Theories

It is widely assumed that consumers do not make independent decisions to purchase individual grocery items at various stores, but decide, instead, where to shop for an entire bundle of products (Holdren 1960, chapter 8; Cassady 1962, p. 122; Preston 1963, pp. 9–18). The assumption seems applicable to other retail purchases as well. Clothing buyers, for example, are likely to purchase a shirt and tie where they have bought a suit. Moreover, a substantial body of research indicates that the perception of a store's relative prices is a major factor when consumers decide where to shop (Engel and Blackwell 1982, pp. 523–24). The job of the retail pricer is, then, not to price products independently, but rather to price them to maximize total profit from the store's entire product line.

There are two explanations for variations in price markups that are based on the effect that individual prices have on the profitability of a store's total product line. One is based on price perceptions, the other on buyer segmentation.

Price-Awareness Hypothesis

Despite the importance that consumers place on price in their store selection, research indicates that their knowledge of the actual prices paid for most grocery items is generally poor (Dietrich 1977; Brown 1971). For only a small percentage of products, generally those bought most frequently, do consumers actually remember prices well enough to enable them to make price comparisons across stores. That observation leads naturally to the *price-awareness hypothesis* (Holton 1957, p. 20; Cassady 1962, pp. 169–71) that buyers make inferences about a store's overall level of prices from only that subset of products that they purchase frequently enough to remember.

If a store can identify those products, it can price them below the average for its product line, misleading consumers (at least initially) who believe that they constitute a representative sample. Consumers may eventually recognize that the sample is biased and therefore not indicative of the absolute level of a store's prices. But if they believe that the bias is equal across competing stores, they may continue using the prices of frequently purchased products to evaluate one store's prices in relation to another. Consequently, a store must price more frequently purchased products with lower markups to remain competitive. This implies the following testable hypothesis:

> All other things equal, products purchased more (lesser) frequently by a typical user will have a greater effect on store patronage, leading stores to price them with lower (higher) markups.

Segmented-Market Hypothesis

An alternative, though not necessarily incompatible, explanation for the differences in markups across products is the *segmented-market hypothesis*. A substantial body of research indicates that there are distinct segments among grocery shoppers (Gabor and Granger 1961; Brown 1968; William, Painter, and Nicholas 1978; Roberts and Wortzel 1979). Some buyers, whom we shall call *convenience shoppers*, are relatively price-insensitive when deciding where to shop. They choose a store based more on its location and services than on its prices. Other buyers, whom we shall call *price shoppers*, compare prices more diligently and adjust the location of their purchases accordingly. Ideally, a store manager would like to price high to convenience shoppers, reflecting the value to them of his location and services, while at the same time pricing low enough to attract price shoppers and keep them patronizing his store. He cannot explicitly charge buyers different prices for the same products, however, because he cannot readily identify individual customers as convenience or price shoppers.

Fortunately for the store manager, customers generally purchase an entire basket of items at a single store since the cost of shopping at multiple stores on a single-purchase occasion usually exceeds the potential savings. Consequently, a store manager can earn greater average markups on sales to convenience shoppers than to price shoppers by considering the frequency with which different types of shoppers purchase particular products. For example, if purchasers of a particular brand of automatic-dishwasher detergent are mostly convenience shoppers, a store can assign that brand a particularly high markup, thus raising the cost of a basket bought by convenience shoppers without driving price shoppers from the store. Likewise, if most purchasers of unadvertised brands of paper products are price shoppers, then pricing those brands with particularly low (perhaps even negative) markups will lower the cost of the basket bought by price shoppers without giving unnecessary concessions to convenience shoppers.

In effect, this is a theory of discriminatory pricing through product bundling (Clemens 1951). The usual discussion of bundling assumes that customers demand products individually and goes on to show how sellers can gain by constraining customers to buy those products in bundles. For customers making retail purchases, however, the cost of shopping at multiple stores can naturally constrain them to demand products in bundles. Sellers can gain simply by recognizing the natural bundling that occurs and thoughtfully pricing the elements of those bundles to include different amounts of profit for different customer segments. This implies the following testable hypothesis:

> All other things equal, products purchased disproportionately by price (convenience) shoppers will have a greater (lesser) effect on store patronage, leading stores to price them with lower (higher) markups.

Implications for Testing

Either the price-awareness or the segmented-market hypothesis (or both) could explain variations in retail grocery markups not accounted for by costs. According to the price-awareness hypothesis, a low price for a frequently purchased product is a more profitable way to pull customers into a store than is a low price for a product purchased less frequently. This is because the price of the frequently purchased product has a greater effect on customer's perceptions of a store's price level. If that explains the variations in grocery-price markups, then markups should be inversely related to a product's purchase frequency.

In contrast, the segmented-market hypothesis implies that a low price for a product bought disproportionately by price shoppers is a more profitable way to increase store patronage than is a low price on a more typical product. The low price is given only to those who are likely to respond to it in their store choice. Consequently, markups should be positively related to those characteristics of a product's purchasers that distinguish price shoppers from convenience shoppers.[2]

Formulating a Test

A Model of Margins

To specify a test of the competing hypotheses explaining variations in retail markups, it is useful to begin with a model of price setting in a multiproduct firm. Consider a model of a two-product firm, pricing to maximize current profits. The firm seeks to maximize

$$\text{profit} = (P_1 - c_1)q_1 + (P_2 - c_2)q_2 - F \tag{1}$$

where P_1 and P_2 are the prices of the two products, c_1 and c_2 are their marginal costs, q_1 and q_2 are the quantities sold, and F is fixed costs. Maximizing (1) with respect to P_1 and P_2 yields expressions for the optimal margin for each product. The optimal percent margin for a product satisfies the equality

$$\frac{P - c}{P} = E \tag{2}$$

E is a composite elasticity term that embodies the effect of the product's price both on its own sales (the own-price elasticity) and on the sales of the store's other products (the cross-price elasticities) that result from changes in total store patronage.[3]

The cost term, c, on the left-hand side of equation (2) represents all marginal costs, not just the wholesale product cost. Thus, the left-hand side is the percent gross margin, not the markup, on the product. To derive the markup, let

$$c = c^w + c^r$$

where c^w is the wholesale product cost and c^r is the total of all other marginal costs of retailing the product. Substituting into equation (2) and rearranging, we can express the percent gross markup for a product as

$$\frac{P - c^w}{P} = \frac{c^r}{P} + E \tag{3}$$

Our test will involve estimating equation (3) using proxies for E suggested by the alternative hypotheses that we wish to test.[4]

The Data

The data we use to test the alternative explanations of variations in grocery markup come from two sources:

A list of prices, sales levels, wholesale costs, case sizes, and manufacturers' allowances for all packaged goods sold in June 1979 by a major grocery chain in one metropolitan area (within which there is a common price list for all the company's stores.

The Simmons Market Research Bureau's *1979 Study of Media and Markets*. This study provides estimates of brand usage across a number of demographic categories.[5]

We matched products from these two sources to obtain a data base of 378 different brands in seventy-two product classes.

There are a number of limitations to these data. First, the Simmons survey is a national sample that may not be adequately representative of consumption patterns in the region for which we have store data. Second, our available data base does not contain as much variation in markups as actually occurred in a store. The reason is that most of this grocery chain's loss leaders were in product classes for which data were unavailable from Simmons (e.g., fresh bakery and dairy products, local brands of some packaged grocery products). Third, the Simmons survey measures usage for all of a brand's sizes taken together, while our store list differentiated between different sizes of the same brand. We addressed this problem by using the store data for the size with the largest dollar volume.[6] We have no reason to suspect that these problems bias the data in favor of either theory, but they inevitably reduce the power of our tests.

From this data base, we selected or constructed variables that, according to one theory or the other, are proxies for variations in E, the composite elasticity term.

Proxies to Test the Price-Awareness Hypothesis

The proxies that we will substitute for E to test the price-awareness hypothesis are measures of average purchase frequency. The price-awareness hypothesis implies that those products bought frequently will have high own- and cross-price effects in demand at an individual store. The rationale for this is that more frequent purchases result in more frequent exposure to a product's price, increasing the probability that it will be remembered when making interstore price comparisons. Unfortunately, the Simmons data measures the share of respondents who use a brand, not the frequency of purchase. Our store data, however, contains units sold. Assuming that buyers purchase only one unit (of any size) on each purchase occasion,[7] we can combine these two variables to create the following measure of purchase frequency by the average user:

$$Q/USAGE = \frac{\text{the total number of units purchased divided by}}{\text{the percentage of the population using the product}}$$

If the price-awareness theory is correct, this variable would be a proxy for price sensitivity and would be inversely related to E

The relationship between $Q/USAGE$ and price awareness is not necessarily linear. One would expect that as purchase frequency approached the rate necessary to assure recall of price, further increase in frequency would have a diminished incremental effect on price awareness. Consequently, we also used the natural log of this variable as an alternative proxy to test the price-awareness hypothesis.

Proxies to Test the Segmented-Market Hypothesis

The proxies that we will substitute for E to test the segmented-market hypothesis are measures of the demographic characteristics of product users. Roberts and Wortzel [1979] found that two objective demographics (income and age) predicted a shopper's "concern for price" or "price-minimization" behavior better than did role-orientation variables. Other studies (Satow and Johnson 1977; Blattberg et al. 1978; William, Painter, and Nicholas 1978) also indicate that particular demographic variables are correlated with shopping behavior.[8]

In our tests, we employ product-usage data for the following demographic categories to distinguish those products bought disproportionately by price or convenience shoppers.

- *Family Income.* Intuitively, one would expect that higher-income shoppers would be less price-sensitive than lower-income shoppers. Gabor and Granger [1961], Blattberg et al. [1978], and Roberts and Wortzel [1979] provide evidence that income levels are associated with price sensitivity in grocery shopping. Consequently, the segmented-market hypothesis predicts that products purchased disproportionately by high-income shoppers should receive higher markups than average, while the converse should be true for products consumed disproportionately by low-income shoppers. We attempt to measure this effect on a product's markup with the variable *COVINCOME*, the covariance of income with usage of the product.[9]

- *Children.* Households with children buy more food in supermarkets, both because they have more mouths to feed and because they eat more meals at home. They, therefore, have a greater incentive to shop for low prices. Moreover, Roberts and Wortzel [1979] argue that the existence of children is associated with families where the wife plays a "traditional" role with time to shop carefully. Consequently, the segmented-market hypothesis predicts that products purchased disproportionately by families with children will have lower markups. We attempt to measure this effect with the variable *%CHILD*, the percentage of a product's usage accounted for by families with children.

- *Female Employment.* Grocery shopping is still a task performed primarily by the woman in a family. According to the Simmons study, 83.7 percent of full-time homemakers and 86.3 percent of employed women are the primary grocery shoppers in the household. If a woman is employed outside the home, her time will be more scarce; therefore, one might suspect that she will be more likely to seek convenience than low prices when shoping. Anderson [1972] showed that working women were more brand-loyal and Blattberg et al. [1978] found that working women as a group were less "deal-prone" than were full-time homemakers. Roberts and Wortzel [1979] also found that women who work outside the home for financial reasons were more price-sensitive than nonemployed women (though there was no significant increase in price sensitivity for women who worked purely for personal satisfaction). Consequently, the segmented-market hypothesis would predict that products purchased disproportionately by employed women would be priced with higher markups. We attempt to measure this effect on a product's markup with the variable %*EMPLOYED*, the percentage of a product's usage accounted for by families with wives who are employed full-time.

- *Home Ownership.* Homeowners generally have more storage space than do apartment dwellers, which should encourage price shopping. A household with more storage space could shop at different stores on alternate weeks, buying enough of the items priced low at each store to last until the next time they visit that store.[10] Consequently, products consumed more by home-owning families should be associated, other things equal, with higher price elasticities and therefore should carry lower markups. Blattberg et al. [1978] used this variable successfully to identify deal-proneness for grocery products. We attempt to measure this effect on a product's markup with the variable %*HOME*, the percentage of a product's usage accounted for by families that own their residences.

- *Household Location.* People who live in high-density urban locations can often walk to a convenient local store, but would have to drive or take public transportation to most competing stores. Thus, price shopping at other than the nearest store is significantly less convenient. In contrast, people who live in low-density suburban locations usually must drive to even their nearest store. Price shopping at other than the nearest store does not involve as much additional inconvenience for the suburban shopper as it does for an urban shopper. Consequently, products consumed more by people who live in high-density urban locations should be associated, other things being equal, with lower price elasticities and should therefore carry higher markups.[11] Supporting this argument, William, Painter, and Nicholas [1978] found "store nearby" a strong predictor of convenience shopping, while "store an easy drive" was not. We proxy this effect with the variable %*CITY*, the percentage of product usage accounted for by families living within the city limits of a metropolitan area.

Controlling for Cost Difference

There is, of course, another factor causing variations in grocery markups that we need to consider. Costs of retailing, other than the wholesale product cost, also vary among products. Some products take up more shelf space, turn over less frequently, or require refrigeration—all adding to the cost of selling them.

The cost most often cited as important for grocery retailing is the opportunity cost of shelf space. Unfortunately, we lacked a direct measure of product size. Noting, however, that products with larger dimensions are packed fewer per case, we developed a proxy for product size: the number of units per case. If the cases of all grocery products were the same size, units per case would show a perfect *inverse* relationship with product size. However, the largest products (with fewest units per case) are packed in larger cases than are smaller products. We accounted for the resulting nonlinearity by using the natural log of units per case, LN(*UNITS/CASE*), as our surrogate for size. It should take a negative sign because the relationship between product size and units per case is an inverse one.

To account for the higher marginal cost of carrying refrigerated and frozen products, we simply included dummy variables, *REFR* and *FROZ*. The final variable included is a nonfood variable, *NFD*. Casual observation of our data indicated a significant difference between the markups of food and nonfood items. We can only speculate as to the theoretical basis for this difference, but it is a systematic variation not captured by our other variables. Consequently, we include it to improve our specification. Table 14–1 summarizes the explanations of these variables and their sources.

Table 14–1
Independent Variables Used in Regression Analysis

Variable (label)	Description	Source [1]	Mean (standard deviation)
Cost intercept [1/P]	The inverse of the brand's price	Store data	1.14 (0.77)
%GM	Retail price minus unit wholesale cost, divided by retail price. Unit cost is adjusted for manufacturers' allowances received by the retailer.	Store data	24.6 (8.55)
LN(*UNITS/CASE*)	Proxy variable for the amount of shelf space taken up by one unit of a product.	Store data	2.77 (0.54)
FROZ	Indicates a product that must be kept frozen in the store.	Store data	1 for frozen, 0 otherwise
REFR	Indicates a product that must be kept refrigerated in the store.	Store data	1 for refrigerated, 0 otherwise

Table 14–1 (Continued)

Variable (label)	Description	Source [1]	Mean (standard deviation)
NFD	Indicates a nonfood product.	Store data	1 for nonfood, 0 otherwise
Q/USAGE	Proxy variable for the relative number of purchase occasions by an average user.	Store and Simmons data	2.16 (9.00)
LN(Q/USAGE)	Natural log of Q/USAGE.	Store and Simmons data	4.04 (1.29)
COVINCOME	The covariance of income (in thousands of dollars) with the usage of the brand by income class.[2]	Simmons data	11.27 (152.83)
%EMPLOYED	The share of total brand usage accounted for by families indicating that the wife was employed full-time outside the home.[2]	Simmons data	21.62 (2.71)
%CHILD	The share of total brand usage accounted for by families indicating that they had children in the home under six years of age.[2]	Simmons data	15.06 (5.30)
%HOME	The share of total brand usage accounted for by families indicating that they owned their homes.[2]	Simmons data	70.03 (4.97)
%CITY	The share of total brand usage accounted for by families indicating that they lived within the city limits of a metropolitan area.[2]	Simmons data	29.46 (3.55)

1. "Store data" refers to a printout of prices, costs, and sales levels of a major supermarket chain in one metropolitan area. "Simmons data" refers to the Simmons Market Research Bureau's *1979 Study of Media and Markets.*

2. "Usage" stands for the percentage of respondents who answered yes to the Simmons survey question, "Do you use [brand name]?"

The Empirical Test

Our test focuses on the ability of proxies for E suggested by both the price-awareness theory and by segmented-market theory to explain differences in product markups. To test the price-awareness theory, we assume that

$$E = \beta_0 + \beta_1 \frac{Q}{USAGE} + u \qquad (4)$$

or that

$$E = \beta_0 + \beta_1 \ln\left[\frac{Q}{USAGE}\right] + u \qquad (5)$$

To test the segmented-market theory we assume that

$$E = \beta_0 + \beta_1 COVINCOME + \beta_2 \%EMPLOYED + \beta_3 \%CHILD$$

$$+ \beta_4 \%HOME + \beta_5 \%CITY + u \qquad (6)$$

In each case, u is an error term with a mean of zero and a constant variance. Simultaneously, we also need to estimate c, the marginal retailing costs other than the wholesale cost of the product. For each test, we assume that

$$c = \alpha_0 + \alpha_1 \ln(UNITS/CASE) + \alpha_2 REFR$$

$$+ \alpha_3 FROZ + \alpha_4 NFD + v \qquad (7)$$

where v is an error term with a mean of zero and a constant variance. Substituting alternately (4), (5), and (6) for E and substituting (7) for c in equation (3), we have our first three regression equations:

Regression I:

$$\%GM = \alpha_0 \frac{1}{P} + \alpha_1 \frac{\ln(UNITS/CASE)}{P} + \alpha_2 \frac{REFR}{P} + \alpha_3 \frac{FROZ}{P}$$

$$+ \alpha_4 \frac{NFD}{P} + \beta_0 + \beta_1 \frac{Q}{USAGE} + \frac{v}{P} + u$$

Regression II:

$$\%GM = \alpha_0 \frac{1}{P} + \alpha_1 \frac{\ln(UNITS/CASE)}{P} + \alpha_2 \frac{REFR}{P} + \alpha_3 \frac{FROZ}{P}$$

$$+ \alpha_4 \frac{NFD}{P} + \beta_0 + \beta_1 \ln\left[\frac{Q}{USAGE}\right] + \frac{v}{P} + u$$

Regression III:

$$\%GM = \alpha_0 \frac{1}{P} + \alpha_1 \ln(\text{UNITS/CASE}) + \alpha_2 \frac{REFR}{P} + \alpha_3 \frac{FROZ}{P}$$

$$+ \alpha_4 \frac{NFD}{P} + \beta_0 + \beta_1 COVINCOME + \beta_2 \%EMPLOYED$$

$$+ \beta_3 \%CHILD + \beta_4 \%HOME + \beta_5 \%CITY + \frac{v}{P} + u$$

If regression equation I or II explains markups well, the price-awareness hypothesis is supported. If regression III explains markups well, it supports the segmented-market explanation.[12]

The Empirical Results

Table 14–2 shows the results of our estimations. The dependent variable for each equation is $\%GM$, the percent gross markup calculated after adjusting the wholesale cost c^w, for any promotional allowances.[13] All of our cost variables have the predicted signs and all but the dummy variable for refrigerated products, $REFR$, are significant. Consequently, we can have some confidence that we have accurately, though no doubt incompletely, controlled for cost differences among products.

Regressions I and II test the explanatory power of the price-awareness hypothesis. $Q/USAGE$, our measure of purchase frequency, is clearly a significant predictor of markup variations within a store. The logged formulation (Regression II) fits the data better, implying that the process by which purchase frequency generates price awareness is subject to diminishing returns.

Regression III tests the explanatory power of the segmented-market hypothesis. The demographic characteristics of a product's purchasers clearly affect the way it is priced. All five demographic variables had the predicted signs. The significant positive coefficient for $COVINCOME$ indicates that products purchased disproportionately by high-income shoppers ($COVINCOME > 0$) carry higher markups while those purchased disproportionately by low-income shoppers ($COVINCOME < 0$) carry lower markups. The significant positive coefficient for $\%CITY$ indicates that products purchased disproportionately by urban dwellers carry higher markups (in a chain store with common prices in both urban and suburban locations). The three other demographic variables—$\%EMPLOYED$, $\%CHILD$, $\%HOME$—did not explain a statistically significant amount of the variation in markups.[14]

Clearly, both the price-awareness and the segmented-market theories can

Table 14–2
Regression Results of Alternative Models with Percent Gross Markup as Dependent Variable

Independent Variables	Predicted Sign	Regressions			
		I	II	III	IV
Cost intercept					
$(1/P)$	−	7.49	7.64	7.97	8.27
$\ln(UNITS/CASE)$	−	−1.97	−1.92	−2.19	−2.13
		(3.33)***	(3.26)***	(3.67)***	(3.65)***
FROZ (dummy)[1]	+	7.19	7.60	6.84	7.41
		(4.69)***	(4.96)***	(4.46)***	(4.87)***
REFR (dummy)[1]	+	2.51	1.61	1.18	1.88
		(1.29)*	(0.93)	(0.69)	(1.10)
NFD (dummy)[1]	?	1.52	1.28	1.56	1.53
		(2.19)**	(1.89)**	(2.25)**	(2.25)
Proxy intercept (β_0)		21.6	25.5	10.5	13.5
$Q/USAGE$	−	−.001			
		(1.98)**			
$\ln(Q/USAGE)$	−		−1.08		−.948
			(3.04)***		(2.63)***
COVINCOME	+			.073	.046
				(2.39)***	(1.56)*
%EMPLOYED	+			.183	
				(1.04)	
%CHILD	+			−.073	
				(0.81)	
%HOME	−			−.051	
				(0.46)	
%CITY	+			.371	.367
				(2.58)***	(3.01)***
Adjusted R^2		.075	.087	.089	.106

Note: Numbers in parentheses are t values.
1. These variables are divided by P in the estimation.
  *Significant at the 10 percent confidence level.
 **Significant at the 5 percent confidence level.
***Significant at the 1 percent confidence level.

explain a significant proportion of the variation in grocery-price markups. But do they compete to explain the same portion of the variation in different ways or do they complement each other by explaining different parts of the variation? Regression IV in table 14–2 answers that question by reestimating the equation using both the logged form of $Q/USAGE$ for the price-awareness hypothesis and the significant demographics for the segmented-market hypothesis. It indicates that the two explanations are primarily complementary, each independently explaining part of the variation in grocery-price markups.

For all of these equations, the residuals are quite well behaved and essentially random with one exception: our model consistently failed to explain the extremely low markups for brands of coffee. Our model did predict that certain brands would have relatively low markups, but not the negative markups they often carry. We considered the possibility that we were inappropriately fitting a linear equation to a nonlinear relationship. Consequently, we fit various quadratic specifications to the data but without any change in the results. There is clearly an additional nonrandom factor that explains variations in markups that we have not captured in our model.

It is also noteworthy that our data contained a number of the chain's private-label brands. We tested for the effect of private-label brands by running each of the regressions in table 14–2 with the addition of a private-label dummy variable. It provided no additional explanatory power, indicating that our model explains the markups for such brands equally as well as it does the markups for national brands.

Finally, we considered the possibility that our "frequency of purchase" variable, $Q/USAGE$, was not measuring the effect of purchase frequency at all, but rather was a proxy for the effect of total expenditure on the product, $PQ/USAGE$. We discovered that the correlation between these two variables was low and that the latter did not explain variations in markups when substituted in the equation.

Discussion

Differences in buyer sensitivity to price were represented by a set of demographic and product-use variables and were then related to the markups chosen by a retailer through a simple model of profit maximization. The results indicate that one can substantially explain differences in the markup variations in a retailer's product line. Though most of the variation stems from differences in costs, much of it comes from differences in buyer price sensitivities. These results have a number of important implications, both explanatory and prescriptive.

First, our results support the oft-stated proposition that people remember and respond more to prices that they encounter more frequently. Consequently, grocery retailers price those products lower to attract patronage. Second, our results support the value of segmented marketing, even in an industry as apparently competitive as grocery retailing. Moreover, while this result is limited to the set of products for which we had data, it has implications that extend to other products found in supermarkets[15] and, indeed, to the pricing problems of different kinds of retailers.[16] It could explain, for example, why retailers with nongrocery product lines also select products for low-price promotions.

Finally, these results imply that retailers need not rely solely on experimentation or imitation when pricing products new to their lines. If they know or can predict purchase frequency and the demographics of the product's purchasers, they can use the information along with costs to select an appropriate markup more directly. Reducing the price of a product in order to increase sales is qualitatively no different from using any other marketing tool; it should be implemented where it is effective and avoided where it is not.

Notes

1. The term *markup* is used to refer to the difference between a product's wholesale cost and its retail price. The percent markup is the dollar markup expressed as a percentage of the retail price.

2. Darden and Reynolds [1971] found precisely such variations in usage by demographic classification in a study of health and personal care products.

3. See appendix 14A-1 for derivation and technical explanation of E.

4. Although our theories attempt to explain cross-price elasticities resulting from store-patronage decisions, our proxies may be related to price markups through both the own- and cross-price elasticities. Little and Shapiro [1980] argue that the generally low level of grocery-price markups indicates that cross-price elasticities resulting from competition among stores dominate the pricing of individual grocery items. This is the only logical explanation for loss leaders that are priced below the store's own wholesale cost. To the extent, however, that the same factors that affect price sensitivity for a consumer's store-patronage decision also affect his price sensitivity for individual-product decisions, we will be unable empirically to distinguish those theoretically separate effects.

5. The Simmons study provides cross-tabulated estimates of the percentage of product users by demographic classification as well as by media exposure. A household is defined as a user when a respondent cites the brand in answer to the question: "Which brands (of a particular product class) are used by your household?" It therefore indicates only whether or not a product is used, not the volume of that usage. The data come from a national probability sample of 15,026 people, all 18 years of age or older, residing in the 48 contiguous states, and interviewed between October 1978 and July 1979. Simmons collects data on some regional brands that, though not included in the published volume, are available from them and are included in our analysis.

6. In some cases, products with the same name come in different varieties (e.g., fruit drinks, cat food, TV dinners). In all cases where the different varieties had similar prices and markups, we treated them as one product. In most cases, prices and markups were identical across varieties. In a few instances (e.g., one brand of frozen

pizza), prices and markups differed substantially across varieties, forcing us to delete those products from the study.

7. Clearly, this assumption is not correct for some product classes. Most buyers, for example, probably purchase multiple units of bar soap or cat food on a purchase occasion. Our measure overestimates price exposures for such products if exposures occur only at the time of purchase. If, however, exposure occurs at the time of use as well, then this measure is appropriate for such products.

8. Unfortunately, demographic characteristics do not entirely capture a consumer's attitude toward grocery shopping. Bucklin [1969] found that whether or not a woman had "liberal" or "conservative" views of her role in the family explained more of the variance in store loyalty across consumers than did differences in objective demographics.

9. This measure is calculated as the covariance of the percentage of households using the product with income (using the midpoint of each Simmons income class as the measure of income). We excluded the lowest income class (less than $5,000 per year) because it contains many retirees whose income is not representative of their wealth.

10. A store would want to attract such shoppers because they would also buy perishable items that could not be stored and items that competing stores priced equally.

11. The distinction between urban and suburban shoppers is relevant for explaining the variations in margins within a store only for a chain that follows a common price policy for all stores (both urban and suburban) in an area.

12. We can make the usual assumption that the error term in our regressions is unbiased. We cannot, however, assume that the error term has a constant variance uncorrelated with the explanatory variables. In fact, the error term for our equations will be $v/P + u$. Our only alternative would have been to estimate regression equations with markup specified in dollars (rather than as a percentage). After substituting for c^r and ϵ, such equations would have an error term $v + Pu$. To choose between these two specifications, we estimated both and then regressed the squared error against $1/P^2$ for the %GM regressions and against P for the equivalent %GM formulation of Regression I. The error term for the %GM formulations were uncorrelated with $1/P^2$, implying that v represents a very small portion of the total error. The squared error term for Regression I, however, was strongly correlated with P^2. Consequently, we chose to work with the %GM formulation.

13. The mean adjusted percent gross markup was 24.6 percent with a standard deviation of 8.6 percent. We estimated the equations using unadjusted gross markups as well. The results are qualitatively the same though the equations did not fit the unadjusted markups as well as the adjusted markups.

14. The insignificance of these three variables may not indicate that they are poor predictors of shopping behavior, but may result from the inability of our data set to associate demographics with purchase sizes. The limitations of our demographic data constrained us to look at only one size class in each product category. It may be that families with children buy the same products as other families, but buy larger sizes. Consequently, the retailer may be setting lower markups on the larger sizes to attract such shoppers. The insignificance of %$HOME$ may be disconcerting to readers familiar with Blattberg et al. [1978] since that paper found that home ownership was a sig-

nificant predictor of deal-proneness. Consistent with that finding, we found that %*HOME* (the percentage of a product's usage by homeowners) was a significant predictor of low markups (coefficient = $-.0016$, $t = 1.85$) in a regression equation *excluding* %*CITY*. The significance was lost, however, when %*CITY* was included. Since Blattberg et al. did not include a location variable, we suspect that the home ownership variable in their study may have had a strong effect only because it was a proxy for a suburban household location.

15. The segmented-market theory could explain why supermarkets carry special promotional items (such as dishes, flatware, and plastic lawn furniture) on which they earn very low or negative markups. If a store finds that the sales of such nongrocery items are more concentrated among price shoppers than are sales of most grocery items, than it can add those nongrocery items to its line and price them to attract price shoppers with less profit leakage to convenience shoppers. The chain used in this analysis was selling stoneware dishes as a promotional loss leader. Each piece sold for 49¢ (with a minimum grocery purchase) though it cost the store 60¢ at wholesale.

16. The reason discount department stores that sell mostly durable goods also carry health and beauty aids at exceptionally low prices could be that those frequently purchased products give the store a generally low price image for its entire product line. The reason that fast-food restaurants price the small single hamburger with a lower markup could be because its price attracts families with children, a price-sensitive segment.

Appendix 14A-1:
Technical Explanation of E

Our profit-maximization model assumes that price is the control variable and quantity sold is a function of the price charged. This differs from most textbook models of product-line pricing that treat price as a function of quantity.

The resulting profit-maximization model for a two-product retailer is

$$\underset{P}{\text{Max}}\,(P_1 - c_1)q_1 + (P_2 - c_2)q_2 - F$$

that yields first-order conditions

$$q_1 + (P_1 - c_1)\frac{\partial q_1}{\partial P_1} + (P_2 - c_2)\frac{\partial q_2}{\partial P_1} = 0$$

$$q_2 + (P_1 - c_1)\frac{\partial q_1}{\partial P_2} + (P_2 - c_2)\frac{\partial q_2}{\partial P_2} = 0$$

These can be solved simultaneously to yield

$$\frac{P_1 - c_1}{P_1} = E_1$$

for good 1 where

$$E_1 = \frac{-\eta_1^{-1} + \eta_{21}^{-1}\dfrac{\left(\dfrac{\partial q_2}{\partial P_1}\right)^2}{\dfrac{\partial q_1}{\partial P_1}\dfrac{\partial q_2}{\partial P_2}}}{1 - \dfrac{\dfrac{\partial q_2}{\partial P_1}\dfrac{\partial q_1}{\partial P_2}}{\dfrac{\partial q_1}{\partial P_1}\dfrac{\partial q_2}{\partial P_2}}}.$$

η_1 is the own-price elasticity (i.e., the percent change in the quantity sold of good 1 for a 1 percent change in its price) and η_{21} is the cross-price elasticity (i.e., the percent change in the quantity sold of good 2 for a 1 percent change in the price of good 1). The equation for the gross margin of good 2 is analogous to that of good 1.

Since η_1 is a negative number (an increase in price reduces sales), the first term in the numerator is positive. Since it is the inverse of elasticity, it implies that the higher the own-price elasticity, the lower the optimal percent gross profit. Unless goods 1 and 2 are substitute brands, η_{21} is less than or equal to zero. It will be less than zero, reducing the optimal margin for good 1, if a low price on good 1 pulls into the store people who also buy good 2. The remaining term in the numerator—the square of the cross-price derivative divided by the own-price derivatives—is simply a weight that indicates the relative importance of good 2 in determining the margin for good 1. The denominator on the right-hand side is a scaling term that is the same for all products. In the multiple-product case, it is the determinant of the matrix formed to solve the multiple–first-order conditions for the profit-maximizing prices.

Part VI
Remaining Issues and Questions

Timothy M. Devinney

T he prior sections of this book have been devoted to addressing specific pricing-related issues and questions. The final section is devoted to two highly critical and related "philosophical" issues. First, how are we to translate and direct pricing-strategy research so that it maintains its academic "rigor" while satisfying the practical demands of managers? Second, in which directions are we to take future pricing-strategy research? With somewhat differential emphasis, the final two chapters examine these issues.

Bonoma, Crittenden, and Dolan provide a case-study perspective aimed at addressing the managerial-relevance, academic-rigor issue. Examining four case studies, they point out that, while the major focus of academic research is on the issue of consumer valuation, managers tend to be concerned about the additional problems of the role of the cost structure and the control exerted by the channels of distribution on the final product price. The authors attribute this difference of emphasis to the academic's reliance on economic-based models (which emphasize value maximization) as well as a lack of pragmatism in the nature of the problems studied by academics. Their solution is twofold. First, they call for more pragmatism in the nature of the problems studied by academics. Clearly, academics should not be constrained to studying only those issues that practitioners deem important to them; however, there exists little shortage of problems of both practical and academic interest. Second, there is the need for a more global examination of the pricing chain—manufacturing, distribution, and valuation. They strongly argue for the necessity of studying the entire pricing chain if any consistent answers are to be achieved about the determinants of successful pricing strategy. Theirs is a call for changing what has been primarily an ends-oriented research program to a means–ends-oriented program.

Monroe and Mazumdar provide a true survey and synthesis of marketing-based pricing research, putting into perspective where we have been and where we need to be going. Prior surveys (see Monroe and Della Bitta [1978]; Rao

[1984]; Nagle [1984]) pointed out four primary shortcomings of pricing research: (1) a lack of clearly specified assumptions, (2) a lack of empirical validation, (3) a lack of understanding of how pricing decisions are actually made, and (4) too heavy a reliance on economic models. Monroe and Mazumdar emphasize that great strides have been made, particularly in the area of the assumptions underlying pricing models; however, they emphasize the need for more empirical validation and, echoing Bonomo, Crittenden, and Dolan, direct research on firms' price-determination process. In addition, they strongly argue for an interdisciplinary approach to the development of a pricing-strategy paradigm, feeling that, even in the late 1980s, too much reliance is made of economic-based models.

Where, then, does this discussion lead us? First, it is clear that the pricing issues, because of its immense practical importance, must have a pragmatic component. It is both poor science and poor common sense to study issues without an understanding of why those issues are important to the decision makers being impacted and without attempting to aid those decision makers. However, to allow academic research to be driven only by issues of current practical importance ignores the fact that much of the strength and longevity of academic endeavors rests on their ability to transcend issues of immediate relevance.

Second, pricing-strategy research must be interdisciplinary. A recognition that economic models are abstractions clearly limits the normative validity of those models in many contexts. However, one can still be interdisciplinary without being totally "democratic." Because of the strong scientific tradition found in economics, as well as the fact that economics is the science of the determination of price in a marketplace, it is clear that pricing-strategy models must be basically economic models. However, the integration of behavioral findings into economic models is not only necessary but also allows pricing strategists to be on the forefront of the integration of two disciplines. Winer's chapter 2 in this book is a perfect example of this interdisciplinary integration.

Third, Bonomo, Crittenden, and Dolan, plus Monroe and Mazumdar as well, clearly point out the necessity of studying the actual pricing process. A great deal of recent economic- and marketing-based pricing research has ignored the positive tradition on which it was based. One is reminded that Adam Smith based much of his economic theory on the pure observation of what was actually happening in markets, not what he thought should have been happening under ideal circumstances.

The fourth and final area of future study is related to the preceding issues. As pricing-strategy research has developed more theoretically sophisticated models, emphasis has moved away from the necessity of empirically validating the models at hand. Monroe and Mazumdar point out two areas where this is critical if our understanding of pricing is to be expanded: dynamic models and the role of the interaction price with other marketing-mix variables. In addition, game-theoretic models will soon lose much of their appeal if they cannot somehow be empirically validated and practically applied.

To conclude, the study of pricing strategy puts a researcher in a unique position, having the opportunity to study questions of immense practical importance while remaining on the forefront between the economic and behavioral science. The next two chapters provide us with both a solid base and a clear direction for future study.

15

Can We Have Rigor and Relevance in Pricing Research?

Thomas V. Bonoma
Victoria L. Crittenden
Robert J. Dolan

T he time is Tuesday, 8:45 AM; the place a marketing conference. A session on "Advances in Pricing Research" featuring three noted pricing researchers from academia is about to begin. Who's in the audience? If our experience is an indicator, the affiliations on the name badges are more likely to be University of Rochester, University of Minnesota, and University of Texas at Dallas rather than Kodak, 3M, and Texas Instruments. The gap between managers' concerns and academics' research is often recognized, bemoaned, and blamed on one party or the other. One practitioner, for example, clearly places the blame for the pricing gap on academics: "Company pricing policy is an area where the academic world has long since retreated in despair of ascribing consistency of principles or rationality of practice" (Alfred 1972). In a more moderate tone, Jeuland and Dolan [1982] present some of the complexities of pricing problems that have limited the relevance of academia's application of modeling technology for managers.

Our purpose here is not to argue about the width of the gap or lay blame for it. Rather, it is more simple and constructive. We aim to contribute to the eventual narrowing of the academic–manager, rigor–relevance gap by clearly identifying some key managerial pricing concerns. Through personal interviews with pricing managers in a variety of industries, we have identified factors that influence how the pricing job is done in a company. Our research shows that the basis for pricing varies systematically across firms depending on internal cost factors, distribution of channel power in the industry, and customers' use of the product (e.g., whether the product is a component or a stand-alone item). The significant variation in what managers are most concerned about signals limited managerial attention to, interest in, and use of the "general-purpose" pricing prescriptions academics strive to establish. Here, in the interest of academic research ultimately having more impact or practice, we provide a framework for more situation-specific pricing research.

The chapter is organized as follows. The next section presents previous research on managerial pricing and our research methodology. The subsequent section presents the raw data for our analysis in the section after that. The "raw data" are descriptions of the price mechanism at four firms in widely divergent industries: numerical controllers, personal care products, computer software, and pleasure boats. That section distills the data of the previous section and clarifies the key influences of cost structure, trade power, and consumer utilization of the product. In the process, we identify the cause of the gap between managerial concerns and academic research. The final section concludes with suggestions for a more fruitful research agenda.

Managerial Pricing and Research

There is a significant gap between the interests of managers and the contributions of academics in pricing. While the normative models developed by academics (see reviews in Monroe and Della Bitta [1978] and Rao [1984]) are impressive in their mathematical sophistication and claims to internal validity, few efforts are marked by the pragmatism necessary to impact managerial practice.

One reason for this is that normative pricing research has not built on the descriptive work reported in the marketing and economics literature. Instead, the normative work in marketing is grounded in microeconomic theory; it eschews descriptive theory development. Since we aim to (1) contribute to the descriptive theory development and (2) suggest that it is from this foundation that pragmatic normative models be constructed, we begin by reviewing the descriptive work through the mid-1980s. There are two relevant research streams: the pricing-determination work occurring largely in the economics literature and the pricing-process work that has appeared in the marketing journals.

Pricing-Determinants Research

This work dates back to Hall and Hitch [1939]. Dean [1951] and Oxenfeldt [1951], on reviewing the studies, concluded the major factors impacting price were the estimate of cost and the firm's desired gross margin percentage. Noticeably absent was any consideration of the "value to the customer" so regularly advocated in the literature of the eighties (e.g., Forbis and Mehta 1981).

Hall and Hitch's [1939] survey of thirty-eight business managers found the general pattern of price setting to be addition of a percentage of overhead costs and profit to the direct cost per unit. Corroboration for the dominance of the cost viewpoint is supplied by the Brookings Studies (Kaplan, Dirlam, and

Lanzillotti 1958; Lanzillotti 1958) and by Barback [1964]. The Brookings Studies examined the pricing policies of large U.S. firms (e.g., U.S. Steel, Du Pont, General Motors); Barback presented similar data for seven British firms.

While cost may be the dominant factor in company pricing, the studies also showed it is not the only consideration. The Brookings interviews revealed that firms consider demand and competitive conditions as well; e.g., while U.S. Steel had a philosophy of cost-plus pricing, they would meet the lowered delivered price of competition when necessary to get the business. Similarly, over half of Hall and Hitch's "cost-plus" firms stated they would cut price if business were depressed.

More recently, Gordon, Cooper, Falk, and Miller [1980] investigated the development of long-run pricing objectives by Canadian and U.S. manufacturing firms. For these firms, both company and marketing conditions are important in determining price; the importance varied with (1) type of product produced, (2) objectives of the firm, (3) intensity of competition, (4) stage of product life cycle, and (5) size of the order backlog. For example, custom-product firms rely more strongly on cost than standardized-product producers, who are more concerned with market factors.

The overall picture emerging from these empirical studies is that the typical firm estimates the cost of producing the product, adds a desired overhead and profit percentage, and then adjusts the resulting figure as necessary to meet demand and competitive situations. Weston [1972] formalizes this type of pricing process as part of a dynamic general equilibrium leading managers to adaptive pricing policies.

Pricing-Process Research

The marketing literature contains many discussions of the decision-making unit (DMU) and decision-making process (DMP) of a company. Often, the decision being referred to is whether to purchase an item. There is, however, a stream of investigations of a firm's DMU and DMP when the firm's decision is a price for its own output. Beginning in the late 1960s, a variety of researchers primarily associated with Columbia University analyzed the identity and interaction of participants in the pricing process. The studies include:

1. Pricing a slightly differentiated product in a market consisting of large and small producers (Howard and Morgenroth 1968),

2. Setting list prices and evaluating requests for temporary price changes (Farley, Howard, and Hulbert 1971),

3. Setting list prices, establishing annual contract terms, and adjusting prices over time (Capon and Hulbert 1975),

4. Making day-to-day price decisions (Capon, Farley, and Hulbert 1975).

The process-tracing research is important in identifying the information needs and key considerations for different types of pricing decisions. While Rao [1984] mentions this work briefly in his review paper "Pricing Research in Marketing," most notable in our view is the lack of any meaningful connection between this descriptive work and the normative work comprising the bulk of Rao's review of the state of the art in marketing.

Our Research Methodology

Our objective is to complement the pricing determinants and pricing-process research by identifying and classifying problems of managerial importance in pricing. In unstructured interviews, we addressed four questions to managers. First, like the pricing-process researchers, we wanted to know, "What is the process by which the firm sets its pricing policy and specific prices?" Our second area of investigation was driven by the fact that the academic literature has largely avoided the issue of complexity of price by considering it a single number. This view ignores issues such as price schedules varying with quantity discounts or other terms and conditions. (Cf. Gould and Sen [1984]). Therefore, we also asked, "What exactly is involved in specifying the firm's price?"

Third, we had a prior hypothesis that one important managerial concern is the ambiguity of the feedback from the marketplace on whether or not the price is "right." This led to the question, "How do you know, even after the fact, if the price is about right, too high, or too low?" Finally, we asked a catch-all question, "What are the most challenging aspects of doing your pricing job well?"

Our criteria for choosing firms to interview were these:

1. We wanted to have a set of firms covering a broad spectrum of pricing situations. Thus, if we consistently found a similar pricing issue arising, we could conclude that it was one with some generality rather than simply an industry-specific phenomenon. We selected firms to obtain variations in:
   • price point
   • extent of industry product differentiation
   • product end users (consumers or business)
   • distribution method

   Table 15–1 lists the four firms interviewed and the characteristics of each along these four attributes. (Firm names have been disguised.) In addition, two other attributes were observed during the interview process and are also noted on the table:
   • end-user pricing system (fixed price list, fixed price list with negotiation, price set by negotiation)
   • special supply considerations

Table 15–1
Description of the Four Situations Analyzed

Product	Typical Price Level	Users	Degree of Product Differentiation	Distribution	End-User Pricing System	Special Supply Considerations
Numerical control manufacturer (Controls)	$50,000	Businesses	High	Direct	Negotiated	Uncertainty about production costs
Personal care products (Personal Care)	$2.00–5.00	Consumers	Low	Intensive indirect	Fixed	Easy entry
Computer software (Software)	$500	Business and consumers	Medium	Selective indirect	Fixed	High fixed, low variable cost
Pleasure boats (Waters)	$20,000	Consumers	Medium	Selective indirect	Fixed with negotiation	None

The next two criteria involve the feasibility of getting the required data:

2. We should have enough knowledge about the firm that we were confident in our ability to identify the key pricing decision makers a priori.
3. We should have a relationship with the firm to permit access to executives for lengthy, personal interviews that would often touch on confidential information.

At this preliminary research stage, our choice of sample size was dictated by our desire to span the characteristics shown in table 15–1. Since we were able to do this with the four firms mentioned, we limited our investigation to them. To us, this represented the appropriate trade-off of breadth versus depth.

Pricing-Process Descriptions

By agreement with the cooperating firms, their names are not used, but no other data are disguised in any way. This section presents the pricing process of each firm independently. The next major section, "Commonalities in the Pricing Process," does the "compare and contrast" analysis necessary to make more general statements.

Firm #1: Controls

Controls builds automated workstations incorporating its proprietary controller technology. The controller's function is to position an item to be assembled precisely under a device such as an adhesive dispenser, pin inserter, or cutting tool. For example, if a six-inch–square piece of plastic needs a dab of adhesive at each corner, 3/8 of an inch from each edge, the controller is programmed to position the four spots sequentially under the dispensing head. Applications range from "low-tech" ones such as gluing to printed circuit board repair. A typical workstation incorporating the controller and many other components might cost $50,000; it would be constructed of standard parts assembled in a custom way. Controls' major customers include Apollo Computer, Digital Equipment Corporation, IBM, Texas Instruments, and Wang. Annual sales are approximately $5 million. Controls sells direct to end users through a nationwide network of manufacturers' representative organizations.

Controls' clearly articulated "pricing policy" is understood by all management-level employees. A 50 percent gross margin is "the guideline we generally expect prices to conform to." Questioned as to what market conditions led to selection of the 50 percent figure as the guideline, a manager replied, "It's out of the blue really, but I know we'll be in business if we hit it." With the 50 percent gross-margin policy, Controls follows a three-step pricing procedure:

1. Price out standard products.
2. Determine charges for assembly and any necessary customization to meet buyer's specification. } Set "target price."
3. Negotiate on individual jobs.

The 50 percent gross-margin rule is applied in step 1. (The product is costed out and price is set to yield a 50 percent margin.) Exceptions to the 50 percent "we generally expect" come from two sources. First, if there is a directly competitive product that can be used as a reference price by the customer, Controls may adjust the product price to be "in line with the competition." Second, a part standard enough to be on the price list does not necessarily mean it is in inventory. For such out-of-stock parts, the actual manufacturing cost is unknown at the time of price quotation, even through previous production provides a guideline. On such items, Controls takes a 60 percent gross margin over the expected cost to protect itself against cost overruns.

For the majority of Controls' price quotes, determining customization charges (step 2) is significant. Customization charges are "where you make it or break it," according to Controls management. These charges present Controls with major problems and opportunities. The problems stem largely from the difficulty of cost estimation, while the opportunity comes from the diversity of the customer base. Commenting on the cost-estimation problem, Controls' president said:

> We must take only business on which we can peg our cost pretty accurately. Cost is the key in our business, and it is the first priority in our pricing. There are very few things we sell where we really know what it's going to cost us to get it out the door and running at the customer's factory. We've taken some pieces of business we shouldn't have. They wound up generating a negative gross margin, because we didn't know our costs.

While presenting problems in cost estimation, customization has a plus side. Two customers may buy a similar set of components with slightly different customization. These buyers differ in:

1. Product applications.
2. Feasible alternatives. As an example, for one buyer, manual methods may be the only way to do the job, while the other could put together a different automation solution.

3. Payback periods used to evaluate capital investments. For example, in electronics, customers do not generally accept paybacks of more than one year, whereas in the automotive industry, it might extend to three years.

Given these differences, the buyers differ greatly in the value placed on Controls' components. Hence, it is to Controls' advantage to move from uniform pricing (as suggested by a price list) to negotiated prices, which can vary across customers in the same degree as customer values vary.

The pricing process takes on new complexity in stage 3. Often we conceive of negotiation as taking place only on price. In Controls' case, negotiation is on product performance and price simultaneously. Figure 15–1 shows the typical relationship between product performance, value to the customer, and expected cost to Controls. Negotiations take place in both the X- and Y-axis directions. This dual dimensionality of negotiations requires Controls to iterate through stages 1 and 2 of the pricing process to estimate the expected-cost curve over a range of product-performance levels, rather than just the cost for the product specified in the original Request for Quotation. Figure 15–1 graphically describes this situation. However, reality is more complicated than figure 15–1 suggests because product performance is a multidimensional construct rather than the unidimensional one shown.

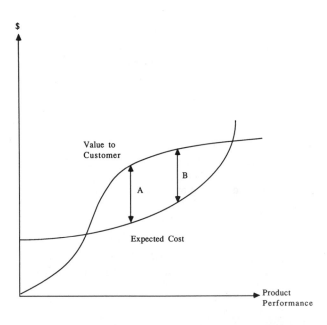

Figure 15–1. The Relationship between Product Performance, Value, and Cost at Controls

A typical pattern is the customer's Request for Quotation, which starts the process at point B, where value to the customer exceeds Controls' expected costs. However, when Controls takes its desired gross margin, the customer reacts by saying, "That's too high." Rather than cutting price and holding product performance, Controls' response typically involves both product and price changes. Hopefully, this is in the direction of figure 15–1's point A, where the cost saving to Controls from the reduction in product performance is greater than the value loss to the customer. This results in a greater "welfare band" (shown by the double-headed arrows) to be split at point A. The key part of this product/price adjustment process for Controls is in iterating back through the cost estimation where, in the words of one manager, it is crucial to "be realistic about the cost savings from simplifying products. In the desire to get business, it's easy to delude yourself about cost savings."

Compared to many textbook descriptions of pricing, Controls offers contrast in the primacy of and, almost paradoxically, uncertainty about cost. Protecting the company from taking jobs that threaten its survival (due to unexpected cost overruns) is a prime function of the pricing mechanism.

One manager summarized the pricing at Controls as the constructive conflict between the market and company cost viewpoints:

> Industrial companies can get into real trouble when pricing is done by one person. The accountants or managers are too rigid on gross-margin percentage. They are not aware of—or responsive to—market realities. The sales and marketing people are not sensitive enough to the cost side and gross-margin-percentage arguments. They always want to cut price or boost performance with no change in price. You must have constructive conflict between these two functions, these different viewpoints.

The predominance of the cost viewpoint within the company evidenced itself in discussion of how Controls knew if the quoted price were right or not:

> All we know is if we price it too low—if it generates a negative margin—we priced it too low. We should have been higher so we wouldn't have booked the business. Other than than, we don't know. If we don't book the business, it's hard to find out who got it and at what price. Plus, the alternative solution is so different from ours that we can't easily determine the price that would have won it for us.

Firm #2: Personal Care

Personal Care is a leading marketer of health and beauty aids such as deodorants, shampoos, and hair sprays. Annual U.S. sales are approximately $400 million. Products are intensively distributed through food and drug outlets and mass merchandisers. Figure 15–2 shows Personal Care's channels of distribution.

Personal Care's pricing policy is "to be competitive." This competitive parity policy stems from several factors. First, consumers perceive little product differentiation in the category. Hence, there is little brand loyalty at the consumer level, which trickles up the channels of distribution, creating a situation of no trade loyalty as well. Second, Personal Care's cost structure leads to a volume orientation. The manufacturing cost of goods sold is only a small percentage of total cost. The product is very easy to make; production rates can be increased by contracting for outside facilities. Advertising expenditures, on the other hand, are budgeted at 30–40 percent of sales. Management's view of the necessity of these high advertising expenditures is attested to by the fact that advertising is referred to as a part of "cost of goods sold." The large advertising fixed cost, small unit cost of manufacture, and easy access to supply make the rule of Personal Care's business "to sell as much as you can." Price is seen as another element of the marketing mix to be used offensively to move product; i.e., its major role is as a sales-promotion device.

Pricing thus has two components at Personal Care:

everyday invoice price (EIP)

trade promotion schedule

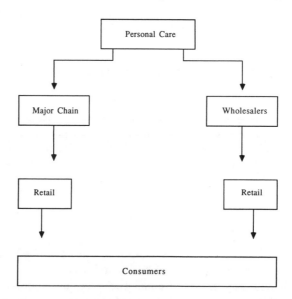

Figure 15–2. Personal Care's Channels of Distribution

The EIP is the price at which Personal Care is willing to sell to the trade at any time. There is a good deal of trade resistance to increases in EIP. The second component is the schedule of temporary price discounts (e.g., rebates, off-invoice, free goods) available to the trade. Four parties are considered in setting these two components:

1. *End consumer:* Since there is little product differentiation, the end consumer should regularly see prices for Personal Care products at parity with, or below, competitive brands.
2. *Trade:* In addition to setting the retail selling price, the trade provides crucial demand stimulation through shelf facing and other displays. Personal Care pricing must overcome trade boredom in a mature category with little product differentiation to get the needed support.
3. *Personal Care sales force:* The company's own sales force must be kept interested in the brand in the same way as the trade.
4. *Personal Care as a company:* Pricing should generate enough volume and unit margins (with large amounts moving off-invoice) to fund overheads of advertising expense and profits.

Currently, the trade-promotion schedule at Personal Care is so extensive that only 20 percent of Personal Care's volume moves at the everyday invoice price. However, the everyday invoice price is a crucial part of the pricing formula at Personal Care because retailers set their everyday shelf prices based on the EIP, not the depth of discounts in the trade-promotion schedule. Consumers see the everyday shelf price regularly because, even though 80 percent of the goods move from manufacturer to trade "on deal," the trade buys forward or simply does not pass along the discounts currently received from the trade.

Trade promotions, together with the low-cost movement of Personal Care's product from one location to another (even internationally), create another control problem for Personal Care: the "diversion market." In the diversion market, goods sold on deal to an authorized Personal Care account are resold to a third party (rather than at retail) at a price less than Personal Care's everyday invoice price. The third party maintains an inventory obtained at slightly above the deal price and competes directly with Personal Care at a later time when the everyday invoice price is in effect.

This description of Personal Care presents an interesting picture of the role of pricing in a market characterized by a very strong trade, a low-interest product, and little product differentiation. While Personal Care would like to view its trade promotions as a proactive sales-promotion device, the reality seems to be that the stronger trade has taken over the pricing and put Personal Care in a reactive, defensive mode by demanding and getting frequent and substantial discounts off-list.

Firm #3: Software

The pricing policy at Software (a leading developer of microcomputer software) is "to obtain fair value for our products, thereby funding future research and development." Like Personal Care, the channels of distribution through which Software sells impact the pricing issues it faces. Software's channel structure is shown in figure 15–3.

As shown, the majority of Software's sales go through a distributor, direct to retail outlets, or to headquarters of chains (e.g., Computerland). They are then sold to users in a "face-to-face" shopping environment. To avoid problems of the sort encountered by Personal Care in losing control of the retail selling price, Software is very selective in its distribution and sets a suggested retail price (SRP). Each class of trade is offered a discount off the suggested retail price as shown in figure 15–3. Each outlet selling Software products must be approved by Software, and one stipulation is the face-to-face selling environment as sales support.

Software's pricing problem is to set the four numbers (SRP and the three off-list discounts, *A*, *B*, and *C*) in figure 15–3. With respect to the off-list discounts, "there are some pretty strong industry traditions on what dealer and

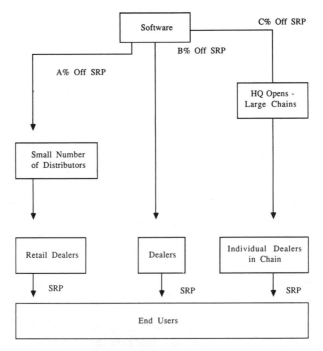

Figure 15–3. Pricing in Software's Distribution Channel

distributor margins ought to be. You would have to have a pretty compelling reason to go against those norms." Essentially, then, Software sets the SRP that determines Software's revenue per unit. The actual retail price is generally close to the SRP because of the selective distribution policy.

Software management feels that software manufacturers in general face some unique issues in setting retail price. First, all buyers are aware of the cost of a floppy disk and, therefore, the supplier's variable cost. Second, while the buyer has a very clear conception of manufacturer's cost, he initially has a very hazy conception of what he will do with the product. This is especially true in "horizontal-market products" (e.g., general applications programs such as spreadsheets, data base management, and word processing).

The conventional wisdom of pricing in such situations is that since the value of the product is not clear to the customer, it is not possible to sustain a "high-price strategy." On the other hand, there is empirical evidence for a number of products and services showing that if benefits are unclear, consumers will use price as a surrogate for the quality. Hence, a higher price creates a greater "value-in-use" perception in the mind of the consumer. Given the pricing policy of "obtaining fair value," Software engages in extensive consumer research to determine what "fair value" is. The research process begins with focus groups with both dealers and users of varying levels of sophistication. These are followed by more precise product-use tests in which users rate competitive products, feature by feature, and are asked specifically about the value of one versus the other as well as about the perceived "fairness" of particular prices.

The product differentiation that Software has achieved allows it to price based on differential value to the customer. Note that the first three firms discussed here differ fundamentally on the basis of the pricing policy statement:

Controls: price relative to cost

Personal Care: price relative to competition

Software: price relative to customer value

By achieving differentiation, Software obtains (1) the right to price not so much on the basis of cost and (2) power over the trade (so sorely lacking in the Personal Care case). Note, however, that Software's pricing policy brings the burden of research and careful inquiry into customer value.

Firm #4: Waters

Waters sells power and sailboat hulls to consumers through an exclusive distribution network. Waters' reputation is to have the highest quality boats in the market at premium prices. Waters' president describes the company pricing policy as: "We price to maximize sales, maximize margin, and have the most beneficial impact on dealer and customer relations." While a somewhat facetious statement, it does show the conflicting desires that are balanced in the pricing process at Waters.

Pricing is influenced to a great extent by the existence of products that customers and dealers will use as reference points in judging a new Waters product's price in terms of its value. These reference products include other Waters boats in the line, used Waters boats, and competitors' offerings.

The pricing process of a new boat begins with an estimate of unit cost:

1. Cost out a bill of materials for the boat.
2. Determine the number of labor hours by skill level and cost out the labor content at appropriate wage rates.
3. Factor in overhead to get a "full manufacturing cost" estimate.

Due to experience with similar production, this cost estimate is pretty precise. Waters takes the average percent company margin from "similar Waters boats" and applies this to the estimated cost to get a tentative dealer price. The standard dealer markup is then applied to the tentative dealer price to see what the customer would have to pay. Waters compares this to competitive offerings to assess if conventional company margins and dealer markups yield a price that its product and high-quality reputation can support. Waters' rule of thumb is that a 15 percent premium over the competition is supportable. While there is no explicit reference to the used-boat market, both Waters and the competition keep an eye on prices in the used-boat market as a downward pressure on new-boat pricing.

In short, Waters uses the company's desired margin to determine "what we'd like to get" and checks it against the competitor's price, plus 15 percent, to see "if we can get it." If the "want-to-get" and "can-get" figures do not match up, there is another iteration through the process. This "rationalization process' is the norm rather than the exception, as the first pass on new-boat pricing typically yields a "want to get" greater than the "can get." The rationalization process is shown in figure 15–4.

Initially, quality-assurance and cost-reduction teams work to improve the mapping in terms of features-to-value and features-to-cost, respectively. Ultimately, if an acceptable features/price package cannot be found, Waters considers the need to deviate from standard margins in order to compete in the segment.

This simultaneous product/base-price determination is the central part of pricing at Waters. However, due to the seasonal nature of the boat business and the need to balance production and shipments to dealers, price promotions are important. Waters uses price promotions to influence the timing of

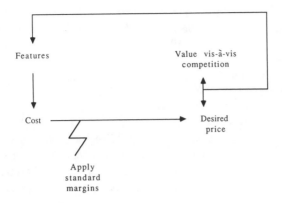

Figure 15–4. Waters' Price-Rationalization Process

demand through discounts in "buy-early" programs, temporary "free-freight" offers, and annual dealer-meeting discounts. Thus, while not at the heart of the pricing process as is the case with Personal Care, trade promotions are an important inventory-loading mechanism for Waters.

Commonalities in the Pricing Process

A risk in choosing such a diverse set of firms is that there may be no apparent similarities or contrasts across the cases. Thus, while the four descriptions may be an interesting collection of facts, there would be no basis for generalization and suggestions for future research. Fortunately, upon examination, the four situations were linked by recurrent and regular factors that we believe provide provocative ground for further investigation. These factors are the role of cost structure, the impact of the trade, and product-use situations.

This section discusses each key influence and presents the "pricing chain" demonstrating the cause of the gap between managerial concerns and academic research. The concluding section draws inferences from these findings to form the basis for future research.

The Dominance of Cost Structure

For years, marketers (e.g., Kotler [1984]), specialists in control and accounting (e.g., Goodman [1972]), and numerous others have counselled academic researchers and managers to avoid cost-based pricing as a primitive tool that leads to suboptimal results. Academics appear to have heeded this advice, basing many of their investigations on consumer-value perceptions. Managers, however, have continued to consider cost as a primary pricing concern. Two specific elements of the cost situation—namely, the significance of the variable costs and the precision of the firm's cost estimate—are particularly influential in how firms set prices.

Our sample includes two high–variable-cost and two low–variable-cost firms. The pricing process differs significantly across these two sets. Controls and Waters, the high–variable-cost firms, follow a "top-down" pricing approach using cost estimates and projected trade margins to eventually get at a user price. In contrast, Personal Care and Software, the low–variable-cost firms, use "bottom-up" pricing; i.e., consumer values and/or competitors' prices are emphasized more directly. The resulting price is then backed up the distribution chain to see if it allows generation of tolerable manufacturer and trade margins.

A second important element of the cost structure is the degree of certainty in the estimate. For both Controls and Waters, variable costs are a significant percentage of price. However, Controls is unable to predict variable costs with accuracy due to the custom nature of much of its production. Combining this uncertainty with the importance of variable costs in the pricing process, gross margins achieved at Controls vary wildly across jobs, while product design is often changed to reflect price positioning. None of the other firms in our sample experience this cost uncertainty and are able to set a price that yields a known unit contribution. While unit volume to be achieved is not known with certainty, there is some stability in these situations. These cost intersections are depicted in figure 15–5.

Confounding the significance of the cost elements is the knowledge each firm has about its competitors. For example, Controls is unable to identify its competition. This lack of clarity about the competition combined with the significance, yet uncertainty, of its variable costs puts Controls in a very vulnerable pricing position, making it difficult to judge—even ex post—the appropriateness of a price quote.

At the other extreme, Waters' and Personal Care's knowledge about costs and competition leads to using price as a strategic positioning tool. Waters is able to adopt a premium price position, while Personal Care follows a parity price strategy. With certainty as to its costs, yet uncertainty as to customers' relative evaluation of competitors, Software follows a strategy of product differentiation leading to price differentiation and, typically, a price premium.

The Impact of the Trade

The second factor markedly influencing the pricing process of our firms is the power of the trade. While many marketing academics (e.g., Cravens [1982]) refer to the influence of the channel upon price, rarely do these references attempt to gauge the extent of this influence and its implications.

FIRM COST KNOWLEDGE

	Uncertain	Certain
High	Pricing Schizophrenia • dramatic price swings • increased chance of pricing too low EXAMPLE: Controls	Pricing Certainty • adoption of firm-wide price position EXAMPLE: Waters
Low	No Instance Studied	Pricing Based on Customer Value and/or Competitors' Prices • High fixed costs (e.g., Advertising, R & D) • Differentiation by non-price means EXAMPLE: Personal Care, Software

VARIABLE COSTS AS A PERCENTAGE OF PRICE

Figure 15–5. Cost Structure's Impact on Pricing Process

Pricing is done very differently in firms facing a powerful trade. At Personal Care, for example, pricing is functionally no longer in the hands of Personal Care's management. The company does not control the shelf price of its products, and it has very little latitude in pricing moves. The trade demands that the everyday invoice price be no higher than competition or else the everyday shelf price seen by the consumer will be higher—a situation that Personal Care cannot tolerate due to the lack of perceived product differentiation. Personal Care tries to influence shelf prices through trade promotions, but the trade is now demanding these promotional schedules months in advance to develop the most economical buying programs. As the trade develops more long-term purchasing strategies, the impact of trade promotions on the contemporaneous shelf price decreases. As a consequence, some firms in Personal Care's markets are forced to unusual merchandising practices (e.g., on-pack price-off coupons for ''instant savings'') in order to bypass the trade and influence the end user's price. In addition, dealing activity has led to diversion markets that are difficult to control.

The Waters and Software cases represent moderate instances of trade power. The manufacturer and the distribution chain appear to jockey back and forth for control of the channel. Both Software and Waters restrict the total number of outlets for their products. Of the two firms, Software seems to have more power over its channels and is even able to establish conditions of sale (e.g., store fronts, face-to-face selling) for qualifying dealers. Waters, on the other hand, yields power to the trade via its dealer commitment programs aimed at increasing total dealer volume. Both firms, however, are plagued by parallel markets. Software has to contend with the grey market, while Waters is impacted by the large used boat market.

Both Waters and Software attempt to exert some control over end-user prices, with Waters being more successful than Software. Software has suggested retail prices for all of its products. However, in a survey of eight microcomputer software dealers, only four were selling Software's latest product for the suggested retail price. Waters is able to keep tighter control of its end-user price by being a more important marketing partner to its dealer (in terms of proportion of dealers' total sales volume) than Software is able to be.

Controls represents the extreme form of manufacturer power and channel weakness. Here, the manufacturer's sales representatives prospect for customers and bring them to Controls. For this, the sales reps receive an established percent commission on each order. Controls maintains complete control of the pricing process and handles all negotiations with customers. The trade-power and pricing-control considerations combine to yield the results in figure 15–6.

Product and Use Dynamics

The nature of the product category and the customer's utilization of the product also have great impact on pricing practices. Differentiating the products sold by each firm on the basis of (1) component versus stand-alone products and (2) clarity of value in use results in different pricing rubrics.

The firms are dispersed along a component/stand-alone continuum, with Controls and Personal Care at the component and stand-alone ends of the spectrum, respectively. In between these end points, Waters is more of a component vendor than Software, since it builds and sells only boat hulls to which dealers later add engines and other accessories. Software sells stand-alone products, yet they are not stand-alone in the same sense as Personal Care's products. Software's products are not bought because they are attractive in and of themselves, but because they can be made to perform specific customer applications. Hence, Software's products are complete when sold, yet they are only a component of the customer's overall application needs.

With respect to the clarity-of-value-in-use dimension, Personal Care and Controls again represent end points. Personal Care, with its line of toiletry products, provides very clear value to the consumer. The value of Control's products, however, is much harder for the consumer to understand. Waters and Software again occupy the middle positions, with Waters' boats demon-

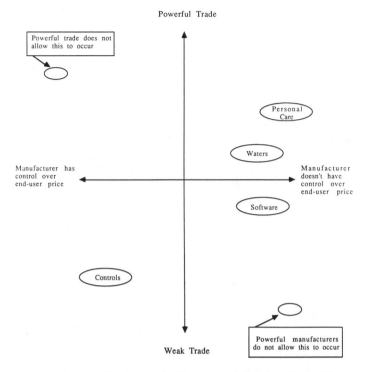

Figure 15-6. Trade Power and Pricing Control

strating more clear value to its prospective use (sailing) than Software's products (a firm's analysis needs). Figure 15-7 outlines these cross-cutting dimensions for the four firms.

Several academic researchers (e.g., Porter [1985]; Forbis and Mehta [1981]) suggest that premium prices are more easily sustainable for products that offer demonstrably better value to the customer. However, our research suggests just the opposite. Component products (e.g., Controls' and Waters') that created value in ways hard to perceive or measure are the premium-priced products. This situation is most evident with Controls' products, which are incorporated into other machines and applications. In such complex systems, the differential value of the Controls' component, relative to the component that a competitor could provide, is not clear.

While the product-completeness/clarity situation is not as dramatic at Waters, the evidence points to similar conclusions. Waters' boat hulls are about half the total value of the "packaged" boat, motor, and accessories. Since the hull is the largest component of the boat, Waters can price hulls high (e.g., a 10 percent increase on a hull is only a 3-5 percent total-package

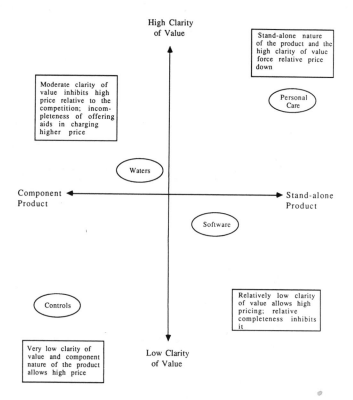

Figure 15-7. Product Completeness and Clarity of Value in Use

increase). But, the relative clarity of value tends to work against the premium-pricing position. There is a constant marketing thrust at Waters to prove that its crafts are substantially better than the competition and, therefore, worth the premium price.

Software occupies a position theoretically opposite that of Waters. Software's products are more complete offerings than Waters', yet the value of the product is harder to discern. Again, there is a pricing tension. The relatively low clarity of value in use, which makes competitive comparisons difficult, fosters high pricing; yet, the relative completeness of the product serves to inhibit a high-price strategy.

Personal Care is in the worst possible position. The functionality of its products is clear, and there is not the uncertainty associated with being part of a larger system. The high clarity of value and stand-alone nature of the products make it easy for customers to identify competitors and impossible for Personal Care to command high prices relative to these competitors.

The Pricing Chain

When the pricing-process commonalities of cost structure, trade power, and product and use dynamics are taken together, the traditional gap between academic and managerial pricing interests is much easier to interpret. Academic researchers have focused a vast amount of attention on aspects of the pricing process that are different from and further down the chain (see figure 15-8) when compared to the concerns of participating managers. Managers appear concerned largely with proximal interrelationships of costs, competition, distribution channels, and the end user's utilization of the product in order to arrive at a price that hopefully represents value added to the end user. Academics have resolutely focused on the distal end state of the pricing process: value provision to the end user.

Figure 15-8 illustrates this "pricing chain" and one interpretation of where the two factions have focused. Viewed in this light, the tension that has been characteristic between academics and managers is less a matter of different pricing theories, methods, or sophistication than it is a necessary consequence of real differences in focus of attention.

A Pricing Research Agenda

While the observations in this chapter in no way meet traditional standards of statistical rigor, our primary purpose was to identify research areas rather than

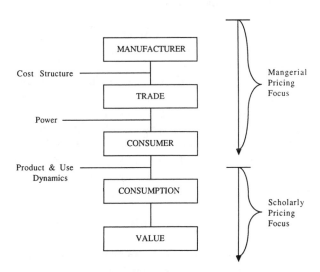

Figure 15-8. The Pricing Chain

resolve a research question. The findings, although tentative, do suggest a profitable research agenda that could forge a new cooperation between managers and academics in the pricing area.

Each of the three areas identified as key influences in the pricing process could serve as the subject of several managerially relevant, but academically rigorous investigations:

A. *Cost structure:*
   1. Most academic pricing models implicitly assume low fixed costs and high variable costs (i.e., $MC = C$) and that variable costs are a significant percentage of price. But, what about those firms faced with just the opposite—high fixed costs and low variable costs? How should we suggest that they price their products in order to receive the optimal return? Can an academically rigorous, yet managerially relevant, pricing model be built for these firms?
   2. Textbook descriptions of pricing assume that the variable cost of producing a product are known. How does the firm that does not know these variable costs price its products when variable costs are a significant percentage of price?
   3. The topic of defensive competitive strategies is an important issue in both marketing and strategic management. But, how does a firm defend itself when it cannot identify its competitors? Specifically, what impact does this have on the pricing process? How does the firm with uncertain, yet significant, variable costs *and* lack of competitor identification determine prices?

B. *Trade power:*
   4. Very little is found in the literature about pricing constraints due to strong channel members. How can a manufacturer facing a powerful trade maximize firm profits?
   5. Should control over the end-user price (in indirect selling) be an important concern to pricing managers? What does selling the product below the suggested retail price indicate to the buyer?
   6. The term *end-user value* may take on different meanings at various levels of the distribution channel. For example, utility to the trade may mean being able to sell the product, and utility to the end user may mean being able to use the product. What is the impact on the pricing process when these differences in definition occur?

C. *Product and use dynamics:*
   7. Contradictory suggestions are made in the literature and in this research for pricing products when customer value is difficult to measure. Is a price premium sustainable in instances of readily measurable value or instances of hard-to-measure value?
   8. Is pricing a component product different than pricing a stand-alone product? What is the relationship between customer value and product completion?

These questions represent only a few of the myriad of research questions that could be derived from this analysis. Examining issues such as those identified here is the link that can serve to narrow the academic–manager, rigor–relevance gap by simultaneously providing scientifically reputable data and managerially actionable advice.

It is not that academics cannot solve managerial pricing problems or that there is no interest in solving them. Rather, it seems that academic researchers have not known, or do not focus on, the key pricing concerns of managers in order to conduct rigorous pricing research. While management has preoccupied itself with many of the partially manipulable or understandable pricing stimuli, the academic community has concentrated its pricing interests on the reactions of consumers and the "value in use" derived from vendor offerings. It is only as a rapprochement between these divergent foci is achieved that truly synergistic, rigorous, *and* relevant pricing work will result.

16
Pricing-Decision Models: Recent Developments and Research Opportunities

Kent B. Monroe
Tridib Mazumdar

Recent Reviews and Criticisms of Pricing Models

In the years since Monroe and Della Bitta [1978] expressed concern about the dearth of comprehensive pricing-decision models, a relatively large number of models have been developed by researchers in marketing. Perhaps stirred by the call for more model development in pricing as well as the efforts to develop research interfaces between economics and marketing, these new models have contributed to a new excitement in pricing research. That this book has been conceived and published is a tribute to the emergence of quantitative modeling in pricing research. While great strides have been made, nevertheless considerably more progress is necessary. One of the objectives of this chapter is to suggest necessary model development and validation to continue the progress made since 1978.

The review by Monroe and Della Bitta [1978] included selected models published prior to 1975. Rao [1984] and Nagle [1984] selectively reviewed model development in marketing and economics through 1983. In each of these reviews, in the commentaries by Narasimhan [1984a] and Raviv [1984] on Nagle's review, and in the commentaries by Oren [1984] and Hauser [1984] on Rao's review, a number of criticisms and suggestions were made to further model development in pricing. To help assess the progress that has been made as well as provide an opportunity to prescribe further research efforts, it is useful to review the nature of these previous assessments on model development in pricing.

Monroe and Della Bitta

Evaluating earlier pricing models on the criteria of realism and clarity of assumptions, specificity of variables and relationships, applicability for managerial decision making, and use of current evidence on buyers' use of price, the review found serious deficiencies in pricing models. Primarily, most models did not have clearly specified assumptions nor were the assumptions usually realistic. It was suggested that this problem stemmed from the historical reliance on the precepts of classical economics, particularly in terms of buyer behavior. While most models seemed to clearly specify the relevant variables, unfortunately the information necessary for model implementation generally was not readily accessible to most business organizations. Frequently, the information required included detailed knowledge of the firm's demand curve and its elasticity as well as its cost structure. Also, the underlying relationships often were not clearly specified, and most models did not use existing research evidence on buyers' use of price information.

Rao

In Rao's review, a number of positive developments were noted, particularly in the area of new-product–pricing models in a dynamic framework. Nevertheless, this review pointed out the formidable problems associated with empirical validation of the models. Concern was also expressed about the lack of incorporating recent behavioral evidence into the structure of these models. Recent research on pricing was characterized as disjointed, and a call for research on how pricing decisions are made in practice was made. On this latter point, it was suggested that a good description of pricing practices would be beneficial to the development of better pricing theory. Other areas needing research included product-line pricing, the role of price in consumer choice, competitive pricing models, and empirical validation of pricing models.

Oren [1984] and Hauser [1984], in commenting on Rao's review, note some of the distinctions between a marketing approach versus an economic approach to developing pricing models. An important issue concerns viewing price as a decision variable (marketing) rather than as a given (economics). Moreover, the normative, equilibrium-type models from economics rarely are validated or calibrated for the acquisition of empirical data. As Hauser noted, marketing science as a discipline is relatively new and is still developing its methods. Thus, he cautioned against uncritically adopting economic concepts, methods, and assumptions for the development of marketing-oriented pricing models. In particular, the assumptions of economics must be scrutinized and adapted in the light of empirical evidence amassed in marketing and consumer behavior. As will be developed in a later section, Hauser's point remains a necessary requirement if model development in pricing is to advance the state of knowledge in pricing.

Nagle

Noting that economic theory is often the basis of pricing models, Nagle cautions against expecting too much from this singular discipline. Simply, economic pricing models are abstractions that hold many real variables constant and, consequently, rarely provide useful prescriptions or descriptions of pricing practice by either buyers or sellers. Economic theory is more concerned with the behavior of aggregates or markets, particularly how persistent and widespread behavior leads to certain stable results called equilibrium. However, Nagle notes some recent developments in economic theory that consider some of the realities of the marketplace: asymmetric information about product quality, buyer information acquisition, segmented pricing, and some specific papers dealing with distribution channels, unique goods, peak loads, priority pricing, and pricing superstars. It was also suggested that in addition to economics and marketing, the disciplines of psychology and sociology provide useful foundations for pricing. To these disciplines, we would add accounting, finance, and the law as necessary sources of knowledge to develop models that eventually are useful in furthering pricing theory.

In their commentaries on Nagle's review of the economic foundations for pricing, Narasimhan [1984a] and Raviv [1984] offer additional suggestions on how economics is useful for pricing research. Both commentaries point out the relative newness of these approaches and, therefore, the limitations that currently exist in terms of useful contributions. While it is clear their commentaries focus on the economic foundations for pricing, it is important to recognize that a strict economic orientation to the development of pricing models ignores other relevant and important foundations for developing pricing theory. It is necessary to utilize useful economic concepts and analytical methods, but at the same time to avoid falling into the trap of being enamored with the mathematical elegance of the structure and ignoring whether real progress in knowledge development has actually occurred.

Overview

Since 1978, a large variety of pricing models have been developed. These models have attempted to capture the dynamic interrelationships between cost- and demand-related factors (Dolan and Jeuland 1981), effects of competitive actions (Mesak and Clelland 1979; Shugan and Jeuland in chapter 10 of this book), effects of price promotion and deals (Rao and Sabavala 1980; Narasimhan 1984b), the role of price in individual choice decisions (Rao and Gautschi 1982; Winer 1985, 1986), and the relationship of price with other marketing-mix variables. However, despite these encouraging efforts, practitioners and academic researchers continue to experience difficulty in using and evaluating the models (Bonoma, Crittenden, and Dolan in chapter 15 of this book; Rao 1984). While some diversity in theoretical approaches is desirable, what remains disturbing is that, at times, mathematical tractability and modeling elegance have led to assumptions that neither fit established theories or empirical evidence nor allow for meaningful generalizations.

While this chapter will present some criticisms of the present state of pricing models, nevertheless the purpose of the chapter is to encourage the development of pricing models. A constructive way to accomplish this goal is to identify a few selected areas in pricing that have received attention, isolate their underlying theoretical assumptions, and delineate the scope and boundaries of their applicability. The review will be general and will include several models that have been reviewed in earlier works as well as the models presented in this book.

The next section will provide a general framework for pricing decisions. It will identify some of the important factors influencing the decision and the interrelationships among these factors. Then a classification scheme is developed to categorize the various pricing models according to their objectives and variables. The chapter will then review the models in this book and several other selected models, critiquing their premises and assumptions. Finally, the chapter will offer an agenda for future pricing-model research.

A Conceptual Framework for Pricing Decisions

A major challenge in making sound pricing decisions lies in resolving the complex interactions among the internal and external factors that need to be considered. Figure 16–1 presents a simplified framework capturing such interrelationships. The basic notion of the model is the determination of an appropriate pricing strategy consistent with the overall positioning of the product (Shapiro and Jackson 1978). If one accepts the importance of customers' views, then the product-positioning decision and, therefore, selection of the pricing strategy should flow directly from demand-related factors such as customers' perceptions of value, existence of distinct price-market segments based on buyers' preferences and price sensitivities, as well as demand interrelationships among multiple product offerings. Guided by an overall marketing and pricing strategy, the firm can develop a set of feasible pricing alternatives, taking into account cost-related factors, anticipated competitive reactions, prevalent trade practices in the distribution channel, and corporate objectives within a legal and public-policy framework.

Setting prices is complex and difficult not only because of the large number of variables influencing the decision, but also because of the interrelationships among them. In an apparently innocuous value-maximizing model, Rao [1984] demonstrated the difficulty these interrelationships present when specifying and estimating cost and demand functions. In particular, the difficulties are illustrated when (1) previous-period cost and demand functions enter the model endogenously and (2) competing products and the marketing-mix variables of other products in the line influence the impact of the product's price. What his model illustrates is the need to partition the complex decision problem into a number of smaller problems in order to obtain reasonable mathematical solutions. Thus, no single modeling effort can be expected to address

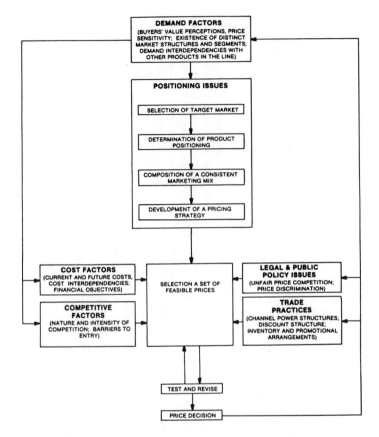

Figure 16-1. Determination of the Pricing Strategy

the entire decision problem. Rather, each pricing model should be evaluated in terms of its ability to formulate and solve specific pricing issues. The next section classifies pricing models on the basis of their objectives and the variables considered relevant for the particular pricing problem.

Classification Framework

Despite considerable diversity in previous modeling efforts, patterns emerge in terms of model objectives and variables included. The pricing models can be broadly classified into the six categories shown in table 16-1. A brief description of each category is provided here. The review does not include competitive bidding or models from the economics literature.

Table 16-1
Classification of Pricing Models

Model Categories	Selected Exemplars	Concepts Used and Variables / Model Objectives	Considered	General Comments
Single-period pricing models	Kunreuther and Richard (1971); Braverman (1971); Mesak and Clelland (1979); Smith (1986); Gerstner and Holthausen (1986); Nagle and Novak (*); Devinney (*)	Setting prices to maximize firm's single-period profits. Other objectives include examination of the effects of price change, interactions between customers and store with multiple products, and price differentiation in a segmented market.	Both buyers and sellers are postulated to use maximizing principles. Variable of interest are demand (deterministic and stochastic), marginal or average costs, inventory costs, buyers' switching costs, segment composition, price differentials, buyers' purchase frequency and price sensitivity.	In general, these models examine specific problems and are interested in one-period optimization. Changes in demand, cost, and competitive reactions over time are not explicitly considered. Some of these models have useful applications in retail pricing.
Dynamic pricing models	Simon (1979; 1982); Robinson and Lakhani (1975); Dolan and Jeuland (1981); Lodish (1980); Kalish (1983a); Clarke and Dolan (1984); Bass (1980); Dhebar and Oren (1985); Rao (*); Lilien and Yoon (*)	Setting prices to maximize present value of profits earned over the life of the product. Focus on combining time-dependent cost and demand functions for arriving at optimality conditions. Effects of competitive entry on penetraton pricing are also examined.	Major concepts used are diffusion of innovation (product life cycle) and experience curve. Buyers' acceptance and product obsolescence are postulated to influence demand. Marginal costs are postulated to decline at a constant rate with increase in cumulative output. Conditions for myopic pricing and dynamic pricing are examined.	These models formalize the qualitative distinctions between skimming and penetration pricing (Dean 1969). Useful applications for pricing new and innovative products when experience effects are present. Additional validation is necessary.
Price-promotion and discount models	Goodman and Moody (1970); Kinberg, Rao, and Shakun (1974); Blattberg, Buesing, Peacock, and Sen (1978); Blattberg, Eppen and Lieberman (181); Narasimhan (1984b;*)	Determination of discount schedules to minimize buyers' and sellers' costs either independently or jointly. Other objectives include examination of brand-switching behavior when competing brands offer price promotions.	In general, the issue is treated as an inventory-management problem. Buyer (or household) as a production unit compares time saving with price inducements; seller offers deals to reduce inventory. Variables of interest include buyers' and sellers' inventory cost, ordering cost, and stock-out cost. Other variables are demand, regular and discounted price, promotion-induced trials, and repeat purchases.	These models have helped to identify the determinants of deal-proneness among buyers and to develop optimal discounting strategy. Potentials exist to model this are incorporating buyers' behavioral factors.

Product-line–pricing models	Setting prices to maximize product-line profits or to maximize contribution per resource units. Also examines the effects of price differentials within an acceptable price range.	Urban (1969); Palda (1971); Monroe and Della Bitta (1978); Monroe and Zoltners (1979); Little and Shapiro (1980); Reibstein and Gatignon (1984); Oren, Smith and Wilson (1982; 1984); Saghafi (*)	In general, the demand and cost interdependencies among products are modeled. Some variables of interest are own-price and cross-price elasticities, sharing pattern of common and scarce inputs, and buyers' evaluations of price range.	Under a relatively static condition, these models identify optimal conditions for product-line pricing. Typically, competitive and buyers' behavioral responses are ignored. Opportunity for modeling bundling and loss-leadership situations exists.
Price and other marketing-mix variables	Examining interrelationships between price and various nonprice variables such as advertisement, product warranty (as a signal for product quality), channel competition and structure, and pricing authority for sales force.	Agarwal and Ratchford (1980); Farris and Albion (1980); Welam (1982); Thompson and Teng (1984); Cooper and Ross (*); Monahan and Nti (*); Shugan and Jeuland (*); Shugan (*)	Variables of interest are advertisement expenditure, product warranty, channel structure, sales-force authority, and product characteristics.	Useful for understanding specific interrelationships between price and other marketing-mix variables and their combined effects on sales and profits.
Price and individual choice	Examining how price and price range enter buyers' product evaluations, utility formation, and ultimate choice. Effects of buyers' perceptions of price change are also examined.	Monroe (1971a); Rao and Shakun (1972); Rao and Gautschi (1982); Srinivasan (1982); Winer (1985; 1986; *); Thaler (1985).	Buyers' psychological factors such as adaptation levels, absolute and differential price thresholds, and decision frames are foundations of these models. Variables used are reference price, evoked price, acceptable price range, price-quality relationships, and buyers' value function.	Modeling efforts in this area are sparse. Potential exists for combining behavioral or consumer-information-processing aspects with economic theories to explain how price references are formed and used.

*Appearing in this book.

Generally, single-period pricing models are concerned with solving specific marketing problems with an objective of selecting a price that maximizes single-period profits. Although there are a number of diverse models in this category, the distinctive feature of them is their assumption that the variables of interest do not change over time.

On the other hand, the dynamic pricing models have explicitly examined changing cost and demand functions over time. These two time-dependent functions are combined to develop a pricing strategy that maximizes the present value of the firm's profit stream. Within this framework, various models have been proposed that incorporate the effects of competitive entry, product obsolescence, and situations where the product's value changes with increased adoption.

The price promotion and discount models primarily have treated the issue as an inventory-management problem. In these models, the sellers' concern is to dispose of inventory with the help of price inducements, and the buyers' objective is to balance the savings of buying on deal against the additional time and storage costs.

The product-line–pricing models examine the cost and demand interdependencies of products in the line in order to maximize the firm's total profits. The major variables of interest include the own-price and cross-price elasticities among products on the demand side and the sharing patterns of input resources on the cost side. In this classification, a variety of models incorporating nonlinear price-volume schedules and the effects of price differentials have been proposed.

The models capturing the interaction between price and other marketing-mix variables have received limited attention. In general, these models have examined how product characteristics, advertising, product warranties, channel competition and structure, and sales-force pricing authority affect pricing decisions and profits.

The role of price in individual choice decisions is an area that has generated considerable interest recently. The basic issues being addressed by researchers include whether price enters at the value formation (utility-formation) stage or whether price serves as an external constraint on buyers' income. Researchers have also examined how buyers' reference prices are formed and how these reference prices affect purchase decisions.

In the next section, each of these modeling areas is examined in greater detail.

Review of Selected Pricing Models

Some of the models listed in table 16–1 are reviewed in this section. Because the review is brief, the original papers should be considered for a more thorough understanding.

Single-Period Models

The classical condition for optimality has been developed in microeconomics as

$$MR = (1 + 1/e_p)p^* = MC \qquad (1)$$

By rearranging terms, the optimal price for a monopolist is
$$p^* = [e_p/(1 + e_p)]MC \qquad (2)$$

where

MR = marginal revenue

MC = marginal cost

e_p = price elasticity of demand

p^* = the price at which a monopolist maximizes single-period profits

Despite the apparent simplicity of this formulation, its application is restricted for at least three reasons. First, and most critical, is the difficulty in formulating and validating the necessary demand and cost functions (Rao 1984). A second problem with this optimality criterion is that it is restricted to the situation when a product is price-elastic; i.e., price elasticity is less than -1. (See Saghafi in chapter 11.) Third, the criterion does not consider changes that take place in demand and costs over time, nor does it include the effects of other marketing-mix variables.

Nevertheless, researchers have used this basic maximizing principle to analyze and model different pricing problems. Kunreuther and Richard [1971] compared the impact of centralized and decentralized pricing and inventory decision making on retail store profits. In a centralized decision system, the pricing and purchase decisions are made simultaneously, whereas in a decentralized system, the decisions are made sequentially (i.e., the pricing decision assumes zero inventory costs). The centralized system was shown to be more profitable when demand was price-elastic, order sizes were small, and ordering costs were relatively high.

Using a Bayesian decision approach, Braverman [1971] concluded that the price at which expected demand equals the quantity produced at the minimum average cost maximizes the firm's expected profits. To apply this model requires assigning subjective probabilities to different price-quality combinations. Moreover, the model assumes the market is relatively free of competition, facilitating the revision of the posterior prices.

A distinctive feature of Mesak and Clelland's [1979] model for low-priced, frequently purchased products is that consumer demand is explicitly considered. Using the concepts of perceived value and upper price threshold (maximum price a buyer is willing to pay), consumers' brand-switching behavior in response to simultaneous competitors' price changes is modeled. The model has two assumptions that need to be mentioned. First, buyers are assumed to be able to detect any price change and to alter their purchase behaviors so long as the new price does not exceed their perceived value. Current behavioral price research raises the question of whether buyers are able to remember previous prices paid for frequently purchased goods (Monroe, Powell, and Choudhury 1986). The ability to detect price changes presumes the buyers know previous prices paid. Moreover, how much of a price difference is necessary behavior buyers shift their purchase behavior (price-differential threshold) is a second behavioral issue not addressed in the model (Monroe 1979). Second, the model assumes that only price changes induce buyers to switch brands. Nonetheless, the researchers show that their competitive-pricing model had better predictive accuracy than an alternative model used by the company.

Three models concern the issue of price segmentation and price discrimination. Gerstner and Holthausen [1986] extend the traditional segmented-pricing approach by allowing buyers in the high-priced segment to move to the low-price segment by incurring a transaction cost. When market segments are not perfectly sealed, it was shown that a price-differentiation strategy would still be profitable when buyers in the high-price market segment incur high transaction costs when shifting to a low-price market. Conversely, when these transaction costs are relatively low, a price-differentiation strategy may not be effective. Using this model, it is also possible to determine the amount of leakage from the high-price market to the low-price market before a price-differentiation strategy is not profitable.

Another model developed by Smith [1986], although dynamic in nature, examines the necessary static conditions for optimality when a market can be segmented in terms of desired quality and levels of market penetration. Assuming different price sensitivities of buyers in different quality segments and assuming one dimension of quality, an optimal-pricing equation is developed. This pricing equation assumes the buyers' objective is to maximize their consumer surplus (maximum price they are willing to pay less the actual price paid) subject to the market-penetration level. In essence, the model assumes that buyers are price-conscious regardless of their quality orientation, possibly a contradictory assumption.

Nagle and Novak's chapter 14 in this book estimates optimal retailer markups when buyers can be segmented in terms of purchase frequency and price consciousness. (Although they use the term *price awareness*, the more appropriate term is *price consciousness* (Monroe 1979)). They make three critical assumptions about buyer behavior:

1. Prices of frequently purchased products are more likely to be remembered.

2. Buyers use these remembered prices to infer overall store-price levels.

3. Shoppers choose stores to shop on the basis of a "low-price" image.

Therefore, given these assumptions, frequently purchased products should be priced with relatively lower markups to maximize store patronage. Shoppers who are not price-conscious are presumed to be convenience-oriented. Thus, items purchased frequently by convenience-oriented shoppers should have higher markups.

There are two major difficulties with the structure of these assumptions. First, research on patronage behavior suggests that shoppers can be typed into other categories or segments as well (Guiltinan and Monroe 1980). Thus, a segmentation strategy based on either price-oriented or convenience-oriented shoppers will not tap a major portion of the market. Second, research on shoppers' ability to remember prices suggests that their recall of frequently purchased goods' prices is not as high as this model assumes.

Nagle and Novak do attempt to empirically validate their model. However, their efforts underscore the difficulty faced by researchers attempting to validate their pricing models. They were able to use actual price, cost, and other relevant store data from one grocery chain in one area. These data were supplemented by aggregate brand-usage data from Simmons Market Research Bureau. Another difficulty they encountered was in operationalizing the concept of buyer price sensitivity. Differences in buyer price sensitivities were represented by a set of demographic and product-use variables and not measured directly. Previous research on buyers' ability to remember prices has not been successful in relating demographics or use to the ability to remember prices (Mazumdar 1987). Despite these difficulties, it is important to encourage modelers to face the very necessary step of providing empirical validations of their models.

Dynamic Pricing Models

Pricing over the life of a product has generated considerable attention from researchers in recent years. The two major concepts used are diffusion of innovation to capture the dynamics of demand and the experience curve to model cost dynamics.

Following social-contagion theory of adoption of innovations (Rogers 1983), Bass [1969] developed a quadratic sales function, the parameters of which express the rate of innovation adoption, imitative effects, and the total market potential. Robinson and Lakhani [1975] followed Bass's efforts and, incorporating the experience-curve concept with the diffusion of innovation, developed a multiperiod pricing model. Bass [1980] presented results of empirical validation of this model using six consumer-durable products. He concluded that the single-period profit-maximization rule will not result in optimizing the profit stream of a product over its life cycle.

Dolan and Jeuland [1981] and Jeuland and Dolan [1982] extended the earlier models in two important ways. First, they considered repeat-purchase situations to apply the model to nondurable products. Second, they assumed the firm's objective was to maximize the net present value of the profit stream. The optimal multiperiod price can be expressed as:

$$P^{\star}_{(t)} = P^{\star}_{m(t)} + dP_{(t)} \tag{3}$$

where

$P^{\star}_{m(t)}$ = the optimal myopic price

$dP_{(t)}$ = an adjustment expressed as a function of the price elasticity, innovative and i effects, market potential, and discount rate.

A number of interesting implications arise from their optimal-price solution:

1. In the absence of demand dynamics, the solution is identical to the classic solution given in equation (2). In such a situation, the myopic optimal prices decline monotonically over time following the experience curve.
2. When future profits are not discounted, three situations are important:
   a. For durable goods where the imitation effect is important for adoption, the optimal-price path follows a pattern of low introductory price, then increases to a peak high price, and declines thereafter.
   b. For durable goods where the imitation effect is unimportant, an introductory high price (skimming) followed by a monotonic decline in price is optimal.
   c. For nondurable goods with frequent repeat purchases, the optimal price path would be an introductory low price (penetration) followed by monotonically increasing price.
3. As the discount rate increases, the present-value factor becomes less important. Eventually, for a discount rate of infinity, the optimal multiperiod pricing strategy is identical to the myopic optimal solution.

Other researchers have offered several extensions and modifications of the Jeuland and Dolan [1982] model. Kalish [1983a and chapter 6 in this book] examined two different effects of adoption on demand. First, demand increases as adoption occurs due to strong word-of-mouth effects. In this situation, the optimal-pricing strategy is similar to the preceding strategy 2a from Jeuland and Dolan. However, when increases in adoption lead to a decrease in demand due to market-saturation effects (durable goods with a finite market size), then the optimal strategy is the preceding 2b.

In an attempt to validate the dynamic pricing model, Bass and Bultez [1982] did a computer simulation and concluded that multiperiod prices should decline over the product's life and will always be less than the single-period optimal price.

This brief overview is indicative of considerable advancements made in dynamic pricing models. However, additional research is necessary to solve some difficult issues. First, the dynamic pricing model needs to be validated and the parameters estimated. For a truly innovative product, the task of estimating eventual market potential, innovative and imitative effects, and repeat-purchase rates is extremely difficult if nigh impossible. It is likely that some surrogate indicators of these variables will be required.

While it is convenient to assume a monopolist market structure, in reality, competition has a strong impact on pricing over a product's life cycle. Recently, researchers have attempted to grapple with this competition effect. Clarke and Dolan [1984] compared skimming and penetration strategies in a duopolist (two-sellers) situation. However, except to illustrate the usefulness of simulation techniques and a game theoretic approach, they do not offer generalizable results. Using a nonzero-sum-differential game, Thompson and Teng [1984] developed an optimal pricing and advertising policy for an oligopolist. Wernerfelt [1985], also using differential game theory, analyzed the dynamics of price and market share over the life of a product. His results suggest that with the experience effect operating, and with a decline of price sensitivity of buyers coupled with a declining growth rate of demand, a strategy of maximizing sales volume in the introductory stage gives a firm a competitive advantage. In chapter 9 of this book, Rao examines the use of penetration pricing (introductory-pricing strategy) to forestall competitor entry. In a duopolist situation and applying game theory, he concludes that a monopolist may delay competitor entry by starting with a low price (and assumed high output levels) and then increasing price over the product's life (while reducing output levels). Of course, what this monopolist does with the initial capacity that required a substantial investment for the introductory period is not addressed by the model.

A third issue with the Jeuland and Dolan [1982] model lies in the assumption of constant price elasticity over the life of the product. But, given the findings of Simon [1979, 1982] and Lilien and Yoon [chapter 12 in this book], the need to incorporate changing price sensitivities over the life cycle is a necessary complexity. Moreover, Jeuland and Dolan assumed that the product's demand was price-elastic throughout its life. Yet, the evidence of Simon as well as Lilien and Yoon refutes the generalizability of this assumption.

While it is evident that much additional work still needs to be done, the research on dynamic pricing models has made substantial progress. It is clear that the preceding models still have not considered the dynamics of buyer behavior over a product's life cycle. For example, for frequently purchased products, there is behavioral-research evidence that an introductory low price followed by a price increase may lead to a substantial dampening of demand over time (Monroe 1979). Such a pricing strategy may actually serve to enhance buyers' price sensitivities and reduce market potential. A second issue for durable products concerns the possibility that there may exist multiple price-market segments with different price sensitivities and different market potentials.

Price-Promotion and Discount Models

In recent years, manufacturers and retailers have made increasing use of coupons, rebates, short-term price reductions, and free samples to stimulate short-term demand for their products. Despite the popularity of these price deals, it is not at all clear that a majority of these deals are profitable. There are a number of perplexing issues that must be resolved if an optimal discount structure is to be developed:

1. Should a price promotion be offered?
2. When should the promotion be offered?
3. How long should the promotion run?
4. How many units should be covered by the promotion?
5. What products should be promoted?
6. What should be the amount of the price reduction?
7. To whom should the deal be offered: dealers or final customers?

In an early model in this area, Goodman and Moody [1970] suggested that the decision be treated as an inventory-management problem of the seller. The seller's objective was to minimize the opportunity costs for excessive quantity sold at a reduced price and lost sales due to stockouts. The model determined the optimal quantity to be offered on deal and the optimal size of the discount. Kinberg, Rao, and Shakun [1974] developed a brand-switching model for when competing brands offer temporary price reductions. There were two price-market segments (price-conscious buyers and quality-conscious buyers) and two brands (private and premium brands). The model developed a schedule of when to promote depending on competitive reaction to maximize incremental sales revenue.

The development of price-promotion models took a different perspective by integrating Becker's [1965] notion of the household as a production unit. In this view, households are postulated to include the value of their time in their buying decisions. Thus, buyers are postulated to make cost-benefit assessments and evaluate the benefits of the deal against the time and storage cost incurred when buying on deal (Etgar 1978). Using this theoretical perspective, Blattberg, Buesing, Peacock, and Sen [1978] identified several demographic characteristics of deal-prone consumers. Then, Blattberg, Eppen, and Lieberman [1981] combined both the consumers' and retailer's perspectives to develop a comprehensive model. At the core of the model lies an assumption that the inventory costs are transferred from the retailer to customers. The optimal quantity to purchase on deal was determined to be proportional to the magnitude of the deal and the consumption rate, but inversely related to buyers' holding costs. Also, the optimal purchase period was positively related to the deal magnitude, but negatively related to buyers' holding costs.

In the retailer model, the retailer's objective is to minimize total cost per inventory cycle. Based on the optimal solutions, the following are implied:

1. The deal magnitude increases with the retailer's set-up cost and buyers' holding costs, but decreases with demand and retailer's holding costs.

2. The retailer's optimal reorder time is directly proportional to the deal magnitude, but inversely proportional to buyers' holding costs.

3. Dealing costs increase with demand, set-up costs, and retailer's holding costs.

4. Dealing frequency is positively related to rate of demand and holding costs of both sellers and buyers, but inversely related to retailer's set-up cost.

In contrast to these models, Narasimhan [1984] developed a model for using coupons to discriminate in price. Using diary panel data, he determined that significant differences in quantities purchased on deal were based on buyers' price elasticities and coupon-usage patterns. Generally, his results confirm the earlier findings of Blattberg, Buesing, Peacock, and Sen [1978].

In chapter 8 of this book, Narasimhan develops the conditions for optimal discounts and frequencies for a monopolist selling to two market segments: loyal and nonloyal. His conclusions indicate that a product with a greater share of loyal customers should offer lower discounts less frequently. Assuming that loyalty for an established product develops over time, a new product would need more frequent and deeper discounts. It would seem that this observation would generalize to products that have low market share (low-loyalty segment) as well.

Since 1978, considerable progress has been made in the development of price-promotion and discount models. However, additional opportunities exist for understanding buyers' behaviors and reactions to deals and discounts. Research in the areas of comparative price advertising, framing, and reference prices would provide additional insights for model developers.

Product-Line–Pricing Models

There are a number of reasons why prescriptions for single-product pricing may not generalize to a multiple-product situation. First, products in the line may be related on the demand side (substitute or complements). Second, there may be cost interdependencies such as shared production, distribution, and marketing expenditures. Third, several products may be sold as a bundle, thereby creating a complementarity among them. Fourth, the price of a product in the line may influence buyers' subjective evaluations of other products. Finally, there may be some overriding corporate objective that influences prices of other products (e.g., a regulated industry or a not-for-profit organization).

Although interest in a single-product–pricing models has been predominant, there have been some efforts to model the multiple-product problem. Urban [1969] examined the interdependencies of prices, advertising, and distribution among brands in a product-line context. Using store audit data for three product lines of related, frequently purchased goods, he developed a procedure for measuring the own- and cross-price elasticities for each marketing variable.

Palda [1971] offered several theoretical solutions for determining the optimal prices for a product line under different demand and cost interdependencies:

independent products	$MR_i = MC_i$
demand-related product	adjusted $MR_i = MC_i$
cost-related products	MR_i = adjusted MC_i
both cost- and demand-related products	adjusted MR_i = adjusted MC_i
demand-related products with one cost function	$MR_i = MC_i$

where MR_i and MC_i are the marginal revenue and marginal costs for the ith product, and the adjustment reflects the effect of price and output changes of the ith product on the cost and revenue of the other products in the line.

Monroe and Della Bitta [1978] derived a single-period profit-maximizing pricing solution under demand and cost interdependencies among products in the line. However, the model is restricted by three assumptions. The linear cost function precludes scale economies in production, distribution, or marketing. Second, the fixed-cost components are separable, making the model a maximizing contribution to profits model. Third, the effects of competition are excluded.

Little and Shapiro [1980] examined the interactions between customers and retail store when several products carried by the store are interrelated. By maximizing the store's single-period profit function subject to consumers receiving a given level of utility, the optimal prices are determined by the products' own- and cross-price elasticities, the nature of demand, and the gross margins. No empirical evidence was provided for the validity of the solution.

Considering three nonlinear, stochastic sales-response functions, Reibstein and Gatignon [1984] developed an optimal pricing model for demand-related products. The optimal solution is identical to the expression derived by Rao [1984] for a deterministic demand situation:

$$P_i^\star = [e_i/(1 + e_i)]MC_i - [e_{ij}/(1 + e_i)]$$

$$\star\ [Q_j(P_j - MC_j)/Q_i]$$

The substantive implication of equation (4) is that the optimal price of a product in a demand-interdependent product line is the single-product optimal price (the first component in equation (4)) corrected by an adjustment factor (the second component in the equation). The adjustment factor is a function of the product's own-price and cross-price elasticities, demand for the products in the line, and the price and marginal costs of the other products in the line. For a stochastic sales-response function, the adjustment factor is also dependent on the variances of the disturbance terms. Using UPC scanner data for the sale of eggs over twenty-five weeks, they concluded that the most realistic estimates were obtained when cross elasticities were included in the model.

Monroe and Zoltners [1979] examined the special case when products related by costs are being produced under conditions of productive capacity. Under this condition, they show, using an iterative mathematical programming model, that maximum profits are obtained when prices and production decisions are made on the basis of the contribution per scarce resource unit.

In chapter 11, Saghafi points out four shortcomings of previous product-line models:

The firm's objective is assumed to be profit maximization.

Average production costs are assumed to be constant.

It is presumed the products should be in a product line.

It is presumed that the firm should always be operating in the elastic portion of the demand curve.

He then develops several models addressing these four issues.

For a traditional single-period-profit–maximizing firm operating under economies of scale, Saghafi determined that the firm would be better off if it produced one product rather than the two substitute products. However, if the products were complements, then both products should be produced, but the products need not be operating in the elastic portion of the demand curve. If the firm is a return-to-cost maximizer and if the products are demand independent, then the product line should be produced. It was also shown that under specific objectives, regardless of demand interdependencies, a simultaneous product-line–pricing strategy should be adopted. As in the other models just reviewed, it is apparent that a necessary piece of information for pricing a product line is the own- and cross-price elasticities for the products—which is not easy information to obtain.

Oren, Smith, and Wilson [1984] examined a special case where prices of successively higher-quality products are determined sequentially. Assuming a single dimension of quality, no competitive reactions, and no changes in consumer characteristics over time, they develop a nonlinear pricing schedule for customers with varying preferences. The behavioral issues of sequential price determination of a product line have been discussed by Monroe and Petroshius [1980] and Petroshius and Monroe [1987]. By developing the price differentials needed for buyers to perceive quality distinctions in the products, a mathematical procedure is available for developing the price schedule (Monroe 1979).

Price and Other Elements of the Marketing Mix

Although price interacts with the other elements of the marketing mix to influence demand, few efforts have been made to model these interactions. There are some models considering the interaction of product and advertising with price. More recently, the interaction of distribution with price has been modeled.

Product and Price. The interrelationship between product and price has been studied using the economics perspective as well as the behavioral perspective. Within the economics paradigm, a product is viewed as a bundle of utility-producing characteristics and buyers are assumed to judge the utility of the product independent of price (Lancaster 1966). Rosen [1974] removed the "infinite-divisibility" assumption of Lancaster's model and devised the "hedonic approach," which was introduced into the marketing literature by Ratchford [1975]. According to the hedonic approach, a product's price is a function of its characteristics:

$$P_j = f(Z_{1j}, Z_{2j}, \ldots, Z_{nj}) \tag{5}$$

Fitting a regression between prices and product characteristics produces an estimate of the contribution each characteristic makes to price. The regression equation can then be used to predict the hedonic price at different levels of product characteristics.

Examples of the hedonic approach can be found in Morgan, Metzen, and Johnson [1979] and in Agarwal and Ratchford [1980]. Assuming a linear hedonic price function, Morgan, Metzen, and Johnson demonstrated the contributions of different characteristics of breakfast cereals to their prices. Agarwal and Ratchford [1980], using a loglinear hedonic price function, explained about 70 percent of the variation in automobile prices. However, they pointed out that the predictive power of the hedonic approach depends primarily on the careful selection of appropriate product characteristics. Ratchford [1975] has also suggested that the difference between actual and hedonic prices occurs because of buyer inertia, buyers' lack of complete information, and other imperfections in the marketplace. The issue of information asymmetry between buyers and sellers has also been addressed by Klein and Leffler [1981] and Nagle [1984]. Also, the role of product warranties in signaling product characteristics, particularly product quality, is addressed by Ross and Cooper in chapter 4 of this book.

In the behavioral paradigm, a buyer's judgment about a product's potential utility is rarely made independently of price. It has been postulated that buyers use price or other intrinsic or extrinsic cues to subjectively evaluate a product's quality or benefits. Cognitively balancing the perceived utility (quality) based on the product's price against the disutility of the price, it is argued that buyers make a subjective judgment about the value of the product offer. Although the empirical evidence about the use of price as an indicator of product quality appears to be inconsistent, a quantitative review of a selected set of studies provides positive evidence of the phenomenon (Monroe and Krishnan 1985). The inconsistency of individual study results seems to stem from the failure of previous research to rigorously establish the scope and boundaries of the phenomenon (Monroe and Dodds 1988).

This brief review of the two perspectives on the interaction between product and price isolates an important issue that needs to be resolved. Does price serve primarily as a constraint on buyers' income, or does price influence the formation of buyers' utilities? Interesting treatments of this issue are presented by Rao and Gautschi [1982], Srinivasan [1982], and Thaler [1985]. These efforts will be discussed later.

Price and Advertising. Research involving the interaction between price and advertising has raised some important managerial and public-policy issues. Depending on the perspective taken, advertising either serves to increase or decrease buyers' sensitivities to price (Farris and Albion 1980). If advertising serves primarily to differentiate the product, then as the seller successfully differentiates the product, buyers become less concerned about the price. The opposing perspective maintains that the increased information from advertising makes buyers more knowledgeable and, therefore, more price-sensitive. Research on the impact of advertising on buyers' price sensitivities has found support for both positions. In a recent field experimental study, Krishnamurthi and Raj [1985] found, for a frequently purchased consumer product, price elasticity decreased with increased levels of advertising. It was also found that the decrease in price elasticity was more pronounced among buyers in the high price sensitivity segment than it was for buyers with less price sensitivity.

Other researchers have developed models for optimal price and advertising strategies over time. Assuming demand to be a multiplicative function of price and advertising, Welam [1982] developed a model with the objective of maximizing the present value of the profit stream, plus a salvage value at the end of the planning period. In this model, as well as in most of the price advertising models, the effect of advertising is assumed to decay over time, but may be replenished by current advertising. He concludes that it is optimal to maintain a constant price and a constant level of advertising throughout the planning period. Interestingly, Welam [1982] found that the popular practice of setting advertising budgets on the basis of the previous year's sales will produce a near optimal decision.

In chapter 7 of this book, Monahan and Nti develop a dynamic pricing and advertising model for a new consumer-nondurable product. Three distinctive features of the model are worth noting. First, the initial trial is assumed to be random because of the uncertainty surrounding the product's performance. Second, the pricing and advertising decisions are assumed to be stochastic functions of the rate of market penetration. Third, the market is segmented between triers and nontriers. The model indicates that if demand is insensitive to price, then a penetration introductory-pricing strategy would be optimal only if advertising in the repeat-purchase market helps to differentiate the product. When the new customer segment is price-sensitive, but this sensitivity declines as the product matures, then a penetration strategy would be preferable. A skimming strategy would be appropriate if the new market demand initially is not price-sensitive, but the repeat-purchase segment becomes price-sensitive.

An important issue developed by this model is the price sensitivity of repeat buyers. Because sales growth is dependent on repeat purchases, the price sensitivity of this segment dominates the firm's strategy. If a low introductory price is chosen to secure a relatively large number of triers, then the question arises as to why they become less price-sensitive after trying the product? If they like the product and recognize that it offers value to them, or if advertising persuades them that the product is useful to them, then, perhaps, within some range of higher prices, these buyers will continue to buy as the price increases. However, if the initial low price becomes the reference price for future purchases, then it is likely that these initial triers will become more price-sensitive rather than less. Evidence from behavioral price research indicates that this lower reference price may serve to increase price sensitivity as the product's price increases (Monroe 1979). Also, to apply this model requires knowledge of price sensitivities prior to introducing the product to the market, a most difficult requirement.

Price and Distribution. There has been little research on the interaction between price and distribution, as noted by Bonoma, Crittenden, and Dolan in the preceding chapter. Lal [1986] investigated the effect of delegating pricing responsibility to the sales force. Using an agency-theory framework and making the usual assumptions about the salespersons' utility function, it was concluded that a necessary condition for salespeople to be given pricing responsibility is for them to have better information about the selling environment than upper management has.

Two additional research efforts consider the interaction between price and distribution. This book's chapter 13 by Shugan develops a model examining the effects of product assortment and shopper types on a store's markup decisions. The objective of the model is to study the effect of price when shoppers select an outlet before selecting a product. The underlying premise is that the price set by the store depends on the store's assortment. Implicitly, the model assumes that the existence of different price-market segments provides the store's motivation to offer an assortment or "product line." Moreover, these different price segments differ in the degree to which buyers are sensitive to prices.

In the model, two different effects of product-line pricing are developed. In the segmentation effect, prices are set so that buyers will perceive the prices of the different products as different. Thus, the prices must be set far enough apart to preclude buyers in a particular price-market segment from selecting a product outside the price segment. In the trading-up effect, the goal is to set prices so that buyers will not perceive that prices between products are different. (It is important to note that a distinction must be made between noticing whether two prices are numerically different and perceiving that two prices are dissimilar.) Although the model indicates that the segmentation effect dominates the trade-up effect, this result depends on the assumption made about the relative size of the acceptable price range for each price-market segment.

Shugan's efforts to validate the model's prediction empirically are noteworthy, not only for the attempt, but also to illustrate the wide differences between the real world of price setting and current modeling efforts. An important finding of the empirical effort is that outlets seldom offer identical products, even when carrying the same brand. Moreover, these outlets find a variety of ways to differentiate their offerings from competitors. Another finding of interest is that the price of an item within an outlet was not significantly correlated with prices of other items in the store. This last point means that it is not necessarily a correct assumption to infer the overall price level of a store on the basis of a small sample of items offered for sale.

In chapter 10 of this book, Shugan and Jeuland extend the earlier work of McGuire and Staelin [1983a] and offer a framework for studying the pricing behavior of channel members under different channel structures and in a duopolistic situation. While the model provides a structure for understanding the motivation to vertically integrate a channel, the model does not consider the effect of price on final demand. In effect, the assumption that the profit-maximizing behavior of channel members causes specific market prices ignores the ability of the final buyer (the end user) to refrain from buying if the price is unacceptable. Their model does demonstrate the destructive nature of price cutting as a competitive reaction. Unfortunately, it is not clear that distributors in reality do recognize this point. Their conclusion that it is imperative to know how pricing decisions are made in practice if we are to further the theory of price setting echoes the argument made in chapter 15 by Bonoma, Crittenden, and Dolan. Indeed, Bonoma et al. argue for pricing theory to recognize that channel members play a major role in the setting of prices and that descriptive research is necessary to understand this role.

Price and Individual Choice

The role that price plays in influencing individual purchase decisions has been a key aspect of price research for a long time. In the classical economic view, price serves as an indicator of how much utility (money) a buyer sacrifices when making a purchase. However, beginning with Scitovszky's essay [1944–45], a body of research has explored when buyers may also use price as an indicator of product quality. From this research, a number of important concepts have been advanced that need to be considered when developing price models. Gabor and Granger [1966] suggested that while a budget constraint may lead a buyer to judge a particular price as too expensive, it is also feasible that a specific price may be judged as too low. Thus, the concept of buyers' acceptable price range was formulated. This acceptable price range is bounded by buyers' absolute price thresholds or limits (Monroe 1973). This price-limit concept was the basis of two early modeling efforts examining the impact of price on consumer choice.

Using the Weber-Fechner law of psychophysics, Monroe [1971b] proposed a lognormal buy-response function expressing the probability that a buyer will consider buying a product at a given price. He also demonstrated the use of probit analysis to estimate the parameters of the buy-response function and to estimate the lower and upper price thresholds. Rao and Shakun [1972] extended the model by incorporating a multibrand situation where buyers could be segmented as either price-conscious or quality-conscious. An excellent review and critique of the model is presented in Lilien and Kotler [1983].

Researchers have also investigated the role of price in buyers' subjective evaluations of a product (Monroe 1973; Monroe and Petroshius 1981), and in buyers' utility judgments (Rao and Gautschi 1982; Srinivasan 1982). Srinivasan argues for including price as an attribute in the utility function because the inclusion incorporates the association between price and other attributes excluded from the model. Thus, the key point is that price plays multiple roles in buyers' product evaluations. That is, price is an indicator of both the buyers' sacrifice (disutility) and product quality when other attribute information is unavailable. Descriptive models incorporating this dual role of price have been proposed by Dodds and Monroe [1985], Zeithaml [1986], and Monroe and Chapman [1987]. The core argument in each of these models is that buyers make a cognitive trade-off between perceived quality or benefits and perceived sacrifice to make an assessment of perceived value. Thaler [1985], using prospect theory, makes a similar argument, as does Keon [1980] in his bargain-value model.

Another behavioral concept that has considerable usefulness for understanding the role of price in individual choice is reference price. A reference price is an internal (memory) or external price that buyers use to compare the price of the product being evaluated (Monroe 1973, 1979). While there is general agreement about the concept of a reference price being used as a standard for comparison by buyers, there is considerable concern about how the internal reference prices are formed and how they influence buyer choice (Monroe 1973; Monroe and Petroshius 1981; Rao 1984; Winer 1985, 1986; Klein and Oglethorpe 1987). In chapter 2 of this book, Winer provides a comprehensive treatment on how this concept may be modeled, and he identifies several ways reference prices may be formed in buyers' minds.

Winer [1986] expressed the unobservable reference price as a function of the last price paid (or exposed to) and a trend factor. Incorporating reference price in a probabilistic choice function, and using panel scanner data for coffee with different price-expectation assumptions, he demonstrated that the relative difference between the reference price and the observed price produced a significant effect on choice in two of three brands. In chapter 2 of this book, Winer extends his earlier demand function by using the Weber-Fechner law:

$$Q_t = a + b \ln[P_t^o - P_t^r)/P_t^r] + cX_t + e_t \tag{6}$$

where Q_t = demand at time t

P_t^o = observed price at time t

P_t^r = reference price at time t

X_t = other nonprice exogenous variables affecting demand

This equation holds only when the observed price is larger than the reference price. Yet, as observed by Thaler [1985], there may be many situations when the reference price is larger than the observed price, introducing an additional value component, transaction value (Monroe and Chapman 1987). Moreover, if the buyers' reference price is the last price paid, the model assumes they are capable of complete price recall. Again, the evidence on buyers' ability to remember prices paid raises a concern about the validity of the assumption (Mazumdar 1987).

Despite these limitations, Winers' chapter 2 in this book makes an important contribution by providing a comprehensive treatment of this important concept. His table 2-1 provides an excellent integration of some important concepts from behavioral price research for the modeling of demand functions. Moreover, he identifies how different demand models may conflict with each other and suggests empirical ways to resolve these conflicts.

Price Signaling

When Scitovsky [1944-45] suggested that when buyers' do not have perfect information about a product's ability to satisfy them, they may use price as an indicator of quality, he implicitly made a crucial assumption. The assumption was that a higher-quality product is more costly to produce, and, assuming a nominal profit margin over production costs, it was rational for buyers to infer that higher-priced products were of higher quality. However, in the usual market situation, price is not set by the impersonal market forces, but by the firm. Hence, in the interest of obtaining higher profits, a firm could set a high price that did not reflect the actual level of quality built into the product. This strategy could succeed only if the buyer either were unable to evaluate the product's attributes before purchase or could not completely evaluate the product's attributes (and quality) after a single purchase (or several purchases). Thus, there is a situation in which the information about a product's quality is known by the seller but not known by the buyer, a condition of asymmetric information. Within the economics of literature, a stream of research has developed to investigate the question of when is it in the interests of the firm to signal to the marketplace the quality of its product using price, advertising, warranties, or other signals. Two chapters in this book (chapter 3 by Devinney and chapter 4 by Cooper and Ross) develop models investigating this issue.

In chapter 3, Devinney provides an introduction to the area of economics of information. The issue of concern is how can external information cues be utilized by the seller to convey information about the product to the marketplace. Specifically, a signal is a piece of information that can be revealed to the market at some cost to the provider. (It is important to note that the perspective of the research is on the seller, not the buyer. Thus, while an aspect of behavioral price research has examined the effects on buyers' perceptions of quality of different external cues such as price, brand name, or store image, signaling theory does not consider the degree to which that external cue is perceived as intended by the seller.) A signal is an observable, alterable (by the seller) characteristic that may affect buyers' assessments of product quality.

For a piece of information (cue) to serve as a signal:

1. There must be observable differences in a characteristic across sellers.
2. There must be differences to the sellers in the cost of providing the cue.
3. The quality level of products in the market must vary directly with the characteristic.

This third requirement is critical, because if buyers know that the quality does not vary as the signal varies, then the signal cannot be used to convey differences in quality across competing products (Rao and Monroe 1988).

In chapter 3, Devinney gives a useful introduction to the economics of information and describes equilibrium conditions for when price, advertising levels, and scale of operations may serve as signals to the market. However, issue must be taken with one conclusion in the chapter. To state that "what makes price . . . a signal is *not* a consumer's feelings, but firms' production functions and the gain and losses from signaling" ignores important behavioral research findings. Whether consumers use price to infer product quality depends, not on the costs producers incur when using price to differentiate their products, but on whether consumers believe there is a positive relationship between the signal and quality, and whether they can compute, cognitively, the actual covariation among the products in the marketplace (Bettman, John, and Scott 1986).

In chapter 4 of this book, Cooper and Ross review an important area of pricing strategy. When a seller has a high-quality product, how can the level of this quality be signaled to buyers, particularly when comparable alternative products are of significantly lower quality? While a significantly higher price than the comparable products' can be a part of the signaling strategy, nevertheless buyers may still not believe the product is as good as the seller expresses through the price signal. By guaranteeing the product's quality through an expressed warranty, the seller may alleviate buyers' concerns that the product's quality is not commensurate with its price. chapter 4 develops some of the issues that need to be researched to provide better information on when sellers should consider offering warranties and the magnitude of the warranties. As the authors point out, there is much to be done on this topic; nevertheless, the chapter opens up an important area of pricing research.

Conclusion

As noted at the outset of this chapter, model building in pricing has made substantial progress since 1978. This brief and selected review has covered a range of pricing issues, many of which had not been subjected to model development before 1978. Moreover, the interest in pricing research—model development as well as empirical efforts—shows a continuing increase in activity. These changes are welcome and necessary if knowledge in pricing is to advance. Nevertheless, despite these notable advancements, some criticisms from previous reviews remain and need to be addressed by researchers in pricing. The purpose of these final comments is to review these critical points in the hope that researchers will begin to examine them in the near future.

Monroe and Della Bitta [1978] called for assumptions in pricing models to be more realistic and to be articulated clearly. The creators of the models in this book as well as the others mentioned have been aware of the need to clarify their assumptions, although there remains room for improvement. Hauser's [1984] point that pricing-model developers must scrutinize traditional economic assumptions in the light of empirical evidence in marketing and consumer behavior primarily has not been followed. Thus, we find assumptions of a monopolist selling to many small buyers who are perfectly informed no later than after one purchase occasion. Prescriptions based on such models have no hope of being adapted either by price setters or by public-policy makers. Moreover, the enormous difficulties of attempting to empirically validate such attempts will lead to the models being relegated to the category of "an interesting intellectual exercise."

In the first chapter of this book, Devinney attempts to provide an integrated framework based on economic concepts for research and management decisions. The goal is an extremely important one for pricing research. Unfortunately, because his attention is focused only on economic concepts, his ideas fall short of this goal. Because only economic concepts and analytical methods are used to develop the integration, he winds up in the trap that Hauser [1984] has advocated it is necessary to avoid. We cannot afford to rely on one research paradigm for the development of pricing knowledge. Pricing necessarily must incorporate information, assumptions, and methods from the areas of economics, marketing, psychology, sociology, finance, accounting, and other disciplines as relevant to the issues under scrutiny. To continue a single-discipline orientation when the area is multidisciplinary in nature is folly and is doomed to fail.

A second area of concern is the low attention paid to the existing and growing base of empirical knowledge on how buyers acquire, retain in memory, and use price information. Many of the models continue to rely on the assumption that buyers either have current and past price information available to them or they are able to extract such information from memory without error. Further, there is the assumption that buyers are able to acquire complete information about the products' attributes no later than after one purchase occasion. Once it is assumed that buyers do have price information, it is also assumed that the "rational" buyer seeks to minimize the price paid (that is, to equate the marginal utility of acquiring one more unit of the product to its price). While such assumptions may be necessary to extract optimal solutions from the model, they do not conform to the empirical realities about buyer behavior, and they become susceptible to the relevance criticisms raised by Bonoma, Crittenden, and Dolan in chapter 15 of this book.

Another important issue is the relative lack of empirical validation for the models that have been proposed. In this book, three attempts aimed at empirically validating pricing-theory propositions are reported. The authors need to be applauded for these efforts. These chapters also illustrate a major difficulty in providing empirical validation. It is difficult to obtain data that conforms to the structure of the theoretical formulation. One source of this difficulty relates to the criticisms of model development previously discussed. However, another critical difficulty concerns the inability or unwillingness of business firms to permit researchers access to data that may be closer to the needs of the model being tested than retail shelf or checkout observations. To enable academic researchers to focus on the pricing issues of concern to management, management must be willing to be accessible to academic researchers and their data needs. For a variety of reasons, it has not been the tradition of management to be "friendly" to the needs of academic researchers in the area of pricing.

In a similar way, the recommendations that more descriptive research on pricing be done need to be followed. Descriptive research has been the unwanted stepchild of academic researchers for some time. However, the philosphy-of-science debate that has been a part of marketing since 1978 seems to have opened up some awareness that descriptive research is both legitimate and necessary for knowledge development. We simply need to know more about the decision processes and heuristics used by managers and buyers concerning price. One of the goals of such research efforts would be to develop a series of scenarios about the pricing environment to provide a focus on when existing models have applicability and when models with different structures need to be developed. Such efforts should also help to move pricing models from the almost exclusive reliance on an uncritical acceptance of the economic paradigm as the framework for these models.

As these criticisms suggest, there are many opportunities for researchers in the area of pricing. Researchers with a behavioral orientation have many opportunities to investigate issues relating to how buyers acquire, remember, and use price information for evaluating product alternatives and for choosing among these alternatives. Researchers with a quantitative-modeling orientation have ample opportunities to use the evidence from behavioral researchers, adapt the many important and useful concepts and theories from economics, and develop models that are useful to the advancement of pricing knowledge. Researchers who are methodologically oriented need to work on the problems and issues related to empirical validation of the models. Researchers with established relationships with managers need to engage in descriptive research to provide better information about the variety of pricing environments that exist in the world of business.

The ability to solve current and future pricing problems will require: (1) new attitudes toward pricing by business and academics and (2) establishing price research programs to provide information on (a) buyers' use of price information, (b) cost, volume, and profit implications of price decisions, and (c) an integration of price in product and market life-cycle strategies. The need for research attention to pricing is critical because pricing is an important and complex aspect of business management and buyer behavior.

References

Abernathy, W., and N. Baloff [1973], "Planning New Product Start-Ups," *Decision Sciences*, 1–20.

Adam, D. [1970], "Consumer Reactions to Price," in B. Taylor and G. Wills (eds.), *Pricing Strategy*. Princeton, N.J.: Brandon Systems Press, 75–88.

Adams, W., and J. Yellen [1976], "Commodity Bundling and the Burden of Monopoly," *Quarterly Journal of Economics*, 90, 475–98.

Adelman, M. [1959], "Pricing Objectives in Large Companies: Comment," *American Economic Review*, 49, 669–70.

Agarwal, M., and B. Ratchford [1980], "Estimating Demand Functions for Product Characteristics: The Case of Automobiles," *Journal of Consumer Research*, 6, 249–62.

Akerlof, G. [1970], "The Market for 'Lemons': Qualitative Uncertainty and the Market Mechanism," *Quarterly Journal of Economics*, 84, 488–500.

Albright, S., and W. Winston [1979], "Markov Models of Advertising and Pricing Decision," *Operations Research*, 27, 668–81.

Alchian, A. [1959], "Costs and Output," in M. Abramovitz et al. (eds.), *The Allocation of Economic Resources: Essays in Honor of B.F. Haley*. Stanford, Calif.: Stanford University Press, 23.40.

Alfred, A. [1972], "Company Pricing Policy," *Journal of Industrial Economics*, 21, 1–15.

Amihud, Y., and H. Mendelson [1983a], "Multiperiod Sales-Production Decisions Under Uncertainty," *Journal of Economic Dynamics and Control*, 249–65.

Amihud, Y., and H. Mendelson [1983b], "Price Smoothing and Inventory," *Review of Economic Studies*, 50, 87–98.

Anderson, B. [1972], "Working Women Versus Non-Working Women: A Comparison of Shopping Behaviors," in B. Becker and H. Becker (eds.), *Marketing Education and the Real World*, Proceedings of the 1972 AMA Educators' Conference. Chicago, Ill.: American Marketing Association, 355–59.

Arnott, R., and J. Stiglitz [1983], "Moral Hazard and Optimal Commodity Taxation," *Journal of Public Economics*, 29, 1–24.

Arrow, K. [1961], "The Economic Implications of Learning by Doing," *Review of Economic Studies*, 29, 155–73.

Arrow, K., and M. Kurz [1970], *Public Investment, the Rate of Return, and Optimal Fiscal Policy*. Baltimore, Md.: Johns Hopkins University Press.

Bain, J. [1956], *Barriers to New Competition: Their Character and Consequences in Manufacturing Industries*. Cambridge, Mass.: Harvard University Press.

Baligh, H., and L. Richartz [1967], *Vertical Market Structures*. Boston: Allyn & Bacon.

Barback, R. [1964], *Pricing of Manufacturers*. London: Macmillan.

Bass, F. [1969], "A New Product Growth Model for Consumer Durables," *Management Science*, 15, 215–27.

Bass, F. [1980], "The Relationship Between Diffusion Rates, Experience Curves, and Demand Elasticities for Consumer Durable Technical Innovations," *Journal of Business*, 53, 551–67.

Bass, F., and A. Bultez [1982], "A Note on Optimal Strategic Pricing of Technological Innovations," *Marketing Science*, 1, 371–78.

Bass, F., and R. Rao [1983], "Equilibrium Dynamic Pricing of New Products in Oligopolies: Theory and Evidence." Working paper, University of Chicago.

Baumol, W. [1967], *Business Behavior, Value and Growth*, 2nd ed. New York: Harcourt Brace Jovanovich.

Baumol, W. [1977], "The Empirical Determination of Demand Relationships," in E. Mansfield (ed.), *Microeconomics: Selected Readings*. New York: W.W. Norton, 55–62.

Baumol, W., J. Panzar, and R. Willig [1982], *Contestable Markets and the Theory of Industry Structure*. New York: Harcourt Brace Jovanovich.

Beales, H., R. Craswell, and S. Salop [1981], "The Efficient Regulation of Consumer Information," *Journal of Law and Economics*, 24, 491–540.

Becker, G. [1965], "A Theory of the Allocation of Time," *Economic Journal*, 75, 493–517.

Becker, G. [1981], *A Treatise on the Family*. Cambridge, Mass.: Harvard University Press.

Bettman, J. [1979], *An Information Processing Theory of Consumer Choice*. Reading, Mass.: Addison-Wesley.

Bettman, J., D. John, and C. Scott [1986], "Covariation Assessment by Consumers," *Journal of Consumer Research*, 13, 316–26.

Blattberg, R., T. Buesing, P. Peacock, and S. Sen [1978], "Identifying the Deal Prone Segment," *Journal of Marketing Research*, 15, 369–77.

Blattberg, R., G. Eppen, and J. Lieberman [1981], "A Theoretical and Empirical Evaluation of Price Deals for Consumer Nondurables," *Journal of Marketing*, 45, 116–29.

Blattberg, R., and S. Sen [1974], "Market Segmentation Using Models of Multi-Dimensional Purchasing Behavior," *Journal of Marketing*, 38, 17–28.

Blume, L., D. Easley, and M. O'Hara [1982], "Characterization of Optimal Plans for Stochastic Dynamic Programs," *Journal of Economic Theory*, 28, 221–34.

Braden, D., and S. Oren [1977], "Pricing Nonlinearly to Reduce Uncertainty About Demand." Working paper, University of Rochester.

Braden, D., and S. Oren [1987], "Dynamic Non-Linear Pricing," Working paper, University of Rochester.

Braverman, J. [1971], "A Decision Theoretic Approach to Pricing," *Decision Sciences*, 2, 1–15.

Bresnahan, T. [1981], "Duopoly Models with Consistent Conjectures," *American Economic Review*, 71, 934–45.

Brown, F. [1968], "Price Perception and Store Patronage," *Proceedings*. Chicago, Ill.: American Marketing Association.

Brown, F. [1971], "Who Perceives Supermarket Prices Most Validly?" *Journal of Marketing Research*, 8, 110–13.

Bucklin, L. [1969], "Consumer Search, Role Enactment, and Market Efficiency," *Journal of Business*, 42, 416–38.

Bulow, J. [1982], "Durable Goods Monopolists," *Journal of Political Economy*, 90, 314–32.

Bulow, J., J. Geanakoplis, and P. Klemperer [1985], "Multimarket Oligopoly: Strategic Substitutes and Complements," *Journal of Political Economy*, 93, 488–511.

Burdett, K., and D. Malueg [1981], "The Theory of Search for Several Goods," *Journal of Economic Theory*, 24, 362–76.

Buzzell, R. [1966], "Competitive Behavior and Product Life Cycles," in J. Wright and J. Goldstucker (eds.), *New Ideas for Successful Marketing*. Chicago, Ill.: American Marketing Association, 46–68.

Capon, N., J. Farley, and J. Hulbert [1975], "Pricing and Forecasting in an Oligopoly Firm," *Journal of Management Studies*, 12, 133–56.

Capon, N., and J. Hulbert [1975], "Decision Systems Analysis in Industrial Marketing," *Industrial Marketing Management*, 4, 143–60.

Cassady, R., Jr. [1962], *Competition and Price Making in Food Retailing*. New York: Ronald Press.

Chamberlin, E. [1936], *Theory of Monopolistic Competition*. Cambridge, Mass.: Harvard University Press.

Chan, Y., and H. Leland [1982], "Prices and Qualities in Markets with Costly Information," *Review of Economic Studies*, 49, 499–516.

Clarke, D., and R. Dolan [1984], "A Simulation Analysis of Alternative Pricing Strategies for Dynamic Environments," *Journal of Business*, 57, S179–200.

Clarke, F., M. Darrough, and J. Heineke [1982], "Optimal Pricing Policy in the Presence of Experience Effects," *Journal of Business*, 55, 517–30.

Clemens, E. [1951], "Price Discrimination and the Multiproduct Firm," *Review of Economic Studies*, reprinted in R. Heflebower and G. Stocking (eds.), *A.E.A. Readings in Industrial Organization and Public Policy*. Homewood, Ill.: R.D. Irwin, 19.

Coase, R. [1972], "Durability and Monopoly," *Journal of Law and Economics*, 15, 143–49.

Conlisk, J., E. Gerstner, and J. Sobel [1984], "Cyclic Pricing by a Durable Goods Monopolist," *Quarterly Journal of Economics*, 99, 489–505.

Conover, W. [1980], *Practical Nonparametric Statistics*, 2nd ed. New York: John Wiley & Sons.

Cooper, P. [1970], "The Begrudging Index and the Subjective Value of Money," in B. Taylor and G. Wills (eds.), *Pricing Strategy*. Princeton, N.J.: Brandon Systems Press, 122–31.

Cooper, R., and T. Ross [1984], "Prices, Product Qualities and Asymmetric Information: The Competitive Case," *Review of Economic Studies*, 51, 197–207.

Cooper, R., and T. Ross [1985], "Product Warranties and Double Moral Hazard," *Rand Journal of Economics*, 16, 103–13.

Coughlan, A. [1985], "Competition and Cooperation in Marketing Channel Choice:

Theory and Application," *Marketing Science*, 4, 110–29.

Cox, W., Jr. [1967], "Product Life Cycles as Marketing Models," *Journal of Business*, 40, 375–84.

Cravens, D. [1982], *Strategic Marketing*. Homewood, Ill.: Richard D. Irwin.

Darby, M., and E. Karni [1973], "Free Competition and the Optimal Amount of Fraud," *Journal of Law and Economics*, 16, 67–88.

Darden, M., and F. Reynolds [1971], "Shopping Orientations and Product Usage Rates," *Journal of Marketing Research*, 8, 505–8.

Day, G., A. Shocker, and R. Srivastava [1979], "Customer-Oriented Approaches to Identifying Product Markets," *Journal of Marketing*, 43, 8–19.

Dean, J. [1950a], "Pricing Policies for New Products," *Harvard Business Review*, 28, 45–55.

Dean, J. [1950b], "Problems of Product-Line Pricing," *Journal of Marketing*, 14, 518–28.

Dean, J. [1951], *Managerial Economics*. Englewood Cliffs, N.J.: Prentice-Hall.

Dean, J. [1969], "Pricing Pioneering Products," *Journal of Industrial Economics*, 17, 165–87.

Dean, J. [1970], "Pricing a New Product," in B. Taylor and G. Wills (eds.), *Pricing Strategy*. Princeton, N.J.: Brandon Systems Press, 534–40.

Della Bitta, A., K. Monroe, and J. McGinnis [1981], "Consumer Perceptions of Comparative Price Advertisements," *Journal of Marketing Research*, 18, 416–27.

Deshmukh, S., and W. Winston [1977], "A Controlled Birth and Death Process Model of Optimal Product Pricing Under Stochastically Changing Demand," *Journal of Applied Probability*, 14, 328–39.

Devinney, T. [1987], "Entry and Learning," *Management Science*, 33, 706–24.

Devinney, T. [1988], "Scale as a Signal of Product Quality," Working paper, Vanderbilt University.

Devinney, T., and D. Stewart [1988], "Rethinking the Product Portfolio: A Generalized Investment Model." *Management Science*, forthcoming.

Dhebar, A., and S. Oren [1985], "Optimal Dynamic Pricing for Expanding Networks," *Marketing Science*, 4, 336–51.

Dietrich, R. [1977]. "Poor Price-Quiz Scores Give Shoppers No Cause for Pride," *Progressive Grocer*, 56, 33.

Dixit, A. [1979], "A Model of Duopoly Suggesting a Theory of Entry Barriers," *Bell Journal of Economics*, 10, 20–32.

Dockner, E. [1985], "Optimal Pricing in a Dynamic Duopoly Game Model," *Zeitschrift für Operations Research*, Series B.

Dockner, E., and S. Jorgensen [1987], "Optimal Pricing Strategies for New Products in a Dynamic Oligopoly." Working paper, Copenhagen School of Economics and Business Administration.

Dodds, W., and K. Monroe [1985], "The Effect of Brand and Price Information on Subjective Product Evaluations," in E. Hirschman and M. Holbrook (eds.), *Advances in Consumer Research*, 12. Provo, Utah: Association for Consumer Research, 85–90.

Dodson, J., and E. Muller [1978], "Models of New Product Diffusion Through Advertising and Word-of-Mouth," *Management Science*, 24, 1568–78.

Dolan, R., and A. Jeuland [1981], "Experience Curves and Dynamic Demand Models:

Dolan, R., and A. Jeuland [1981], "Experience Curves and Dynamic Demand Models: Implications for Optimal Pricing Strategies," *Journal of Marketing*, 45, 52–62.

Dolan, R., A. Jeuland, and E. Muller [1986], "Models of New Product Diffusion: Extensions to Competition against Existing and Potential Firms over Time," in V. Mahajan and Y. Wind (eds.), *Innovation Diffusion Models of New Product Acceptance*. Cambridge, Mass.: Ballinger, 117–50.

Doob, A., J. Carlsmith, J. Freedman, T. Landauer, and S. Seleng, Jr. [1969], "Effect of Initial Selling Price on Subsequent Sales," *Journal of Personality and Social Psychology*, 11, 345–50.

Doraiswamy, K., T. McGuire, and R. Staelin [1979], "An Analysis of Alternative Advertising Strategies in a Competitive Franchise Framework," *American Marketing Association*, Educator's Conference, 463–67.

Eaton, J., and J. Brander [1984], "Product Line Rivalry," *American Economic Review*, 74, 323–34.

Eliashberg, J., and R. Chatterjee [1985], "Analytical Models of Competition with Implications for Marketing: Issues, Findings and Outlook," *Journal of Marketing Research*, 22, 237–61.

Eliashberg, J., and R. Chatterjee [1986], "Stochastic Issues in Innovation Diffusion Models," in V. Mahajan and Y. Wind (eds.) *Innovation Diffusion Models of New Product Acceptance*, Cambridge, Mass.: Ballinger, 151–202.

Eliashberg, J., and A. Jeuland [1986], "The Impact of Competitive Entry in a Developing Market Upon Dynamic Pricing Strategies," *Marketing Science*, 5, 20–36.

Eliashberg, J., and R. Steinberg [1984], "Marketing-Production Decisions in a Channel of Distribution." Working paper, University of Pennsylvania.

Emergy, F. [1970], "Some Psychological Aspects of Price," in B. Taylor and G. Wills (eds.), *Pricing Strategy*. Princeton, N.J.: Brandon Systems Press, 98–111.

Engel, J., and R. Blackwell [1982], *Consumer Behavior*. Chicago, Ill.: Dryden.

Erickson, G. [1983], "Dynamic Pricing in Oligopolistic New Product Markets." Working paper, University of Washington.

Etgar, M. [1978], "The Household as a Production Unit," *Research in Marketing*, 1. Greenwich, Conn.: JAI Press, 79–98.

Farley, J., H. Howard, and J. Hulbert [1971], "An Organizational Approach to an Industrial Marketing Information System," *Sloan Management Review*, 13, 35–54.

Farris, P., and M. Albion [1980], "The Impact of Advertising on the Price of Consumer Products," *Journal of Marketing*, 44, 17–35.

Feichtinger, G. [1982], "Optimal Pricing in a Diffusion Model with Concave Price-Dependent Market Potential," *Operations Research Letters*, 1, 236–40.

Feichtinger, G., and E. Dockner [1985], "Optimal Pricing in a Duopoly: A Non-Cooperative Differential Games Solution," *Journal of Optimization Theory and Applications*, 45, 199–218.

Fershtman, C., and M. Kamien [1984], "Price Adjustment Speed and Dynamic Duopolistic Competitors." Working paper, Northwestern University.

Fershtman, C., V. Mahajan, and E. Muller [1983], "Advertising, Pricing and Stability in Oligopolistic Markets for New Products." Working paper, Southern Methodist University.

Fershtman, C. and E. Muller [1984], "Capital Accumulation Games of Infinite Duration," *Journal of Economic Theory*, 33, 322–39.

Forbis, J., and N. Mehta [1981], "Value-Based Strategy for Industrial Products,"

Business Horizons, 24, 32–42.

Fouilhe, P. [1970], "The Subjective Evaluation of Price: Methodological Aspects," in B. Taylor and G. Wills (eds.), *Pricing Strategy.* Princeton, N.J.: Brandon Systems Press, 89–97.

Friedman, J. [1979], "Non-Cooperative Equilibria for Exit Supergames," *International Economic Review,* 20, 147–56.

Fruhan, W., Jr. [1972], "Pyrrhic Victories in Fights for Market Share," *Harvard Business Review,* 50, 100–7.

Fudenberg, D., and J. Tirole [1983a], "Learning-by-Doing and Market Performance," *Bell Journal of Economics,* 14, 522, 530.

Fudenberg, D., and J. Tirole [1983b], "Capital as a Commitment: Strategic Investment in Continuous Time," *Journal of Economic Theory,* 31, 227–50.

Fudenberg, D., and J. Tirole [1985], "Pre-Emption and Rent Equalization in the Adoption of New Technology," *Review of Economic Studies,* 52, 383–401.

Gabor, A. [1977], *Pricing: Principles and Practices.* London: Heinemann Education Books.

Gabor, A. [1979], "Determining Your Price Structure at Home and Abroad," *Management Decision,* 17, 649–60.

Gabor, A., and C. Granger [1961], "On the Price Consciousness of Consumers," *Applied Statistics,* 10, 170–88.

Gabor, A., and C. Granger [1964], "Price Sensitivity of the Consumer," *Journal of Advertising Research,* 4, 40–44.

Gabor, A., and C. Granger [1966], "Price as an Indicator of Quality: Report on an Inquiry," *Economica,* 33, 43–70.

Gabor, A., and C. Granger [1970], "The Pricing of New Products," in B. Taylor and G. Wills (eds.), *Pricing Strategy.* Princeton, N.J.: Brandon Systems Press, 541–55.

Gabor, A., and C. Granger [1973], "A Systematic Approach to Effective Pricing," in L. Roger (ed.), *Marketing Concepts and Strategies in the Next Decade.* London: Cassell, 171–94.

Gabor, A., C. Granger, and A. Sowter [1971], "Comments on 'Psychophysics of Prices'," *Journal of Marketing Research,* 8, 251–52.

Gardner, D. [1971], "Is There a Generalized Price-Quality Relationship?" *Journal of Marketing Research,* 8, 241–43.

Gardner, D. [1975], "Deception in Advertising: A Conceptual Approach," *Journal of Marketing,* 39, 40–46.

Gaskin, D. [1971], "Dynamic Limit Pricing: Optimal Pricing under Threat of Entry," *Journal of Economic Theory,* 3, 306–22.

Gerstner, E., and D. Holthausen [1986], "Profitable Pricing When Market Segments Overlap," *Marketing Science,* 5, 55–69.

Gold, B. [1981], "Changing Perspective on Size, Scale, and Returns: An Interpretive Essay," *Journal of Economic Literature,* 19, 5–33.

Goodman, D., and K. Moody [1970], "Determining Optimum Price Promotion Quantities," *Journal of Marketing,* 34, 31–39.

Goodman, S. [1972], *The Marketing Controller.* New York: AMR International.

Gordon, L., R. Cooper, H. Falk, and D. Miller [1980], *The Pricing Decision.* Canada: Society of Management Accountants of Canada.

Gould, J., and S. Sen [1984], "Issues in Pricing Research," *Journal of Business*, 57, iv–vii.

Griliches, Z. [1961], "Hedonic Price Indexes for Automobiles: An Econometric Analysis of Quality Change," in *Price Statistics of the Federal Government*. New York: National Bureau of Economic Research, 173–96.

Grossman, S., and O. Hart [1983], "An Analysis of the Principal-Agent Problem," *Econometrica*, 51, 7–45.

Grossman, S., and J. Stiglitz [1980], "On The Impossibility of Informationally Efficient Markets," *American Economic Review*, 70, 393–408.

Grover, R., and W. Dillon [1985], "A Probabilistic Model for Testing Hypothesized Hierarchical Market Structures," *Marketing Science*, 4, 312–35.

Guadagni, P., and J. Little [1983], "A Logit Model of Brand Choice Calibrated on Scanner Data," *Marketing Science*, 2, 203–38.

Guiltinan, J., and K. Monroe [1980], "Identifying and Analyzing Consumer Shopping Strategies," in J. Olson (ed.), *Advances in Consumer Research*, 7. Ann Arbor, Mich.: Association for Consumer Research, 91–96.

Gurumurthy, K., and J. Little [1986], "A Pricing Model Based on Perception Theories and its Testing on Scanner Panel Data." Working paper, Massachusetts Institute of Technology.

Hall, R., and C. Hitch [1939], "Price Theory and Business Behavior," *Oxford Economic Papers*, no. 2.

Harrell, S., and E. Taylor [1981], "Modeling the Product Life Cycle for Consumer Durables," *Journal of Marketing*, 45, 68–75.

Harsanyi, J. [1967–68], "Games with Incomplete Information Played by 'Bayesian Players'," parts I, II, and III, *Management Science*, 14, 159–82, 320–24, 486–502.

Hauser, J. [1984], "Pricing Theory and the Role of Marketing Science," *Journal of Business*, 54, S65–71.

Hauser, J., and S. Shugan [1983], "Defensive Marketing Strategies," *Marketing Science*, 2, 319–60.

Heal, G. [1977], "Guarantees and Risk Sharing," *Review of Economic Studies*, 44, 549–60.

Helson, H. [1964], *Adaptation-Level Theory*. New York: Harper & Row.

Heyman, D., and M. Sobel [1984], *Stochastic Models in Operations Research, Vol. II: Stochastic Optimization*. New York: McGraw-Hill.

Hicks, J. [1935], "Annual Survey of Economic Theory: The Theory of Monopoly," *Econometrica*, 3, 1–20.

Holdren, B. [1960], *The Structure of a Retail Market and the Market Behavior of Retail Units*. Englewood Cliffs, N.J.: Prentice-Hall.

Holmstrom, B. [1979], "Moral Hazard and Observability," *Bell Journal of Economics*, 93, 541–62.

Holmstrom, B. [1982], "Moral Hazard in Teams," *Bell Journal of Economics*, 13, 324–41.

Holton, R. [1957], "Price Discrimination at Retail: The Supermarket Case," *Journal of Industrial Economics*, 6 (1), 13–32.

Horsky, D. [1987], "The Effects of Income, Price, and Information on the Diffusion of New Consumer Durables." Working paper, University of Rochester.

Horsky, D., and L. Simon [1983], "Advertising and the Diffusion of New Products," *Marketing Science*, 2, 1–17.

Howard, J., and W. Morgenroth [1968], "Information Processing Model of Executive Decision," *Management Science*, 14, 416–28.

Jacoby, J. [1976], "Consumer and Industrial Psychology: Prospects for Theory Corroboration and Mutual Contribution," in M. Dunnette (ed.), *Handbook of Industrial and Organizational Psychology*. Chicago, Ill.: Rand McNally, 1031–61.

Jacoby, J., and J. Olson [1977], "Consumer Response to Price: An Attitudinal, Information Processing Perspective," in Y. Wind and M. Greenberg (eds.), *Moving Ahead with Attitude Research*. Chicago, Ill.: American Marketing Association, 73–86.

Jeuland, A. [1979], "Epidemiological Modeling of Diffusion of Innovation: Evaluation and Future Directions of Research," *Proceedings of the 1979 Educators' Conference*. Chicago, Ill.: American Marketing Association, 274–78.

Jeuland, A. [1981], "Parsimonious Models of Diffusion of Innovation: Part B, Incorporating the Variable of Price." Working paper, University of Chicago.

Jeuland, A., and R. Dolan [1982], "An Aspect of New Product Planning: Dynamic Pricing," in A. Zoltners (ed.), *TIMS Studies in the Management Science*, Special Issue on Marketing Planning Models. Amsterdam: North-Holland, 18, 1–21.

Jeuland, A., and C. Narasimhan [1985], "Dealing—Temporary Price Cuts—by Seller as a Buyer Discrimination Mechanism," *Journal of Business* 58, 295–308.

Jeuland, A., and S. Shugan [1983a], "Managing Channel Profits," *Marketing Science*, 2, 239–72.

Jeuland, A., and S. Shugan [1983b], "Coordination in Marketing Channels," in D. Gautschi (ed.), *Productivity and Efficiency in Distribution Systems*. New York: Elsevier, 17–38.

Jeuland, A., and S. Shugan [1988], "Channel of Distribution Profits When Channel Members Form Conjectures." Working paper, University of Chicago.

Johnson, M. [1984], "Consumer Choice Strategies for Comparing Noncomparable Alternatives," *Journal of Consumer Research*, 11, 741–53.

Johnson, M. [1986], "Modeling Choice Strategies for Noncomparable Alternatives," *Marketing Science*, 5, 37–54.

Jorgensen, S. [1983], "Optimal Control of a Diffusion Model of New Product Acceptance with Price-Dependent Total Market Potential," *Optimal Control Applications and Methods*, 4, 269–76.

Jorgensen, S. [1986], "Optimal Dynamic Pricing in an Oligopolistic Market: A Survey," *Dynamic Games and Applications in Economics*. Lecture Notes in Economics and Mathematical Systems, 265. New York: Springer-Verlag, 179–237.

Jorgensen, S. [1987], "Optimal Dynamic Price and Advertising Policies for a New Product." Paper presented at workshop on "Model Building and Operations Research Applications in Marketing," European Institute for Advanced Studies in Management, Brussels, November 17–18.

Kahn, A. [1959], "Pricing Objectives in Large Companies: Comment," *American Economic Review*, 49, 670–87.

Kahn, C. [1986], "The Durable Goods Monopolist and Consistency with Increasing Costs," *Econometrica*, 54, 275–94.

Kahnemann, D., and A. Tversky [1979], "Prospect Theory: An Analysis of Decision Under Risk," *Econometrica*, 47, 263–91.

Kalish, S. [1983a], "Monopolist Pricing with Dynamic Demand and Production Costs," *Marketing Science*, 2, 135–59.

Kalish, S. [1983b], "An Application of a New Diffusion Model Incorporating Price, Advertising and Uncertainty." Working paper, University of Rochester.

Kalish, S. [1983c], "New Product Diffusion Model with Price Advertising and Uncertainty." Working paper, University of Rochester.

Kalish, S. [1984], "Comments on 'A Simulation Model for the Evaluation of Pricing Strategies in a Dynamic Environment'," *Journal of Business*, 57, S205–9.

Kalish, S. [1985], "New Product Adoption Model with Price, Advertising and Uncertainty," *Management Science*, 31, 1569–85.

Kalish, S., and G. Lilien [1986], "A Market Entry Timing Model for New Technologies," *Management Science*, 32, 194–205.

Kalish, S., and S. Sen [1986], "Diffusion Models and the Marketing Mix for Single Products," in V. Mahajan and Y. Wind (eds.), *Innovation Diffusion Models of New Product Acceptance*. Cambridge, Mass.: Ballinger, 87–96.

Kambhu, J. [1982], "Optimal Product Quality Under Asymmetric Information and Moral Hazard," *Bell Journal of Economics*, 13, 438–92.

Kambhu, J. [1983], "Product Liability Rules and Moral Hazard in Incentive Contracts." Working paper, Columbia University.

Kamen, J., and R. Toman [1970], "Psychophysics of Prices," *Journal of Marketing Research*, 7, 27–35.

Kamien, M., and N. Schwartz [1981], *Dynamic Optimization: The Calculus of Variations and Optimal Control in Economics and Management*. London, England: North Holland.

Kaplan, D., J. Dirlam, and R. Lanzillotti [1958], *Pricing in Big Business*. Washington, D.C.: Brookings Institution.

Karlin, S., and K. Carr [1962], "Prices and Optimal Inventory Policy," in K. Arrow et al. (eds.), *Studies in Applied Probability and Management Science*. Stanford, Calif.: Stanford University Press.

Katona, G. [1960], *The Powerful Consumer*. New York: McGraw-Hill.

Keon, J. [1980], "The Bargain Value Model and a Comparison of Managerial Implications with Linear Learning Models," *Management Science*, 26, 1117–30.

Kihlstrom, R., and M. Riordan [1984], "Advertising as a Signal," *Journal of Political Economy*, 92, 427–50.

Kinberg, Y., and A. Rao [1975], "Stochastic Models of Price Promotion," *Management Science*, 8, 897–907.

Kinberg, Y., A. Rao, and M. Shakun [1974], "A Mathematical Model for Price Promotions," *Management Science*, 20, 948–59.

Klein, B., and K. Leffler [1981], "The Role of Market Forces in Assuring Contractual Performance," *Journal of Political Economy*, 89, 615–42.

Klein, B., and J. Oglethorpe [1987], "Cognitive Reference Points in Consumer Decision Making," in P.F. Anderson and M. Wallendorf (eds.), *Advances in Consumer Research*, 14. Provo, Utah: Association for Consumer Research.

Kotler, P. [1965], "Competitive Marketing Strategies for New Product Marketing Over the Life Cycle," *Management Science,* 12, B104–9.

Kotler, P. [1971], *Marketing Decision Making: A Model Building Approach.* New York: Holt, Rinehart and Winston.

Kotler, P. [1980], *Marketing Management: Analysis, Planning and Control,* 4th ed. Englewood Cliffs, N.J.: Prentice-Hall.

Kotler, P. [1984], *Marketing Management: Analysis, Planning, and Control,* 5th ed. Englewood Cliffs, N.J.: Prentice-Hall.

Kotowitz, Y., and F. Mathewson [1979], "Advertising, Consumer Information, and Product Quality," *Bell Journal of Economics,* 10, 566–88.

Kreps, D., and R. Wilson [1982a], "Reputation and Imperfect Information," *Journal of Economic Theory,* 27, 253–79.

Kreps, D., and R. Wilson [1982b], "Sequential Equilibria," *Econometrica,* 50, 863–94.

Krishnamurthi, L., and S. Raj [1985], "The Effect of Advertising on Consumer Price Sensitivity," *Journal of Marketing Research,* 22, 119–29.

Kunreuther, H., and J. Richard [1971], "Optimal Pricing and Inventory Decisions for Non-Seasonal Items," *Econometrica,* 39, 173–75.

Kydland, F. [1985], "Noncooperative and Dominant Player Solutions to Discrete Dynamic Games," *International Economic Review,* 16, 321–35.

Lakatos, I. [1978], *The Methodology of Scientific Research Programmes: Philosophical Papers,* J. Worrall and G. Currie (eds.). Cambridge, England: Cambridge University Press.

Lal, R. [1986], "Delegating Pricing Responsibility to the Salesforce," *Marketing Science,* 5, 159–68.

Lambin, J. [1970], *Modeles et Programmes de Marketing.* Paris, France: Press Universitaires de France.

Lancaster, K. [1966], "A New Approach to Consumer Theory," *Journal of Political Economy,* 74, 132–57.

Lancaster, K. [1971], *Consumer Demand: A New Approach.* New York: Columbia University Press.

Lancaster, K. [1979], *Variety, Equity, and Efficiency.* New York: Columbia University Press.

Lanzillotti, R. [1958], "Pricing Objectives in Large Companies," *American Economic Review,* 48, 921–40.

Lazear, E. [1986], "Retail Pricing and Clearance Sales," *American Economic Review,* 76, 14–32.

Levitt, T. [1980], "Marketing Success Through the Differentiation of Anything," *Harvard Business Review,* 58, 83–91.

Lilien, G., and P. Kotler [1983], *Marketing Decision Making.* New York: Harper & Row.

Lippman, S., and J. McCall [1976], "The Economics of Job Search: A Survey," *Economic Inquiry,* 14, 155–89, 347–68.

Little, J. [1979], "Aggregate Advertising Models: The State of the Art," *Operations Research,* 27, 629–67.

Little, J., and J. Shapiro [1980], "A Theory for Pricing Non-featured Products in Supermarkets," *Journal of Business,* 53, s199–209.

Liu, L., and D. Hanssens [1981], "A Bayesian Approach to Time-Varying Cross-Sectional Regression Models," *Journal of Econometrics,* 15, 341–56.

Lodish, L. [1980], "Applied Dynamic Pricing and Production Models with Specific Application to Broadcast Spot Pricing," *Journal of Marketing Research*, 17, 203-11.

Loomes, G., and R. Sugden [1982], "Regret Theory: An Alternative Theory of Rational Choice Under Uncertainty," *Economic Journal*, 92, 805-24.

Lund, D., K. Monroe, and P. Choudhury [1982], *Pricing Policies and Strategies: An Annotated Bibliography*. Bibliography Series. Chicago, Ill.: American Marketing Association.

Lutz, N. [1985], "Discrete Warranties, Signaling and Consumer Moral Hazard." Working paper, Stanford University.

Mahajan, V., P. Green, and S. Goldberg [1982], "A Conjoint Model for Measuring Self and Cross-Price/Demand Relationship," *Journal of Marketing Research*, 19, 334-42.

Mahajan, V., and E. Muller [1979], "Innovation Diffusion and New Product Growth Models in Marketing," *Journal of Marketing*, 43, 55-68.

Mahajan, V., and R. Peterson [1978], "Innovation Diffusion in a Dynamic Potential Adopter Population," *Management Science*, 24, 1589-95.

Mahajan, V., and R. Peterson [1985], *Models for Innovations Diffusion*. Beverly Hills, Calif.: Sage.

Mann, D., and J. Wissink [1983], "Inside vs. Outside Production: A Contracting Approach to Vertical Integration." Working paper, University of Pennsylvania.

Marshall, A. [1980], *Principles of Economics*. London, England: Macmillan.

Maskin, E., and J. Riley [1984], "Monopoly and Incomplete Information," *Rand Journal of Economics*, 15, 171-96.

Mazumdar, T. [1987], *The Effects of Learning Intentions and Choice Task Orientations on Buyers' Knowledge of Price: A Experimental Investigation*. Unpublished Ph.D. dissertation, Virginia Polytechnic Institute and State University.

McCall, J. [1965], "The Economics of Information and Optimal Stopping Rules," *Journal of Business*, 38, 300-17.

McGuire, T., and R. Staelin [1983a], "An Industry Equilibrium Analysis of Downstream Vertical Integration," *Marketing Science*, 2, 161-92.

McGuire, T., and R. Staelin [1983b], "The Effect of Channel Member Efficiency on Channel Structure," in D. Gautschi (ed.), *Productivity and Efficiency in Distribution Systems*. New York: Elsevier, 3-15.

Mesak, H., and R. Clelland [1979], "A Competitive Pricing Model," *Management Science*, 25, 1057-68.

Mickwitz, G. [1959], *Marketing and Competition*. Helsingfors, Finland: Centratryckerick.

Milgrom, P., and J. Roberts [1982a], "Limit Price and Entry Deterrence," *Journal of Economic Theory*, 27, 280-312.

Milgrom, P., and J. Roberts [1982b], "Predation, Reputation, and Entry Deterrence," *Journal of Economic Theory*, 27, 280-312.

Milgrom, P., and J. Roberts [1982c], "Limit Pricing and Entry Under Incomplete Information: An Equilibrium Analysis," *Econometrica*, 50, 443-60.

Milgrom, P., and J. Roberts [1986], "Price and Advertising Signals of Product Quality," *Journal of Political Economy*, 94, 796-821.

Monahan, G. [1983], "Optimal Advertising with Stochastic Demand," *Management*

Science, 29, 106–17.

Monahan, G. [1984], "A Pure Birth Model of Optimal Advertising with Word-of-Mouth," *Marketing Science*, 3, 169–78.

Monroe, K. [1971a], " 'Psychophysics of Prices': A Reappraisal," *Journal of Marketing Research*, 8, 248–50.

Monroe, K. [1971b], "The Information Content of Prices: A Preliminary Model for Estimating Buyer Response," *Management Science*, 17, B519–32.

Monroe, K. [1973], "Buyers' Subjective Perceptions of Price," *Journal of Marketing Research*, 10, 70–80.

Monroe, K. [1979], *Pricing: Making Profitable Decisions*. New York: McGraw-Hill.

Monroe, K., and J. Chapman [1987], "Framing Effects on Buyers' Subjective Product Evaluations," in P. Anderson and M. Wallendorf (eds.), *Advances in Consumer Research*, 14. Provo, Utah: Association for Consumer Research.

Monroe, K., and A. Della Bitta [1978], "Models for Pricing Decisions," *Journal of Marketing Research*, 15, 413–28.

Monroe, K., and W. Dodds [1988], "A Research Program for Establishing the Validity of the Price-Quality Relationship," *Journal of Academy of Marketing Science* (forthcoming).

Monroe, K., and R. Krishnan [1985], "The Effects of Price on Subjective Product Evaluations," in J. Jacoby and J. Olson (eds.), *Perceived Quality: How Consumers View Stores and Merchandise*. Lexington, Mass.: Lexington Books, 209–32.

Monroe, K., and S. Petroshius [1980], "A Theoretical Approach for Determining Product Line Prices," in C. Lamb, Jr., and P. Dunne (eds.), *Theoretical Developments in Marketing*. Chicago, Ill.: American Marketing Association, 21–24.

Monroe, K., and S. Petroshius [1981], "Buyers' Perceptions of Prices: An Update of the Evidence," in T. Robertson and H. Kassarjian (eds.), *Perspectives in Consumer Behavior*, 3rd ed. Glenview, Ill.: Scott Foresman, 23–42.

Monroe, K., C. Powell, and P. Choudhury [1986], "Recall vs. Recognition as a Measure of Price Awareness," in R. Lutz (ed.), *Advances in Consumer Research*, 13, Provo, Utah: Association for Consumer Research, 594–99.

Monroe, K., and A. Zoltners [1979], "Pricing the Product Line During Periods of Scarcity," *Journal of Marketing*, 43, 49–59.

Montgomery, D. [1975], "New Product Distribution: An Analysis of Supermarket Buyer Decisions," *Journal of Marketing Research*, 12, 255–64.

Moorthy, S. [1984], "Market Segmentation, Self-Selection, and Product Line Design," *Marketing Science*, 3, 288–305.

Moorthy, S. [1985], "Using Game Theory to Model Competition," *Journal of Marketing Research*, 22, 262–82.

Morgan, K., E. Metzen, and S. Johnson [1979], "An Hedonic Index for Breakfast Cereals," *Journal of Consumer Research*, 6, 67–75.

Moyer, R., and T. Landauer [1967], "Time Required for Judgments of Numerical Inequality," *Nature*, 215, 1519–20.

Myerson, R. [1984], "Two-Person Bargaining Problems With Incomplete Information," *Econometrica*, 51, 461–88.

Nagle, T. [1984], "Economic Foundations for Pricing," *Journal of Business*, 57, S3–26.

Nagle, T. [1987], *The Strategy and Tactics of Pricing*. Englewood Cliffs, N.J.: Prentice-Hall.

Narasimhan, C. [1984a], "Comments on 'Economic Foundations for Pricing'," *Journal of Business,* 54, S27–34.

Narasimhan, C. [1984b], "A Price Discrimination Theory of Coupons," *Marketing Science,* 3, 128–47.

Narasimhan, C. [1987], "Modeling Consumer Price Expectations in New Product Models." Working paper, University of Chicago.

Narasimhan, C. [1988], "Competitive Promotional Strategies." *Journal of Business,* forthcoming.

Narasimhan, C., and R. Rao [1984], "Models of Price Promotion Under Endogenous Search." Working paper, University of Chicago.

Nelson, P. [1970], "Information and Consumer Behavior," *Journal of Political Economy,* 78, 311–29.

Nelson, P. [1974], "Advertising as Information," *Journal of Political Economy,* 81, 729–54.

Nelson, P. [1978], "Advertising as Information Once More," in D. Tuerck (ed.), *Issues in Advertising: The Economics of Persuasion.* Washington, D.C.: American Enterprise Institute.

Nelson, R. [1981], "Research on Productivity Growth and Productivity Differences: Dead Ends and New Departures," *Journal of Economic Literature,* 19, 1029–64.

Nerlove, M. [1958], "Distributed Lags and Estimation of Long-Run Elasticities of Supply and Demand: Theoretical Considerations," *Journal of Farm Economics,* 15, 301–11.

Nerlove, M., and K. Arrow [1962], "Optimal Advertising Policy Under Dynamic Conditions," *Economica,* 22, 129–42.

Nevin, J. [1974], "Laboratory Experiments for Estimating Consumer Demand: A Validation Study," *Journal of Marketing Research,* 11, 261–68.

Norton, S. [1987], "The Coase Theorem and Suboptimization in Marketing Channels." *Marketing Science,* 6, 268–85.

Nwokyoye, N. [1975], "An Experimental Study of the Relationship Between Responses to Price Changes and the Price Level for Shoes," in M. Schlinger (ed.), *Advances in Consumer Research,* 2. Ann Arbor, Mich.: Association for Consumer Research, 693–703.

Oi, W. [1967], "The Neoclassical Foundation of Progress Functions," *Economic Journal,* 78, 579–94.

Olander, F. [1970], "The Influence of Price on the Consumer's Evaluation of Products and Purchases," in B. Taylor and G. Wills (eds.), *Pricing Strategy.* Princeton, N.J.: Brandon Systems Press, 50–69.

Oliver, R., and R. Winer [1987], "A Framework for the Formulation and Structure of Consumer Expectations: Review and Propositions." *Journal of Economic Psychology* 9, 469–99.

Olson, J. [1980], "Implications of an Information Processing Approach to Pricing Research," in C. Lamb, Jr., and P. Dunne (eds.), *Theoretical Developments in Marketing.* Chicago, Ill.: American Marketing Association, 13–16.

Oren, S. [1984], "Comments on 'Pricing Research in Marketing: The State of the Art'," *Journal of Business,* 54, S61–64.

Oren, S., S. Smith, and R. Wilson [1982], "Nonlinear Pricing in Markets with Interdependent Demand," *Marketing Science,* 1, 287–313.

Oren, S., S. Smith, and R. Wilson [1984], "Pricing a Product Line," *Journal of Business*, 57, S73–100.

Oxenfeldt, A. [1951], *Industrial Pricing and Market Practices*. Englewood Cliffs, N.J.: Prentice-Hall.

Oxenfeldt, A. [1966], "Product Line Pricing," *Harvard Business Review*, 44, 137–44.

Palda, K. [1971], *Pricing Decisions and Marketing Policy*. Englewood Cliffs, N.J.: Prentice-Hall.

Palfrey, T., and T. Romer [1983], "Warranties, Performance, and the Resolution of Buyer–Seller Disputes," *Bell Journal of Economics*, 14, 97–117.

Parsons, L. [1975], "The Product Life Cycle and Time-Varying Advertising Elasticities," *Journal of Marketing Research*, 12, 476–80.

Pasternack, B. [1984], "Optimal Pricing and Return Policies for Perishable Commodities." Working paper, California State University at Fullerton.

Payne, J. [1976], "Task Complexity and Contingent Processing in Decision Making: An Information Search and Protocol Analysis," *Organizational Behavior and Human Performance*, 16, 366–387.

Peltzman, S. [1981], "The Effects of FTC Advertising Regulation," *Journal of Law and Economics*, 24, 403–48.

Pessemier, E. [1960], "An Experimental Method for Estimating Demand," *Journal of Business*, 33, 373–83.

Petroshius, S., and K. Monroe [1987], "Effect of Product Line Pricing on Product Evaluations," *Journal of Consumer Research*, 13, 511–19.

Phlips, L. [1983], *The Economics of Price Discrimination*, Cambridge, Mass.: Cambridge University Press.

Pintel, G., and J. Diamond [1977], *Retailing*. Englewood Cliffs, N.J.: Prentice-Hall.

Polli, R., and V. Cook [1969], "Validity of the Product Life Cycle," *Journal of Business*, 42, 385–400.

Porter, M. [1985], *Competitive Advantage*. New York: Free Press.

Preston, L. [1963], *Profits, Competition, and Rules of Thumb in Retail Food Pricing*. Berkeley, Calif.: Institute of Business and Economic Research of the University of California.

Priest, G. [1981], "A Theory of Consumer Product Warranty," *Yale Law Journal*, 90, 1297–352.

Pritchard, R. [1969], "Equity Theory: A Review and Critique," *Organizational Behavior and Human Performance*, 4, 176–211.

Qualls, W., R. Olshavsky, and R. Michaels [1981], "Shortening of the PLC—An Empirical Test," *Journal of Marketing*, 45, 76–80.

Radner, R. [1981], "Monitoring Cooperative Agreements in a Repeated Principal—Agent Relationship," *Econometrica*, 49, 1127–48.

Raj, S. [1982], "The Effects of Advertising on High and Low Loyalty Consumer Segments," *Journal of Consumer Research*, 9, 77–89.

Raman, K. [1986], "A General Test of Reference Price Theory in the Presence of Threshold Effects." Working paper, Auburn University.

Rao, A., and M. Shakun [1972], "A Quasi-Game Theory Approach to Pricing," *Management Science*, 18, 110–23.

Rao, R. [1986a], "Skimming Pricing for a Class of Diffusion Models," *Optimal Control Applications & Methods*, 7, 209–15.

Rao, R. [1986b], "Pricing and Promotions in Asymmetric Duopolies." Working paper, University of Texas at Dallas.

Rao, R., and F. Bass [1985], "Competition, Strategy, and Price Dynamics: A Theoretical and Empirical Investigation," *Journal of Marketing Research*, 22, 283–96.

Rao, R., and K. Monroe [1987], "The Moderating Effect of Prior Knowledge on Cue Utilization in Product Evaluations." Working paper, University of Minnesota, Minneapolis.

Rao, R., and D. Rutenberg [1979], "Pre-empting and Alert Rival: Strategic Timing of the First Plant by Analysis of Sophisticated Rivalry," *Bell Journal of Economics*, 10, 412–28.

Rao, V. [1984], "Pricing Research in Marketing: The State of the Art," *Journal of Business*, 57, 839–60.

Rao, V., and D. Gautschi [1982], "The Role of Price in Individual Utility Judgments: Development and Empirical Validation of Alternative Models," in L. McAlister (ed.), *Choice Models for Buyer Behavior*. Greenwich, Conn.: JAI Press, 57–80.

Rao, V., and D. Sabavala [1980], "Allocation of Marketing Resources: The Role of Price Promotions," in R. Leone (ed.), *Proceedings of the Second Marketing Measurement Conference*. Providence, R.I.: TIMS College of Marketing and the Institute of Management Science.

Ratchford, B. [1975], "The New Economic Theory of Consumer Behavior: An Interpretive Essay," *Journal of Consumer Research*, 2, 65–75.

Raviv, A. [1984], "Comments on 'Economic Foundations for Pricing'," *Journal of Business*, 54, S35–38.

Rea, S. [1981], "Workmen's Compensation and Occupational Safety Under Imperfect Information," *American Economic Review*, 71, 80–93.

Reibstein, D., and H. Gatignon [1984], "Optimal Product Line Pricing: The Influence of Elasticities and Cross-Elasticities," *Journal of Marketing Research*, 21, 259–67.

Ricardo, D. [1948], *The Principles of Political Economy and Taxation*. Originally published 1817, New York: E.P. Dutton.

Riley, J. [1975], "Competitive Signaling," *Journal of Economic Theory*, 10, 174–86.

Rink, D., and J. Swan [1979], "Product Life Cycle Research: A Literature Review," *Journal of Business Research*, 7, 219–42.

Roberts, J., and G. Urban [1988], "New Consumer Durable Brand Choice: Modeling Multiattribute Utility, Risk and Belief Dynamics," *Management Science*, 34, 167–85.

Roberts, M., and L. Wortzel [1979], "New Life-Style Determinants of Women's Food Shopping Behavior," *Journal of Marketing*, 43 (Summer), 28–39.

Robertson, T. [1967], "The Process of Innovation and the Diffusion of Innovation," *Journal of Marketing*, 31, 14–19.

Robinson, B., and C. Lakhani [1975], "Dynamic Price Models for New-Product Planning," *Management Science*, 21, 1113–22.

Robinson, J. [1933], *Economics of Imperfect Competition*. Cambridge, England: Cambridge University Press.

Rogers, E. [1983], *Diffusion of Innovations*, 3rd ed. New York: Free Press.

Rosch, E. [1975], "Cognitive Reference Points," *Cognitive Psychology*, 7, 532–47.

Rosen, S. [1972], "Learning by Experience as Joint Production," *Quarterly Journal of Economics*, 86, 365–82.

Rosen, S. [1974], "Hedonic Prices and Implicit Markets: Product Differentiation in Pure Competition," *Journal of Political Economy*, 82, 34–55.

Ross, S. [1983], *Introduction to Stochastic Dynamic Programming*. New York: Academic Press.

Rothschild, M. [1973], "Models of Market Organization with Perfect Information: A Survey," *Journal of Political Economy*, 81, 1283–308.

Rubin, P. [1978], "The Theory of the Firm and the Structure of the Franchise Contract," *Journal of Law and Economics*, 223–33.

Russo, J., B. Metcalf, and D. Stephens [1981], "Identifying Misleading Advertising," *Journal of Consumer Research*, 8, 119–31.

Saghafi, M. [1987a], "Market Share Stability and Marketing Policy: An Axiomatic Approach," in J. Sheth (ed.), *Research In Marketing*, 9, Greenwich, Conn.: JAI Press.

Saghafi, M. [1987b], "Product Line Pricing Under Different Firm-Specific Objectives." Working paper, University of Southern California.

Salop, S., and J. Stiglitz [1977], "Bargains and Ripoffs: A Model of Monopolistically Competitive Price Dispersions," *Review of Economics and Statistics*, 54, 493–510.

Satow, K., and D. Johnson [1977], "Will the Real Working Woman Please Stand Up and Approach the Check-out Counter?" Paper presented at a meeting of the Chicago chapter of the American Marketing Association.

Sawyer, A., and P. Dickson [1984], "Psychological Perspectives on Consumer Response to Sales Promotion," in K. Jocz (ed.), *Research on Sales Promotion: Collected Papers*. Report 84–104. Cambridge, Mass.: Marketing Science Institute.

Scherer, F. [1980], *Industrial Marketing Structure and Economic Performance*, 2nd ed. Chicago, Ill.: Rand McNally.

Schmalensee, R. [1978], "A Model of Advertising and Product Quality," *Journal of Political Economy*, 86, 485–504.

Schmalensee, R. [1979], "Market Structure, Durability and Quality: A Selective Survey," *Economic Inquiry*, 17, 177–96.

Schmalensee, R. [1982], "Product Differentiation Advantages of Pioneering Brands," *American Economic Review*, 72, 349–65.

Schwartz, A., and L. Wilde [1983], "Imperfect Information in Markets for Contract Terms: The Examples of Warranties and Security Interests," *Virginia Law Review*, 69, 1387–485.

Scitovsky, T. [1944–45], "Some Consequences of the Habit of Judging Quality by Price," *Review of Economic Studies*, 12, 100–5.

Seglin, L. [1963], "How to Price New Products," *Chemical Engineering*, 67, 181–84.

Seierstad, A., and K. Sydsaeter [1977], "Sufficient Conditions in Optimal Control Theory," *International Economic Review*, 18, 367–91.

Sethi, S. [1977], "Dynamic Optimal Control Models in Advertising: A Survey," *SIAM Review*, 19, 685–725.

Shapiro, B. [1973], "Price Reliance: Existence and Sources," *Journal of Marketing Research*, 10, 286–94.

Shapiro, B., and B. Jackson [1978], "Industrial Pricing to Meet Customer Needs," *Harvard Business Review*, 56, 119–27.

Shapiro, C. [1983], "Premiums for High Quality Products as Returns to Reputations," *Quarterly Journal of Economics*, 98, 659–79.

Shavell, S. [1979a], "On Moral Hazard and Insurance," *Quarterly Journal of Economics*, 93, 541–62.

Shavell, S. [1979b], "Risk Sharing and Incentives in the Principal and Agent Relationship," *Bell Journal of Economics*, 10, 55–73.

Sheffrin, S. [1983], *Rational Expectations*. Cambridge, England: Cambridge University Press.

Sherif, M., and C. Hovland [1961], *Social Judgment*. New Haven, Conn.: Yale University Press.

Shoemaker, R. [1986], "Comment on 'Dynamics of Price Elasticity and Brand Life Cycles: An Empirical Study'," *Journal of Marketing Research*, 23, 78–82.

Shugan, S. [1983], "The Distribution of Unbranded Brands." Working paper, University of Chicago.

Shugan, S. [1984], "Comments on 'Pricing a Product Line'," *Journal of Business*, 57, S3–6.

Shugan, S., and V. Balachandran [1976], "A Mathematical Programming Model for Optimal Product Line Structuring." Chapter in unpublished Ph.D. dissertation, University of Rochester.

Simmons Market Research Bureau [1979], *The 1979 Study of Media and Markets*. New York: Simmons Market Research Bureau.

Simon, H. [1959], "Theory of Decision Making in Economics and Behavioral Sciences," *American Economic Review*, 49, 253–80.

Simon, H. [1965], *Administrative Behavior*, 2nd ed. New York: Macmillan.

Simon, H. [1979], "Dynamics of Price Elasticity and Brand Life Cycles: An Empirical Study," *Journal of Marketing Research*, 16, 439–52.

Simon, H. [1982], "PRICESTRAT—An Applied Strategic Pricing Model for Non-Durables," in A. Zoltners ed., *Marketing Planning Models*. TIMS Studies in the Management Sciences, 18. New York: North Holland, 23–41.

Smiley, R., and S. Ravid [1983], "The Importance of Being First: Learning Price and Strategy," *Quarterly Journal of Economics*, 97, 353–65.

Smith, S. [1986], "New Product Pricing in Quality Sensitive Markets," *Marketing Science*, 5, 70–87.

Snedecor, G., and W. Cochran [1980], *Statistical Methods*, 7th ed. Ames: Iowa State University Press.

Sobel, M. [1971], "Production Smoothing with Stochastic Demand II: Infinite Horizon Case," *Management Science*, 17, 724–35.

Spatt, C. [1981], "An Intertemporal Theory of Sales." Paper presented at the American Economic Association meeting, Washington, D.C.

Spence, A. [1973], "Job Market Signaling," *Quarterly Journal of Economics*, 87, 355–74.

Spence, A. [1974], *Marketing Signaling*, Cambridge, Mass.: Harvard University Press.

Spence, A. [1977a], "Consumer Misperceptions, Product Failure and Producer Liability," *Review of Economic Studies*, 44, 561–72.

Spence, A. [1977b], "Entry, Capacity Investment and Oligopolistic Pricing," *Bell Journal of Economics*, 8, 534–44.

Spence, A. [1979], "Investment Strategy in a Growing Market," *Bell Journal of Economics*, 10, 1–19.

Spence, A. [1980], "Multi-Product Quantity-Dependent Prices and Profitability

Constraints," *Review of Economic Studies*, 47, 821–41.

Spence, A. [1981], "The Learning Curve and Competition," *Bell Journal of Economics*, 12, 49–70.

Srinivasan, V. [1982], "Comments on the Role of Price in Individual Utility Judgments," *Choice Models for Buyer Behavior*. Greenwich, Conn.: JAI Press.

Stanford Research Institute [1975], *Chemical Economics Handbook*. Stanford, Ca.: Stanford Research Institute.

Stapel, J. [1972], " 'Fair' or 'Psychological' Pricing?" *Journal of Marketing Research*, 9, 109–10.

Stern, L., and A. El-Ansary [1982], *Marketing Channels*. Englewood Cliffs, N.J.: Prentice-Hall.

Stigler, G. [1961], "The Economics of Information," *Journal of Political Economy*, 69, 213–25.

Stigler, G. [1968], *The Organization of Industry*. Homewood, Ill.: Richard D. Irwin.

Stoetzel, J. [1970], "Psychological/Sociological Aspects of Price," in B. Taylor and G. Wills (eds.), *Pricing Strategy*. Princeton, N.J.: Brandon Systems Press, 70–74.

Stokey, N. [1979], "Intertemporal Price Discrimination," *Quarterly Journal of Economics*, 93, 355–71.

Stokey, N. [1981], "Rational Expectations and Durable Goods Pricing," *Bell Journal of Economics*, 12, 112–28.

Stout, R. [1969], "Developing Data to Estimate Price–Quantity Relationships," *Journal of Marketing*, 33, 34–36.

Stuart, C. [1979], "Search and the Spatial Organization of Trading," in S. Lippman and J. McCall (eds.), *Studies in the Economics of Search*. New York: North-Holland, 17–34.

Sweezy, P. [1939], "Demand Under Conditions Of Oligopoly," *Journal of Political Economy*, 47, 568–73.

Taylor, B., and G. Wills (eds.) [1969], *Pricing Strategy*. Princeton, N.J.: Brandon Systems Press.

Taylor, L. [1975], "The Demand for Electricity: A Survey," *Bell Journal of Economics*, 6, 74–110.

Teng, J., and G. Thompson [1983], "Oligopoly Models for Optimal Advertising," *Management Science*, 29, 1087–101.

Thaler, R. [1985], "Mental Accounting and Consumer Choice," *Marketing Science*, 4, 199–214.

Theil, H. [1971], *Principles of Econometrics*. New York: John Wiley & Sons.

Thompson, G., and J. Teng [1984], "Optimal Pricing and Advertising Policies for New Product Oligopoly Models," *Marketing Science*, 3, 148–68.

Thorelli, H., and S. Burnett [1981], "The Nature of Product Life Cycles for Industrial Goods Businesses," *Journal of Marketing*, 45, 97–108.

Topkis, D. [1978], "Minimizing a Submodular Function on a Lattice," *Operations Research*, 26, 305–21.

Tull, D., R. Boring, and M. Gonsior [1964], "The Relationship of Price and Imputed Quality," *Journal of Business*, 37, 186–91.

Uhl, J. [1970], "Consumer Perception of Retail Food Price Changes." Paper presented at the First Annual Meeting of the Association for Consumer Research.

Uradnisheck, J. [1978], "Estimating When Fiber Optics Will Offer Greater 'Value in Use'," *Electronics*, 51, 118–24.

Urban, G. [1969], "A Mathematical Modeling Approach to Product Line Decisions," *Journal of Marketing Research*, 6, 40–47.

Urban, G., and J. Hauser [1980], *Design and Marketing of New Products*. Englewood Cliffs, N.J.: Prentice-Hall.

Webster, F., Jr. [1981], "Top Management's Concerns about Marketing: Issues for the 1980's," *Journal of Marketing*, 45, 9–16.

Welam, U. [1982], "Optimal and Near Optimal Price and Advertising Strategies for Finite Horizons," *Management Science*, 28, 1313–27.

Wernerfelt, B. [1985], "The Dynamics of Prices and Market Share Over the Product Life Cycle," *Management Science*, 31, 928–39.

Wernerfelt, B. [1986], "A Special Case of Dynamic Pricing," *Management Science*, 32, 1562–66.

Wertheimer, M. [1938], "Numbers and Numerical Concepts in Primitive Peoples," in W. Ellis (ed.), *A Source Book of Gestalt Psychology*. New York: Harcourt, Brace.

Weston, J. [1972], "Pricing Behavior of Large Firms," *Western Economic Journal*, 10, 1–18.

Wilde, L. [1979], "Equilibrium Comparison Shopping," *Review of Economic Studies*, 46, 543–53.

Wilde, L. [1980], "The Economics of Consumer Information Acquisition," *Journal of Business*, 53, 543–53.

Wilde, L., and A. Schwartz [1982], "Consumer Markets for Warranties." Working paper, California Institute of Technology.

Wildt, A. [1976], "The Empirical Investigation of Time Dependent Parameter Variation in Marketing Models," in *Educators' Proceedings*. Chicago, Ill.: American Marketing Association.

Wildt, A., and R. Winer [1983], "Modeling and Estimation in Changing Market Environments," *Journal of Business*, 56, 365–88.

Wilkinson, J., J. Mason, and C. Paksay [1982], "Assessing the Impact of Short-Term Supermarket Variables," *Journal of Marketing Research*, 19, 72–86.

William, R., J. Painter, and R. Herbert [1978], "A Policy-Oriented Typology of Grocery Shoppers," *Journal of Retailing*, 54, 327–42.

Wilson, R. [1985], "Multi-Dimensional Signaling," *Economic Letters*, 19, 17–21.

Winer, R. [1980], "Estimation of a Longitudinal Model to Decompose the Effects of an Advertising Stimulus on Family Consumption," *Management Science*, 26, 471–82.

Winer, R. [1985], "A Price Vector Model of Demand for Consumer Durables: Preliminary Developments," *Marketing Science*, 4, 74–90.

Winer, R. [1986], "A Reference Price Model of Brand Choice for Frequently Purchased Products," *Journal of Consumer Research*, 13 (2), 250–56.

Wolinsky, A. [1983], "Prices as Signals of Product Quality," *Review of Economic Studies*, 50, 647–58.

Wright, P. [1975], "Consumer Choice Strategies: Simplifying vs. Optimizing," *Journal of Marketing Research*, 12, 60–67.

Yelle, L. [1979], "The Learning Curve: Historical Review and Comprehensive Survey," *Decision Sciences*, 10, 302–29.

Yoon, E. [1984], *New Product Introduction Timing Methods: R&D and Marketing Decisions Considering Diffusion Dynamics*. Ph.D. dissertation, Pennsylvania State University.

Zeithaml, V. [1984], "Issues in Conceptualizing and Measuring Consumer Response to Price," in T. Kinnear (ed.), *Advances in Consumer Research*, 11, 612–16.

Zeithaml, V. [1986], "Defining and Relating Price, Perceived Quality, and Perceived Value." Working paper. Marketing Science Institute, Cambridge, Mass.

Zeithaml, V., and K. Graham [1983], "The Accuracy of Reported Reference Prices for Professional Services," in A. Tybout (ed.), *Advances in Consumer Research*, 10, 607–11.

Zusman, P., and M. Etgar [1981], "The Marketing Channel as an Equilibrium Set of Contracts," *Management Science*, 27, 3.

About the Contributors

Thomas V. Bonoma is professor of business administration and chairman of the M.B.A. Program at Harvard Business School. His recent research project on marketing implementation is concerned with the effective execution of marketing strategy and plans. His books include *The Marketing Edge: Making Strategies Work, Managing Marketing: Text and Cases, Psychology for Management*, and *The Executive Survival Manual*.

Russell Cooper (associate professor of economics at University of Iowa) received his Ph.D. from the University of Pennsylvania. He has publised articles on the economics of information and on the microfoundations of macroeconomics in *American Economic Review, International Journal of Industrial Organization, Journal of Labor Economics, Rand Journal, Review of Economic Studies*, and *Quarterly Journal of Economics*.

Anne T. Coughlan, assistant professor of marketing at the Kellogg Graduate School of Management at Northwestern University, holds a Ph.D. in economics from Stanford University. Professor Coughlan's research interests include pricing, distribution, and sales-force management. She has published in *Marketing Science, Journal of Marketing*, and *Journal of Accounting and Economics*.

Victoria L. Crittenden is a doctoral student at Harvard Business School. Her research interests include pricing and the interface between marketing and manufacturing. She has published a number of articles and is writing a thesis on the interrelationship between manufacturing and effective marketing.

Robert J. Dolan is professor of business administration and chairman of the marketing area at Harvard Business School. His previous pricing research appears in *Bell Journal of Economics, Industrial Marketing Management, Journal of Business*, and *Journal of Marketing*.

Abel P. Jeuland is professor of marketing in the Graduate School of Business of the University of Chicago. He has published articles on brand choice, new-product management, dealing, and advertising in *Operations Research, Management Science, Marketing Science, Journal of Business,* and *Journal of Marketing.*

Shlomo Kalish is associate professor of marketing and operations research at the William E. Simon Graduate School of Business Administration at the University of Rochester and also a lecturer at the Recanati Graduate School of Business at Tel-Aviv University in Israel. He holds a Ph.D. from MIT and has published articles in *Management Science, Marketing Science,* and *Journal of Business* plus chapters in various books.

Gary L. Lilien is research professor of management science in the College of Business Administration at Pennsylvania State University, where he is research director of the Institute for the Study of Business Markets. Editor-in-chief of the journal, *Interfaces,* he in addition serves on the Advisory Panel of the National Science Foundation's Program in the Decision and Management Sciences.

Tridib Mazumdar, assistant professor of marketing and innovation management in the School of Management at Syracuse University, holds a Ph.D. from Virginia Polytechnic Institute and State University. His research has appeared in the proceedings of the national conference of the American Marketing Association.

George E. Monahan is associate professor of decision and information sciences in the College of Commerce, University of Illinois at Urbana-Champaign. He received his Ph.D. in managerial economics and decision sciences from Northwestern University.

Kent B. Monroe (D.B.A., University of Illinois, Champaign-Urbana) is Robert O. Goodykoontz Professor of Marketing at Virginia Polytechnic Institute and State University in Blacksburg, Virginia. He has pioneered research on the information value of price and has chapters on pricing in *Modern Marketing Management,* in *Marketing Handbook, Vol. 2: Marketing Management,* and in Handbook of Modern Marketing. He is the author of *Pricing: Making Profitable Decisions.*

K. Sridhar Moorthy is associate professor of marketing at the Yale School of Management (where he teaches pricing and marketing management) and a member of the editorial board of *Marketing Science.* His research focuses on competitive strategy, market segmentation, distribution channels, and consumer behavior.

Thomas T. Nagle is associate professor of marketing at Boston University. He has published *The Strategy and Tactics of Pricing* and articles on pricing in *Journal of Law and Economics, Journal of Business, Business Horizons,* and *Strategic Planning Management.*

Chakravarthi Narasimhan is an associate professor of marketing in the Graduate School of Business at the University of Chicago. His research interests are in theoretical and empirical investigation of competitive marketing strategies. His articles have appeared in *Marketing Science, Journal of Business,* and *Journal of Marketing.*

Kenneth Novak is a doctoral candidate at the University of Chicago Graduate School of Business and an advertising financial analyst at Montgomery Ward. The research discussed in his article is not connected to Montgomery Ward.

Kofi O. Nti is associate professor of management science in the College of Business Administration at Pennsylvania State University. He holds a B.S. from Yale University, an M.A. from the University of Rochester, and a Ph.D. in administrative sciences from Yale. His research applies game theoretic ideas to problems in marketing and oligopolist competition.

Ram C. Rao (associate professor of management at the University of Texas at Dallas) holds a Ph.D. from Carnegie-Mellon University. He received his M.S., M.E., and B.E. from UCLA, Indian Institute of Science, and University of Madras, respectively. His articles have appeared in *Management Science, Bell Journal of Economics,* and *Journal of Marketing Research.*

Brian T. Ratchford is professor of marketing at the State University of New York at Buffalo. He received an A.B. from Canisius College and M.B.A. and Ph.D. from the University of Rochester. He has published articles dealing with the application of economics to marketing in *Marketing Science, Management Science, Journal of Consumer Research,* and *Journal of Marketing Research,* among others.

Thomas W. Ross is an assistant professor of economics at Carleton University in Ottawa, Canada. After receiving his Ph.D. from the University of Pennsylvania, he was a research fellow at the Center for the Study of the Economy and the State at the University of Chicago. He has written on imperfect information, regulation, and antitrust in *Review of Economic Studies, Rand Journal of Economics, Journal of Law and Economics, Journal of Business,* and *International Journal of Industrial Organization.*

Massoud M. Saghafi is in the faculty of marketing at the College of Business Administration at San Diego State University in California. He received his

Ph.D. in economics from University of Southern California. He has been published in *Research in Marketing, Journal of Development Economics,* and *National Tax Journal.*

Steven M. Shugan is professor of marketing at the University of Chicago, Graduate School of Business. He received his Ph.D. from Northwestern University in Managerial Economics and Decision Sciences. He is an associate editor of *Management Science* and is on the editorial board of the *Journal of Consumer Research* and *Marketing Science.* He is currently the president of the Institute of Management Science College of Marketing.

Russell S. Winer is an associate professor of management at the Owen Graduate School of Management of Vanderbilt University in Nashville, Tennessee. He received his B.A. in economics from Union College and his M.S. and Ph.D. in industrial administration from Carnegie-Mellon University. Author of over thirty articles in various journals and conference proceedings, he is on the editorial boards of *Journal of Consumer Research* and *Journal of Business Research.*

Eunsang Yoon is assistant professor of marketing at Auburn University in Auburn, Alabama. He also serves as a research associate for the Institute for the Study of Business Markets at Pennsylvania State University. He received his B.A. from Seoul National University, his M.B.A. from University of Georgia, and his Ph.D. from Pennsylvania State University.

Anthony J. Zahorik is associate dean and assistant professor of management at the Owen Graduate School of Management at Vanderbilt University in Nashville, Tennessee. He holds a Ph.D. from Cornell University and has published articles in *Management Science* and *Journal of Consumer Research.*

About the Editor

Timothy M. Devinney is assistant professor of management at the Owen Graduate School of Management of Vanderbilt University in Nashville, Tennessee. He received his B.Sc. from Carnegie Mellon University in psychology and holds an M.A. in public policy studies, an M.B.A. in economics and statistics, and a Ph.D. in business economics, all from the University of Chicago. Professor Devinney is an applied economic whose work covers such diverse topics as firm pricing decisions, the role of bank screening policies and bank–customer relations, the impact of taxation on firms' investment choices, and game theory. He has published the monograph *Rationing in a Theory of the Banking Firm* and articles in *Management Science, Journal of Institutional and Theoretical Economics,* and *Journal of Marketing.*